THE ORTHODOX CHURCl

The Orthodox Church in the History of Russia

by

DIMITRY V. POSPIELOVKSY

ST VLADIMIR'S SEMINARY PRESS
CRESTWOOD, NY 10707
1998

Library of Congress Cataloging-in-Publication Data

Pospielovsky, Dimitry, 1935-
    The Orthodox Church in the history of Russia / by Dimitry V. Pospielovsky.
        p.   cm.
    Includes bibliographical references and index.
    ISBN 0-88141-179-5
    1. Russkaia pravoslavnaia tserkov—History.   2. Orthodox Eastern Church—
Russia—History.   3. Orthodox Eastern Church—Russia—Influence.   4. Russia—
Church history.   I. Title.
BX485.P67   1988
281.9'47—dc21   98-26971
                                                                                      CIP

THE ORTHODOX CHURCH IN THE HISTORY OF RUSSIA

ISBN 0-88141-179-5

PRINTED IN THE UNITED STATES OF AMERICA

Contents

To the blessed memory of Father John Meyendorff, whose example and advice inspired me to concentrate on the controversial and tortuous history of the Russian Orthodox Church as the central subject of my reasearch. He and the late Father Alexander Schmemann taught me that *truth* must be the aim of history writing, even when the subject is too close for comfort.

PREFACE

This is meant as a college textbook in courses on the history of the Russian Orthodox Church, as well as a supplementary textbook for any Russian history courses, as Russian culture and history are inseparable from the Orthodox Church as she unfolded herself through Russian history and influenced its course. I owe the idea of writing this book first of all to Colorado College in Colorado Springs, which invited me in 1988 to teach such an *ad-hoc* course there on the occasion of the Millennium of Christianity in Russia. The notes prepared for that course were later expanded and enriched, as I began teaching specialized courses dealing with Church-State relations, the history of the Church under the Soviet Regime and survey courses of Russian Church history at the seminaries and other educational institutions in post-*perestroika* Russia. In 1993 I taught a survey Russian Church history course at St Vladimir's Orthodox Theological Seminary in Crestwood, NY. This led me to the idea of writing two parallel textbooks: one for Russian and the other for the English-speaking students. The Russian edition was published in Moscow in November 1996.

As most textbooks are, this one is mostly a compilation based predominantly on published secondary sources. As I am primarily a student of twentieth-century Russia and the Soviet Union, much of the material on that century contained in the book is based on my original research in Russian as well as Western archives and libraries. I have been fortunate enough to intensively research former Soviet and early twentieth century Russian archives every year since 1990. And I am very grateful to archivists of the Moscow "State Archive of the Russian Federation," the "Russian Center for the Collection of and Research in the Documents of Contemporary History" and the Leningrad/St Petersburg "Central State Historical Archive," particularly its senior archivist Irina Poltavskaia for her help and guidance. I should also like to express my sincere gratitude to the University of Western Ontario and the, unfortunately now defunct, Canadian academic exchange agreements with the USSR for financially enabling me to travel and research in Russia every year since 1990. The grants were not for a textbook. It is thanks to those grants that I have been able to publish a new scholarly work on the history of the Russian Church in the twentieth century in Moscow (*Russkaia Pravoslavnaia Tserkov' v XX veke*, 1995), which is an improved, expanded, and updated version of my earlier two-volume *The Russian Church under the Soviet Regime* (St Vladimir's Seminary Press, 1984). I am continuing to collect archival material for an expanded and updated English version of that book. Nevertheless, the textbook, at least its last eight chapters, are largely a byproduct of that archival research made possible by the above travel grants.

To conclude, I am extremely grateful to the literary and theological editor of this work, Professor Paul Meyendorff of St Vladimir's Seminary. English is not my native tongue. Then I wrote the English text almost simultaneously with the Russian one; therefore, the latter inevitably and inadvertently influenced my English style and sentence structure. Moreover, whatever English I possess, it is British, which Professor Meyendorff Americanized for the North-American readership—I would not have been able to do this. As I am not a theologian, I am particularly grateful for Paul Meyendorff's review and corrections of the theological passages in the textbook.

Nevertheless, should he have overlooked any inaccuracies or mistakes of any kind in the text, I bear full responsibility for them.

Regarding footnotes and source references I have followed the usual license tolerated in textbooks by giving exact source references only in regard to controversial issues, assertions that might be questioned by the reader. Otherwise, most of the footnotes constitute comments or parenthetical additional remarks, information or details, meant for the most inquisitive reader.

There are numerous first class books on particular aspects and period of the Russian Church history (most of them have been listed at the end of the respective chapters), but neither in English or in Russian is there a text surveying the whole millennial road traveled by the Orthodox Church in Rus', Russia, the Soviet Union and CIS. I hope this textbook will be able to fill the empty niche in this field.

CHAPTER 1

A PREHISTORY OF RUSSIAN CHRISTIANITY: BYZANTIUM, ROME AND THE SLAVS

Many peculiarities of the Russian Church history, of her relations with the state, particularly the twentieth century crisis, can be traced to the "Constantinian legacy," and, more exactly to Justininan's sixth-century doctrine of Church-State Symphony.

The first step in the process of the legalization of Christianity in the Roman Empire was the 311 Edict of the Emperor Galerius, which said that since attempts to annihilate Christianity had failed, it should be allowed to exist and to form its assemblies, i.e., churches. This was followed by Emperor Constantine's Edict of Toleration of 313 which gave the Christian Church a legal status equal to that of the pagan cults.

Constantine was a very controversial figure. A ruthless and bloody murderer of his son and most of his immediate relatives, he nevertheless claimed to have frequent mystical visions, one of which, on the eve of the 312 battle against the usurper Maxentius, appeared to him in the form of a cross with the words "With this thou willst conquer." This vision, and the subsequent victory, he claimed, led him to issue the Edict of Milan. Although he was not baptized until the last days of his life, and although he was baptized by a heretic, the Arian bishop Eusebius, from the moment of the Milan Edict he considered himself Christian. He actively interfered in the life of the Church, convened the first Ecumenical Council of Nicea and presided at its opening. In the latter part of his reign he supported Arians and their persecution of the Orthodox Christians, including that of St Athanasius the Great by the above mentioned Eusebius in 337. In Fr John Meyendorff's opinion, the reason Constantine postponed baptism until his deathbed was that he appreciated the contradiction between the brutal force and acts of violence resorted to by the emperor and the virtues required of a Christian. Be that as it may, the dilemma of a double standard remains: whereas an ordinary mortal had to be baptized before he could claim to be a Christian, an emperor in the person of Constantine appeared to be exempt from that condition. Allowance for such an exception, in the apt words of Fr Alexander Schmemann, placed the emperor above the Church and introduced into Christianity the pagan deification of emperors, leading to the heresy of caesaro-papism.

That heresy is popularly associated with Eastern Christianity, as Constantine had moved his capital from the old Rome to the new Rome—Byzantium (renamed Constantinople after his death). About a century later, the Western Roman Empire collapsed, but the near-deification of emperors was true of the whole Roman Empire, both eastern and western. Psychologically and historically, the appearance of that heresy is easy to comprehend. After three centuries of persecutions the Christian Church was not merely legalized by Constantine, but, soon after his reign, two edicts issued in 391-92 by Emperor Theodosius banned "pagan cults, public or private..." At this point, the Empire became constitutionally and legally a Christian state.[1] It ought to be remembered that, during the early Christian centuries, a sense of the immediacy of the Second Coming was still the general rule in the daily life of Christians. In this context the legalization of Christianity was perceived as the inauguration of the apocalyptic kingdom ruled by a God-chosen king on the eve of the Second Coming. Thus the Christian emperor was perceived to be God-anointed, and those very Christians who had only recently preferred martyrdom to the God-like adulation of pagan emperors were now ready to adulate the Christian emperors as temporal heads anointed by God to lead their Christian flock to salvation. Theodosius (379-395) formally divided the Roman Empire into the Eastern and Western Empires, choosing Constantinople for his capital. This linked Eastern Christianity much more directly with the cult of emperors than was the case for the geographically distant Western Empire, which was soon to collapse anyhow.

The next crucial move in Church-State relations occurred under Emperor Justinian (527-65) when the doctrine of Church-State Symphony was coined. It taught that the emperors cared for the terrestrial needs of their Christian subjects, which included such issues as promotion of Church missions, education, welfare; while the Church, personified by her clergy ranked in structures parallel to civil administration, were the spiritual advisors to the Emperor and his government on all levels, had charge over moral issues and behavior, and administered penance. Even emperors were subject to the moral authority and disciplinary actions of the Church.

1 John Meyendorff, *Imperial Unity*, 8.

Here, one would have thought, an equilibrium was established. Not so. Firstly, all the fullness of power and force remained in the hands of the emperor, while the moral authority of the bishops could restrain only very pious and just rulers who needed such restraints much less than power-greedy and religiously cynical tyrants who simply ignored the Church and her advice. Secondly, although the concept of symphony was first coined by Justinian, there was more of it during the Constantinian period than under Justinian. Constantine abided by the conciliar decisions (although he eventually leaned towards wrong councils and counsels), humbly repented for the persecutions under his predecessors, and kissed the eye-sockets of the Nicean Council delegates blinded by their torturers. Thus, as the Russian theologian N.A. Zaozerskii points out, whereas under Constantine there had been a symphony of sorts between Church and State, Justinian's Sixth Novella (which used the symphonia formula) really spoke only about symphony between the secular ruler and the Church hierarchy. Consequently, "The Church sank into the civil structure, merged with it to form a Christian State," and in order to achieve this aim "that champion of Orthodox statehood," continues Zaozerskii, most cruelly persecuted all pagan faiths, "having shed more blood of his subjects than any other subsequent [Roman] emperor," dealing a very heavy moral blow to Christianity.

According to the findings of both Zaozerskii and N. Aksakov, another noted Russian theologian of the late nineteenth-early twentieth centuries, the very term "patriarch" was for the first time applied to the bishops of capital cities by Justinian's bureaucracy in its pursuit of a state clericalism and a hierarchical structure paralleling that of the state bureaucracy.[2] The decrees of Ecumenical Councils of the time still use the term "bishops," while "patriarchs" are mentioned only in state documents. Not unjustly, Justinian has been called the creator of the ideology of a "Christian" state, and, as with all ideologies, its triumph was very bloody. All ideologues and ideologies are dangerous because they confuse the *temporal* with the *eternal*. Fr Schmemann points out that Justinian had wrongly said that the State was the body of the empire, and the Church, its soul, ignoring the Church as the mystical body of Christ. Believing that it was a duty of the state to protect the Church, the emperor not only persecuted heretics but took the liberty to decide what constituted heresy; and, toward the end of his reign, persecuted Orthodox Christians for their strict

---

2 Kartashev adds that, whereas Constantine considered himself to be the "external bishop" of the Church, Justinian saw himself as a bishop of its internal life as well. He appointed all patriarchs himself: elections survived only in choosing popes in distant Rome. Thus, not unreasonably, Kartashev sees him as a predecessor of Peter the Great.

adherence to the Creed adopted at the very councils convoked by him, and for the reverence of icons. The triumph of the iconoclasts continued until the Seventh Ecumenical Council of 787, which the Empress Irene convoked in Nicea rather than in the still militantly iconoclastic Constantinople.

We ought to remember that, at the time when Christianity became the state religion of the Roman Empire, the Church, except for the much more centralized (old) Rome, consisted of a myriad of tiny autonomous episcopates united only in faith and through frequent local and infrequent ecumenical councils, while imperial power was centralized and autocratic. As the idea of patriarchates was born under Justinian, with his de-facto subordination of the Church to the State, the institution did not necessarily give the Church more power or independence vis-à-vis the State.

On the contrary, no sooner had the concept of symphony been spelled out, than, as a result of Justinian's ideology, it was abused, and in that abused form came to be known as *cesaropapism*. In contrast, *papocesarism* prevailed in the West, after the last emperor of the Western Roman Empire, Romulus Augustus, had been deposed by the Goths in 476. Technically most of Italy was still a province of the Eastern Roman Empire: the pope pledged allegiance to the emperor in Constantinople and there was an imperial governor (*exarch*) in Rome. Nevertheless, in the power vacuum created in the West by barbarian invasions, the pope became a quasi-emperor, not only over parts of Italy directly under his control, but over the multitude of new barbarian kingdoms and principalities. The rulers of many of them were recently baptized (mostly for political reasons, realizing that you had to be a Christian to be accepted into the "family" of civilized nations of Europe) by the Roman pope or his bishops. The pope therefore used his position of exterritoriality to arbitrate in their feuds, form alliances, crown some dukes as kings, and to raise the title of the Frankish king, Charles the Great, to that of the "Holy Roman Emperor" in the ninth century, challenging the Byzantine-Roman Empire and moving ever closer to the Great Schism of 1054. As the pope gained more and more temporal power, he began to use quasi-theological justifications for a special and unique position among Christian bishops as well as monarchs, claiming power over the former and authority over the latter.

Byzantium: for and against...

Not everything about the institutional Church-State symbiosis was negative. While the collapse of the Western Roman Empire resulted in the so-called

Dark Age in western Europe, the Eastern Empire during that very time period experienced a glorious flowering of Byzantine culture. Thanks to the preservation of statehood, the University of Constantinople (*academy* in the Greek terminology) enjoyed a practically uninterrupted continuity from the time of its foundation by Constantine the Great to the fall of Constantinople in 1453. The Greek population of the core of the Byzantine Empire was the direct heir of the Greco-Roman civilization, continuing the sophisticated Greek tradition of philosophizing in the marketplaces—philosophy and theology being everybody's business. Particularly so, because in the East, in contrast to the Latin Rome, services were translated into the vernacular right from the beginning: Syriac as early as the second century, probably simultaneously with Coptic, followed by Armenian in the fourth, Georgian in the fifth... Just as state documents had to be translated into local languages, so similarly the documents of the Church, for there was no concept of division between the secular and the ecclesiastic spheres. The term *liturgy* was applied not only to the church service, but also to state service rendered by a civil servant. Both forms of service, were believed to be performed to the glory of God—the civil servant participated in that universal catholic liturgy by serving the Christian State, the catholicity in this case being the citizens, the people of God whom the civil servant served.

The only institutional limitations on the autocrat were the intricate bureaucracy with its rules, regulations and laws, namely the fifth century Code of the Emperor Theophilus and the sixth century Code of Justinian. Both are known as Roman Law; in fact both were produced in the Byzantine-Roman Empire.

However autocratic the Roman emperors (both in the East and in the West) may have been, there were moral limitations to their arbitrariness. One such limitation was the readiness of religious zealots to die for their faith. These mostly consisted of monks who, in the words of George Every, "were especially formidable critics, for persecution made them martyrs." Thus, for instance, when the parade of the triumph of Orthodoxy took place in Constantinople on the occasion of the final victory of the defenders of icons, it was an endless march of monks maimed by torturers during the preceding decades. "The Greek monk," Every points out, "was often a politician, like the Greek citizen."

And indeed it was one of such politician-monks of the sixth century, the hierodeacon Agapetus, who defined moral limitations on the autocrat in the following words:

Though an emperor in body be like all others, yet in power of his office he is like God ... for in earth he has no peer. Therefore, as God, be he never chafed or angry; as man, be he never proud. For though he be like God in face, yet for all that he is but dust, which thing teaches him to be equal to every man.

In this apparent contradiction—human image, God's image, and dust as essential components of the emperor—the Byzantine author is trying to express the great moral limitations on the sovereign: his responsibility to God for all his deeds, wherefore before God he is like any other mortal, equal to all of them. But his office, placing him in charge of the temporal life of millions of Christians, is so lofty that in the eyes of men the emperor is like God, and his powers cannot be circumscribed by his subjects.

However paradoxical, that definition makes sense and sets serious moral limits on the monarch, provided he is sufficiently virtuous to feel bound by moral tenets. But the authority of the Patriarch was never defined even as vaguely as the powers of the emperor, because, from the eastern perspective, only Christ Jesus is the head of the Church as His mystical body. Bishops, including patriarchs, are only her temporal administrators, supervisors, to use a verbatim translation of the Greek term. In contrast, the powers of the king are of this world, therefore they can be described or/and defined in human terms.

The institution of monarchy may have been sacred, a carryover from the pagan centuries of the Roman Empire, transfigured to a new meaning through the conversion of Constantine. In addition, the Old Testamental tradition of prophets anointing kings rendered itself to diverse interpretations, especially if the clergy were treated as a substitute for prophets. But besides the Judeo-Roman monarchic institution, Byzantium also inherited the Greek democratic tradition and the Christian personalism which emphasized the moral and social responsibilities of each individual person not only for one's own destiny, but also for the destinies of one's neighbors. These elements precluded the development of stable aristocratic and royal dynasties with stable and undisputed rights and privileges inherited by birth. Therefore, with the sole exception of the Macedonian Dynasty which ruled from 867 to 1056, dynasties changed frequently, often overthrown either by mobs, armies or court plots. There could be a mass demonstration right in the cathedral (Hagia Sophia) against a heresy supported by a given emperor, or against heavy taxation; there could also be a rebellion in the army or navy. Imperial incumbents included an illiterate rope-trader (Justin I), a Syrian sheep-driver

(Leo III), an Armenian horse tamer (Basil the Macedonian). The grim side of the picture was the bloodiness of such a system. Often, upon the death of a monarch, his daughters and the sons of his sisters would be slaughtered to prevent their attempts at taking the throne, and on a monarch's rebellious deposition, a similar fate often befell his sons.

Byzantium was a highly regulated welfare state, to use a modern term, where the minister for orphans was one of the most important officials in the cabinet. Women had full real estate inheritance rights separately from their husbands, as well as the right to initiate divorce. Hospitals and educational institutions were widespread and run jointly by the State and the Church. There were many women doctors in the hospitals.

In contrast to west-European feudalism with its absence of a conception of economy, the Byzantine economy was rationally regulated, and extravagance was frowned upon. Even emperors were not spared, and indeed some of them were very thrifty in running their household: for example, the thirteenth century emperor John Vatatzes bought his empress a new crown called 'eggy,' because it was financed from the sale of the chicks and eggs from her kitchen garden. Only people having a job or a business in Constantinople could settle there permanently. The able-bodied unemployed were assigned to public works of street cleaning, weeding public gardens, or working in the bakeries and silk factories which were state monopolies.

While there was considerable bloodiness in connection with imperial succession, the law of the country, obviously influenced by Christianity, avoided the death penalty. When in western Europe people were being hanged for stealing a pair of shoes, for instance, in Byzantium not a single person was executed during the 25-year reign of John Comnenus. In place of execution, bodily mutilation was often used. As Every points out, the preference for mutilation was dictated by the Christian principle of giving a chance for the criminal to repent for his crimes.

As mentioned above, church services in the vernacular familiarized the laity with the contents and meaning of the service and with the doctrines of the Church. Every Orthodox liturgy is an enactment of the theology of the Church, and punctual attendance at the whole annual cycle of services exposes practically the whole Church doctrine to the believer; in the Orthodox Church, worship is theology and is inseparable from the doctrine. Moreover, Justinian ordered that no part of the service be mumbled quietly by the clergy.

All parts must be clearly and loudly pronounced for the whole congregation to hear, so that nothing be concealed from the worshiper who should participate fully and consciously in the service.

The practice of whispering the most sacred prayers of the Eucharist must have developed after Christianity had been granted the status of the state Church. Then masses of yesterday's pagans ignorant of the Christian theology began to fill the churches. It was apparently at that time as well that communion became less frequent and confession began to be demanded from these neophytes as preparation for communion and as a substitute religious education. Nevertheless, the Eastern liturgy has never become a priest's mass for the people as in the medieval Latin West. In the Orthodox church there would always be a psalmist, some type of a choir, often two—one on each side in the front of the church, just before the sanctuary, thus not separated from the congregation. The choir's geographic position would invite the congregation to sing along. The entrances, when the clergy come out of the altar to the center of the church, give movement and dynamism to the service and break the separation of the clergy from the laity. There developed many popular offices, such as memorial services for the dead and *akathist* (paraclyses) with the clergy in the middle of the nave surrounded by the faithful singing along with the clergy. Likewise, the laity received Communion in two forms, just like the clergy, and communed in the early Byzantine Church weekly.

Clericalism was unknown in the East, where lay monks (there were up to 100,000 of them in the Byzantine Empire in the tenth century, roughly at the time of Russia's conversion) were often more important as spiritual leaders than the clergy, and often acted as father-confessors not only to laity, but even to priests and bishops. These monastic holy fathers or elders earned their recognition not by any clerical titles or administrative positions, but by the holiness of their behavior recognized as such by the faithful.

Eastern monasticism knows no separate monastic orders—with the sole exception of the Order of the Protectors of the Sepulchre in Jerusalem. Monasteries are simply voluntary communities of men or women choosing to live a chaste and virtuous life of prayer and dedication to God. Each monastery devises its own statute or rule. Some statutes, such as those of the Stoudion in Constantinople, became particularly popular and were emulated or simply adopted by other monastic communities. Many monasteries are very small. In other cases a network of large and small monasteries in a single area links up and elects a joint administration for the whole group of monastic settlements; the most famous is the peninsular monastic republic of Mount Athos, which has survived to the present day. At its peak it contained an international male monastic contingent of up to 40,000. At present it has about 1,700—almost all of them are Greeks, owing to the Greek government's nationalistic policy of near totally excluding monks from the Slavic countries, who used to make up some 70 percent of the population of Mount Athos.

The tradition of married parish priests also militates against clericalism: married priests and their wives share all the problems common to most parishioners and thus understand each other better than an exclusive caste of celibates. However, there have long been tensions among the clergy between the married and the celibate, i.e., predominantly monastic, clergy. At least since the seventh or eighth century, almost exclusively celibates have been consecrated bishops. In most cases they came from the monasteries, although among the most famous bishops and patriarchs there have been many widowed parish priests and even lay scholars and state officials tonsured[3] and consecrated after having been elected to the episcopate. Such, for instance, was the case with the Patriarch Photius in the ninth century, who was responsible for organizing the mission of Saints Cyril and Methodius to the Slavs. In fact, of the two brothers who would devise an alphabet for the Slavs, translate the Scriptures and service books into that new written language and lead the missions to the Czechs (the Great Moravia of the time) and Bulgars, Cyril set out on his missionary work while still a lay professor of languages at the University of Constantinople, known as Constantine the Philosopher. He took monastic vows with the new name of Cyril much later, already in the midst of his missionary work in Moravia, probably under the influence of his brother, the monk-bishop Methodius.

It was this close interflow between the clergy and the laity, the lack of clerical elitism and of the clergy's unquestionable authority in relation to the laity, the use of the vernacular and the laity's active participation in church services that led the fourth-century St Gregory of Nyssa to complain that in Greece a baker and a bath keeper would debate in a public bath the nature of Christ or

3 Apparently at first even monastic tonsure was not obligatory as long as the candidate gave a vow of celibacy. The last known case of a non-monastic bishop (i.e., apparently without a preliminary tonsure) belongs to the 15th century. As monasticism became the only path to high positions in the Church, careerism rather than spiritual dedication to monasticism became a frequent motivation for choosing monastic vows. Such "monks" in name only have been responsible for the development and growth of tension between the *white* (married) and *black* (monastic) clergy.

the position of the Holy Spirit in the Trinity. Of course such lay theologizing decreased once the Church became an obligatory state institution with masses of nominal Christians. Still, such phenomena as the schism between the new and old ritualists, a predominantly grass-roots movement in seventeenth-century Russia, are a testimony that St Gregory's complaint remained relevant even to that remote heir of the Church of the Eastern Fathers.

That is the reason we see so many heresies and theological debates in the East, with active participation by the laity, often leading to bloody clashes between opposing parties. In the West, by contrast, where the mass was not understood by the laity (except in Italy, where Latin was as close to the vernacular as Slavonic to the early Russian), as a rule the masses did not participate in theological debates.

In the words of Kartashev, during the centuries of the ecumenical councils the domains of the Roman pope were quietly dormant, and the niceties of the eastern theological debates were not even understood in Rome, let alone appreciated. The pope commanded and his bishops disseminated his commands among an ignorant laity. The passionate debates in the East caused the Latin West to think of the East as a bunch of heretics. The East responded likewise when the pope failed to distinguish the fine points separating the Orthodox teaching on the nature of Christ and that of the less obvious heretics and accepted them (such as Marcellus in the fourth century), giving them refuge and full recognition as clergy in Rome. These were among the early signs of mutual distrust, leading eventually to the Great Schism of 1054 between the Latin West and the Greek East.

The Franks, Missions to the Slavs, and the Great Schism.

The Western Roman Empire ceased to exist in 476. The pope's security began to depend on the barbarians, among whom the Franks became the most formidable force by the eighth century. As the pope's protectors, they eventually practically forced the East-West Church split on him.

The Byzantine remnant of the Roman Empire was not a safe haven either. It began shrinking from the east in the seventh century as a result of the Islamic offensive, which soon deprived Byzantium of her possessions in the Middle East and northern Africa, thus cutting off the patriarchates of Antioch, Alexandria and Jerusalem.

Let us, however, return to the Franks. Their ambitious kings were now trying to step into the Italian power vacuum, tear away Italy with the pope from even a formal political dependence on the East Roman emperors, and thereby replace them as masters of Western Europe. The most expedient way to achieve this was to foment a theological East-West split.

First, the Franks began to eradicate the use of Greek in the church services within their domains. The paradox of the seventh-eighth centuries was that while the predominant liturgical language in Ravenna or Rome was Greek, the center of the Latin liturgy was the Frankish capital of Aachen.

At first, Charles the Great (Charlemagne) tried to raise his status by marrying into the Byzantine imperial family, but he was turned down with the words that a purple-born (πορφυρογέννητος, i.e., born in the imperial palace) princess does not marry barbarians. The pope responded by crowning Charlemagne emperor, a title the Greeks refused to recognize, continuing to refer to him as Frankish king. Clearly, a second Roman empire without the consent of the true Roman emperor could not be legitimized unless the latter was declared a heretic, as the pope continued to be in communion with the Church of Constantinople and therefore technically remained a subject of the Byzantine emperor.

A theological peg for a schism was the *filioque*, a phrase inserted into the Creed by the Franks in Spain, claiming the procession of the Holy Spirit not merely from the Father, but also from the Son. For two centuries the popes continued to resist this insertion. The Creed continued to be recited in Italy in its original formulation, but in the territories directly controlled by the Franks it was recited with the insertion. The papacy finally gave in to the Frankish version in 1009. Similarly the Franks won their battle for the universal use of Latin in the West.

Another phenomenon which distinguished the Christian West from the East was the eleventh-century Cluniac Movement, which led to a ban on married clergy in the Western Church. The Franks were likewise advocates of celibacy. They finally had it their way when the split between the papacy and the Church of the East took place: when the papal delegates arrived in Constantinople and delivered the papal edict of excommunication against the Patriarch of Constantinople, the refusal of the Church of the East to insert the *filioque* clause into the Creed and the practice of ordaining married men to priesthood figured very prominently among the reasons for the excommunication—even though both the celibate clergy and the *filioque* were very recent innovations in Rome itself. In fact, Pope Leo III had inscribed the original text of the Creed without the *filioque* on silver shields hung on a wall of St Peter's Basilica for everybody to see that that was the only true text of the Creed.

Now, once the Frankish kings had been crowned emperors, they attempted to apply cesaro-papist policies to the Church, in imitation of the Roman (Byzantine) emperors' policies towards the patriarchs and, formerly the pope. According to Meyendorff, until the eleventh century "the bishops of Rome [i.e., the popes] were hardly more than mere tools in the hands of the Western [Frankish] emperors." Several eleventh-century popes, however, succeeded in resisting total Frankish control. The multiplicity of rulers and the atomization of authority in feudal Europe eventually secured the "triumph of the papacy over the Empire." And, as Meyendorff concedes, the ability of the popes to break out of the imperial shackles allowed the Church to rise high above petty politics, raise morals and fight simony. "The results of their efforts was the birth of a Christian Europe and a new civilization."

The duel between the Franks and Byzantium, however, directly affected the destinies of Christianity among the western Slavs. In 862, Prince Rastislav of Great Moravia, a Slavic Kingdom which engulfed most of today's Czechoslovakia, parts of Austria, Hungary and southern Poland, including Cracow, appealed to the Roman Emperor in Constantinople to send Christian missionaries to his country. Nominally, the Moravian Kingdom was a vassal of Charlemagne's Frankish Empire, and it was invaded by German clergy using Latin in the liturgy, which was incomprehensible to the Slavs. The Byzantine emperor and his patriarch, Photius, chose two learned Slavic-speaking Macedonian brothers, the Philosopher Constantine and the monk-priest Methodius, to head a mission to Moravia. Constantine, who would later be tonsured under the name of Cyril, had already devised an alphabet for the Slavs, and with his Slavic disciples Naum and Clement [of Ohrid], had translated the main liturgical texts and parts of the Scriptures into the Slavonic dialect spoken in the Salonica area [Bulgaro-Macedonian], the language now generally known as Old or Church Slavonic. At the time, the differences between the diverse Slavonic dialects were still relatively minor; thus, the language 'created' by Cyril soon became the official common literary language of all Slavs embracing the Eastern Orthodox faith.

With their imperial ambitions, the Franks were not prepared to tolerate any Byzantine influence in Central Europe. This was another reason for them to seek an excuse to achieve an ecclesial break between Constantinople and Rome. They upheld the theory that worship was legitimate only in the three languages in which the inscription, "Jesus, the King of the Jews," was made on the Cross, i.e., Latin, Greek, and Hebrew. On these grounds, the Franks persecuted the Slavic missionaries. In 864, the Franks under Prince Louis invaded Moravia and forced Rastislav to recognize their suzerainty over him. The Byzantines were unable to help Rastislav, as they were hard-pressed by their militant Bulgarian neighbors and by the Islamic threat from the east. Cyril's and Methodius' only hope was the Pope, who was eager to curb Frankish ambitions. When the brothers arrived in Rome in 867-68, Pope Hadrian II officially authorized the use of the Slavonic liturgy and appointed Methodius as the bishop of all Slavonic churches in Moravia, Panonia (modern Hungary), and probably Croatia (judging by the geography of the time). Nevertheless, on his return to Moravia Methodius was soon arrested and imprisoned by the Franks for two and one half years. According to a popular hypothesis, some Slavonic churches with the Byzantine rite survived in the East-Carpathian region of twentieth-century Slovakia (now south-western Ukraine) and Poland. That is how the so-called sub-Carpathian Ruthenians like to explain the origin of the Orthodox and later Byzantine-Rite Catholic Church of the region.

In the ninth century, however, under the impact of German persecutions, most of Methodius' Slavic clergy followed their teacher Cyril (after Methodius' death in Rome) to Constantinople in 881. Most likely, it was they who disseminated Christianity in the vernacular among the Bulgars and Serbs. The best known disciples of the Macedonian brothers were Clement and Naum of Ohrid, who established in that city the first Slavonic university (or academy), with over 3,000 students. That school and the Ohrid diocese became the missionary center for the Slavs. It is likely from there that came to Russia most of the clergy and teachers in the late tenth century following Vladimir's conversion.

The process of the conversion of Bulgaria was the reverse of what occurred in Moravia. The bellicose Bulgars were a constant threat to the very existence of the Byzantine Empire, constantly attacking it from the north, having formed their own tsardom in the immediate neighborhood of Constantinople. Because adopting Christianity from Byzantium meant becoming its vassal (or, to use D. Obolensky's terminology, a member of the "Byzantine Commonwealth"), Tsar Boris of Bulgaria concluded an alliance with the Frankish King Louis in the early 860's, promising him to accept Christianity from Frankish missionaries. But, by that time, Byzantine-rite Christianity had already taken root in Bulgaria. Forestalling allied military actions the Byzantine Emperor Michael III moved his naval and land forces to the shores of Bulgaria. Boris capitulated and agreed to accept the Byzantine Rite as the state religion of Bulgaria in return for the lifting of the military blockade. But before Boris completed the conversion of his nation he had to suppress a rebellion by his pagan clan leaders. Thereafter, in Obolensky's words, Bulgaria became "the first big and well organized state of Eastern Europe to adopt Byzantine Christianity."

FOR FURTHER READING

Aksakov, N.P. "Sobory i patriarkhi." *K tserkovnomu soboru—sbornik gruppy Peterburgskikh sviashchennikov* (St Petersburg, 1906), pp. 149-182.

Beck, Hans. *Geschichte der orthodoxen Kirche im byzantinischen Reich* (Göttingen, 1980).

Blane, A. & Thomas Bird, eds. *The Ecumenical World of Orthodox Civilization. Essays in Honor of George Florovsky*, 3 vols. (The Hague: Mouton, 1974).

Bolotov, V.V. *Lektsii po istorii Drevnei Tserkvi*, 4 vols. (Moscow, 1994).

Dvornik, F. *The Slavs in European History and Civilization* (Rutgers University Press, 1962).

Every, George. *The Byzantine Patriarchate.* (London, 1962).

Florovsky, G. *Aspects of Church History* (Belmont, Mass.: Nordland Press, 1975).

Iliin, I.A. *O monarkhii i respublike* (New York, 1979).

Kartashev, A. *Vselenskie sobory* (Moscow: "Respublika," 1994).

Meyendorff, John. *The Byzantine Legacy in the Orthodox Church* (Crestwood: St Vladimir's Seminary Press, 1982).

_____, *Imperial Unity and Christian Divisions* (Crestwood: St Vladimir's Seminary Press, 1989).

Obolensky, D. *The Byzantine Commonwealth* (Crestwood: St Vladimir's Seminary Press, 1989).

_____, *The Byzantine Inheritance of Eastern Europe* (London: Variorum, 1982).

Schmemann, Alexander. *The Historical Road of Eastern Orthodoxy* (Crestwood: St Vladimir's Seminary Press, 1977).

Thomas, John. *Private Religious Foundations in the Byzantine Empire*. Dumbarton Oaks Studies, v. 24 (Washington, D.C., 1987).

Zaozerskii, N. His Reports in *Zhurnaly i protokoly zasedanii Predsobornogo prisutstviia*, vol. I (St Petersburg, 1906), pp. 321-46.

Zernov, N. *Eastern Christendom: a Study in the Origin and Development of the Eastern Orthodox Church* (Putnam, 1961).

CHAPTER 2

THE CONVERSION OF RUS' TO CHRISTIANITY AND RELATED CONTROVERSIAL ISSUES

The Periodization of Russian History

The distinguished Russian Church historian Anton Kartashev divides pre-revolutionary Russian Church history into six distinct periods. We shall simplify that periodization by reducing it to the following four periods and then add the post-revolutionary era, which could be treated either as a single 'Post-Constantinian' era or be divided into the Communist and the Post-Communist periods.

Period 1. The pre-Mongolian Kievan period of the Christian conversion of Rus'. This period was marked by a particularly high status of the Church, her bishops, priests, and especially monastic holy fathers. Their moral status and authority were undoubtedly higher than those of the secular rulers. Monks built their monasteries mostly in the cities or their immediate vicinity, with the typically neophytic belief in the possibility of truly christianizing the state and spiritually influencing the behavior and policies of the ruling princes and their advisers.

Period 2. This was the era of the so-called Tatar (or Mongol) Yoke, lasting formally from 1238 to 1480, but more accurately until 1447, when the last major royal succession dispute was settled not by appeals to the Mongol rulers, but by decision of a council of five Russian bishops in favor of direct succession from father to the eldest son. This period of over two centuries was marked by mutually feuding appanages and the division of the Rus' lands into domains under the control of Mongols, Lithuanians, and Poles, with the gradual rise of Moscow as the new Russian core and its ecclesiastic and political center. A large part of that period could be considered as Russia's Dark Age.

Period 3. This era begins with the break of Russia's ecclesiastic dependence on Constantinople and the unilaterally declared autocephaly of the Russian Church following Constantinople's brief subordination to the papacy after the Council of Florence (1438-39). This period includes the elevation of the Russian Church to the status of a patriarchate in 1589, and it ends with the enforced abolition of the patriarchate by Peter the Great, *de facto* in 1700, *de jure* in 1721.

Period 4. This is the era of the so-called "Holy Synod," a system devised by Archbishop Feofan (Theophanes) Prokopovich, Peter's chief adviser on Church affairs. This system deprived the Church of any semblance of autonomy, subordinating her to the secular state bureaucracy. This theologically untenable polity survived until the revolutions of 1917.

Kartashev stops there. But logically Periods 5 and perhaps 6 should be added as well, as mentioned above:

Period 5. This period begins with the restoration of the patriarchate in 1917 and continues through the seven-odd decades of Communist dictatorship. If we stress the institution of the patriarchate as the decisive characteristic of the period, then the post-Communist era, which began in 1991 could be treated as the continuation of that period. But should our criteria be the status of the Church vis-à-vis state and society, then the present post-Communist era should be treated as *Period 6.*

Some Puzzles Related to the Baptism of Rus'

The commonly accepted date for the conversion of Rus' to Christianity is 988, but pockets of Christian communities had existed on the territories of that which was recently known as the Soviet Union much before 988.

There were Greek colonies with numerous Christian churches in several spots along the Black Sea coast, at least since the fourth century. There was even a Diocese of Surozh (now the town of Sudak) in Crimea. The Armenian Kingdom, which stretched across much of eastern Anatolia (modern eastern Turkey) in addition to the territory north of Mt Ararat that it occupies today, was the first nation in the world to adopt Christianity as its official state religion—in the early fourth century, even before the Roman Empire did so. The conversion of Georgia, Armenia's immediate neighbor to the north, also began in the fourth century, Christianity becoming its state religion in 609. The Patriarchate of Antioch granted the Georgian Church complete autocephaly in 1053-54 with her own patriarch (finally recognized by the Ecumenical Patriarchate [Constantinople] in the 1980s).

Then there was the great Church of Assyria persecuted for its Nestorian heresy which denied the Virgin Mary the title of Mother of God. Nestorians claimed that Jesus was born an ordinary child in whose flesh God came to reside as a separate entity—they thus denied Jesus' consubstantiality with God and the completeness of the two natures in Jesus. Persecutions pushed the heresy eastwards, and in the eighth-tenth centuries it had thriving dioceses in Bukhara and Samarkand in Central Asia, and missions as far to the east as China and probably Japan.[1]

The first Diocese of Rus', known under that name, was established in the 860s in the city of Tmutorokan' on the northwestern shore of the Caucasus, just opposite Crimea, by St Cyril, still known at that time as the philosopher Constantine. Tmutorokan' was in the southwestern corner of the Hazar Empire, a loose multi-tribal conglomerate whose official religion was Judaism. This, however, seemed to have been only the religion of its emperor-*kakhan* and the ruling elite. Most of the rest of the population consisted of pagans in the north, northeast and northwest, Muslims in the south and Christians in the southwest. Christians had been complaining to the Byzantine emperor about persecutions to which their Hazar overlords subjected them. In 860, Byzantium negotiated with the Hazars a visit of the philosopher Constantine to the Hazar court, where he would be allowed to hold a public debate with the Jewish, Muslim, and pagan wizards.

According to Byzantine chronicles, Constantine's theological erudition impressed the Hazar kakhan so much that he promised Constantine never to persecute Christians again, and allowed him to establish a diocese. According to the Byzantine sources, the language of that diocese's services was Russian. But who were the Tmutorokan' Rus'?

As early as the fourth century, St John Chrysostom, the archbishop of Constantinople, mentioned a Gothic Church on the Black Sea littoral worshipping in their language and making tremendous missionary progress. Hence, some historians (including the late George Vernadsky of Yale) think the Black Sea Rus' were a Gothic tribe. Others believe they were Slavs, and that the liturgical books "in Rus' letters," as mentioned in some Byzantine sources, were in fact in Slavonic. Should this be so, then Cyril and Methodius' translations into Slavonic had to have been accomplished before their Moravian mission of 864. Or else, some Slavonic scriptural translations must

---

1 The Nestorian view on Christ and the Theotokos was very similar to Islam's, wherefore the appearance of Islam was mistaken by Christendom as another version of Nestorianism, and its crushing offensive into Palestine, Asia Minor and northern Africa caught Christians unawares.

have existed prior to those of the Macedonian brothers. But then the question arises, what alphabet did they use? Glagolithic? But the general opinion now is that the Glagolithic script (still used on some isolated Adriatic islands) was the first Slavonic script produced by Constantine the Philosopher; while what is now known as the Cyrillic alphabet was the work of his disciples Clement and Naum of Ohrid, who gave their invention the name of their teacher.

Be that as it may, the name "Rus'" coincides with the name of the Kievan state which appeared on the historical scene as the center of Rus' in 882, a good thousand miles to the northwest of Tmutorokan'. Were the Kievan Ruses "also" Goths? Hardly; because the Russian Chronicles (which began to be written some two centuries after the events) whenever they talk about the Swedes, Germans or any other foreigners, mention interpreters between them and the Slavic language of the Kievans, but no interpreters are mentioned in connection with Slavs or the Rus'.[2] This has led some historians to conclude that both the Tmutorokan' and the Kiev Ruses were Slavs.

The Conversion of Rus' and Its Effects

It is still uncertain which Russian princes were the first to convert the East Slavs to Christianity. Some historians believe that there were two conversions of Kiev, or at least of its elites. The first was that of the two Kievan princes, Askold and Dir, in 860-61, after their abortive attempt to seize Constantinople. According to Greek sources, besieged by the Rus' the population of Constantinople, led by Patriarch Fotios and the Emperor, prayed for a miracle to save them. They dipped the alleged tunic of the Virgin Mary into the sea begging for a storm. Their prayers were heard: a storm destroyed the Russian fleet. Shaken by the miracle, remnants of the Russians returned to negotiate peace with the Byzantines, and were baptized.

Other historians argue that those baptized Russians were in fact from Tmutorokan'. There is total silence on any baptism of Askold and Dir in the early Kievan Chronicles (it is mentioned only in the Moscow Nikonian copy of the Chronicles, where it is believed to have been a later insertion).

Much more reliable information in the Chronicles includes that in 882 a river flotilla of northern Russians from Novgorod, calling themselves the

---

2 Neither are interpreters mentioned in connection with the Varangians, which leads such anti-Normanist historians as Alexander Riasanovksy, for instance, to conclude that Varangians could not have been Scandinavians, but were western Slavs from the Baltic littoral close to Denmark, an area that was being linguistically and politically germanized in the 9th-12th cc.

Ilmen' Slovenians, commanded by their Prince Oleg, descended upon Kiev, killed the Kievan ruling princes Askold and Dir, and made Kiev their new capital, "the mother of all Russian cities," in Oleg's words. Oleg and his immediate successors—Igor', Olga, Sviatoslav and Vladimir—were definitely pagans. Hence, if there had been at least a partial conversion of Kiev under Askold and Dir, then the coming of Oleg and his heirs was a pagan restoration (not unlike the reign of Julian the Apostate in Byzantine Rome). Christianity, nevertheless, was gradually winning over converts in Kiev, as by the mid-tenth century there were at least two Christian churches in the city; i.e., there must have been Christian missionaries in Kievan Rus' prior to its official conversion.

The most famous of the early Kievan Christians was the widow of Prince Igor', Princess Olga, who converted to the Byzantine form of Christianity around 955. She failed, however to convert her son, the warrior-prince Sviatoslav, who is alleged to have told his mother that his warriors would laugh at him if he were to become a Christian. In other words, Christianity was associated in the minds of the Russians with pacifism—a clear sign that the Church the Russians were familiar with came from Byzantium, where military exploits were seen as barbarism, and not from the West with its Frankish-Teutonic tradition of knighthood and military honor.[3]

Sviatoslav was killed in 971 in a battle with the Patsinacks, a nomadic tribe from the Black Sea steppes. His death was followed by an internecine struggle for Kiev between his sons, lasting until 978 when, after the murder of his elder brother Yaropolk, Prince Vladimir, Sviatoslav's bastard son, ascended the throne. Circumstantial historical facts indicate that Vladimir's victory may have been the triumph of a militantly pagan party, as Yaropolk was married to a former Greek nun, while the early part of Vladimir's reign was marked by the only known period of Russian history when human sacrifices were made to pagan gods and Christians were actively persecuted.

Vladimir, however, was not only a passionate pagan, but also a very wise statesman. He achieved control over the whole of Rus', and in a series of successful battles enlarged its territory by annexing what are today Galicia and Carpathian Ruthenia from Poland and the land of the Lithuanian tribe of Yatviags. He understood that in order to unify these diverse Slavonic, Finnic, and Lithuanian tribes into a single union, they must share a common faith;

3 This point is being made because of the claims of some western historians that there was a German-Roman connection to early Russian Christianity and to Olga's baptism.

or, as we would put it today, a common unifying ideology had to be established. And so Vladimir began by erecting in Kiev a pantheon of sculptures representing the pagan gods of all these tribes.

But, apparently, Christianity had already become too influential a force in Rus' to be written off. Vladimir must also have realized that monotheism was prevailing throughout Europe and was a must to be accepted as a part of European civilization. By 988, he decides to replace the pagan conglomerate with Christianity as the new, nationally unifying, factor.

The Chronicles tell us of two stages in the process. First, Vladimir invited representatives from the various monotheistic faiths. He rejected Judaism (probably from the Hazars), supposedly on the grounds that the Jews had no homeland. He is alleged to have said: "If God dispersed the Jews in foreign lands because of their sins, should we bring a similar destiny on our heads?" To the Muslim ambassadors (from the Volga Bulgars, apparently, as they had adopted Islam almost a century before Russia's baptism) he is alleged to have said that Russia's happiness is in food and drink, hence a religion that forbids wine is not suitable. He thus chose Christianity, but which version—the Greek or the Latin? To solve that problem, we are told by the Chronicles, he sent ambassadors to the Germans and the Greeks. They returned with reports on gloominess and boredom of the Latin mass, but a glorious description of the Greek liturgy: "In St Sophia Cathedral it was so beautiful. We did not know whether we were on the earth or in Heaven during the service," they are alleged to have reported on their return. And so, Vladimir chooses to baptize himself, his retinue, and the whole nation to the Greek version of the still technically undivided Christianity. There is no way to establish real facts in this legend. But what is significant in it is the factor of beauty that is posed out as the final argument in favor of a faith. This association of beauty with virtue and truth has remained an important characteristic of the Russians' world view, reflected in iconography, in the architecture of Russian churches and their adornment; finally, in the words of Dostoevsky that Beauty will save the World, or Gogol's horror that celestial beauty can be combined with evil or prostitution—as reflected in his "Nevskii Prospekt."

But let us return to the conversion and its consequences. To begin with, let us point out the crucial historical, religious, cultural and geo-political importance to Western civilization of Vladimir's choice of Christianity over Islam. Had he chosen Islam, Europe would have been faced with a three-pronged Islamic onslaught: one through northern Africa, another through the Balkans, and a third by the north-central route through Russia. Had this occurred, there would probably not have developed the European Christian civilization as we know it. Thus Byzantium in the south and Russia to the north became the bulwark saving Europe, at a very high cost to themselves. That sacrifice has never been fully acknowledged or appreciated by the West, which instead responded with hostility and with invasions of their Eastern Christian brothers.

Let us now look at the internal aspects of Vladimir's action. We shall not discuss here Vladimir's strategy of how to adopt the faith from the Greeks without humiliation for himself and his country. What is more important is the effects of the baptism on Vladimir himself and on his policies, which indicate that the conversion was not merely a political act on his part. According to the Chronicles, his behavior and governance were drastically altered after his conversion. He introduced what we would today call the principles of a welfare state, ordered free distribution of food and clothing to the needy. The Chronicles, obviously exaggerating, claim that before his conversion he had 800 wives and concubines; but upon conversion he released them all and kept only one wife, Anna, sister of the Byzantine Emperor, whom he received along with baptism as a price for returning Crimea to Byzantium. According to the Chronicles, Vladimir even stopped punishing criminals in accordance with the commandment: "Thou shallt not judge." Allegedly, it was the Greek clergy who convinced Vladimir to reestablish the courts and even to apply the death penalty in extreme cases. Dimitri Likhachev, a leading expert on Old Russian civilization, cites, as additional evidence of the religious sincerity of Vladimir's conversion, his preoccupation with Christian education, with building churches, and with composing a Church Statute which gave the Church much wider powers than those known in Byzantium. Likhachev argues that no such activities were evident in the post-baptismal behavior of St Stephen, the baptizer of Hungary, or in that of the Polish and Czech princes who brought Christianity to their countries.

Also, in contrast with Hungary, where Stephen had to wage war against Hungarian princes and clans to force them to accept Christianity, in Russia there were reports of only two local rebellions against the new religion—the first in Novgorod in 1073, led by *volkhvy*, some Slavonic pagan priests, oracles and prophets; and the other in the Finnish Quarter of the northeastern town of Suzdal in the 1030s. It is interesting that both rebellions occurred in areas with large Finnish populations, and in the case of Suzdal, it is plainly stated that this was a Finnish rebellion. There is no historical evidence of any Finnish resistance to the Slavonic expansion into their territory. This is self explanatory: the rural population was very sparse in the north, living and farming in temporary forest clearings. The Finns made their clearings, the Russians made theirs, and they did not bother each other. But Finnish resistance to Christianity was rather stubborn and prolonged. Soviet archaeologists have found numerous cases of whole Finnic clans reacting to the spread of Christianity in the north by suicidal migrations to the far North, where they could not cultivate sufficient food and died out in their isolated dugouts. In fact, one of the Finnic peoples, the contemporary Mari Republic in the Volga-Urals area has recently declared paganism an official national religion, along with Orthodox Christianity.

There is very little reliable information about Russian paganism, as pre-Christian Russians had no alphabet. Literacy was associated with Christianity, hence it is possible that the *volkhvy* remained illiterate as an act of resistance against Christianity. The nineteenth-century Russian-Ukrainian writer, Nikolai Gogol, left us some mementos of the remnants of pagan traditions and superstitions in the Ukraine in his collection of stories, *The Evenings at the Farmstead near Dikan'ka*. Such celebrations as the carnival of the Cheesefare week just before Lent have their roots in the pre-Christian pagan spring feast. But that is about all.

Yet, that some form of written communication had existed in pre-Christian Rus' is evident from the Byzantine documents which say that, for instance, the peace treaties between the Rus' and the Byzantines of 911 and 944 were drafted in Greek and in Russian. The story of Constantine's visit to the Hazars says that on his way, in Crimea, he saw a Gospel "written in Russian." This indicates that some alphabet was used by Russian Christians even before the work of Cyril and Methodius. Could that have been an early form of the Glagolithic, improved by the Macedonian brothers and then simplified and hellenized by their disciples? Or did the pre-Cyrillian Slavs simply use Greek characters (phonetically insufficient for Slavonic sounds)? The questions remain unanswered. Significant, however, is that in all cases except the peace treaties, literacy is associated with Christianity. The most reliable historical hypothesis is that, as only Christians could write, and writing was necessary for international treaties and other documents of the Prince's chancellery, the pre-Christian Russian rulers simply hired local Christians to run their chancellery. Thus our original thesis, that literacy came with

Christianity and that the Slavonic pagan wizards were illiterate, still stands. But the question arises as to why hardly any examples of Russian writing of the pre-conversion era have survived.[4] The answer seems to lie in the fact that the vast majority of Christians in Rus' before 988 was concentrated in the south (Tmutorokan' and Kiev), areas most savagely and repeatedly devastated by invasions of the steppe nomads. Even Kievan documents of the post-conversion era have survived almost exclusively in copies stored in Novgorod, Vladimir-Moscow, or in the western cities of Lvov and Vilna (Vilnius).

The relatively peaceful process of Christianization of the original multi-tribal land of Rus' may at least partly be attributed to the use of the near-vernacular Slavonic (or Old Bulgarian, as it is often called), which made the Christian message more clearly understandable than did the use of Latin in the West. Yet such secular historians as Paul Miliukov, for instance, have used the term *dvoeverie* or "duality of faith" to describe the early Russian Christian, claiming that for several centuries there remained a mixture of paganism and Christianity in the religious beliefs of the common man. The great contemporary Russian Christian scholar, Dmitri Likhachev, however, rejects this term as the invention of a bureaucrat. You can believe either in Jesus or in pagan deities, he argues, but not in both simultaneously. What occurred, according to Likhachev, was that some pagan traditions and pantheistic ideas of the early Slavs penetrated the world of the Russian peasant and remained a part of his life, neither conflicting with nor debasing his/her faith in God and Jesus as the Son of God. Such, in his opinion, was the personification of the *Moist Mother-Earth*. A more recent example of the symbolism of the *Moist Mother Earth* can be seen in Dostoevsky's *Crime and Punishment*, when Raskolnikov kneels and kisses the earth, the source of life, in an act of atonement for the sin of murder. Likhachev argues that this veneration of the Earth had nothing to do with *dvoeverie*—simply that some pre-Christian traditions became a part of a Russian's, particularly a peasant's, life, devoid of any rationalization on his part. In believing, say, in a house spirit (*domovoi*) the peasant did not place him on the same level as Christ or as any Christian saint. At the most he treated pagan survivals as bad, often satanic, spirits.

Fedotov, in his *The Russian Religious Mind*, pointed out that the "worship" of the Earth as a cult of fertility and motherhood in pre-Christian Rus' found its way into the particularly popular Russian veneration of the Mother

---

4   There is the notorious clay jug with a few Glagolithic letters, which anyhow seems to be of Balkan-Slavonic origin.

of God, where the motherhood has been stressed to a greater degree than the virginity of Mary. He believed that that veneration of motherhood, of femininity, resulted in certain ethical characteristic of the Russian male as well: "The mother taught him kindness and fidelity, not freedom and valor—the male virtues." According to Fedotov, this was one of the basic character formation differences between the Russians and the West Europeans. The latter developed their traditions of knighthood, with the sword being the tool to defend the rights and dignity of individual knights. The Russians, said Fedotov, saw society as an extended family and the *rod* (clan being the nearest English rendition of the term), as the continuity of the family through generations (the use of the patronymic in Russian, the name of the *pater familias,* being its expression). In this scheme of things, the tsar was seen as the father of the nation as an extended family, his subjects being his children. The nineteenth-century Slavophiles continued that tradition in their vision of an organic unity between the nation and its tsar.

Fedotov believed that one of the reasons why the primacy of individual freedom never became deeply rooted in Russian mass culture was the vision of society as a family or as a social organism, where the cult of motherhood and the female values of fidelity, humility, and a degree of fatalism took the place of Western pride and honor. In Fedotov's view, the particular national veneration of Boris and Gleb proved the accuracy of his thesis.[5] According to the Chronicles and the princes' *vitae*, their only qualification for sainthood was that in the fratricidal struggle unleashed, allegedly, by Sviatopolk the Dread, their eldest brother, they had refused to put up any resistance to him, stating that after their father's death, the eldest brother's authority over them was as absolute as that of their father. They thus went to the slaughter like lambs, refusing to heed the advice of their retinue to put up a fight. The Church in Constantinople at first resisted accepting their sainthood on the grounds that they had been not martyrs for faith, but victims of an internecine war. But eventually the Mother-Church too accepted the universal cult of the two brothers in Rus'.

But let us go back to St Vladimir and look at his Church Statute. Not only was it very generous to the Church, but it also reflected a society that was

---

5 Andrzej Poppe, the Polish authority on the spiritual history of Kievan Rus', places the beginning of the Boris and Gleb cult in the 1070's. He emphasizes the Orthodox tradition of a saint's cult arising "from below," i.e., at the initiative of the population of the locality where the saints lived or were martyred, or of the local bishop. This tradition, he points out, was particularly characteristic of Byzantium and early Rus'. Cf. *Russia Mediaevalis*, pp. 6-29.

quite different from Byzantium which, with its concept of symphony, had known no division between the secular and the ecclesiastic spheres, even at the level of legal courts. A plaintiff or a defendant had the right to choose between a bishop as president of the court set up to judge his case, or a lay presiding judge. But in Russia, the sources (and therefore the hierarchy) of authority of the prince, a local Barbarian chieftain, and that of the Metropolitan-Archbishop of Kiev were radically different. The Metropolitan was either a citizen of the illustrious East Roman Empire, or even if he was a native Russian, he was nevertheless ordained by the Ecumenical Patriarch in Constantinople and approved by the Roman Emperor himself! Thus, as long as the Russian Church remained a subordinate branch of the great Church of Constantinople, her chief hierarch's status stood far above that of the local prince. This special position of the Church was reflected in the first Russian Church Statute. The late British historian John Fennell noticed also another aspect related to the non-Russian origin of most metropolitans of Kiev: the rarity of their interference into interprincely relations and other purely internal Russian political matters. The cases, of their active mediation in inter-princely feuds during the pre-Mongol period of Russian history (with positive results), as reported in the Chronicles, could be counted on the fingers of one hand. More common were the cases of active intervention and mediations by particularly revered local monks or even by some ad-hoc councils of parish clergy (*sbory iereiskie*). Thus Grigori, abbot of St Andrei's Monastery in Kiev, with the help of such a *sbor* of all priests of Kiev "in 1128 managed to avert war" between the prince of Kiev, Mstislav, and his nephew, prince of Chernigov. Nevertheless, the question remains: would their voice have been as effective as it was had their hierarchical administration not been somewhat extra-territorial?

St Vladimir established an ecclesial court structure apart from the secular one. The ecclesial courts received jurisdiction over all moral transgressions of the laity: matrimonial and divorce matters, polygamy, blasphemy, foul language, matters relating to dowry, kidnapping of brides, rape, property disputes between husbands and wives, adultery, assaults and physical fights within families. St Vladimir's Statute made it clear that royal power was derivative from and circumscribed by the superior norms of Christian moral teachings; and it stressed that the limitation on secular rulers would be forever binding. That moral limitation subsequently remained the only restriction on the powers of Russian autocrats. The Statute stated that these limitations on the prince's powers related only to his Christian subjects, while his powers over the pagans was unlimited, because they were not subject to the authority of the Church. It may be of interest that the same idea is found in the writings of St Augustine, with which Vladimir could not have been familiar, as a Russian translation of Augustine's writings was not available until the sixteenth century. Of course, some of the Greek clergy engaged in baptizing the Russians could have been familiar with Augustine's writings.

The Statute further prescribed that ten percent of the State budget be given to the Church. Ecclesial judicial functions became another important source of income for the Church, as most penalties in the early Russian codes were in the form of monetary fines of diverse value. The Statute became the basis of all subsequent legislation on the judicial powers of the Church in Russia. Laws on marriage and divorce and some other family matters were based on St Vladimir's Statute until 1917.

The Church and the Nation

Size, ethnic and cultural diversity, and extremes of climate making communications very difficult also exacerbated the advance of the Christian culture. The demand for priests far exceeded both the supply and the capacities of the educational establishments. As Russia advanced eastward, northward and toward the northeast, the gap between supply and demand only increased. This forced the hierarchy to ordain more and more uneducated, sometimes practically illiterate priests for the more distant and isolated parts of the country. Thus, in the first centuries after the conversion, the general educational and cultural level of the clergy declined, particularly in comparison to the period of the conversion and immediately after, when the still limited urban flock had been served mostly by missionaries from the Balkans (probably Bulgars and Macedonians) and their Russian disciples. The low level of the subsequent generations of priests and monastic scribes resulted in some errors and textual discrepancies in the service books, which would become one of the factors of controversy in the Great Schism of the seventeenth century.

Most historians have accepted the fact that, as Orthodox Christianity was being assimilated, it acquired the character of a truly Russian national religion. The highly secular and agnostic historian Paul Miliukov saw the process dialectically. In the Kievan period, he argued, the relatively well educated missionary clergy and the new schools and libraries in the major Russian cities stood far above the cultural level of the nation. The Orthodox Church was then the religion of the elite. As she embraced the nation, the clergy's and the Church's level of sophistication began to decline even as the nation's culture was rising. The intellectual decline of the clergy, however, was more rapid than the cultural rise of the nation. The two met roughly in the second half of the fourteenth century—the time of St Sergius of Radonezh, Metropolitan Alexis of Moscow, etc.—and from then on the Church and the national culture became one and began to grow culturally in harmony with each other, even if very slowly. The scenario makes sense, except that personalities such as Sts Alexis of Moscow and Sergius of Radonezh, not to mention Metropolitan Cyprian (Tsamblak), were highly educated individuals, definitely far above the average level of the nation. So the meeting of the nation and the Church had to occur earlier than Miliukov has suggested, perhaps by the very beginning of the fourteenth century.

The view that the "inculturation" of the Church had occurred considerably earlier than Miliukov had suggested was held by George Fedotov, a very perceptive Church historian. He argued that the use of the near-vernacular Slavonic turned the Church into a native institution rather rapidly, and to a much greater degree than the Latin Roman Catholic Church ever achieved in any country except, perhaps, in the near-Latin speaking Italy. Fedotov, however, sees both positive and negative consequences in that "inculturation."

Latin and Greek were almost interchangeable as languages in which the writings of both Antiquity and Christianity were available. Therefore, the fact that not only the Church but all education in the West functioned in Latin made the intellectual and theological legacy of the Greco-Roman world readily accessible to every literate person in Western Europe. In the Eastern Church, by comparison the use of the near-vernacular brought the Scriptures and their lessons into every Christian's daily life (and not only for the ones who could read, for even the illiterates could still hear the Gospel lessons at each church service). The Church became much more a part of the daily life of the Russian, reflected in his/her piety, humility, constant references to the teachings of Christ. A multitude of common expressions invoking God ("thank God," "God-permitting," "God grant," "with God's help") became so common that even Soviet Communist leaders used them in their speeches. The Russian expression of thanks is either "May God save you" or "I invoke blessings on you," and the word for Sunday is *voskresenie*, i.e., resurrection. But the use of the vernacular by the Church and in education limited the educated Russian's access to the treasures of the Greco-Roman culture. As even a literate Russian could very rarely read Greek, he had to wait for translations. Cyril and Methodius and their disciples made many translations, but much remained to be done. Very few Russian ecclesiastics knew either Greek or Latin, and it is unlikely that the schools established by Vladimir and his son Yaroslav-the-Wise, taught much Greek if any. Hence the early Russian library was quite limited. With time, more linguists and translations would have become available; but Kiev's and Byzantium's decline in the twelfth-thirteenth centuries and the subsequent Mongol-Tatar invasions, which ended the Kievan era and caused Russia's statehood to move to the primitive and isolated northeast, as well as the sacking of Constantinople by the crusaders in 1204, from which the Empire never fully recuperated, delayed Russia's enlightenment by a good two centuries.

Peter Struve, a famous Russian economist and philosopher of history, expressed another dimension of the role of Church Slavonic in early Russia. He pointed out that it was the Bulgaro-Macedonian language that was brought into Russia, not a language spoken by the Russians. Yet the Slavonic tribal dialects of the time were still sufficiently close to each other for the new Church language to be commonly understood by all Slavs. As Church Slavonic became the synthetic common literary language of the whole loose federation of Russian princes, it functioned as a national coalescing agent, forging the diverse eastern Slavonic tribes into a single nation. In other words, Russians had had a common national language before they formed a single Russian nation. This leads Struve to conclude: "The single Russian nation is older than the single Russian state." This undoubtedly facilitated Moscow's task of molding the nation into a single Great Russian State during the fourteenth-sixteenth centuries.

Nevertheless, it cannot be disputed that the use of Slavonic did slow the transplantation onto Russian soil of the intellectual heritage of Greek antiquity, as well as of the Church Fathers. But the amazingly rapid advancement of the early Kievan Christian civilization with its mushrooming schools, including probably the first women's college in Europe outside of Byzantium, would have soon made up the gap through translations, had the growth not been stopped by adverse historical events. And undoubtedly Slavonic, being so close to the vernacular, was an important channel for such rapid cultural growth. Clearly illustrating this is the richness of expression and vocabulary found in the earliest written Russian documents, such as the *Chronicles* or the *Sermon on Law and Grace* delivered in the newly-erected magnificent St Sophia Cathedral around 1040 by the Archimandrite Ilarion of the Kievan Caves Monastery, who would become the first Russian native metropolitan about a decade later. Taking into consideration that it was written a mere half-century after the introduction of literacy, its richness of expression has no parallels in the vernacular writings of Europe of the period. The Sermon is not merely an exercise in elegant oratory. Ilarion unfurls a thesis in the philosophy of history, which he sees as a dialectical process of law and grace:

a. The strain of the law given by Moses is the strain of slavery, for to live by law is to live in spiritual slavery;

b. The strain of grace brought by Jesus is the way of freedom. The development of humanity through history is a process of the gradual replacement of law by grace and of a gradual expansion of grace, as more and more countries become christianized.

This contempt for law as belonging to the sphere of slavery, compulsion, force, and hence to human and ungodly passions of hate, envy, and pride, is typical of the Eastern Church, which draws the lesson from the Gospel that the only law worthy of mankind is the law of love (e.g., St Paul's words that in God's Kingdom even faith will disappear, because we shall see God, but love will remain eternally).[6] Metropolitan Ilarion then goes on to praise St Vladimir's baptism of Rus', which he compares to the work of the Apostles. He sees Vladimir as the ideal prince who combines piety with power and rules his land with justice, courage, and reason.

Secular power, he argues, should concern itself with the interests of the faith. A good prince, such as Vladimir, has the right to subjugate unenlightened nations, even by the sword, spreading to them the light of Christianity. Yet every secular power must respect the instructions of the Church. This, of course, corresponds to the Byzantine *symphonia* theory.

Ilarion asserted in his sermon the glory and independence of the Christian Russian state, thus implicitly rejecting Byzantine claims of suzerainty over Russia. He claims a global missionary (or messianic) importance of the conversion of Russia, thus foreshadowing the "Third Rome" and the "Holy Russia" ideologies of the sixteenth and seventeenth centuries.

Another remarkable document was the *Instruction* of Vladimir Monomakh to his children written in the first quarter of the twelfth century.

6 This may be so in absolute terms, but in the fallen world such contempt for worldly laws and regulations in the Christian East has been conducive to the reign of despots, while the eventual prevalence of legalistic concepts in the West led to the birth of modern democracy.

Although he was the last Kievan prince to unite the Russian principalities into a relatively powerful unified state, his *Instruction* is remarkable in its deep appreciation of Christianity and its sense of true Christian humility. Vladimir criticizes our tendencies to avenge each case of personal insult, to subdue our enemies by the sword, and says that the only true and sure way of overcoming our enemies, as taught by Jesus Christ, is: "repentance, tears and charity ... I beg you in the name of God," Monomakh continues, "remember these three, however hard it may be to abide by them."

He then implores his children never to forget to pray, with humility and prostrations, both in church and at home. "Pray even while riding a horse... and if no other prayer comes to you, then secretly, in your mind, repeat constantly: 'Lord, have mercy,' for that prayer is so much better than all sorts of ungracious thoughts." This instruction reveals Vladimir's knowledge of Orthodox theology and of the Eastern monastic teaching on the constant silent repetition of the Jesus prayer: "Lord, Jesus Christ, be merciful to me, a sinner." This prayer, according to the hesychast school of monasticism, ought to become a subconscious process accompanying every breath. "Most of all," Vladimir continues, "don't ignore the poor and, as much as you can, give alms to orphans and give protection to widows. Don't let the mighty of this world oppress any human being." Then Vladimir raises his voice against capital punishment: "Do not deprive of life either the innocent or the guilty, and do not order anyone killed. Even if his guilt deserves execution, still do not deprive of life a Christian soul." Then he instructs his children not to swear and never to break a promise. Vladimir sees laziness as a source of much wrongdoing:

> Do not take your armour off in a hurry, for man perishes when he is overcome by sloth and takes no precautions. Beware of lies, drunkenness, lechery—thereof perishes the soul, as well as the body...do not allow your retinue to hurt anybody, whether our own or a stranger...so that no one damns you ...Visit the sick, pay your last respects to the deceased, for we are all mortal. Do not pass a human being without greeting and saying a friendly word to him. Love your wife but do not allow her to rule over you. Everything in your life should be founded on a fear of God.

> ...Do not forget the good things you have learned and learn those things you do not know, as my father[7] did, who sitting at home learned five languages—this assures respect from other nations.

7 The great prince Vsevolod, a son of Yaroslav the Wise and the husband of a daughter of the Byzantine emperor from the House of Monomakhos, hence Vladimir's second name, Monomakh.

After confessing his own misdeeds, Vladimir justifies himself somewhat by saying that he never allowed either a poor peasant or a humble widow to be oppressed. He then asks his children or any other prospective reader not to be too critical of him who never praised himself but "praised God and glorified His kindness upon me, the sinful and unworthy one..." Vladimir warns against those who say "I love God, but I do not love my brother." "This is a lie," Vladimir warns: "If you do not forgive your brother's sins, then neither will you be forgiven by your Heavenly Father." This is followed by other Gospel quotations.

"The Library" of the Kievan Intellectual

We have mentioned the problem of the transfer of culture through translations. Let us see what translations and what local writings were available to the reading public of the period.

Among the first theologico-philosophical works to have been translated into the Slavonic and circulated during the pre-Mongol era was *The Source of Knowledge* by St John of Damascus. The opus explains basic philosophical concepts, systems and terms of Aristotle, Socrates, Plato, Heraclites, and Parmenides. Thus the educated Kievan elite was familiar with ancient philosophy, although only through secondary sources.

St John then explains the theory of knowledge and classifies scholarly disciplines into speculative philosophy and practical philosophy. The former includes theology, physiology (sic), and mathematics, which is further subdivided into arithmetic, geometry, astronomy, and music (theory of sounds). Practical philosophy includes ethics, economy (household), and politics. But the most significant part of the Damascene's work is his philosophically substantiated and passionately defended notion of the freedom of the will, his criticism of determinism, including astrology with its attempts to predict human destinies by attaching some secret meaning to natural phenomena. St John's essentially Orthodox doctrine of freedom contrasts sharply with St Augustine's concept of predestination, which came to dominate Western theology, and was later inherited and brought to the extreme by Calvin—thence finding its way into Hegel's philosophy of history and eventually into Marxist historical determinism.

Early Rus' also produced her own interesting thinkers in addition to the above mentioned Metropolitan Ilarion, including Metropolitan Clement

Smoliatich, St Cyril, Bishop of Turov and others. On the occasion of Clement's elevation to the Kievan see in 1147, a chronicler noted that such a philosopher there had never been in the land of Rus'. Unfortunately only one of his works has survived to our day. It is a well-argued defense of an allegorical, rather than a literal, interpretation of the Old Testament. When he turns to the New Testament, just as Ilarion he emphasizes the priority of grace brought by Jesus to replace the Old Testament Law. Grace, he writes, is freedom; law is subjugation. In his arguments and illustrations, taken eclectically from Greek and Alexandrian sources, Clement demonstrates considerable scholarly erudition. Fedotov believed that Clement's use of these sources indicates the existence of a rather large body of Slavonic translations from the Greek by the twelfth century, as there is no evidence that Clement knew Greek. Many more writings by Cyril of Turov have been preserved to our day; but very little is known of him as a person, except that he was bishop of the small Belorussian appanage town of Turov during the mid-twelfth century. His works fall into three categories: letters, sermons, and prayers. Like Clement, he favored and defended the allegorical interpretation of the Old Testament. He often illustrated his arguments by citing some Oriental parable. His sermons show him to have been a great orator, often emulating the style of St John Chrysostom and other Byzantine fathers. Cyril's style was that of a high, unemotional, intellectual poetry. In Fedotov's words, his writings were "oriented towards the divine, not the human." He sought inspiration not in the Gospel, but in the liturgical tradition of the Church. Surprisingly he knew the Old Testament much better than the New, in referring to which he occasionally committed such errors as, for instance, saying that Jesus had fed 500 people instead of 5,000. That such errors remained uncorrected by Russian scribes and copyists until the seventeenth century reveals something of their level of education.

So far, we have discussed Kiev and southwestern Rus', but the less developed north, namely the Novgorod lands, did not remain silent. A sample of the Novgorodian theological thought has been preserved in the writings of Luka Zhidiata, a bishop of Novgorod. His thought and its expression, however, lacked the graceful style and ornateness characteristic of the southwest. His vocabulary is direct, almost conversational in style. The ethics he preaches are instructive and practical in character. Both in Novgorod and the northeast (Suzdal', Vladimir, Moscow), the main theological expression was in the form of spiritual art—iconography and church architecture, both of which became truly native in this area, in contrast to Kiev's close imitation of Byzantium or simply the employment of imported Byzantine masters.

During the thirteenth century, most of Russia's traditional skills, including architecture, disappeared, as skilled craftsmen were captured by the invading Tatar-Mongols and taken as slaves to Central Asia and other Tatar centers. But the Tatars, pagans at first and then converting to Islam, had no use for iconography. Their respect for the Russian Church, however, and the immunities given to her monastic institutions, spared the monasteries from destruction. Hence the art of iconography, mostly concentrated in monasteries, was not only preserved under the Tatar Yoke, but even reached its artistic apex in the fourteenth-fifteenth centuries. With the decline of education after the fall of Kiev and the Tatar invasions, the art and practice of preaching virtually disappeared in the Russian northeast, although there were a few exceptions, such as the sermons of Serapion, a thirteenth-century bishop of Vladimir. Altogether, the church service in the near-vernacular Slavonic made the sermon less necessary than in the Latin West, where preaching basically consisted of a free translation of the Bible lesson of the day, which was read in incomprehensible Latin. In post-Kievan Rus', the average priest would often read from one of the volumes of Commentaries on Scriptural readings instead of attempting to compose his own sermon. The revival of preaching had to wait until the seventeenth century.

The lay literature of the time—based mostly on biblical, quasi-biblical, and historical themes—also reached considerable sophistication of style and expression. The most famous literary work of the time was *The Lay of the Prince Igor's Host,* an epic poem about an unsuccessful minor campaign of a local prince against the Polovtsians in 1185, written apparently by a campaign participant. Its literary mastery remained unmatched in Russian literature until the early nineteenth century. Fedotov expressed the opinion that a work of such mastery could not have been an isolated event; it could only be the product of a certain culture which must have produced other works of a similar niveau that have not survived to our day. In fact, even *The Lay* was discovered only at the end of the eighteenth century, in a provincial Russian monastery library in a single copy.

Although other extant literary products of the period are inferior to *The Lay,* the volume of the literary output of both periods is both abundant and diverse, consisting of hagiographies, historical tales, travelogues. The early Kievan *Chronicles*, in fact, are of very high literary quality. Some critics have claimed that they have no parallel in other European historical chronicles of the time. The vocabulary of the Kievan *Chronicles* is in excess of 12,000 words, an amazing achievement within a century of gaining an alphabet. The chronicler, a learned monk in most cases, was not a mere recorder of historical events: he served "the higher cause" of the state, his prince and the Church. In Nicholas Riasanovsky's words, the chronicler was less interested in the "structure and development of human society, than in the ethical sense of events, and the possible moral conclusions therefrom. His attitude is moral-historical. History for him is a constant struggle between the Good and the Evil for the human soul."

Our brief review of the amazing intellectual and cultural progress of Rus', within a mere century and a half of its conversion to Christianity and the introduction to literacy that accompanied it, would be incomplete without citing the words of St Cyril, the enlightener of the Slavs, pronounced in the ninth century about the Slavic race as such: "Indeed, the Slavonic tribe is now flying ahead as if on wings."

Yet that surge forward was short-lived. In the west, the Slavs were forcefully Latinized and Germanized; in the Balkans, the progress was cut short by the Turkish invasion and the subsequent Ottoman yoke of nearly four centuries; in Rus', internal fragmentation and eventually the Tatar-Mongol Yoke of over 200 years clipped her wings for several centuries.

But not everything can be blamed on external factors (which, of course, became internal once the countries in question had lost their independence). In the case of Russia an interesting hypothesis has been put forward by Georges Florovsky. He believed simply that "the package" received by Rus' from Byzantium was too sophisticated for the young and primitive country to digest. The sophistication, civilization, and theology of the old Rome which "fed" the young Barbarian cultures of Western Europe were considerably more primitive than those of Byzantium. Moreover, most of the Western countries were rising on territories formerly controlled by the defunct Roman Empire, i.e., their original cultural terrain was not a *tabula rasa,* as was the case for Rus'. Hence, the development in the West was gradual, whereas in Russia, the entire complex Byzantine legacy, with its intricate civil service, a minutely developed legal system with codes and rules, its welfare system of hospitals, hospices, its sophisticated education, poetics, oratory, philosophizing and, most of all, its complex theology—was all at once pushed down the throat of the infantile nation. Nothing, it seemed, was left to the imagination of the Russians. No room was left for creativity, all was ready-made, and all that remained for the Russians to do was to digest that huge package. A few great individuals managed to swallow most of it, and even to produce interesting regurgitations of that food. But the country as a whole choked on that rich nourishment. Very likely, Rus' as a whole would eventually have been able to digest it and to be inspired by it for further creativity. But its disintegration, caused by external and internal factors in the thirteenth century, delayed the process by some four centuries, by which time, alas, Russia was much more interested in imitating Western Europe than in a creative readaptation and revival of her true and essential legacy.

FOR FURTHER READING

Bulgakov, S., *The Orthodox Church* (Crestwood, NY, 1988).

Dunlop, D., *The History of the Jewish Khazars* (Princeton, N J, 1954).

Dvornik, F., "Byzantine Political Ideas in Kievan Russia," *Dumbarton Oaks Papers* 9 and 10 (1956).

_____, "The Kiev State and Its Relations with Europe," *Transactions of the Royal Historical Society* 29 (1947).

_____, *The* Slavs, Their Early History and Civilization (Boston, 1956).

Fedotov, George, *The Russian Religious Mind*, vol. I (Belmont, MA: Nordland Press, 1975).

_____, *A Treasury of Russian Spirituality* (New York, 1948).

Kaiser, Daniel H, *The Growth of the Law in Medieval Russia* (Princeton University Press, 1980).

Kartashev, A., *Ocherki po istorii Russkoi Tserkvi*, vol. I (Moscow, 1992).

Klyuchevsky, V., *Course of Russian History*, vol. I (New York, 1911).

_____, *Zhitiia sviatykh, kak istorichekii istochnik* (Moscow, 1871).

Miliukov, P, *Outlines of Russian Culture*, vol. 1 (Philadelphia, 1942).

Obolensky, D, "Byzantium, Kiev and Moscow: a Study in Ecclesiastical Relations," *Dumbarton Oaks Papers* 11 (1957).

_____, "Russia's Byzantine Heritage," *Oxford Slavonic Papers* 1(1950).

Poppe, A, *The Rise of Christian Russia* (London: Variorum, 1982).

Priselkov, M.D., *Ocherki po tserkovno-politicheskoi istorii Kievskoi Rusi X -XII vv.* (St Petersburg, 1913).

Riasanovsky, A., *The Normanist Theory of the Origin of the Russian State: a Critical Analysis* (Ann Arbor: University Microfilms, 1974).

Riasanovsky, N. V. *A History of Russia* (Oxford University Press, 1993).

Runciman, S., "Byzantium, Russia and Caesaropapism" *Canadian Slavonic Papers* 2 (1957).

Russia Mediaevalis, tomus I (Munich: Fink Verlag, 1973).

Smirnov, S.I., *Drevne-russkii dukhovnik; issledovanie po istorii tserkovnogo byta* (Moscow, 1914).

Soloviev, S.M., *Istoriia Rossii s drevneishikh vremen*, v. I (Moscow, 1950).

Vasiliev, A., *The Goths in the Crimea* (Cambridge, MA, 1936).

Vernadsky, G. *Kievan Russia* (New Haven, CT, 1948).

_____, *Medieval Russian Laws*. (Records of Civilization, No. 41) (New York, 1947).

Zenkovsky, S., *Medieval Russian Epics, Chronicles and Tales* (New York: Dutton, 1974).

Zernov, N., "Vladimir and the Origin of the Russian Church," *Slavonic and East European Review* 28 (1949-50).

CHAPTER 3

CHURCH AND STATE IN MEDIEVAL RUSSIA

According to the Franco-Russian historian Eck, the Kievan or pre-Mongol period is the Russian Antiquity, the thirteenth-seventeenth centuries are the Medieval age, of which the last century and a half is a transitional period from the Medieval to the Modern Age, or a pale reflection of the European Renaissance.

According to this periodization, in this chapter we treat the Muscovite Middle Ages, of which the thirteenth century could be considered the Russian Dark Age. Fedotov calls the thirteenth-fourteenth centuries Russia's "Age of Silence." By silence Fedotov means the absence of literature, of a written Russian self-expression. However, writing there was, particularly from the second half of the fourteenth century. Therefore Fedotov's term can to some extent be applied only to the thirteenth and the early fourteenth centuries. Even then *Chronicles* and other forms of writing continued. But certainly the greatest Russian contribution to world culture during this period was in the form of iconography and frescos.

With the collapse of a single undisputed center of Rus', and its replacement by the proliferation of practically independent appanages busy fighting one another,[1] the concept of a single Russian state or of a common heritage of Rus' was practically erased from the memory of both politicians and the general populace. The only institution that remembered the term Rus' was the Church. Only her chief bishop bore the title of "Metropolitan of Kiev and All Rus'," which the metropolitans retained even after having moved their de-facto residence to the northeast. Therefore the "capital" of what remained of the country was not where a great prince or grand duke sat,[2] but where the metropolitan of All Rus' resided. Frequent riots against the Tatars were caused mostly by their crude and oppressive tax collecting system: the collectors, *baskaks* in Tatar, regularly raided towns and villages with an armed cavalry detachment collecting the tax directly, often taking more than the official tithe,

---

1 Lack of inter-princely solidarity and cooperation was the main reason for the success of the Mongols in subjugating all of them, one by one.

2 In accepted English terminology Kievan princes are called Great Princes, Moscow princes of the 14th-16th cc. are known as Grand Dukes, although in Russian both are called *velikii kniaz'*.

plundering and raping along the way. In revenge, *baskaks* and their retinue were often killed. Enraged, the Tatar *khan* would undertake a bloody, punitive operation against the region or against the ruling prince of the given principality. Since the Tatars had great respect for the Church, it was one of the most important functions of the metropolitans and other bishops to mediate between the *khan* and a Russian prince, trying to protect the latter and his subjects from Tatar revenge. They also mediated between feuding Russian princes, often calling for *national* unity in the *Russian* land in the hope of one day achieving freedom from foreign domination.

In the performance of these mediatory functions, double dealing, hypocrisy, cunning, flattery, and deception were inevitable, as exemplified, for instance, by Metropolitan Kirill II (or III, according to some historians), a Galician (West-Ukrainian by modern terminology) archimandrite, chosen for the post by the mighty Galician-Volynian Prince Daniel Romanovich. Owing to the conquest of Constantinople by the Crusaders and the establishment there of a temporary Latin "Empire," Kirill returned from his consecration in Nicea (the temporary capital of the Orthodox Byzantine Empire) in 1248, only to discover much to his dismay, that his prince was negotiating with the pope to launch a joint campaign against the Tatars. Having witnessed what the papacy had done to the Orthodox in Byzantium, Kirill talked Daniel out of the agreement and left for the northeast to support the Grand Duke Alexander Nevsky in his decision to acquiesce to the Mongol authority in order to fight the Teutonic Knights, who had been blessed by the pope to conquer Russia for the Latin Church. He realized that, whereas the Tatars respected the Church and left the infrastructure of Russia basically intact, the Westerners sought to destroy the Orthodox Church and impose conversion to Roman Catholicism.

In his active support for Alexander, Kirill just as actively engages in humiliating flattery toward the Tatars, assuring them of eternal loyalty, while in confidential letters to Russian princes he expresses his hope for eventual national freedom. He is constantly on the road, visiting Russian towns, encouraging the population to restore the devastated country. At the same time, in 1261, he gains from the Tatar Khan Mangu-Temir the right to establish an Orthodox diocese in Saray, the capital of the Golden Horde, the Khanate running Russia. The same *khan* grants a charter of immunities to the Orthodox Church in 1279, according to which the Church is freed from all forms of taxation and duties owed the Tatars; her lands and real estate are declared off-limits to the Tatars. Having gained these privileges, the Church (and particularly her monasteries) becomes the storehouse, as it were, of the national capital, as well as the preserver of whatever remains of education, arts and crafts, and a refuge for the population from Tatar excesses.

Kirill II died in 1281 in Alexander's temporary capital of Pereiaslav-Zalesski, but in accordance with tradition, he was buried in the crypt of St Sophia Cathedral in Kiev, the last All-Russian metropolitan to be buried there. His successor, the Greek Metropolitan Maxim, after arriving in Kiev and seeing the devastation there, also chose the northeast, de facto transferring his seat to the city of Vladimir, less than 150 kilometers east of Moscow, at that time a small outpost of the Vladimir Grand Duchy. The next candidate for the metropolitanate, a Volynian archimandrite named Peter, again betrayed the hopes of his Galician patron, Prince Leo, son of the late Prince Daniel. On his return from Constantinople (regained by the Greeks in 1260), Peter chose to establish Vladimir as his seat. Often visiting Moscow, whose prince Ivan Kalita was the first Moscow prince to receive the title of Grand Duke from the *khan*, Peter died there in 1326 and in his will allegedly requested to be buried in Moscow. His example was followed by his successor, the Greek Theognostos,[3] who spent much time in Moscow. His Russian successor, Metropolitan Alexis (1354-78), proved to be an outstanding statesman and diplomat, winning the strong confidence of the Tatar *khan,* whose wife he cured from blindness. Russians believed this to have been a miracle, and this was one of the factors leading to his canonization by the Church. His canonization, as well as that of Metropolitan Peter, solidified Moscow's position as the ecclesiastic capital of Russia.

Grand Duke Dimitri Donskoi and the Church

Dimitri, the son of Ivan II of Moscow, was grandson of the first Moscow grand duke. He ascended the throne in infancy, and the state was at first ruled by a council of guardians presided over by Metropolitan Alexis. Busy with his political functions, Alexis ignored the southwest, which by then had been annexed by Lithuania or, as it was known at the time, the Lithuanian-Russian Grand Duchy, because 80 percent of its population consisted of West Russians (now known as Ukrainians and Belorussians), and the official language of the state was Russo-Slavonic. The ethnic Lithuanians were still pagans, but

---

3 At this time Russians and Greeks, or rather Byzantine citizens, alternated on the Russian metropolitan throne.

some of the ruling princes and the Russianized aristocracy adopted Orthodox Christianity. Despite their new faith, they did not want their Orthodox subjects to be in the jurisdiction of a bishop who identified himself completely with the interests of Moscow, Lithuania's chief rival. This became their chief argument (and later that of the Polish kings as well) in favor of a separate metropolitan for West Russia in their numerous appeals to Constantinople, which only reluctantly and irregularly appointed separate metropolitans for Western Rus', e.g., in Galich in 1371.

Several crucial events in Russian secular and ecclesiastic history are associated with the reign of Dimitri. The most important was the Battle on the Kulikovo Field in 1380, in which for the first time a united Russian force of some 150,000 warriors, led by over twenty Russian princes under Dimitri's command, routed a Tatar force of 200,000 commanded by Mamai. With this victory, the first Russian victory over the Tatars in a major confrontation, Moscow's leadership of eastern Russia became a foregone conclusion, especially since the battle had the blessing of the highly revered Saint Sergius of Radonezh. According to his *vita* and the *Chronicles*, before setting out towards the Kulikovo Field on the banks of the Don River, due south of Moscow, Dimitri went 70 kilometers northeast to the Trinity Monastery to receive a blessing from its abbot, St Sergius. The latter is alleged to have inquired first whether all means of peaceful settlement had been exhausted. Dimitri assured him that this was so. Only after a long conversation between them did St Sergius agree to bless the confrontation, and he is even alleged to have allowed two monks, former warriors Peresvet and Osliabia, to join Dimitri's forces. Then Sergius prophesied that Dimitri would win.

According to some Soviet-Russian historians there was more at stake in this battle than just the fear of Tatar leaders that Russia was on its way to unification and to emancipation from their control. Allegedly Mamai was a Muslim fundamentalist of sorts and was on the march to conquer Russia for Islam. If this hypothesis is true, then Sergius' support for the battle, or rather the crusade, is even more meaningful and prophetic.

Sergius' era signifies a transition of the concept of sainthood in Russian mentality. He closes, as it were, the era of canonizing warrior-princes. Whereas during the Kievan period only two princes were canonized, Boris and Gleb (St Vladimir was entered into the lists of Russian saints only in the seventeenth c.), and neither of them for military exploits, in the thirteenth and early fourteenth centuries almost all canonizations were of princes, with no pretense to their piety or spiritual virtue. The most famous saint of the period was Prince Alexander Nevsky, whose only claim to sainthood was his successful defense of Novgorod from the Swedes and Germans, which his contemporaries treated as a miracle because of the enemies' greater numbers and better armaments. Even more shocking may seem the canonization of the fourteenth century Lithuanian prince Dovmont. While a pagan, he killed his father. Later, he was baptized into the Orthodox Church and invited by the city of Pskov to become its prince. The Pskovians canonized him for delivering the city from a German invasion. All these "saintly" warrior-princes took the tonsure shortly before their death, or on their death beds. The Osliabia-Peresvet story indicates that even monks could, under certain conditions, take up arms, and that this was quite acceptable to the Russian mentality of the time.

Certainly all Christian writings, including those of the period under discussion, condemn aggression and the unleashing of war. Nevertheless, the warrior-princes are praised for defending their people, i.e., for their readiness to lay their lives for their friends (Jn 15:13). It can therefore be concluded that there was a concept of just and unjust wars, the former being wars of defense, understood as a sacrificial service to fellow-men, similar to the monastic vocation. Hence, under these conditions, there was nothing wrong with exchanging the monastic robe for the sword, and vice versa. Life was full of misery, insecurity and danger. Those who helped to protect life and give some hope of security were seen as saintly deliverers.

Hesychasm in the Balkans and in Russia

Only after some semblance of stability was achieved by the mid-fourteenth century did people begin to venerate the more traditional Christian values, and the "warrior-saints" gave way to the eremitic and monastic saints. This coincides with what the late John Meyendorff called the Orthodox hesychastic pre-renaissance. In the Balkans, it began about a century earlier than in Russia. The Greek re-conquest of Constantinople in 1260 was followed by a revival of theological scholarship and the appearance of the last great Fathers of the Church, Gregory Palamas and his pupil Nicholas Cabasilas. St Gregory promoted and defended the so-called "hesychast" movement. *Hesychia* in Greek means silence, quietude. This school of monastic spiritual concentration emphasized an individual road to self-perfection via a ceaseless intellectual prayer (or prayer of the mind), repetition, special movements of the body, even a system of breathing, dividing the prayer, "God be merciful to me a sinner," between inhaling and exhaling, making it a psychosomatic process. Thus, in contrast to the schools of extreme asceticism prevalent particularly in the medieval West, the hesychasts restored the notion of body as a God-created vessel of the spirit, and taught that human spirituality can be achieved only in a harmony between the spirit and the body, controlling the latter by the spirit, but not mortifying the body. The highest mystical experience is the vision of the uncreated light of God (the divine energies), achieved through prayer, spiritual concentration, and asceticism. The energies can be perceived through prayer before an object of concentration. Thus, for example, God's miracles can be mediated through icons, before which so many prayers had been directed to God. In this process man becomes a co-creator with God in accordance with the theology of *theosis* (divinization): Jesus became man, so that man might become God.

Palamas' successful defense of hesychasm at the 1341, 1347 and 1351 councils of Constantinople encouraged the spread of the movement to all Orthodox countries, including Russia. At these councils, Palamas' adversaries were led by Barlaam of Calabria (southern Italy); he, though accusing Palamas of paganism, promoted a full revival of ancient Greek philosophy and art, which in Italy would a century later lead to the Renaissance. Palamas and the hesychasts did not reject Aristotelian philosophy, but they taught that the study of creatures was a purely human function and could lead only to a relative knowledge within the sphere of the Creator. The absolute transcendence of God could not be identified with anything created. God can be witnessed only in a personal experience by one who searches for the experience in his own intellect of the heart. According to Meyendorff, pre-Renaissance humanism did not evolve into a full Renaissance precisely because of the hesychastic victory in these debates over the nature of man. Renaissance humanism was secular, carnal, leading to a separation of the corporeal from the spiritual. It was precisely this hesychastic Orthodox concentration on man as a wholesome reflection of the Divine and as a channel for inner contact with the Divine that led to the achievement of the greatest artistic-spiritual heights in iconography as a physical representation of the spiritual.

Since the hesychasts saw humans as God's co-creators, they did not preach complete isolation from the world, but rather active participation in bringing Christ into the life of nations. Hence their victory in Constantinople had a direct impact on the policies of bishops, and even of statesmen.

Among such learned hesychastic (or at least pro-hesychast) clergy was Cyprian (Tsamblak), a hellenized Bulgarian chosen for the Russian metropolitanate even before the death of Metropolitan Alexis in 1378. For thirteen years, Cyprian contested the Russian metropolitanate with Metropolitan Alexis. Alexis had been wrongly accused of simony by his enemies. A thorough investigation in Constantinople eventually vindicated him, but the Patriarchate had sent Cyprian to Russia without waiting for the conclusion of the investigation. As Cyprian could not reside in Muscovy after Alexis' vindication, he stayed in Lithuania as the leader of the Orthodox flock there, thus dividing the Russian Church. Dimitri, bearing a grudge against Cyprian for having opposed Alexis, and preferring a Russian metropolitan who could be controlled, refused to let Cyprian into Moscow even after Alexis' death. When Cyprian arrived, the Grand Duke had him arrested and expelled from Moscow.

Instead, in 1379, Dimitri sent his father-confessor Mitiai (Michael) to Constantinople for consecration. Mitiai was very handsome, had a beautiful voice, was well educated and widely read, but disliked monasticism. One thing Mitiai did have in common with the hesychasts and Cyprian was his opposition to monastic wealth. Even when still a candidate for the metropolitanate, he started to cruelly punish monks for loose living. But his anti-monasticism in general put him squarely into the anti-hesychastic camp. Not surprisingly, St Sergius opposed Mitiai's candidacy (as a result, Dimitri's relations with the saint were not very cordial either). Just before reaching Constantinople Mitiai died. His companions then placed the name of another cleric in their company on the petition, that of a certain archimandrite Pimen, and proposed him for consecration. The Ecumenical Patriarchate chose to ignore the forgery and in 1381, without Dimitri's knowledge, consecrated Pimen as Metropolitan of Russia. After learning about the forgery, Dimitri had Pimen arrested, and finally accepted Cyprian as the Metropolitan of Moscow. Less than two years after the great Kulikovo victory, another Tatar ruler, Tokhtamysh, appeared unexpectedly on Russia's borders. In panic, Dimitri fled to Kostroma in the north; Cyprian followed suit, but did not go as far. It seems that the Metropolitan had criticized the Prince for abandoning his subjects to their own devices, because after his return to the ruins of Moscow after the bloody Tokhtamysh raid, Dimitri refused to let Cyprian return to his see. Instead, he decided to send another Russian bishop, Dionisii, to Constantinople for consecration as Russia's metropolitan. Dionisii, however, died in Constantinople in 1384. Three years later the Ecumenical

Patriarchate condemned Pimen for forgery and reaffirmed Cyprian as the sole Metropolitan of Rus'. Nevertheless, Cyprian was prevented from entering Moscow until Dimitri's death in 1389. Meyendorff remarks in this connection that, by trying to impose a weak and insignificant native metropolitan in place of a truly outstanding figure, Dimitri demonstrated both his nationalistic provincialism and the first despotic effort to subordinate the Church, to make her serve the state, the prince, the tsar...[4]

Dimitri's son, Grand Duke Vasili I (Basil) brought Cyprian back to Moscow, whence he ruled over both parts of the Russian Church until his death in 1406. Kartashev believes that Constantinople's double dealing in this affair greatly undermined its prestige in Russia's eyes and paved the way for the severance of ties between the Russian Church and Constantinople. The first move in that direction appears to have been a temporary discontinuation of prayers for the Byzantine Emperor, for which the Ecumenical Patriarch scolded Basil I. In demanding public prayers for the emperor at the liturgy, the patriarch unfolded a whole cesaro-papist doctrine, according to which the Church could not exist without the emperor. The final break came in 1441, when the Greek Metropolitan of Moscow, Isidore, returned from the 1438-39 Roman Council of Florence as a Roman cardinal.

The last Byzantine emperor, besieged by the Ottoman Turks, appealed to the pope for armies to rescue Constantinople. As a condition, the pope demanded a reunion of the Orthodox Church with the Roman Church and the recognition of the pope as head of the Church. Grand Duke Basil II agreed to send Isidore to the council of reunion on the latter's promise that he would not betray Orthodoxy and would not submit himself to the pope. Under terrible pressure from both the Byzantine emperor and the pope (with tortures and threats according to some reports) the Greek delegation finally signed the agreement of union, which marked a total capitulation to Roman theology. Isidore signed as well. In Greece itself, outside of Constantinople, the union was never accepted, nor did any troops materialize from the West. After the fall of Constantinople in 1453, the union was declared null and void by the Greek Church. Isidore, on his return to Moscow, was arrested on Basil's order. When attempts to convince him to renounce the union had failed, he was

---

4 The 1980 canonization of Dimitri by the Moscow Patriarchate was a clear case of *political* canonization, in connection with the Kulikovo Battle's 600th anniversary, celebrated at the time with great fanfare by the Soviet Government. The Patriarchate by that canonization wanted to demonstrate to the Communists the national-historical significance of the Church.

apparently allowed to escape from prison and fled to the West. Isidore's betrayal of Orthodoxy, however, caused the Russians to decide to sever all ecclesiastic connections to the Greek hierarchy. In 1448, a council of Russian bishops convoked by the Grand Duke elected Jonas, archbishop of Riazan', the first Metropolitan of all Rus', independent from Constantinople. The Russian Church was now autocephalous in all but name. The autocephaly, however, did not lead to any increase in the power of the Church. On the contrary, now having their own subjects as metropolitans, the Russian rulers could achieve that which Dimitri Donskoi probably wanted when he tried to install Mitiai as metropolitan.

During the fifteenth century the locally chosen metropolitans, though they were in fact appointed by the grand dukes, still tried to stand up to the sovereigns. As late as 1481, Metropolitan Gerontii agreed to return to office after a quarrel with Ivan III only after that proud prince, who was the first Russian ruler to call himself autocrat, had publicly repented and asked Gerontii for forgiveness. But, as Kartashev points out, such conflicts occurred because the rulers now began to interfere into ecclesiastical affairs, which they had not dared to do so obviously while the metropolitans still had the "extraterritorial" Constantinopolitan connection. In the era of autocephaly, individual battles could be still won by bishops, but the eventual outcome was, predictably, not in their favor.

By the end of the fifteenth century, the Moscow Grand Duchy was an empire (or tsardom) in all but name, and it needed an ideology to justify her expansion. As the Byzantine Roman Empire, or rather a shadow of what had once been an empire, had ceased to exist in 1453, and Russia, finally breaking with her Mongol overlords in 1480, remained the only independent Orthodox state, she obviously became the heir of the Second Rome. But all that had to be "rationalized" in the historico-ideological concepts of the period. And this "rationalization" first appeared in the form of *The Tale of the White Cowl*, a legendary account on how a white cowl worn by the Roman popes was first transferred to the New Rome (Constantinople) after the popes had fallen into heresy. Then, because of the sins of the Greeks, it abandoned Byzantium and appeared in Novgorod, to be worn by the archbishops of that city. Its conclusion that Russia has thus become the Third Rome is hardly logical, since the leadership rested with Moscow, and not with Novgorod. But a more consistent exposition of the Third Rome doctrine fell to a monk from Pskov, Philotheus (Filofei in Russian), who argued that, after the fall of all other Orthodox states to the Muslim Turks, the resurgence of Russia puts special moral responsibilities on her rulers. Two Romes have fallen, Moscow has become the Third Rome, and there will never be a fourth, he writes. This makes Russia a protector of all Orthodox Christians and requires of her a purity of faith. Should she fail to preserve the purity of Orthodoxy, that would bring about the end of time. This doctrine is consistent with the medieval belief that, since Jesus Christ had been a citizen of Rome, therefore the Roman Empire in some form will survive to the second coming: Jesus will appear as King and Judge over the empire in which he had been crucified.

Contrary to a common western misinterpretation of the Third Rome doctrine, Philotheus' version of it had nothing to do with imperialism and carried no direct political content. It first arose in direct consequence of the annexation of Pskov by Basil III, whom Philotheus reproached for his administrators' corruption and unjust government of the territory. His message was that Basil, as the only existing Orthodox monarch, was duty bound to rule justly and fairly as a true Christian, not as a tyrant, and that he had moral duties not only in relation to Russians, but also in relation to all Orthodox Christians in the world.

The Russian "Pre-Renaissance"

In iconography Russia reached her apex in the fifteenth century, although the previous century also produced masterpieces, particularly those of Theophanes the Greek. Theophanes' great disciples, Andrei Rublev and Daniel the Black, likewise began to paint in the fourteenth century. The last of the greats was Dionisius and his circle of the late fifteenth-early sixteenth centuries.

The hesychast influence also produced a certain reanimation in education and writing. The greatest Russian saint of the late fourteenth century, St Sergius of Radonezh, came from Rostov-the-Great, where at the time of his youth resided a learned Greek bishop. One of its monasteries had an excellent library by the standards of the period, containing many Greek manuscripts. It is more likely than not that Sergius knew Greek. At least two of his contemporaries were also proficient in Greek: Metropolitan Alexis, who was busy working on a new Slavonic translation of the New Testament from the Greek; and St Stephen, Enlightener of the pagan Finnic Perm tribe, for which he created an alphabet and translated the services, a precedent that would be followed by nineteenth-century Russian missionaries in Siberia, Alaska, and Japan.

Fedotov calls St Sergius the first Russian mystic. He introduced the hesy-chastic prayer of the mind to Russia, a prayer by then widespread among East-ern monastics, particularly on Mount Athos, which it reached from the Middle East. The earliest *vitae* of Sergius cite testimonies of members of his monastic community that they saw visitations of St Sergius by the mystical, heavenly, uncreated light, as well as by the Virgin and angels. At a church service, he was seen assisted at the altar by an angel, and Sergius is reported to have said to the monks who witnessed the sight:

> My children, how can I conceal the secret from you if the Lord has revealed it to you? The one you saw was an angel of the Lord; and not only today but always I, the unworthy, serve with Him. Having seen Him, don't spread the word as long as I am still in this world.

As a hesychast, Sergius did not despise this world and its problems. First, he agreed to fulfill the Moscow Grand Duke Dimitri's request to visit several Russian appanage princes and to plead with them to cooperate with Dimitri, to recognize his supremacy over them, and not to undertake any acts against him. In this Sergius was only partly successful: in the case of Nizhni Novgorod, he even resorted to the sealing of all churches in order to break the resistance of the local prince. Dimitri's crucial 1380 Battle of Kulikovo, at which the Russians defeated the Mongols for the first time, had the blessing and prayers of St Sergius, but only after he was persuaded by Dimitri that all attempts at a peaceful settlement of the conflict had been exhausted.

Outside of these few incidents, Sergius shunned worldly politics and led a semi-eremitic life of humility, absolute rejection of worldly treasures, fasting, individual as well as communal prayer combined with manual work. He prac-ticed the typically hesychastic freedom of individual choice, freedom from the standard, strict forms of collective discipline. But his monastic community, dedicated to the Holy Trinity, grew, and the monks insisted that he be or-dained as their abbot. The Patriarch of Constantinople then sent him the Stu-dite monastic statute of cenobitic life.[5] Sergius accepted this statute and the role of abbot only very reluctantly. His name and memory attained national veneration, and with it generous donations began to pour into his monastery. Soon after Sergius's death, the Trinity Monastery, to which Sergius's name was

---

5 In the Orthodox Church there are no individual monastic orders. Each monastery is free (at least in theory) to set up its own statute. With time, most new monasteries came to borrow statutes from the most famous monasteries, one of which was the Studite Monastery of Constantinople. Those monasteries which practice communal life, with no property owned by monks individually, are called cenobitic.

added after his canonization, became extremely wealthy, contrary to his original intentions and to hesychastic convictions. The most dedicated monks soon left the monastery in search of solitude and freedom in the wilderness north and northeast of the upper Volga. Thus the trans-Volga *startsy* (elders) and *sketes* (small monastic communities consisting of an elder and a small group of monks who had chosen him as their teacher) began to be founded. These would play an important role in Russia's spiritual history of the fifteenth-sixteenth and again of the nineteenth-early twentieth centuries.

The monastic movement directly contributed to the theological discussions of the fifteenth-sixteenth centuries and enlivened religious writing. Among the most popular collections of religious readings of the time were the so-called *Izborniki* ("Miscellanies").[6] These were collections of didactic, ethical, and historical writings mixed with excerpts from the Bible and from the Church Fathers, as well as the *vitae* of popular saints. Their popularity is borne out by the fact that several hundred manuscripts containing these collections have survived to our time.

They were meant to serve as daily readings for Christian families. Curiously, they contain more stories from the apocrypha than from the canonical Gospels. Apparently, their fantastic character—one of the main reasons the early Church concluded they were not accurate accounts of Jesus—inspired the imagination of Russians of the time more than the sober Gospel accounts. As the scribes compiling and copying the *Izborniki* were either clerics or monks, Fedotov concludes that the indiscriminate conglomerate of canonical and non-canonical writings is another indication of a lack of clericalism in medieval Russia, with no significant difference in the education of the clergy and that of literate laity. Moreover, although Metropolitan Cyprian brought a Byzantine Index to Russia, it was never applied; generally, pre-typographical Russia knew no indexes, no real censorship.

The Russian medieval reader was so thrilled with the art of literacy that every book for him was *The Book*. There were no gradations of quality, no discrimination. Thus one of the most popular *Izborniki*, called the *Izmaragd*, contained mutually exclusive moral lessons found side-by-side, without, it seems, bothering the logic of either the scribe-compiler or most readers. Thus,

---

6 They had been in existence in Rus' since the 11th century, but became particularly widespread in the 15th, as witnessed by the number of copies of that period that have survived to our time. Indeed, they might have been equally widespread in the 11th century as well. The subsequent invasions, first by the Polovtsians, then by the Tatars, destroyed most pre-Mongol Russian libraries.

in one copy of the book one instruction, of Byzantine origin, to a master on how to treat slaves allows a maximum of thirty lashes as punishment, adding: "Be not excessive in treating any flesh. If you have a slave whose goodness has been tested, treat him as your brother..." Adjacent to it is an instruction by a Russian author which prescribes no lashes and implores: "Mercy more than any lashes will make them tremble and edify you. If you act in this way, you will also find mercy instead of punishment on the departure of your soul."

The most frequently attacked sins, hence obviously those most common, are drunkenness and adultery. Women are treated very harshly, as temptresses, flesh-centered, perfidious, and unreliable—which indicates monastic authorship. Fedotov remarks that the harshness of the book regarding vices of the flesh contrasts sharply with the actual tolerance of the Russian Church towards sensual vices.

It was during that period that a new translation of the New and of some books of the Old Testament was completed, mostly by Pachomius the Serb. The first sizable libraries were established in the late fourteenth century: the Metropolitan's Catalogue mentions 212 manuscripts in the Beloozero-St Cyril Monastery Library (in the north) and 300 at the Holy Trinity-St Sergius Monastery Library.

Metropolitan Cyprian introduced into Russia the new Sabaite liturgical ritual, in use in the Orthodox Church universally to this day; while Pachomius brought from Serbia a new and highly ornate, formalistic style of hagiographic writing.

Spiritual Problems of the Church in Politics

By the late fourteenth century, after some wavering, the Church leadership both in Russia and in Byzantium took side with Moscow. When the Church saw that the time was right for Mongol control to end and that there was no peaceful alternative to the Kulikovo confrontation, she gave the Battle on the Don her blessing. A century later, the Church gave her blessing to the final confrontation with the Tatars: when Ivan III, instead of attacking Khan Akhmat, remained in a state of indecision on one side of the River Ugra, while the Tatar force stood just as indecisively on the opposite bank, Vassian, the archbishop of Rostov, sent a long letter encouraging Ivan to follow the example of Dimitri Donskoi and expel the Tatars from Russia for good. Eventually, there was no battle: one foggy November morning, the Tatars simply went back home, devastating the countryside on their way. Thus the mighty Mongol Yoke ended "not with a bang but a whimper."

Having played the role of chief national diplomats for over 240 years of the Mongol Yoke, the Church leadership was forced to engage in double-talk and other unsavory diplomatic tactics; these had to reflect negatively on the moral stature of the bishops and on the fabric of the whole Church establishment. The holy men of the Church tried to avoid participation in Church politics of this kind and sought escape from worldly temptations in the wilderness of the north. Here, in dense forests, hundreds of new monasteries arose between the fourteenth and seventeenth centuries. Most were built by disciples of St Sergius or by their followers. The following summarizes the direct or indirect results of that monastic "migration":

1. Finnic tribes of the sub-Arctic and Arctic of the European Russian and later Turkic and Mongolian tribes of Siberia were being gradually converted to Christianity by these monastic outposts.

2. Peasants and other seekers after spiritual leadership often followed the monks and built their settlements in forest clearings around the monasteries.

3. After the appearance of peasant settlements, some monks would move further out into the wilderness; and the process would repeat itself. Naturally, new settlers were soon followed by government officials and military detachments, formally annexing the territories to the crown. This was one of the ways of the Empire's expansion in which the eremitic or semi-eremitic monks became unwittingly agents of "Russian imperialism."

Theology and Heresies

No sooner had the (Muscovite) Russian Church begun to speak with her own voice, than heresies began to appear, reflecting both sincere religious quests and theological ignorance. Most heresies came from Novgorod, a culturally more advanced area than Moscow, with considerable contacts among West European merchants at the precise time when heresies and Protestantism were rapidly spreading in the West.

The *Chronicles* report that a 1311 Russian church Council in Pereiaslav Zalesski condemned a Novgorodian archpriest for rejecting monasticism. We know nothing more about that case. Toward the end of the fourteenth century, another heresy appeared in Novgorod: the *Strigol'niki*. The etymology of this word comes from "cutting" or "shearing." Were they barbers, tonsurers, or did they preach and/or practice the shaving of beards? No written records survive to explain the term or the details of their teachings. All that is known from the *Chronicles* and other documents is that the *strigol'niki* protested against the fees bishops would charge clergy candidates for ordination. This practice, which contradicted the canons, was common in Greece, but the Russian zealots could not believe that their original teachers of faith could be in breach of the canons. When the Ecumenical Patriarchate cleared Metropolitan Alexis of the charges of simony, even though the Bishop of Tver' had reported to them that the Metropolitan had been charging a tax for ordination, a zealous monk, Akindin, was sent to Constantinople to investigate the situation in Greece. The Greeks wiggled out of the embarrassing situation by telling him that they did not charge for ordination, but merely collected the cost of the expenses incurred in ordination. Akindin took this to mean that ordination fees were condemned by the Greeks. In his report to the Moscow Grand Duke, he condemned the practice as simony and declared that a priest thus ordained was not a canonical priest. The *strigol'niki* concluded from this that the whole Russian clergy was canonically invalid. Subsequently, they rejected all the sacraments except baptism (because it could be administered by laity), as well as the historical Church after apostolic times. There appears to have been a split in their ranks: the more moderate ones returned to the Church in the fifteenth century, demanding only her purification; the extremists eventually rejected even the New Testament, the afterlife, resurrection, and the belief in Christ as the Savior. They accepted only the Lord's prayer, and they confessed their sins to the *Moist Mother Earth*, or to the sky and the stars as God's universe.[7] Although after the mid-fifteenth century we find no more mention of the *Strigol'niki*. Their more moderate members or those influenced by their teachings must have played a role in the 1503 Russian Church Council's condemnation of ordination fees.

From the Novgorodian *Chronicle*, we know that at least three extremist *Strigol'niki* were drowned in the Volkhov River by order of the *Veche* (the city assembly which ruled the Novgorodian Republic). Fedotov stresses that this was a secular decision, as both the Russian Metropolitan Photius and the Patriarch of Constantinople wrote letters pleading with the Novgorodians and the neighboring Pskovians not to use force against heretics, but only

---

7 Their descendants may have been the sect of *dyrniki*, so named after the word *dyrka*, meaning a hole which they made in the roof of their dwelling in order to pray to the Heavens. A. Prugavin found that sect still in existence in the late 19th century.

exhortation and admonition. In extreme cases the Orthodox, they advised, should avoid breaking bread with the heretics.

Another heresy, which came to be known as the Judaizers (*zhidovstvuiushchie*, in Russian), appeared in Novgorod around 1470. There is no evidence that there was any connection, whether in persons or in ideas, with the *Strigol'niki*, but the atmosphere for any challenge to Orthodoxy was undoubtedly prepared by them.

Novgorod had a tradition of inviting princes to rule the republic, but they had very limited power, circumscribed by the *Veche*, the *Gospoda* (a House of Lords of sorts), and its chairman, the *Posadnik*. When the heresy began the prince was Alexander Olel'kovich, from the Kievan Orthodox branch of the Lithuanian dynasty. Alexander's personal physician, a Jew named Zachariah or Skharia, and his two Jewish merchant-companions, Mosed Hanush and Joseph Shmoilo Skarabei, introduced the Judaizer heresy. In debating theology with Novgorodian priests, they argued that the New Testamental concept of the Trinity, which Skharia falsely interpreted as three gods, contradicted the Old Testamental teachings about one single God. As a Jew, Skharia absolutely rejected the idea that God took human flesh, and he claimed that Christ could not have been the Messiah who, supposedly, would appear just before the end of time. In other words, he rejected the belief in the two appearances of the Messiah: the first one as the suffering Christ, and the other as Christ-the-King, accepting only the latter. Stressing Christ's words that He came into the world to fulfill the Old Testament, not to destroy it, they argued that the Old Testament was eternal, and therefore more important than the New. Consequently, Skharia taught that Christ was only a holy prophet in the Old Testamental tradition. He rejected icons, crosses, monasticism, rituals, fasting, and the need for a formal Church altogether. Skharia taught a mixture of the rationalistic, anti-trinitarian heresies, fashionable in Europe at the time, and Judaism. His erudition impressed the poorly-educated Russian priests, and several of them secretly joined the heresy. Kartashev stresses the secret character of this sect; for example, Skharia convinced a priest Alexis not to undergo circumcision for conspiratorial reasons.

Ivan III, visiting Novgorod in 1479, met two Judaizer priests, Abraham (former Alexis) and Dennis, was thrilled by their theological erudition, and appointed them rectors of the two main Kremlin cathedrals in Moscow. There they converted the widow of Ivan's eldest son, the Moldavian princess Elena, as well as Ivan himself, as he later confessed to his father-confessor.

By this time, however, Novgorod was no longer the only source of that heresy. Ivan's chief diplomat, Theodore Kuritsyn, brought an identical or at least very similar anti-trinitarian teaching from Hungary, from where he returned in 1486 after a four-year mission abroad. He was fluent in German, Polish, Greek and Hungarian, and had established intimate contacts in high society circles there. With his education and wide foreign travels Kuritsyn was very influential at Ivan's court. This allowed him to continue to disseminate the heresy within Moscow high society at the very time when the sect was being actively persecuted by Archbishop Gennadi in Novgorod.

In Novgorod, the heresy lost its secrecy in typically Russian fashion. Two Judaizing clerics got drunk at a bar, grabbed an axe, and began to hack icons. Arrested and questioned they easily broke down and gave away many names. This resulted in a first round of arrests. All the arrested were forgiven and released after showing what was believed to be honest repentance. Most of them then escaped to Moscow under the protection of Kuritsyn. Zachariah went to Crimea in 1485, where he met Kuritsyn, who had been ambushed on his way back from Hungary and brought captive to Crimea. There Kuritsyn was released by the Crimean *khan* and allowed to proceed to Moscow. The Judaizers remained strong in Moscow: a Judaizing metropolitan, Zosima, was even elected in 1490.

The tireless opponents of the Judaizers at the time were Archbishop Gennadi and the Abbot Joseph. A local council in Novgorod was convoked in 1490 under their pressure. Gennadi and Joseph demanded that the ringleaders be burned at the stake, but the trans-Volga hesychasts Nilus of Sorka and his companions protested against the death penalty; as a result nine Judaizer clerics were condemned to monastic imprisonment in Novgorodian monasteries, from which they eventually escaped abroad.

In Moscow high society, however, the heresy continued unchecked. Whereas the Novgorodian priests had been attracted to the heresy as a religious teaching, Moscow high society was attracted to its alchemical aspects, including astrology, its pseudo-scientific claims of determination of human behavior and fate by natural phenomena, and fortune-telling based on "stars"—all this was part of that semi-Judaic heresy. After the death of Gennadi, Joseph led his campaign against the Judaizers very cautiously. First, he succeeded in having a local council in 1494 depose Zosima for sodomy, debauchery, and the denial of Jesus' resurrection and life after death. In the meantime Joseph wrote and disseminated a book, *The Enlightener* (*Prosvetitel'*) against the Judaizers. But even the election of Simon as the new metropolitan in 1495 changed little. Kuritsyn remained the royal chancellor and continued to promote Judaizers to high positions in the Church.

Only after Kuritsyn's death in 1497 could Joseph begin his decisive fight against the heretics. Two local councils in 1503 and 1504-1505, addressed the Judaizer heresy. Ivan III had supported the non-possessor monks,[8] headed by Nilus of Sorka, who opposed the death penalty for heretics. But Ivan was ill and dying at the time of the 1505 council, and the aging Nilus was absent (he died in 1508). Ivan's son, Basil III, supported the possessors, apparently in return for their support of his candidacy for the throne.[9] Although Nilus' disciple, the monk Vassian Patrikeev, protested against the death penalty, he was overruled by Joseph of Volotsk, who had the support of Basil III. The *Chronicles* list six names of leading Judaizers condemned to death at the stake, and then adds that many others were executed as well; but Kartashev doubts that there were many more than the six, including Volk Kuritsyn, apparently a brother of the deceased Theodore. In addition, several dozen were sent to monasteries for repentance, most of whom were eventually released. It is because there were so few victims, in comparison to the large numbers involved, that Kartashev suspects a deeply conspiratorial character of the heresy.

Some historians treat the Judaizer heresy as an offshoot of anti-trinitarian anabaptism, fashionable at that time in Western Europe, including in neighboring Lithuania; Kartashev, however, sees it as a Judaic "fifth column" of sorts. He points out that Jews were never interested in proselytism, treating Judaism in its pure form as a tribal religion. The Judaizer heresy then was a watered-down version of Judaism for the *goim*, taking the form of a freethinking rationalism which upheld the supremacy of the Old Testament. He sees confirmation of his thesis in the few surviving literary documents of the Judaizers, which include: a translation of the Pentateuch directly from the Hebrew (rather than from the Greek) into the West Russian vernacular of the time (not Church Slavonic); and a book of pseudo-psalms with texts similar to those of the regular psalms but without any hints at a foresight of Christ. If he is correct, then the existence of several so-called "Hebrew" villages in

8 See the next chapter for details on the possessors and non-possessors.

9 Ivan's eldest son, Ivan the Young, had died several years earlier, leaving a son Dimitri. The issue was whether the throne should pass to a grandson born of the legal heir or to a junior son by the second marriage. At first, Ivan opted for Dimitri, but then changed his mind and had Basil crowned as his co-ruler and heir.

central Russia, consisting of ethnically pure Russian peasants but professing Judaism, would appear to be a remnant of the fifteenth-century Judaizers.[10]

The appearance of these heresies stimulated Orthodox theologizing, which was not limited to Joseph's *Enlightener* alone. For example, Archbishop Gennadi, though not particularly well-educated himself, gathered a group of translators, among them a Croat Dominican monk named Benjamin (who, having spent some time in Spain, informed Gennadi and Joseph of the Spanish inquisition, which inspired them to apply its methods against the Judaizers). They prepared the first translation of the entire Bible into Slavonic. At that time, neither the East nor the West possessed such a full translation into any language close to vernacular (there being only Hebrew, Greek and Latin Bibles). Owing to the delay in the introduction of book printing into Russia, however. the manuscript had to wait another eighty years before finally being published—with corrections and improvements—in 1580-82 at the printing house of the Ostrozhskii princes in Volynia; this first complete Slavonic Bible is thus known as the *Ostrozhsky* (or Ostrog) Bible.

FOR FURTHER READING

Andreyev, N.E. "O dele diaka Viskovatogo," *Seminarium Kondakovianum* 5 (Prague, 1932).

_____, *Studies in Muscovy* (London: Variorum, 1970).

_____, "Was the Pskov-Pechery Monastery a Citadel of the Non-Possessors?" *Jahrbücher für Geschichte Osteuropas* 17 (1969).

Birnbaum, M. and M. Flier, eds., *Medieval Russian Culture* (U. of California Press, 1984).

Bosley, R., "The Saints of Novgorod," *Jahrbücher* 32 (1984).

Bushkovich, Paul, "The Limits of Hesychasm," *Forschungen zur osteuropaischen Geschichte* 38 (Berlin, 1986).

Dewey, H., "The Blessed Fools of Old Russia," *Jahrbücher* 22/1 (1974).

Fennell, J., "The Attitude of the Josephians and the Trans-Volga Elders to the Heresy of the Judaizers," *Slavonic and East European Review* XXIX (1951).

_____, *The Emergence of Moscow, 1304-1359* (U. of California Press, 1968).

_____, *Ivan the Great of Moscow* (London, 1961).

Florovsky, G., "The Problem of Old Russian Culture," *Slavic Review* XXI (March, 1962).

Fuhrmann, J. "Metropolitan Cyrill II and the Politics of Accommodation," *Jahrbücher,* 24/2 (1976).

10 Some of these peasants emigrated to Israel in the early 1980's.

Goldfrank, D., ed. and trans., *The Monastic Rule of Joseph Volotsky* (Kalamazoo, Mich.: Cistercian Publications, 1983).

Halperin, Ch., "A Chingissid Saint of the Russian Orthodox Church: the Life of Peter, Tsarevich of the Horde," *Canadian-American Slavic Studies* 9 (1975).

Hosch, E., *Orthodoxie und Haresie in alten Russland* (Wiesbaden, 1975).

Hurwitz, Ellen. *Prince Andrej Bogolibskij: the Man and the Myth* (Florence, 1980).

Kartashev. *Ocherki...*, vol. I.

Kazakova, N.A., *Vassian Patrikeev i ego sochineniia* (Moscow, 1960).

Kliuchevskii, V., *Drevnerusskie zhitiia sviatykh, kak istoricheskii istochnik* (Moscow, 1988).

Kondakov, N.P., *The Russian Icon* (Oxford, 1927).

Lilienfeld, F. von., *Nil Sorskij und seine Schriften: der Bruch der Tradition im Russland Ivan III* (Berlin, 1963).

Medlin, W.K., *Moscow and East Rome* (Westport: Hyperion Press, 1952).

Meyendorff, John, *Byzantium and the Rise of Russia* (Crestwood, NY, St Vladimir's Seminary Press, 1989).

Ostrowski, D., "Church Reform and Monastic Land Acquisition in 16th c. Muscovy." *Slavonic and East European Rev.* 64 (1986).

Popov, A.N. *Istoriko-literaturnyi obzor drevne-russkikh polemicheskikh sochinenii protiv latinian* (XI -XV vv.) (London: Varioirum, 1972).

Raba, J., "Church and Foreign Policy in the 15th Century Novgorodian State," *Canadian-American Slavic Studies* 13, 1-2 (1979).

Shpakov, A., *Gosudarstvo i Tserkov' v ikh vzaimnykh otnosheniiakh v Moskovskom gosudarstve,* 2 vols (Kiev-Odessa, 1904-1912).

Thompson, Ewa., *Understanding Russia: the Holy Fool in Russian Culture* (University Press of America, 1987).

Utechin, S., *Russian Political Thought* (London: J.M. Dent, 1963).

Wieczynski, J., "Archbishop Gennadius and the West," *Canadian-American Slavic Studies* 6/3 (1972).

Zenkovsky, S., ed. *Medieval Russia's Epics, Chronicles, and Tales* (Dutton, 1974).

Zernov, N., *St Sergius, Builder of Russia* (London, 1938).

Zguta, R., "Aristotelevy vrata as a Reflection of Judaizers...," *Jahrbücher...* 26/1 (1978).

CHAPTER 4

FROM POSSESSORS AND NON-POSSESSORS TO THE GREAT SCHISM OF THE 17TH CENTURY

The Possessors and the Non-Possessors.

Fedotov considers that the Monastic Statute of St Nilus of Sorka and Joseph's tract against the Judaizers (*The Enlightener*) were Russia's first theological works. Although initially these two leaders of fifteenth-sixteenth-century Russian monasticism were not that far apart in their views, and some specialists even believe that the first chapter of *The Enlightener*, "Epistle to an Iconographer," was written by St Nilus, eventually Nilus and Joseph and their two works came to represent two opposite streams within the Orthodox Church. Joseph's line prevailed after 1504 and remained the ideology of the Russian Church establishment; while that of Nilus survived among numerous monastics as well as among many humble laymen and priests. The victory of the *possessors* became directly relevant to the Great Schism of the seventeenth century, to the secularization of the Church and her complete subordination to state bureaucracy by Peter the Great, and even to the Bolshevik victory of militant atheism in the Russia of the twentieth century.

Nilus (1433-1508) was born into a peasant family of Maikovs, but received a rather good education by the standards of the period. He worked as a book copyist, then spent several years on Mt Athos, where he became a passionate follower of hesychasm, which he disseminated among Russian monks, creating in the woods of the northern trans-Volga regions small sketes in the hesychastic tradition. Very little is known about the Elder Nilus, because, in his extreme humility, he refused to leave or dictate his biography. In conformity with the Orthodox tradition, Nilus treated pride and vainglory as one of the eight gravest sinful temptations. What is less usual for Orthodoxy is Nilus' request that his body be buried not in a grave, but "cast ... in the desert[1] to be eaten by beasts and birds; for it has sinned much before God and is not worthy of a funeral..."

His monastic statute, consisting of eleven chapters, is remarkable for its emphasis on personal freedom in the search for the most appropriate method

---

1 Desert—a deserted and humanly uninhabited place—meant for the north Russians a dense forest. Hence hermitages and small monasteries deep in the forests are called *pustynia*, i.e., a desert habitation.

of monastic self-restraint, prayer, discipline, etc. The emphasis is on spiritual life. It analyses various forms of self-denial, concentration for prayer, the role and function of tears in repentance and prayer, the necessity to keep one's death always in mind. There is surprisingly little in the way of hard and fast rules and prescriptions. Only intellectual or mental prayer is discussed at length, as well as ways to make it a continuous cycle of repetition of the Jesus prayer, both in conscious life and in sleep, when it thus becomes a prayer of the heart.

In contrast to Nilus, the monastic statute of St Joseph of Volotsk concentrates on the externals. It contains minute regulations on discipline, food and fasting, silence during meals, attendance at services… Both Nilus and Joseph practiced great personal bodily severity. But whereas Nilus teaches that each person achieves his spiritual aims in his own way and evolves his own regime, Joseph imposes very harsh but uniform rules for all. But he does make an exception for tonsured boyars (lords, aristocrats), who are accustomed to luxuries and would not therefore join a very severe monastery.

Nilus originated the skete type of monastery in Russia. A skete is a small cottage where two or three monks live together. Nilus found this to be more conducive for prayer and spiritual growth than either a large, cenobitic monastery, with its minute and rather mechanical regulations of communal life, or a hermitage, where an isolated individual can fall prey to temptations more easily than if there are two or three companions ready to support each other in spiritual growth. Monks, Nilus taught, should earn their living, no more than the bare necessities, by working with their hands. Only in exceptional cases could alms be accepted, but just in a quantity necessary to sustain life. Needless to say, Nilus opposed any monastic wealth and landed estates, though he recognized the necessity for some income producing properties for episcopal centers to finance education and charity projects. Hence Nilus' followers came to be known as the "Non-possessors"(or "Non-acquisitors"), while those of the prevailing Josephites were called "Possessors" (or "Acquisitors").

Joseph's monastery was a large cenobitic institution with minutely detailed rules and regulations. It also engaged in much charity and help to the neighboring population. A peasant whose horse had died or whose plough had broken down would go to Joseph and invariably received the money necessary for replacement or repairs. Joseph wrote letters to local landowners imploring them to be good to their peasant-tenants and slaves. A very practical administrator, he explained in these that a badly treated worker will work badly, causing material losses to the landowner in the long run. Similarly, in running his monastery, he raised the necessary funds by encouraging the wealthy to bequest their estates in return for prayers for the deceased. For Joseph, Fedotov remarks, "externally ascetic deeds and a wide activity take that place which St Nilus devotes to the prayer of the mind."

Joseph was a disciple of St Pakhomii of Borovsk, who had been a follower of St Sergius. From Sergius, Joseph inherited charity, kindness to the poor, personal asceticism, and industriousness (Joseph humiliated his pride and body by hard manual work); but it is inconceivable that the kind hearted and loving Sergius would have approved of Joseph's harshness, severity, and his merciless cruelty towards heretics. Favoring the Spanish inquisition, Joseph argued that if the death penalty was applied to murderers of the body, there is even greater reason to deprive of life those who murder the soul. In contrast, Nilus favored the spiritual re-education of heretics and, in extreme cases, their isolation from society by placing them under arrest into monasteries. A repentant heretic, Nilus said, should be welcomed like the prodigal son in the Bible. Joseph disagreed: repentance under duress, he said, should not fool anybody and should result at best in a milder form of punishment, not in forgiveness.

Such harshness was atypical for the Russian Church. Even as far back as the thirteenth century, Serapion, Bishop of Vladimir, protested in his sermons against witch hunts by ignorant laity: "You are still holding on to pagan traditions: believing in magicians and burning innocents at the stake. Even those of you who have not taken part in the murders but did not protest against them are murderers by complicity..." We know that the idea of burning heretics at the stake was suggested to Joseph by Archbishop Gennadii's Croatian secretary, who had recently come from Spain; but it is also interesting that whereas Nilus was of Great Russian stock, Joseph was a descendent of Russo-Lithuanian gentry who had emigrated to Muscovy. It is possible that from the Catholic tradition, he might have inherited his religious rigidity, as well as his emphatically social monasticism and certain papo-caesarist ideas.

Joseph was so strict and super-ascetic that he allowed no beardless youths or women on the grounds of his monastery (just outside the present town of Volokolamsk, 70 km north-west of Moscow). He refused even to see his mother, a nun, who came to visit her son. And yet, as mentioned above, he made exceptions for boyars who, he said, were needed for two reasons: to bring wealth to monasteries and to be candidates for the episcopacy. Wealth, he argued, was necessary for the establishment and support of hospitals, homes for the aged, for orphans and other needy persons, as well as for financing schools. Indeed, Joseph can be credited with having institutionalized monastic hospitals and social asylums, having opened a home for orphans and the aged at his monastery, and in years of famine he regularly fed 700 people. He commanded his monks to buy such quantities of bread that no pilgrim would ever depart hungry from the monastery. His vita reports at least one riot by his monks because he had given away the last crumb of food to visitors. Joseph's order was: "Pray!" Within a short while, horse-drawn carts full of grain appeared and the corn-bins were filled to the brim.

The reason aristocratic bishops were necessary, Joseph argued, was that without them the Church could have no influence on state policies, as princes and boyars respect the opinions only of those of their own class. His Statute therefore contains three degrees of asceticism, depending on the type of promise the newly-tonsured monk voluntarily gives. The degrees differ in the number of dishes per meal and in the quality and quantity of the wardrobe. But even here everything is minutely detailed.

The Consequences of the Possessors' Victory

After the victory of the possessors, many heretics found refuge in the compassionate, trans-Volga sketes. The fact that, almost two centuries later, the area north of the upper Volga (although mostly to the north of Nilus' skete, closer to Onega Lake and to the White Sea) housed a major concentration of the most persistent Old Believers, particularly those who became known as the "priestless" branch, which in the eighteenth-nineteenth centuries gave birth to a variety of heretical sects (*dukhobors, molokans,* etc.), may perhaps indicate some influence of the descendants of the Judaizers on the priestless Old Believers.

As to Nilus' disciples, in the sixteenth century, the triumphant Josephites accused them of heresy. The accusations proved to be not entirely groundless. At his heresy trial in 1531 the most prolific writer among Nilus' followers, the monk Vassian Patrikeev,[2] defended a monophysite heresy by rejecting Jesus' full humanity.

As to the triumphant Josephites, a leading scholar in the field, the late N. Kazakova, found an incompatible duality in their school of thought. On the

2   He was a second cousin of the ruling Grand Duke Basil III and a friend of Maxim the Greek, an Athonite scholar working as a translator of theological works in Moscow.

one hand, Joseph was a pioneer in Russia of "the theory of the theocratic character of royal prerogatives";[3] on the other, knowing full well that a centralized autocracy could lead to the liquidation of monastic property, he in practice supported appanage princes. Moreover, he formulated a theory of disobedience to tyrants using the following terms:

> Should a tsar ... fall prey to ugly passions and sins, greediness and rage, cunning-ness and lies, pride and violence or, what is even worse, want of faith and slan-der—such a tsar is not God's but devil's servant; he is not a tsar but a tyrant...and thou shouldst not fulfill such a tsar's orders...even if tortured and threatened with murder.

Although the distinction between a righteous tsar and a tyrant was known in Russia from the writings of St John Chrysostom and Basil the Great, this was the first time that it was spelled out in such a detail by a Russian author. The doctrine was then further elaborated by Metropolitan Daniel of Moscow, who stressed that tsars and princes had power only over human bodies, not their souls. Therefore, he wrote, one should not obey a ruler if he orders to kill or to do something else harmful to the soul. "God," Daniel wrote, "has created the soul to be free and independent," capable of distinguishing between good and evil.[4]

One would have expected this doctrine to come from the non-possessors, but they were not really interested in state affairs and argued that if God had meant to create man absolutely free, there would be no kings. Yet, while the possessors preached disobedience to tyrants, they maintained that royal power ruled supreme over that of bishops in all administrative matters. Therefore, it is also the duty of kings to punish heretics (since the Church cannot deprive any-body of life); while the Church ought to participate actively in the affairs and politics of the state, though presumably as a junior partner, if the supreme authority of the king encompassed both secular and ecclesiastical affairs.

One would have thought a synthesis of the possessors' and non-possessors' ideas might produce a well-balanced Christian society. It could have been a synthesis of the command that "faith without works is dead" with St Paul's words that no works will save a man if he lacks an all-forgiving love. The Josephite line pointed toward an active social Christianity, Nilus', to

3 His formula was that tsars and princes are God's representatives on earth. *Ocherki istorii russkoi obshchestven-noi mysli*, 108.

4 Alas, Daniel's activities (he imprisoned Maxim the Greek, for instance) had nothing in common with his writings.

spiritual and moral purity and to self-improvement. Unfortunately, the visible, institutional victory fell to the Josephites; and as Josephianism preached an active participation of the Church in politics, a partnership of the two swords. But the physical sword would sooner or later vanquish over the spiritual sword, and this would eventually deprive the Church as institution of any sword. The Josephite teaching on resistance to heretical kings (i.e., the very idea that a baptized and anointed Orthodox Tsar can be a heretic!) also allowed the Old Ritualists in the seventeenth century to proclaim the ruling tsar to be a servant of Satan, and thus to refuse to follow his orders. As we shall see, the cruelty of the confrontation between the established Church and the Old Ritualists was exacerbated by the fact that both sides were Josephites, and the struggle was not merely for the right to coexist but to be the state religion.

But let us return to the sixteenth century. At least initially the de facto appointment of metropolitans by the Russian autocrats did not yet mean their complete obedience to the autocrats. Nor did the victory of the possessors bring an immediate disappearance of the non-possessors from leading positions in the Church. Thus, Metropolitan Varlaam (1511-21), a non-possessor, openly criticized Basil III for his devious methods of eradicating the last appanages by inviting the relevant princes to Moscow, guaranteeing their safety, but then arresting and often killing them. Varlaam's behavior led eventually to his retirement to a monastery, imposed on him by the Grand Duke. He was replaced by the Josephite Daniel, who—although he wrote about freedom of conscience—as metropolitan pursued the other line of Josephite teaching: close collaboration with the ruler, and the priority of *raison d'état* above all else. It was he who allowed Basil III to place his allegedly barren wife Solomonia into a convent and to marry another woman in order to have an heir—even though the Ecumenical Patriarch, the Athonite monks, and the Russian bishops prior to Daniel categorically maintained that barrenness was not a sufficient cause for divorce, as procreation was not the only purpose of marriage.[5]

For the second time in fifty years the prestige of the Russian Church establishment was falling very low—the first time being during Zosima's tenure. Some hope arose when soon after Basil's death Daniel was deposed and replaced by the

---

5 A Russian historian recently advanced a hypothesis that it was Basil who was impotent, and that his two sons by his second marriage to Elene Glinskaia were fathered by her lover, Prince Obolensky, which makes Ivan the Terrible a bastard. His decimation of practically all the boyars who had surrounded the throne during his childhood and of most of his relatives could then be explained by his fear that, if the secret were revealed, the throne would be claimed by his cousins.

saintly non-possessor Ioasaf. But Ioasaf's moral integrity did not suit any of the court parties. Refusing to return favors to those who had installed him, he was deposed three years later (in 1542) by that very same party.

Metropolitan Makarii and Ivan IV

Ioasaf was succeeded by Metropolitan Makarii, a possessor who was deeply preoccupied with state affairs. A man of high moral integrity and of considerable administrative talents, he was to have a very beneficial influence on the young Ivan IV. His tenure (1543-63) is considered to have sealed the possessors' victory as the official ideology of the established Church. He had proved his administrative talents as archbishop of the very difficult diocese of Novgorod (1526-42), which also included Pskov. He was the first archbishop accepted by both cities since the abolition by Ivan III of elections of the Novgorod archbishops by the city assembly (*veche*). The first Moscow-appointed archbishop, Sergius, was boycotted and went insane. The second, Gennadi, got along well in Novgorod, but was totally ostracized by Pskov. The third, Serapion, a non-possessor, aroused the opposition of the Novgorodians by his open hostility to Joseph of Volotsk, who was very popular with the anti-Judaizer majority. Serapion was removed in 1509, and in punishment Basil III deprived the city of a bishop for 17 years. Makarii won popular admiration in Novgorod. He succeeded in lowering the taxes levied on the city by Moscow, improved the well-being of the clergy, and stood up for innocents wronged either by the Novgorod authorities or by the Grand Duke himself.

As an ideological Josephite eager to raise the prestige of both Church and state, Makarii convinced Ivan IV in 1547 to be crowned as the first Russian tsar, i.e., "emperor." Then he found him an excellent bride, Anastasia Romanovna Zakhariina, whose grand nephew would become the first Romanov tsar sixty-six years later. She had a very beneficial moral influence on her obviously unstable husband, keeping him away from excesses of cruelty as long as she lived.

To match the growing strength and centralization of the state, Makarii began to streamline and centralize the Church administration. In 1551, he convoked the *Stoglav* ("Hundred-Chapters") *Council*, so called because it adopted a Church statute consisting of 100 articles. In addition, heeding a request from the Tsar, the Council (or *sobor*, in Russian) resolved to establish a national network of permanent schools: schools teaching basic literacy were to be attached to each parish, while a college of advanced learning, with a curriculum including theology and training for priesthood was to be established at each diocesan center. The council also resolved to undertake a massive correction of Church related books, in which many differences in texts had accumulated over the centuries. With the advance of printing presses the problem now arose as to which copies were to be used as models. To address this problem, it was decided to collect ancient manuscripts available in Russia, as well as from the rest of the Orthodox world. However, few of the decisions could be implemented as all of Ivan's efforts and the national resources were directed to the wars for the Baltic coast. Then, after Anastasia's sudden death in 1560, who Ivan wrongly believed was poisoned, Ivan's reign of terror began, leading the nation finally into the Time of Troubles, which included Polish and Swedish invasions. The projected reforms were initiated only in the mid-seventeenth century. Makarii also increased the number of dioceses in Russia, carried out an investigation regarding all locally venerated Russian saints. Ignoring the most dubious of them, Makarii created a "pantheon" of national saints, composing and commissioning vitas for most of them. He also compiled a multi-volume *Menaion* of *vitaes* and teachings of most saints universally recognized by the Orthodox Churches.

One of the painful problems of Makarii's period was the fate of the learned Athonite monk, Maxim the Greek. Although Constantinople did not officially recognize the unilaterally declared autocephaly of the Russian Church, it accepted it *de facto*, as can be seen from its positive response to the request of Basil III to send a learned Greek cleric to Russia to translate theological works from Greek and Latin. Constantinople's gift to Russia was the above-named Maxim, who had been highly educated in several Italian universities, and had for a while been a Roman Catholic monk. Disappointed in Roman Catholicism, he returned to Orthodoxy, became a monk on Mt Athos, and even wrote several polemical tracts against the Latins.

Residing in the Chudov Monastery at the Moscow Kremlin Maxim the Greek, a hesychastic monk, not only worked on translations, but engaged in polemical writing, in which he lamented Russia's break with Constantinople and criticized Russian piety for its theological ignorance and absolutization of ritualism. As he was undoubtedly the best and most erudite scholar in Russia at the time, his monastic apartment became an intellectual salon of the Moscow elite. Thus his ideas, which were not to the liking of the possessors, became influential. Maxim's knowledge of Slavonic was very limited, and his translations were thus often inaccurate. Metropolitan Daniel and his

Josephite party jumped at this and accused Maxim of heresy, tried him in 1525 and sentenced him to life imprisonment in a monastery. Not satisfied with this, Daniel arranged a new trial in 1531. Accusing Maxim of spying for Turkey and of non-recognition of the metropolitans of Moscow,[6] Daniel condemned him to particularly strict monastic imprisonment in Tver'. The local abbot, however, had great respect for the learned monk, associated with him in a friendly manner and secretly improved his conditions of imprisonment, giving him ink and paper, so he could continue his theological endeavors. Only after the deposition of Daniel in 1539 was Maxim freed, but he was still not allowed to leave the city of Tver'.

After Makarii became metropolitan, he wrote to Maxim that he was kissing his chains in tears of compassion, but that he could not annul the sentence as long as Daniel was alive and refused to do so. Finally, the "Hundred-Chapters" *Sobor* allowed the abbot of the Trinity-St. Sergius Monastery, Artemii, to settle Maxim with comfort at his monastery, where he enjoyed complete freedom of writing, preaching, and associating, as well as great honor from the monks, but was still not officially rehabilitated as his "judge" was still alive. Maxim's petitions to the Tsar to be allowed to return to Greece were rejected. In 1556, he died and was buried with honor in the refectory church of the monastery. In 1988, at the Millennial Sobor of the Russian Orthodox Church, Maxim was canonized as a saint.

The Church and Ivan's Terror

With the death of Metropolitan Makarii in 1563, Ivan's paranoia lost all restraints. He set up a special terror police called the *oprichnina*. Looking for an obedient metropolitan, he thought he found one in Afanasii, who at first agreed to tolerate the *oprichnina*, whose alleged purpose was to "sniff out treason." Two years later, however, protesting against the terror, Afanasii retired to a monastery, where in a short while he died "of mysterious causes." Ivan then turned to German (Herman), an outstanding missionary and eccliastic diplomat who, as the archbishop of the former Tatar kingdom of Kazan', which was annexed to Russia in 1552, gained many converts from paganism and even Islam without antagonizing either party and without ever using force or repressing the Muslims. German demanded the abolition of the *oprichnina* as his

---

6 Indeed, Maxim did criticize the Russian Church for breaking with Constantinople and suggested that the Russian Church should once again become subordinate to the Ecumenical Patriarchate. In other words, he criticized the autocephalous status of the metropolitans, but never questioned their canonical validity as bishops.

condition of accepting the metropolitanate. In anger, Ivan expelled him from Moscow, and just as his predecessor, he soon died in a monastery. Ivan's third choice was his childhood friend and former warrior, a boyar's son, Fillip (Kolychev), who was abbot of the Solovki Arctic White Sea island monastery, where he achieved remarkable feats of engineering. He built canals and dikes, created scientifically regulated fisheries, erected hothouses where he grew tomatoes and southern fruits, and turned the monastery into a school of literacy as well as of trades (carpentry, masonry, fishing, etc.) for the peasant sons of the Russian Arctic littoral. Fillip agreed to accept the office on condition of his right to intercede on behalf of the unjustly oppressed. Two years later, at a Sunday service in the Kremlin Dormition Cathedral after a terror spree by Ivan, Fillip refused to allow Ivan to venerate the cross with the following words, stated loudly for all worshipers to hear: "Sire,... don't you fear God? We here are rendering the bloodless sacrifice for the salvation of the world, but beyond the sanctuary the blood of innocent Christians is being shed." The tsar, uttering angry threats, departed. Soon there was a parody of a trial: Fillip was deposed, imprisoned in a monastery, and soon strangled by Ivan's chief *oprichnik*, Maliuta Skuratov.

That spelled the end of Church leaders' vocal opposition to Ivan's terror. The silence of the Church once again left the nation without visible moral leadership. This undoubtedly contributed to the instability of power and absence of authority once Ivan died (1584); and the violence of the state translated itself into violence of society. This period is known as the Time of Troubles, a dynastic crisis after the death of Ivan's childless heir, Theodore, in 1598—the last tsar of the Riurikid dynasty.

The Church and the Time of Troubles.

Theodore was a sickly, kind and very pious person who spent most of his time assisting at church services, praying for the forgiveness of his father's sins, while the governing was done by his brilliant brother-in-law, Boris Godunov.

Undoubtedly the most important single event of Theodore's reign was the elevation of the status of the Russian Church to a Patriarchate, and the recognition of her autocephaly by all four eastern patriarchs: the Ecumenical of Constantinople, and the patriarchs of Alexandria, Antioch and Jerusalem. Ecumenical Patriarch Jeremiah II came to Moscow in 1588 to beg for alms for his Church, which had been devastated by the Turks. The Russian Government received him with great honor, settled him and his entourage in luxurious conditions at the Kremlin, but in fact kept the Patriarch under house arrest, letting him understand that he would not return to Constantinople until he recognized the autocephaly of the Russian Church and participated in the enthronement of her first patriarch. Jeremiah eventually agreed, and the first Russian Patriarch, Job, was installed in 1589. On his return to Constantinople, Jeremiah informed the other patriarchs of the deed, and the Russian Patriarchate received a charter of recognition signed by all the other heads of local Orthodox Churches, modestly accepting the fifth place in seniority (after the four ancient patriarchates of the East).

But the elevation of the Russian Church into a Patriarchate did not make her more powerful. Job was Godunov's creation. As soon as Boris had died, his son murdered, and the False Dimitri had entered Moscow in 1605, Job was deposed and sent to a monastery for refusing to recognize the Impostor as the true son of Ivan IV, who in fact had either accidentally killed himself in a fit of epilepsy or had been murdered (allegedly by Godunov's agents). The Impostor, who seems to have been a servant in the Romanov household before his escape to Poland, from which he marched on to Russia as a pretender to the throne, had Filaret (Romanov) consecrated as metropolitan.[7] The first bishop to recognize the Pretender as the true tsar was a Greek bishop of Riazan', Ignatius, whom the Pretender had elected as Patriarch. A year later, after the Pretender had been deposed and murdered, the new tsar, Basil IV (Shuisky), deposed Ignatius and replaced him with Hermogen, the metropolitan of Kazan'.

Patriarch Hermogen, however, proved to be much more than a favorite. He was a disciple and successor of the Kazan' missionary archbishop German. The Kazan' missionary archbishopric was established by a Russian Church Sobor in 1555, three years after that Khannate's annexation by Russia. The establishment and the early story of the Kazan' archdiocese was one of the brighter developments of Ivan's otherwise gruesome reign. Ivan's missionary guidelines for the conquered Tatar kingdoms of Kazan' and Astrakhan' stipulated that conversions were to be only voluntary, by education and conviction, not by coercion. Although the mission did not ignore the Muslims, it concentrated on the predominantly Finnic, pagan tribes which constituted a majority of the population of the Kazan' Khannate's domains. The Muslim Tatars, as monotheists, were even indirect allies of the Russian mission. The first Archbishop of Kazan' was Gurii, a pious monk of the Volokolamsk

---

7 Filaret, originally the boyar Theodore, Anastasia Zakhariina's nephew, was tonsured by force by Godunov for plotting against him. He would be enthroned as patriarch after the Time of Troubles

Monastery and a kind and wise missionary, who died in 1563. He was replaced by German. After the establishment of the Moscow Patriarchate, Kazan' became a metropolitanate; its first metropolitan was Hermogen. The Kazan' mission laid the foundations for future Russian Orthodox missions in Siberia, Central Asia, and eventually Alaska and Japan.

Hermogen's patriarchate coincided with the peak of the Time of Troubles, 1606-12. The Patriarch circulated appeals to the Russian people to expel the Poles and the Swedes from Russia and to defend their faith. The Poles occupying Moscow imprisoned him in a Kremlin dungeon, but he still found ways of smuggling out his patriotic appeals. In 1612, Hermogen died of starvation in the dungeon, even as a national rebellion's army approached Moscow. The Church canonized Hermogen as a martyr for the faith.

The Aftermath of the Time of Troubles and the Zealot Movement

The prestige of the Church as the defender of the integrity of the faith and nation rose very high in those trying years. Hermogen was not an isolated phenomenon. The Trinity-St Sergius Monastery held out for sixteen months against a Polish siege. The Poles were eventually forced to retreat without taking the walled monastery. The spiritual leaders in the siege were Archimandrite Dionisius and the monk Abraham (Palitsyn), a chronicler of the Time of Troubles. The Pskov Monastery of the Caves also put up a successful defense.

The Swedish invasion in the north and the Polish one from the west were the first large scale encounters between Muscovite-Russia and Western Europe. These encounters left bad scars. As a consequence some Russians became very defensive and isolationist, seeking to protect the country from western influences, while others became pro-westerners. Contemptuous of Russian backwardness, the latter blamed the Orthodox Church and became admirers of Catholicism and/or Protestantism. Nearly everyone, however, realized that Russia was far behind the West and had to learn its crafts and sciences. The state sought a middle course: it began to invite thousands of instructors, engineers, doctors, military experts and other professionals (banning Roman Catholics, however) to work in Russia, but settled them in separate settlements and forbade them from mingling with Russians after working hours.

Somewhere between the two opposite trends in society stood the *zealots*, a movement founded by the above-mentioned Dionisius and consisting of numerous better educated and enlightened clergy (mostly married or "white" in the

Russian common usage, in contrast to the monastic or "black" clergy). They hoped to restore Orthodoxy to its original purity and spiritual beauty, so as to morally uplift and enlighten the nation. They restored the sermon as a moral weapon, preaching not only in churches, but in the streets and market places, unmasking corrupt administrators, cruel and unfair judges, dishonest merchants...

Patriarch Filaret, father of the first Romanov tsar, shared with his son the title "Great Sovereign" and in fact ruled the country until his death in 1634. He was a power-hungry politician, not a theologian, and had little sympathy for the zealots (*bogoliubtsy* in Russian, i.e., lovers of God). There are numerous blemishes in his biography, including a very questionable link to the Impostor. As for the zealots, their time came after Filaret's death, and particularly under the second Romanov tsar, Alexei, who sympathized greatly with their cause. But now the new code of laws of 1649 (*Ulozhenie* in Russian) stood in the zealots' way, as it placed all monastery lands under the administration of a Monastery Department run by state bureaucrats, thus severely limiting Church resources. The code also contained an article placing all clergy below the rank of patriarch, as well as lay persons working for the Church, under the jurisdiction of secular courts, which had the right to sentence clergy and church workers to corporal punishment for abusing or slandering a state official. Consequently, after 1649 zealot preachers were often severely beaten for daring to criticize a mayor or a local governor.

But these adverse conditions did not deter the zealots. They recruited lay people to preach. The zealots received full control over the joint State and Patriarchal printing house and increased its output to levels unsurpassed for more than a century. Not limiting themselves to religion and theology, they also published large numbers of primers and other school textbooks, as well as translations of west-European works on geography, history, anatomy, medicine, and other sciences. They also began preparatory work for the publication of liturgical books in accordance with the Hundred Chapters Sobor's resolutions. They began by sending messengers to ancient monasteries on Mount Athos, elsewhere in Greece and the Middle East, and to monastic book collections in Russia, to find the originals or the most reliable copies to be used as models.

The zealots also struggled against the practice of *mnogoglasie* ("polyvocality"), i.e., that several parts of the service are said at once: the priest's words, the deacon's litanies, the choir's responses, the reader's chants, all at the same time, rendering the service totally incomprehensible. The practice of *mnogoglasie* developed because of the unmanageable length of the services and because of the Russian desire to omit nothing. Between the thirteenth-fifteenth centuries, the Orthodox Churches had adopted a monastic office, whose services lasted close to eight hours per day, much longer than in the "cathedral rite" formerly used in parish churches. But whereas Greece and other Orthodox countries developed an abbreviated form for parish use, Russia has not done so to the present day, and each priest is left to abbreviate the services by cutting out parts as best he can. The mistake of the zealots was that, instead of cutting out repetitions or other less important parts of the services, they insisted on keeping every word; the resulting length of the service was unrealistic in the secular world. Since the tsar supported them (he used to spend several hours in church every day and up to seven-eight hours on Sundays and feast days), the zealots went ahead with the restoration, creating mortal enemies for themselves, especially among state officials and merchants. The latter hated the zealots even more for pushing through a law banning alcohol sales on Sundays and during Great Lent and closing bars on those days. This hurt the traders' profits.

Although the Hundred Chapters' Sobor had banned "polyvocality," the zealots' struggle encountered a decisive resistance of most bishops, priests and particularly lay ecclesiastical workers. A special one-day *sobor* in February 1649 re-confirmed "polyvocality" and requested of the tsar to punish the zealots for opposing and insulting the bishops (in the heat of debates the tsar's confessor called Patriarch Joseph a wolf). But the tsar protected his confessor and continued to support the zealots. This led the Russian Patriarch to ask the Ecumenical Patriarch's advice on the matter. The latter condemned "polyvocality" in his response, stating that five words pronounced clearly are of greater value than a flood of incomprehensible sounds. Consequently, another Sobor gathered in 1651 which banned the use of "polyvocality" in church services and ordered the publication of a new service book for "monovocal" services. These two *sobors* also revealed a growing antagonism between the "white" clergy and the monastic episcopate which would reveal itself once again in the twentieth-century anti-monastic Renovationist schisms. At least the following reasons were behind that growing gap between the two branches of clergy. Whereas in the early Russian Church many bishops were consecrated from the ranks of widowed parish priests, even without the necessity of their monastic tonsure, with the collapse of non-monastic schools in thirteenth-century Russia, monasteries remained the only places where relatively educated candidates for the episcopate could be found. Moreover Russia had very few bishops, only eleven, for instance, in the mid-seventeenth century. The dioceses were huge: over 3,000 parishes in the Moscow Diocese, close to 1,500 in the Novgorod Diocese. Thus, bishops became too distant and isolated from the daily needs of the parish clergy, let alone those of laity. Then there was the colossal discrepancy between the wealth of the bishops and the material poverty of the priests. All this came into the open at the 1649 Sobor, undoubtedly impacting the future Old Ritualist Schism. But for the moment the zealots were clear victors in 1651.[8]

They were also at the height of their power: the tsar's confessor Stephen Vonifatiev, was a zealot, and the tsar, who wanted a zealot as patriarch, offered the title to him. He refused because of old age, and instead proposed the candidacy of Nikon, Archbishop of Novgorod and an active zealot. Alexei agreed. According to custom, Nikon declined the offer twice; when it was offered the third time, he agreed, but only on condition that he be given the right to use the title "Great Sovereign" in imitation of Filaret. Nikon forgot, however, that whereas Filaret had been the father of a tsar, he was but the son of a humble Mordovian village church reader. Tsar Alexei agreed to allow Nikon to use the title, causing the predictable and vengeful envy among the aristocratic courtiers of the tsar, who saw Nikon as an unbearable plebeian upstart.

Patriarch Nikon and the Great Schism.

Nikon was the very embodiment of action: imperious, short tempered, impatient. He supported the printing of books, but had no patience to wait for a scholarly analysis. Instead, he used as models the seventeenth-century Greek and Kievan printed books, although the Greek books of the period were published in Venice and contained a few Latin insertions, while the Kievan Academy was thoroughly Latinized. This sudden rehabilitation of Kievan Orthodox scholarship shocked the zealots, who remembered the time of Patriarch Filaret who, after an eight-year imprisonment in a Polish dungeon, hated everything related to Poland so much that he ruled that even Orthodox monks from Poland be re-baptized before being permitted to officiate in Russia. As for the Greeks, the Russians doubted their orthodoxy ever since the Council of Florence.

8 S. Zenkovsky, *Russkoe Staroobriadchestvo*, pp. 119–43.

But the patriarch and the young tsar were now dreaming of liberating the Balkan Christians from the Turkish Yoke, restoring the Byzantine Empire, with the Russian Tsar and the Moscow Patriarch celebrating the midnight Paschal service together with the Ecumenical Patriarch in Constantinople. These dreams were constantly being encouraged by the innumerable Greek and other Balkan "pilgrims" to Russia: patriarchs, bishops, monks, priests, as well as merchants and shady adventurers—all flocking into Russia begging for alms, ostensibly for the needs of the Church, but most often simply for personal enrichment. In their naiveté, the Russian tsars of the sixteenth and seventeenth centuries generously rewarded them with furs, money, gold, silver, and vestments and church plate of all kinds. To please the tsars, these "pilgrims" constantly flattered them, calling them the new Byzantine emperors, leaders of the whole Orthodox Christendom, and assured them that should the Russians send even a small army into the Balkans, all the Christians would rise and the Ottoman Empire would collapse. Paisios, Patriarch of Jerusalem and Ecumenical Patriarch Ioannikios II were among such petitioners. They petitioned both the Ukrainian Cossack Hetman Bohdan Khmel'nitsky, who had led the most eventful anti-Polish rebellion in 1648, and Tsar Alexei to join forces with them in a campaign against the Ottoman Empire.[9] Surprisingly, it was not the emotional and daydreaming Alexei, but the most sober Peter the Great, who succumbed to these promises by leading a small expeditionary force into Moldavia in 1701; but no general uprising ensued and Peter lost the campaign, narrowly escaping Turkish captivity.

Imagining himself in a church celebration with the Ecumenical Patriarch, Nikon foresaw the difficulties that would arise from the differences of ritual between the Greeks and the Russians, and he was eager to remove them by aligning Russian Church ritual with Greek practice—especially since the visiting Greek clergy constantly criticized Russian practice and assured the Russians they were wrong. For instance, Greeks processed around the church counter-clockwise, the Russians processed clockwise; the results could be quite messy. As many Greeks had received their higher education in Italian universities, their erudition impressed many Russians, including Nikon.

Receiving a delegation of Greek merchants on Easter day in 1653, Tsar Alexei asked them if they would want him to liberate their country from the Turks. Their response was enthusiastically positive. Deacon Paul of Aleppo,

9 See N. F. Kapterev, *Kharakter otnoshenii Rossii k pravoslavnomu Vostoku.*

present at the meeting, reported that the tsar said that, God willing, he would undertake such a campaign, and that he was ready to exhaust all his resources and shed his blood for their freedom.

After Khmelnitsky had brought Ukraine under the Russian tsar's scepter at the Pereiaslav Council of January 1654, the Russian and Ukrainian forces began their joint campaign against Poland, which at first was very successful. The Balkan Christians seriously believed the war would grow into a general Balkan war of liberation, according to S. Zenkovsky. On the other hand, the merger of the Ukraine with Russia raised a more immediate problem for Nikon: he undoubtedly wanted to bring the Orthodox Church in the Ukraine into the fold of the Moscow Patriarchate. Yet, the Ukrainian Church followed Greek practices and their service books differed from those of Muscovy. Hence Nikon's impatience with the defenders of the Old Russian rituals, the Old Believers or, more accurately, the "Old Ritualists."

The struggle intensified. The Old Ritualists now turned their wrath not only upon Nikon, but also upon the Tsar for supporting Nikon. By the end of the seventeenth century some twenty Old Ritualist leaders were either burned at the stake or otherwise executed (mostly after the death of both Alexei and Nikon, during the regency of Princess Sophia, Alexei's eldest daughter and Peter's half-sister). Many more were held prisoner in monastic prisons. About 20,000, however, burned themselves to death in mass immolations, believing that the age of Antichrist had arrived and seeking to die a martyr's death for Jesus. Up to one-third of the population of Russia at the time might have joined the schismatics openly or secretly. Their descendants soon split into numerous sects.

Nikon's tragedy, however, was that in this struggle the Zealots of Piety, his former allies, became enemies, while his former enemies became temporary allies. The zealots succeeded in obtaining a ban on alcohol sales on Sundays and during Great Lent. This turned the merchants and many other sections of the population against them and the Patriarch. Nor did the lengthening of church services as a result of the abolition of *mnogoglasie* endear many people to them either. Obviously, state officials of all ranks hated the zealots both for what they had managed to implement and for what they were trying to achieve. Their support of Nikon, after his fellow-zealots had turned against him, was only tactical, and at the first convenient moment they turned against him for having supported and implemented the zealots' reforms. In any case, except for the very few who sincerely supported the Greek-Ukrainian innovations in Church ritual out of conviction and who could be considered the early Russian Westernizers, most supporters of the official "Nikonian" Church were either religiously lukewarm or simply passive. Having lost the support of the zealots, most of whom became Old Ritualists ready to die for the faith, the State Church became a relatively spineless body, unlikely to offer much resistance against another onslaught by the secular government or by a powerful ruler bent on subordinating the Church to the State.

As Nikon was an extremely temperamental and intolerant person, the Old Ritualists zeroed in on him in the early stage of the schism. It was during Nikon's tenure that some of the most revered Old Ritualist leaders, including the Archpriest Avvakum, were sent into cruel exile. At least one bishop opposing Nikon was killed or died of starvation in prison, and another ended his life in exile. So, argues Kartashev, when Nikon had retired from active service to the New Jerusalem Monastery in 1658, after a quarrel with the tsar (induced by the courtiers hostile to Nikon), the schism with the Old Ritualists could still have been healed. At the Russian Church *sobors* of 1665 and 1666 the Russian bishops unanimously accepted the new rituals but did not, however, condemn the old books; they agreed to leave alone those who continued to serve according to the old books, as long as they did not condemn the new. But now, in addition to the Old Ritualist issue, the Church also had to solve the Nikon issue which had arisen out of his claim of the primacy of the patriarchal office over that of the tsar. The problem was that Nikon had retired to the monastery without abdicating his position. The Church was thus left without her chief executive, and major church issues had to be resolved by the tsar. Yet until Nikon retired no new patriarch could be elected. But he could be forced into retirement only after his concept of the primacy of the patriarch's office was condemned as heretical, as this was the issue underlying his quarrel with the tsar. Nikon needed that formula for his fight against the articles of the 1649 Law Code which restricted the income of the Church, i.e., in order to win his "war" against the bureaucracy. For this very same reason, the bureaucracy wanted to eliminate Nikon.

To solve these and to put an end to the patriarchal interregnum, Tsar Alexei invited the Eastern patriarchs to join the Council of 1666-67. Indeed, in November of that year, the patriarchs of both Antioch and Alexandria arrived in Moscow. Their advisers and interpreters included a former metropolitan, Paisios Ligarides, and a Greek monk, Arsenios. The former had been defrocked and excommunicated for illegally abandoning his Diocese of Gaza and for switching between Orthodoxy and Roman Catholicism, as suited him at the moment. Lying to the tsar that he needed huge amount of money, furs and gold to bribe the Turks and thus to protect his diocese, he obtained all he had asked for, but appropriated it for himself. Taking advantage of Nikon's retirement, he replaced Nikon as the leading adviser to the tsar on religious matters, impressing the latter by his erudition, acquired in Jesuit academies in Italy. He was the chief accuser against the Old Ritualists and against Nikon at the 1666-67 Council at which Greek hierarchs dominated and which condemned both the Old Ritualists and Nikon. Also associated with the indictments against the Old Ritualists was Arsenios, a learned Greek monk, educated in Florence and Rome where he had converted to Roman Catholicism. Later in the Ottoman Empire, he converted to Islam, then became a Uniate (Eastern-rite Catholic) while staying in Poland. In the 1650s he came to Moscow pretending to be a strict Orthodox monk and scholar. Here he became Nikon's main and most trusted translator and editor, until he was unmasked by the Patriarch of Jerusalem as a person who had been excommunicated for his religious swindles and sent to the Solovki monastic prison. Returning to Moscow in 1666, Arsenios joined the chorus condemning his former patron, Patriarch Nikon. Needless to say, the Greek patriarchs and their learned advisers were very generously bribed by the tsar to make sure that their judgment would be in accordance with tsar's expectations.[10]

On the basis of nothing more than minor differences in ritual, the Eastern Patriarchs condemned the Old Ritualists as heretics and anathematized them, even though originally the Greeks had ridiculed the Russians for ascribing such importance to such trivial differences. Then they condemned and deposed Nikon for his sun-moon theory, calling it, not without reason, "a papist heresy." As Kartashev remarked, for Russians the gravity of the Greek judgment was not so much in ritual details but in the fact that, at this council, without any protests on the part of the Russian bishops, those Greeks "placed all Moscow Church history in the dock and condemned it."

Nikon's fall dealt a double blow to the Russian Church and to her autonomy within the state. First, the Church lost her strongest adherents,

10 It ought to be added that the patriarchs of Constantinople and Jerusalem took no part in the proceedings of that unseemly trial. In fact the Ecumenical Patriarch warned the Russians in a letter against condemning the Old Ritualists, pointing out that as long as the doctrine of the faith was the same, minor ritual differences were not important.

becoming weak vis-à-vis the growing strength and sectarianism of the autocratic state. Second, the Patriarch, in losing his battle for supremacy, lowered the prestige and power of the patriarchal office. Subsequently, the Russian Orthodox Church lost her capacity to resist effectively the monarchic absolutism of the tsars and their offensive against the rights of the Church.

The Greek prelates condemned not only the old rituals, but also the Hundred Chapters Council of 1551, which had proclaimed the correctness of the two-fingered sign of the cross and other Russian customs, as well as its convener and chairman, Metropolitan Makarii, whom they called "an ignorant and erring metropolitan." They also banned such works as: *The Story of the White Cowl*, with its legend of the miraculous migration of the patriarchal white cowl from Rome then to Constantinople, then to Russia, after the Greeks had betrayed Orthodoxy in Florence; *The Hundred Chapters Sobor's Statute*; and *The Vita of St Euphrosinius*, with its affirmation of the two-finger crossing. Both S. Zenkovsky and Kartashev agree that the trial and its resolutions were the Greeks' vengeance for Russia's condemnation of their temporary capitulation to Rome in the fifteenth century.

The Council upheld Nikon's position only on two counts: ritual reforms with the adoption of the new Greek books, and his insistence that the Monastery Department be returned under the jurisdiction of the Church. Indeed, under the energetic administration of Patriarch Joachim in the 1670s and 1680s it was brought back under the Church, and state officials were replaced by church people in all the administrative offices of the Church in 1675. But the victory was short-lived.

In 1667, The Greek prelates at the Sobor formulated the relationship between the tsar and the patriarch as follows: "The tsar has priority in civil matters, the patriarch, in church matters." This, says Zenkovsky, subsequently made it possible for the tsar to replace church leaders at will for reasons of state, whereas prior to this the high handed removals of metropolitans by Ivan the Terrible, for instance, had been condemned by Tsar Alexei himself.

Attempts to come to terms with the Old Ritualists were undertaken in the 1680s, when the Regent Sophia announced public debates between the patriarch and his clergy on the one hand, and the Old Ritualist leader, on the other. Unfortunately, these came to naught when the Old Ritualists, supported by some Court infantry (*strel'tsy*), instead of debating, began abusing the Patriarch and his party, first by hurling insults, but then by spitting and throwing rocks at him. The debate ended with a counter-attack by regular troops, which was followed by the most massive persecution of the Old Ritualists to date. These persecutions attracted wide sympathy for the persecuted, many of whom fled to Poland and Turkey. The island Monastery of Solovki in the White Sea became the most famous Old Ritualists center of resistance. Besieged by the regular troops from 1668 to 1676, it was finally sacked, and its defenders, both laymen and monks, were massacred.

As often happens, once the Old Ritualists were left to themselves, they began to split into numerous sects, some moving far from their Orthodox roots, such as the *Dukhobors*, the *Molokans,* or the *Khlysty*, a variant of shakers. Others remained quite Orthodox in their theology, although separating into so-called "priestly" and "priestless" groups. Persecutions of the Old Ritualists, which continued with varying degrees of intensity and with some intervals of toleration, lasted until 1905. These persecutions were probably among the causes of the collapse of the monarchy in 1917. As natural conservatives and deep patriots ready to die for their national and religious traditions, Old Ritualists were the natural stuff for the most dedicated support of the Crown. Yet the Crown forced them into opposition, radicalized them, alienated them. Thus, when the revolutionary crisis arrived, those in the nation who in the very core of their being should have been the cornerstone of the monarchy, were not prepared to support it.

FOR FURTHER READING

Andreyev, N.E., *Studies in Muscovy* (London: Variorum Reprints, 1970).

—— *O Dele Diaka Viskovatogo. Seminarium Kondakovianum* 5 (Prague, 1932).

Avvakum, "The Life of Priest Avvakum by Himself," in Zenkovsky, S., ed., *Medieval Russia's Epics ...*

Bushkovich, *Paul, Religion and Society in Russia. The Sixteenth and Seventeenth Centuries* (Oxford University Press, 1992).

Fedotov, G., St Filipp, *Metropolitan of Moscow: Encounter with Ivan the Terrible* (Belmont, MA: Nordland Press, 1978).

Fennell, J., ed. and trans., *The Correspondence between Prince A.M. Kurbsky and Tsar Ivan IV of Russia* (New York, 1955).

Florovsky, G., *Aspects of Church History* (Belmont, MA: Nordland Press, 1975).

Fonkich, B.L., *Grechesko-russkie kul'turnye sviazi v XV-XVII vv.* (Moscow, 1977).

Gorchakov, M., *Monastyrskii prikaz* (1649-1725) (St Petersburg, 1868).

Haney, Jack., *From Italy to Muscovy: the Life and Works of Maxim the Greek* (Munich, 1973).

Ikonnikov, V.S., *Maxim Grek i ego vremia* (Kiev, 1915).

Iosif Volotsky, *Poslaniia* (Moscow, 1959).

Kazakova, N.A., *Vassian Patrikeev i ego sochineniia* (Moscow-Leningrad, 1960).

_____, and Y.S. Lurie, *Antifeodal'nye eretichekie dvizheniia na Rusi XIV-nachala XVI vv.* (Moscow, 1955).

Kapterev, N.F., *Patriarch Nikon i tsar' Aleksei Mikhailovich*, 2 vols. (Sergiev Posad, 1909-1912).

_____, *Kharakter otnoshenii Rossii k pravoslavnomu vostoku v XVI i XVII stoletiiakh* (Sergiev Posad, 1914).

Kartashev, A., *Ocherki....*, vol. II (Paris, 1959).

Kharlampovich, K.V., *Malorossiiskoe vliianie na velikorusskuiu tserkovnuiu zhizn'* (Kazan', 1914).

Klibanov, A.I., *Reformatsionnye dvizheniia v Rossii v XIV i pervoi polovine XVI vv.* (Moscow, 1960).

Klyuchevky, V., *Course of Russian History*, vols. 2 & 3 (New York, 1911-1931).

Kotoshikhin, G., *O Rossii v tsarstvovanie Alekseia Mikhailovicha* (St Petersburg, 1906).

Kruglov, F., *Ispravlenie knig v XVII stoletii i staroobriadcheskii raskol* (St Petersburg, 1911).

Lilienfeld, Fairy von, *Nil Sorskii und seine Schriften: der Bruch der Tradition im Russland Ivans III* (Berlin, 1963).

Lupinin, N., *Religious Revolt in the XVIIth Century: the Schism of the Russian Church* (Princeton, NJ: Kingston Press, 1984).

Medlin, W., *Moscow and East Rome: a Political Study of the Relations of Church and State in Muscovite Russia* (Westport, CT, 1981).

_____, *Renaissance Influences and Religious Reforms in Russia: Western and Post-Byzantine Impacts on Culture and Education (16th-17th cc.)* (Genève: Droz, 1971).

Meyendorff, Paul, *Russia, Ritual and Reform* (Crestwood, NY: St Vladimir's Press, 1991).

Nil Sorskii, *Predanie i ustav. Pamiatniki drevnei pis'mennosti i iskusstva*, vol. 179 (St Petersburg, 1921).

Palitsyn, Avraamy, "Pseudo-Dmitry" and "Answer of the Defenders of the Holy Trinity-St. Sergius Monastery to the Polish Request to Surrender" in Zenkovsky, *Medieval...*

Platonov, S.F., *The Time of Troubles* (The University Press of Kansas, 1970).

Smolitsch, Igor., *Russisches Monchtum: Entstehung, Entwicklung und Wesen, 988-1914* (Würzburg, 1953).

Soloviev A.V., *Holy Russia: the History of a Religious-Social Idea* (New York, 1959).

Soloviev, S.M., *Istoriia Rossii s drevneishikh vremen*, vv. II & III (Moscow, 1960).

Utechin, S.V., *Russian Political Thought: a Concise History* (New York & London, 1964).

Vernadsky, George, *Russia at the Dawn of the Modern Age* (New Haven: Yale U. Press, 1959).

_____, *The Tsardom of Moscow*, 1547-1682 (Yale U. Press, 1959).

Zenkovsky, S., *Russkoe staroobriadchestvo* (Munich: Fink Verlag, 1970).

Zernov, N., *Moscow, the Third Rome* (London, 1945).

Zimin, A.A., I.S. *Peresvetov i ego sovremenniki* (Moscow, 1958).

Zyzykin, M.V., *Patriarkh Nikon i ego gosudarstvennye i kanonicheskie idei*, 3 vols. (Warsaw, 1931-38).

CHAPTER 5

THE CHURCH IN WEST RUSSIA: FROM ORTHODOXY TO THE UNIA AND AGAIN TO ORTHODOXY

The Mongol-Tatar invasion of 1238-42 was equally destructive to all parts of Russia except Novgorod. Kiev, located so close to the southern steppe, the natural habitat of all nomads, including the Mongol-Tatars, suffered several additional devastating raids. Of these, the most destructive was the raid of 1299 when, according to the chronicler, the city was almost totally destroyed. Whereas in the rest of Russia Tatars allowed the Russian political infrastructure to continue, the former principalities of Kiev and Pereiaslav, as well as Podolia, were simply annexed to the Golden Horde and ruled by a baskak appointed by Batyi, the conqueror of the Russian lands.[1] In general, Kiev's fate in the period between the Mongol conquest in 1241 and its annexation by the Lithuanian prince Vitovt in the early fifteenth century remains unclear. The Russian historian M. Liubavsky claimed that early in the fourteenth century the Mongols handed the governorship of Kiev over to the Russian prince of Putivl'. According to Kartashev, the Tatars entrusted Kiev to the Grand Duke of Vladimir in 1245, whereupon "the resident-Prince Mikhail of Chernigov and his bishop Peter (Akerovich), who had called himself a metropolitan, retreated to Hungary." All we know about Peter is that he participated in the Union Council of Lyons, where he presented himself as the Russian metropolitan and concelebrated with Latin bishops, after which he disappears from the historical horizon. Prince Mikhail returned to his Chernigov and ended his life as a martyr in the Tatar capital after refusing to partake of what he considered to be blasphemous pagan fire rituals required prior to being admitted before the face of the khan. For this, he was later canonized by the Church. It appears that, just as Grand Duke Daniel of Galich, Prince Mikhail of Chernigov went to seek allies in the west for a common struggle against the Tatars; and, dreaming of restoring Kiev to its former glory, he called his bishop a metropolitan.

The collapse of Kiev left two potential political centers of gravity for the Russians: one was in the backwoods of the lands of Vladimir-Suzdal', where

---

1 Baskaks were Tatar armed tax collectors who also acted as viceroys for the khan in conquered lands. See: George Vernadsky, *The Mongols and Russia*.

the young town of Moscow eventually prevailed over other cities in the region; the other was the Grand Duchy of Galicia-Volynia, in the extreme south-west corner of Russia. During the reign of its two talented leaders, Prince Roman Mstislavich of Volynia who in the late twelfth century amalgamated the two principalities, and his son Daniel Romanovich, who ruled in the thirteenth century, the Grand Duchy of Galicia and Volynia was undoubtedly the strongest of the Kievan successor states. It was also the wealthiest, owing to the beneficent southern climate, the excellent black soils of Volynia, and its river trade routes connecting the duchy to markets in Poland, Hungary, Bohemia, and the Baltic Sea. Three separate factors helped to seal its fate: first, the wealth and independence of its landed gentry, who often plotted with the neighboring Polish and Hungarian dukes against their ruler; second, the proximity of Roman-Catholic states hostile to Orthodoxy and envious of Daniel's might; third, the Mongols, who totally devastated the land in 1240-41, a situation of which Poland and Lithuania would later take advantage.

At first, Daniel sought help from the West, through the intermediary of the pope, to form a crusade against the infidel Tatars. As a price for such assistance, the pope requested church union with the papacy and the prerogative to crown Daniel as king. Daniel at first agreed. During the same time his candidate for the all-Russian metropolitanate, Kirill II, (Kirill III, according to Golubinsky), was in Nicea awaiting consecration. The pope, meanwhile, failed to raise a military force for Daniel, and Kirill returned from Nicea with reports about the anti-Orthodox vandalism of the Latin crusaders. Apparently he was able to talk Daniel out of the Union, because in 1249 Daniel rejected the royal crown, broke off his negotiations with the papacy, and proceeded to the Golden Horde to beg the khan's forgiveness. The Khan Batyi magnanimously forgave Daniel and took him into his vassalage; but apparently Daniel's religious vacillations convinced the Metropolitan to choose the northeast rather than the southwest as Russia's ecclesiastical center. As described in chapter 2, Kirill left for Vladimir-Suzdal' and became a strong supporter of Alexander Nevsky's policy of close alignment with the Tatars. Kirill was an excellent Church administrator. He convened a local council in Vladimir which took strong measures to raise the moral standards of the clergy, banning simony, reforming and regulating religious services, and adopted the canon law of the Greek Church which had been translated by St Sava of Serbia. Kirill died in 1281 in Pereiaslav-Zalesski, Alexander Nevsky's temporary capital. Choosing the Vladimir-

Suzdal' land as the de facto seat of the metropolitans of Rus' was crucial to the future formation of the national capital in that area.

Kirill's tenure marked a turning point in the Greek insistence that the ruling metropolitan of Rus' be a Greek. Kirill's predecessor, Iosif, was a Greek who arrived in Kiev in 1237, but who seems to have defected in the face of the Tatar invasion. Kartashev suggests that the Greeks agreed to consecrate a Russian not only because of a sense of shame that their compatriot had abandoned his flock, but also because the Byzantines were at the time negotiating with the Golden Horde for support in their effort to get the crusaders out of Constantinople. It would have been embarrassing for the metropolitan of Rus', a Byzantine national, to be a subject of the khan. True, the next metropolitan after Kirill was a Greek, Maxim, but by then the Greeks had regained Constantinople, so there was no longer any need of a partnership with the Tatars. In addition, the Russian princes had regained much of their autonomy from the Mongols, and it was thus not so humiliating for the Byzantines to have one of their subjects under the khan's suzerainty. In any case, from this time appeared the unwritten custom of alternating Russians and Greeks as metropolitans of Rus'.

Metropolitan Maxim arrived in Kiev around 1286-87, after first paying homage to the Golden Horde. After the Mongol raid on Kiev in 1299, however, he moved to Vladimir and mostly remained there until his death in 1305. In approximately 1286-87 he convoked a local council, apparently to inform the Russian clergy about the Council of Lyons, to assure them that the Greek Church had rejected the union with Rome, and that the Patriarch had excommunicated the emperor Michael Paleologos for uniting with Rome.

The Rise of Moscow

Now that two consecutive metropolitans had chosen the northeast over the southwest, Daniel's grandson, the Galician grand duke Iurii L'vovich, put pressure on Constantinople to appoint a separate metropolitan for his land. Constantinople, which preferred to see a single, undivided Church administration in Russia, this time gave in to the Galician pressure and, in 1302-03, consecrated a certain Nifont, with the new title of a "Metropolitan of Galicia," not of Kiev and All Rus'-that title was retained by Maxim.

Both Maxim and Nifont died around 1305. Two candidates were then sent to Constantinople: one by the grand duke of Vladimir and Tver'; the other, Peter, a Volynian monk, was sent by the Galician grand duke.

Constantinople, returning to the principle of one metropolitan for both parts of Rus, consecrated Peter, who, after only a year in Galicia and Kiev, moved to the northeast. Prince Mikhail of Tver', who at that time held the grand-ducal patent (from the Tatars), however, was hostile to Peter, because his own candidate had not been consecrated. Probably in order to assuage Michael and to demonstrate his impartiality, Peter became a wandering metropolitan, often visiting Volynia and Galicia, thus keeping the Galician ruler satisfied. But most of his time Peter spent in the small appanage town of Moscow, where he died and was buried in 1326 (allegedly according to his will), two years after the Moscow prince Ivan I, Kalita, first managed to obtain the grand-ducal patent from the Tatar khan. The interment in Moscow of that outstanding leader of the Church, who was soon canonized as a saint, raised Moscow's status to that of de facto "national capital."

The Grand Duchy of Lithuania and the Division of the Russian Church

In the meantime, threatened by the German Teutonic knights who had already overrun Lithuanian-speaking East Prussia and exterminated most of its pagan population, the leader of one of the Lithuanian clans, Prince Gediminas, united all the uninvaded Lithuanian clans. The new and highly militant Lithuanian state, squeezed by German invaders from the west, began to annex Russian territories to its immediate east. By the second half of the fourteenth century, Lithuanian territory included most of western Rus': Kiev, Belorussia and Volynia; while Galicia and parts of Podolia and western Volynia were annexed by Poland. Ethnic Lithuanians, still predominantly pagan in the fourteenth century, constituted a mere 20 percent of the population of this new Russo-Lithuanian Grand Duchy. The west-Russian version of Slavonic became the state language, the ethnic Lithuanian aristocracy and members of the royal family began to convert to Orthodoxy, the majority religion. Since the Orthodox Church did not use force to bring Lithuanians to the baptismal font, Christianity's progress among ethnic Lithuanians was very gradual. One of the explanations for this slowness may have been the reluctance of the Ecumenical Patriarchate to break up the Russian Church into two, while the proud Lithuanian princes did not want to convert their natives to a religion based in Moscow, their major rival.

Under pressure from Lithuanian princes, and even more from Polish kings, who threatened to impose Roman Catholicism on their Orthodox subjects unless a hierarchy separate from Moscow was set up for their territories,

Constantinople occasionally gave in and appointed separate metropolitans either for Galicia or for Lithuania, but this remained the exception. The Ecumenical See remained opposed to the idea. One of the factors militating against two separate Churches in the fourteenth century may have been the uncertainty over whether the final center of Russia would be in Moscow or in Vil'na (now Vilnius, the capital of Lithuania). The end to such speculations came in 1386, when Polish magnates arranged a matrimonial union between the Lithuanian Grand Duke Jagiello (in Russian, Yagailo, baptized in the Orthodox Church as Jacob) and Queen Jadwiga (Hedwig), a daughter of the last Polish king of the Piast dynasty. Jagiello was to become the king of Poland on condition that he convert to Roman Catholicism, open Lithuania to the Roman Catholic missionaries, and make Roman Catholicism the only legal religion of the Grand Duchy. To all this Yagailo agreed, and he was crowned as King Wladyslaw.

The ethnic Lithuanian population remained at least as reluctant to become Roman Catholics as they had resisted conversion to Orthodoxy. Even at the end of the seventeenth century, after all the coercion to push the Orthodox population into Roman Catholicism, of either Western or Eastern rite, the entire Lithuanian territory had only 700 Roman Catholic, as against 5,000 Orthodox churches. Language might have been one of the factors: Latin was as foreign to the Samogidians of western Lithuania as Slavonic.

In the end, at least in the Lithuanian part of the Commonwealth of Poland and Lithuania, the Orthodox fared much better than Yagailo's original Krewo Agreement with the Poles might have suggested. Yagailo's ambitious cousin Vitovt (Vitautas) fought a prolonged war against him. The war ended in a treaty in 1413, according to which Lithuania regained its independence within the loose commonwealth. Its ruling prince, Vitovt at the time, was only a vassal to the king of Poland, and Lithuania continued to be ruled by its own laws which were based on those of Kievan Rus', thus de facto re-legitimizing the Orthodox Church.

After the Polish-Lithuanian union, there could no longer be any question that the center of East Slavonic Orthodoxy would be in Moscow. In 1448, however, Moscow broke its ecclesiastic dependence on Constantinople, and that changed the latter's position on the question of a separate Orthodox Church for Poland and Lithuania.[2] Having lost control over and income

2 Ever since the Union of Florence, the Russians have been somewhat contemptuous of the Greeks as "traitors of Orthodoxy." In fact, the Russians have little reason to be proud of their own fidelity, because it was Grand

from the Moscovite Russian Church, Constantinople, devastated and impoverished by the Turkish occupation, was now eager to retain at least a part of the Russian Church in its fold. In 1458, a certain Bulgarian priest, named Gregory, was consecrated in Rome as the Byzantine-Rite bishop for Lithuania. At the liturgy he publicly commemorated both the pope and the Ecumenical patriach, after which the West Russian clergy and laity refused to recognize him as their bishop. Gregory went to Constantinople, repented, was forgiven by the patriarch for his apostasy and restored to the ranks of Orthodox bishops. in 1469 he was appointed Metropolitan of Kiev, though de facto residing permanently in Vil'na.[3] Thus, as of 1469, there were two separate Russian Orthodox Churches: the autocephalous Church of Moscow and All Russia, and the Church of Kiev and Little Russia,[4] under Constantinople but virtually autonomous. This was not the original intention of the Ecumenical Patriarch. He appealed to all Russian bishops, including the metropolitan of Moscow, to recognize Gregory as the Metropolitan of All Russia. But the Moscow government's response to this appeal was to ban the entry into Muscovy of Gregory and of any bishops subordinate to him.

The Orthodox laity of Poland and Lithuania, however, continued to doubt Gregory's Orthodoxy and began to form lay brotherhoods to protect the Church from the unreliable and usurpatory bishops. Indeed, the next metropolitan, Misail (Pestruch) of Smolensk, elected under pressure from the Polish king, also flirted with Rome, trying to revive the Union of Florence. The Ecumenical patriarch apparently knew of Misail's correspondence with Rome, because he never confirmed him as Metropolitan of Kiev, and in 1480, after Misail's death, appointed a Great Russian (although a Lithuanian subject), Spiridon, as Metropolitan of Kiev. The grand duke of Lithuania ordered his arrest, allegedly as a Turkish spy (!). Two years later Spiridon was expelled to Muscovy, where he lived the rest of his life in monastic retirement, because of his pro-Constantinopolitan orientation. As Spiridon had been very popular with the Orthodox clergy and laity of Lithuania and Poland, the episode

Duke Basil II who had refused to accept the Union and ordered the arrest of Isidore, not the bishops whose response was a silent acceptance of Isidore, i.e., of the Union. By contrast, in Greece, the whole Church, including the laity, rejected the Union, which de facto became a brief union of the emperor, his court and the Ecumenical patriarch with Rome, not of the Greek Church as a whole.

3 The capital of Lithuania, now Vilnius. Kiev apparently was still too unstable to be the real seat of the metropolitans.

4 The terms "Little Russia" and "Great Russia" (respectively Μικρο and Μεγαλι), were of Byzantine origin and meant respectively the core or original Russia and the expanded larger possessions of the original core.

apparently served as an early warning to the king about the pro-Moscow orientation of his Orthodox subjects at a time when Moscow was expanding at Lithuania's expense, winning back old Russian territories. This fear, as well as the need to keep his Orthodox subjects happy, forced the king to respond favorably to their appeals to elect their metropolitans at local councils of bishops, clergy and laity. From this time metropolitans were thus elected, with a legate of the patriarch confirming the metropolitan-elect on the spot. This practice further increased the role and authority of the brotherhoods and parish clergy in the life of the Church.

The Orthodox Church in the Polish-Lithuanian Commonwealth suffered not so much from direct persecutions-although, according to a letter by the metropolitan-elect Misail to the pope, Orthodox clerics were often abused, even beaten, maimed and murdered by the Latins-as from an uncertain legal status. Officially, lands and estates belonging to Orthodox churches and monasteries were royal property. And as the Roman Catholic king was no protector of the Orthodox, he distributed these lands as patronage to West Russian magnates for services rendered to the king. Many of these magnates were Orthodox only in name. To support their high living, they often sold their patronages, including even episcopal titles, if the given property included a diocesan center. In this way, some magnates bought episcopal positions for themselves together with the property. Becoming a bishop, such a lord would continue to live with his wife, contrary to the requirement of episcopal celibacy, and occupy part of a monastery, where he might arrange balls and other secular entertainment. Nevertheless, because of the weakness of Constantinople after its seizure by the Turks, as well as the absence of any clear legal status for the Orthodox Church and the practically unlimited powers of the aristocracy in the Commonwealth, the Orthodox magnates were the only intercessors for the Church before the king.

Obviously, a college of bishops controlled by these magnates and consisting mostly of their scions could not effectively defend the faith. Moreover, hard pressed by a Muscovite military offensive, Lithuania was forced to join Poland in a federal, rather than confederal, union in 1569, and the Orthodox aristocracy of Lithuania lost the right to sit in the Senate (Rada). As a result, its political clout was greatly curbed. Although any member of the gentry could participate in the local and the central diet (respectively: *sejmiki* and *sejm*), these did not meet regularly. Day-to-day affairs were conducted in the senate, permanently in session, which could veto any royal decision. And in the seventeenth century the veto power was extended to each individual senator-no decree could pass without complete unanimity. This was the so-called *liberum veto*, and it was enjoyed only by the Latin-rite, Roman Catholic aristocracy. Even the Eastern-rite "Uniates" were not given the privilege. This was the reason most Lithuanian aristocrats converted to the Western Rite Roman Catholicism in the course of the seventeenth century, and particularly those who had joined the Unia—as a result, the Unia became known in Poland as the peasants' religion.

Prior to 1569, the status of the Orthodox in Lithuania was incomparably better than in Poland. In fact, medieval Lithuania had undoubtedly been the most religiously tolerant state in Europe. Even Poland, prior to the mid-sixteenth century, was much more religiously tolerant than any west-European state, or Muscovy for that matter. For this reason, diverse Protestant and even proto-Protestant movements freely disseminated their ideas in the Commonwealth. Protestant schools (mostly Calvinist in Lithuania, and Lutheran in Poland) were widespread, and through them Protestantism became very widespread among the nobility, particularly in Lithuania, where numerous, formerly Orthodox, aristocratic families converted to Calvinism.

All this changes in the second half of the sixteenth century, largely as a result of external factors. Muscovite Russia becomes a serious threat to the territorial integrity of the Commonwealth, and the large Orthodox population is clearly sympathetic to Muscovy's advance. In the north-west both Brandenburg (West Prussia) and East Prussia adopt Lutheranism, and both duchies, separated by the Polish corridor, are ruled by members of the same Hohenzollern dynasty. Orthodoxy and Lutheranism thus become geopolitical threats to the very survival of Poland. The former is identified with the Russian Tsardom, the latter with the potential of German aggression. In response, Poland begins to link Roman Catholicism with Polish identity: only a Roman Catholic can be a true Pole; and therefore, in order to achieve national security, all Polish subjects should be converted to Roman Catholicism.

To overcome the role of Protestant schools in disseminating Protestantism, the Polish king, Sigmund-August II, invited the Jesuits into Poland in 1564 and gave them huge endowments of land to establish a network of schools and colleges (academies) across the country. With these rich endowments, the Jesuit institutions charged no tuition fees, in contrast to the expensive Protestant schools. And in contrast with Protestant schools, Jesuits did not require the pupils of their general education schools to convert to Roman Catholicism. The Russian gentry thus began to send their children to the Jesuit schools. Despite being officially secular, they succeeded in luring many pupils to Catholicism. These new converts would then often pressure their Orthodox peasant serfs to join the Roman Church. Often living beyond their means, the gentry would impose special fees for the use of an Orthodox church situated on their estates. Those who lived in Krakow, Warsaw, or even Paris, as absentee lords would appoint a local Jewish shopkeeper or miller to manage their properties. Pressed to raise more and more money for their lords, these Jewish managers would keep the key to the local church and impose high fees for each use, e.g., for each liturgy, baptism, etc. This practice became particularly widespread after the 1596 Union of Brest, when the Orthodox Church was outlawed and the majority of nobles joined the Roman Church to maintain their privileges, while most peasants and artisans remained Orthodox. Thus Jews came to be identified in the eyes of the general populace with religious oppression. This was the origin of so-called Ukrainian antisemitism, and the cause of the wild Cossack pogroms during all the anti-Polish rebellions by the West Russians in the late sixteenth to the eighteenth centuries.

Realizing the threat to Orthodoxy posed by Protestant and Catholic schools, the Orthodox mutual-aid brotherhoods, formed by guilds of craftsmen and artisans, began to set up Orthodox schools. They also took parish churches under their protection, built and maintained them, and, being distrustful of their bishops, sought and received charters from the Ecumenical Patriarch granting them autonomy from bishops and the right to control brotherhood churches and their clergy. Constantinople was in no position to do any more. It did provide some teachers for the brotherhoods' schools, but not in sufficient numbers or quality. At first, therefore, the Orthodox schools could not compete, although they tried as much as possible to imitate the Jesuit system of education. Remaining inferior to Roman Catholic institutions, the brotherhood schools catered almost exclusively to the children of craftsmen, artisans, and tradesmen, while the gentry sent their children to the Jesuit academies, where they were quickly polonized and religiously romanized.

Brotherhood schools and churches were registered in accordance with the Magdeburg Law accepted by Poland, which recognized guilds as autonomous institutions governed by their own laws, whose estates and buildings enjoyed territorial immunity. Not trusting their bishops, the brotherhoods obtained charters from the Ecumenical Patriarchate granting them the right to appoint and expel priests and teachers, and immunity from episcopal interference. In 1589, Ecumenical Patriarch Jeremiah II, returning from the consecration of the first patriarch in Moscow, passed through Poland and in response to their complaints about the immorality and corruption of their bishops, issued a new statute which forbade the bishops to interfere in the brotherhoods' affairs in any way and compelled them to confirm all excommunications initiated by the brotherhoods.

The Road to the Union of Brest

The 1590s were rife with rumors that the bishops were secretly negotiating with Rome. Many among the Orthodox, including one of Poland's wealthiest and most powerful magnates and a staunch protector of Orthodoxy, Prince Constantine of Ostrog (*Ostrozhskii* in Russian), favored a Church reunion. But they believed it could be accomplished only by a joint and representative council, at which both sides would have equal say, could debate each other's theological positions, and through such a dialogue first achieve doctrinal unity, and then administrative unity. The bishops, admitting to the prince that Rome would never agree to such a council of equals, nevertheless deviously assured him of their staunch Orthodoxy, and denied any secret negotiations with Rome.

In fact, the Polish king received a secret memorandum in 1594, signed by four Orthodox bishops and addressed to the pope, apparently to test his reaction. Indeed, after the addition of the signature of the Metropolitan of Kiev (Mikhail Rogoza), who had just assured Prince Ostrozhsky of his unwavering fidelity to Orthodoxy, the memorandum was forwarded to Rome. Its authors explained their appeal to the pope as resulting from a desire to restore order and discipline in the Church, under the single leadership of the pope, in order to end the dissemination of heresies fomented by dissensions in Orthodoxy, as every bishop claimed to speak the ultimate truth. The memorandum lists ten conditions for their submission to the pope:

1. The inviolability of the Eastern rites and traditions;

2. The inviolability of monastic properties, episcopal cathedrals, and of the hierarchical subordination of the priests to their Orthodox (sic!) bishops;

3. The inviolability of the liturgical ordo and of the Julian Calendar;

4. Due honor rendered [to the bishops] in the diet and seats in the senate;

7. The abolition of the brotherhoods' immunity, granted to them by the Eastern patriarchs, because allegedly, the brotherhoods have become a source of sectarianism;

8. The consecration of Russian bishops only by the Metropolitan of Kiev, who is to be elected, as now, by councils of West-Russian bishops and only confirmed by the pope;

9 and 10. The confirmation of these articles by both the Pope and the Polish king, so that the Russian bishops may have the same rights and privileges as those enjoyed by Latin-rite bishops.

Note the point regarding the brotherhoods. Clearly, their independence was one of the incentives for the appeal to Rome: the West-Russian bishops wanted to have the same power over their flock and clergy as that enjoyed by their Latin confreres. Surprisingly, the document totally ignores the doctrinal differences between the two Churches. The bishops were concerned only with their own privileges and with the ritual.

Rome ignored all these conditions, promising only that the metropolitan of Kiev would have full control over the ancient Kiev Monastery of the Caves. Nevertheless, the Russian bishops now drafted a "Conciliar Address" to the pope, consisting of twenty-six articles, which was to be delivered by two bishops, Ipatii-Potii of Vladimir-Volynsk, and Kirill (Terletsky) of Lutsk. The articles included both a confession of faith and a number of requests, e.g.:

1. The Holy Spirit proceeds from the Father through the Son;

2. All Orthodox liturgies and other rites should remain unchanged;

3. The Eucharist is to continue to be distributed under both species, according to the Orthodox tradition;

4. No objection to purgatory, "but we want to be true to the teaching of the Church."[5] The new calendar can be accepted but the Paschal cycle should remain untouched, as well as those Orthodox feasts which are absent from the Roman Church, e.g., Epiphany;

6. The retention of married clergy;

5 Roman Catholic or Orthodox? This is not clarified.

7. That only Russians or Greeks may be consecrated as bishops;[6]

8 and 9. (Identical to the eighth and tenth articles in the previous memorandum);

11. No Greek bishops are to be allowed on the Commonwealth's territory, and none of their bans are to be valid in the Commonwealth;

12 and 20. Defections to the Roman rite and the transformation of Eastern churches into Latin-rite ones is to be forbidden;

21. Colleges and brotherhoods, should they join the Unia, are to be subordinated to the bishops [!];

26. "Some of ours" have gone to Greece to report [on us] in order to be appointed to posts "superior to ours." Let the King of Poland prevent their re-entry into his domains.

Uniate historians have claimed that this document had a theological character. But the only theology here relates to the *filioque* and purgatory, and on both issues the bishops meekly agree to accept whatever the pope decides. Yet even this petition did not receive a proper response from the Vatican. After vainly waiting for it in Rome, the bishops were simply brought before the pope, were handed the Latin texts of the Latin episcopal oath, which they were made to pronounce while kneeling before the pope. Then, after reciting the Creed with the *filioque*, they were reconsecrated by the pope as Roman-Catholic bishops pure and simple. The confession of faith included in the oath affirmed that only the Roman Church possessed the fullness of truth, and that they accept all the traditions, rites and sacraments of the Roman Church. Only a month later, in January 1596, the Pope magnanimously handed the bishops a short statute for the Uniate Church, permitting it to retain those of their traditions and rites which did not contradict the teaching of the Roman Church. All the other demands made in the two memoranda-such as autonomy, the election of bishops, etc.-were totally ignored by Rome. Ipatii and Kirill then returned to the Commonwealth as bishops of the Eastern Rite, but with no guarantee that that rite would be respected and retained.

It ought to be said in Rome's defense that the Pope had been misled by the title of the second petition, believing that it was indeed conciliar, i.e., that it represented the real opinion of the entire Church. Moreover, accustomed to

---

6 This reflects the fear that Poles might try to infiltrate the Church and gradually latinize and polonize it.

the authoritarian clericalism of the Roman Church, the Vatican thought that once the bishops had joined the Roman Church, there could be no more questions from their flock. But the Orthodox *sobornal* ("conciliar") mentality, however abused, militated against such clericalism, and the will of the bishops was by no means tantamount to the agreement of their flock. In fact, the laity, the parish clergy, and particularly the brotherhoods refused to accept the union with Rome. The protest movement developed and spread quickly, joined at first by a single bishop, Gideon (Boloban) of Lvov. The King gave in to these pressures and authorized the convening of a local council of those bishops, clergy and laity of the Roman and Greek Church who accepted the papacy—i.e., those who did not accept the Unia were not invited.

The Council met in the city of Brest on October 6, 1596. In order to prevent a parallel Orthodox council in any of the numerous Orthodox churches in the city, the Metropolitan of Kiev sealed all Orthodox churches on the day before the Council was to begin, except for the cathedral where the Council was to take place. The Orthodox, nevertheless, converged on Brest as well, with Prince Ostrozhskii and his private army at the head. Failing to find an open church, and after waiting in vain for an invitation from the Uniates, they accepted the offer of a Protestant church school hall for a separate Orthodox Council. The Uniate Council passed a resolution excommunicating all the Orthodox clergy and laity participating in the Orthodox Council. The Orthodox in turn suspended all the clergy and lay participants in the Uniate Council and addressed a petition to the King, asking him to deprive "the traitors" of their dioceses and parishes. But the King decided otherwise: his edict of October 15 legalized only those Byzantine-rite Christians who joined the Unia; it decreed the Orthodox Church null and void and all its clergy excommunicated; while continuing membership in the Orthodox Church was declared to be an act of treason against the state.

After Brest

The struggle now shifted to the 1597 Warsaw Diet, where the Orthodox and the Protestants acted in a united front. But decisions of the diet had to be adopted unanimously in order to be valid. As a result, neither the Orthodox nor the Uniates could get their bills through the Diet. This allowed the Orthodox to continue to exist "semi-legally," as it were. Moreover, the government could not legally shut down those churches which belonged to the self-governing brotherhoods, which enjoyed immunity under the Magdeburg

Law. Nor could the King close a church built on a private estate; and a minority of the landed gentry, such as the Prince Ostrozhskii for instance, were still Orthodox and had Orthodox churches built on their estates. But the safest haven for the Orthodox was the territories controlled by the Cossacks, i.e., the lower Dnieper area, including Kiev.

There were two groups of Cossack militia in the Commonwealth, the "registered" and the "non-registered." The former were commanded by a Crown-appointed general, called *Hetman*. They consisted of West Russians (Ruthenians), and the frontier area they controlled was known as *Ukraine*, i.e., the "Frontier Land." Although the Cossacks were Orthodox, the Polish Crown could ill afford to quarrel with them because they protected Poland's eastern and southeastern frontier, which was constantly threatened by the Turks, Tatars, and Muscovites. Being of the same faith as the Muscovites or Great Russians, and tracing their origin to the same Kievan roots, the Cossacks suffered from divided loyalties and showed readiness to switch to the Russian side whenever they were irritated by Polish policies. Such a switch of loyalties, as happened in the seventeenth century, at a time when Muscovite Russia was already strong enough to take on the Polish-Lithuanian Commonwealth militarily, meant the loss of almost one half of the Commonwealth's territory to Russia.

The non-registered Cossacks presented an even greater danger to Poland. These were predominantly recent fugitives from oppressive Polish serfdom, which expanded across the whole Commonwealth after the Union of Lublin in 1569. Not a few of them were common criminals fleeing from justice and finding a safe haven in the so-called *Zaporozhie Sich*: a group of islands in the lower Dnieper rapids which none but dare-devil Cossacks dared to navigate. The Polish government never extended recognition to the Zaporozhie Cossacks, i.e., it was technically in a permanent state of war with them. As the elders (*starshina*) of the Cossack Host did not allow the Cossacks to farm, in peace time the Zaporozhie Cossacks, who obviously received no salary from the Polish state, did some fishing and hunting, but mostly supported themselves by raiding trade caravans, usually foreign or Polish, as well as by robbing the local population, i.e., their own compatriots. Yet, in times of military conflict with the Turks and Tatars, the Zaporozhie Cossacks, geographically in the forefront, became the first and often successful defenders of the Commonwealth, the first to take on the external enemy. At such times, the Polish State unofficially provided them with ammunition.

The persecution of the Orthodox Church by the Polish State after 1596 suddenly gave the Zaporozhie Cossacks an honorable *raison d'être*: overnight they became defenders of the faith, particularly since their ranks were greatly swelled by the masses of Orthodox refugees fleeing the persecutions. The Registered Cossacks, not wanting to lose face in the eyes of the local Russian population, had to follow their example. As a result, the Orthodox Church not only survived in the Dnieper area, but even began to establish and improve Orthodox schools, including a college in Kiev which later evolved into the first Orthodox university in the Russian lands, with the name of "Greek-Slavonic Academy."

But the battles were far from over. It rapidly became clear that, as far as the Poles were concerned, the Unia was but the first step towards the latinization and then the polonization of the West-Russians. The Union of Brest was followed by the Polish exclamation, *"Niema Rusi!"*-Russia is no more!-which echoed across the Commonwealth. In fact, the first agent of latinization was the successor of Metropolitan Mikhail, Ipatii-Potii, enthroned in 1603 with the curious title, "Metropolitan of Kiev, Galicia and All Russia"-not Rus', but Russia. This fact negates the twentieth century Ukrainian nationalists' claim that the term "Russia" was applied only to the Tsardom of Muscovy and to the Petrine and post-Petrine Russian Empire. In fact, while the seventeenth-century Muscovites were still using the term "Rus'," and the patriarch's title was that of "Moscow and All Rus'," the Kievan Uniate metropolitan's title was "of Russia," though this applied only to the Polish-Lithuanian Commonwealth. This indicates that, contrary to the modern Ukrainian nationalist claims, seventeenth-century Ukrainians (known at the time as Little Russians or Ruthenians) and Belorussians did not differentiate between "Russia" and "Rus'." Had they felt there was a difference, the Polish architects of the Unia, very sensitive to such issues, which related to the very survival of the Commonwealth in the face of Muscovy's claims to the whole Kievan legacy, would not have given such a title to the Kievan Uniate metropolitan.

Potii's latinization began with his twelve-point Instruction to his clergy, demanding that they accept all Roman doctrines and only the papal interpretations of the Scriptures, recognize that salvation can come only through the Roman Catholic Church and that the pope is the terrestrial vicar of Christ, and reject all the theological teachings and writings of the Orthodox Church.

Potii's chief assistant in the latinizing process was Joseph Veliaminov-Rutskii, son of the Russian boyar Veliaminov. He had abandoned Muscovy for Poland, received higher education in Rome, from which he returned to Poland as a Roman Catholic fanatic in a monk's habit. He persecuted those who continued to resist the Unia and annexed to the Unia the Orthodox Monastery of the Holy Trinity in Vilna-whereupon all its monks left the monastery and established the Orthodox monastery of the Holy Spirit on the property of one of the Orthodox brotherhoods. For the Uniates, Rutskii established the monastic order of Basilians, entirely modeled on the Jesuits; and all Uniate educational institutions were transferred to the Basilians' jurisdiction. Hundreds of Jesuits simply transferred to the Basilian Order, which was subordinated directly to the Vatican, rather than to the local Uniate bishops. Even the Uniate metropolitan of Kiev could not choose an assistant for himself without the Order's approval.

Upon Potii's death in 1613, Rutskii became Metropolitan of Kiev. The Orthodox were desperate. Their last bishop, Gideon (Boloban) of Lvov, who had officially joined the Unia but secretly continued to ordain priests for the Orthodox Church,[7] died in 1607. Some relief came in 1620 when Patriarch Theophanes of Jerusalem, returning from the enthronement of Patriarch Filaret (Romanov) in Moscow, deliberately detoured to Kiev, and in the crypt of the St Sophia Cathedral secretly consecrated seven Orthodox bishops for the Polish-Lithuanian Commonwealth. In his sermon, he reprimanded the Cossacks for having taken Poland's side in the wars against the Russian Tsardom and made them give pledge never to participate in any wars against Orthodox Russia and to defend the Orthodox Church at home.

The newly-consecrated bishops, however, were not recognized by the Crown and therefore had to reside in the Diocese of Kiev, which enjoyed the protection of the Cossacks. The desperate situation of the Orthodox was colorfully described by Lavrentii Drevinskii, an Orthodox nobleman at the Warsaw Sejm of 1620:

> Our urban churches have been sealed and livestock is being housed in our monasteries. Children die without baptism; people are buried without a funeral service, like beasts. Men live in sin with their wives ... the Orthodox are refused membership in craftsmen's guilds. Orthodox monks are hunted down, beaten and thrown into jails.

---

7 Kartashev questions the canonical validity of such ordinations, and points out that apparently many Orthodox at that time were not sure on the matter either, as many priestly candidates preferred to cross the border into Moldavia for ordination rather than be ordained by a bishop who had given a formal oath to the Pope while secretly claiming to remain Orthodox.

But the appearance of a canonical college of bishops breathed new life into this semi-clandestine Orthodox Church. The new Orthodox metropolitan of Kiev convoked a *sobor* of clergy and laity in 1621 which produced an effective program to enhance anti-uniate and anti-Latin preaching, to publish Orthodox apologetic literature, to strengthen the brotherhoods, to arrange for more frequent councils, and to dispatch monks to Mount Athos, which served as a practical school of Orthodox monasticism. Despite all its defects the Kiev Academy, opened in 1615, managed to produce sufficiently serious theological works even to attract converts, among whom the most famous were two German converts, Laurentius Zizanii and Adam Zoernicav:[8] both became leading professors of theology at the academy and prolific writers.

The Polish government could also ill afford continuous persecutions of the Orthodox. A war with Turkey loomed on the horizon, and in 1621 the Cossacks presented an ultimatum to the Polish Crown, stating that unless all persecutions of the Orthodox Church ceased, they would refuse to fight the Turks. In response, the 1623 *Sejm* declared toleration of the Orthodox Church and permitted the legitimization of Orthodox bishops and the restoration of their dioceses.

But the joy of the Orthodox was short-lived. The legalization of the Orthodox Church resulted in a mass return to Orthodoxy of the uniates, particularly in Eastern Belorussia, where the Unia had been imposed only recently, and where the fanatical Uniate bishop Josaphat (Kuntsevich) of Polotsk and Vitebsk responded with bloody attacks on Orthodox households and churches with the help of locally stationed regular troops at his disposal. Even Metropolitan Rutskii in vain called on Josaphat to exercise moderation. Then the citizens of Vitebsk rose in revolt, lynched the bishop, and threw his body into the Dvina. A few days later the body was recovered from the water by the Uniates, and Kuntsevich was proclaimed a martyr-saint, highly revered by the Ukrainian Eastern Rite Catholics to this day.

Roman Catholic revenge was immediate and brutal. Ten citizens of Vitebsk were executed, the city lost its immunities granted under the Magdeburg Law, and all Orthodox churches, including those situated on the brotherhood lands, were closed and confiscated. Everywhere in the Commonwealth, the Orthodox lost the right not only to build but even to repair churches; and Pope Urban VII

---

8 This is how he spelled "Chernigov," the city whose bishop had brought him to Orthodoxy.

proclaimed that any Roman Catholic who dared to oppose the use of sword against the Orthodox would be excommunicated.

In the meantime Rutskii, realizing the hopelessness of converting all West Russians to the Unia, and through it to complete latinization, came up with a new idea: create a single West Russian Church of the Eastern Rite, which would commemorate both the Pope and the Ecumenical Patriarch at services. He persuaded even the Pope to accept this idea; and in a measure stressing their autonomy, the Pope issued an encyclical in 1624 forbidding Uniates to join the Latin-rite Catholic Church and instructing them to convene a local council every four years. This angered the Poles, but, as the Ukrainian historian Fedoriv remarks, it kept the Unia from dissolving into the Polish Catholic sea. Once again, theological differences between Rome and the Orthodox were ignored, as if any unification was possible without solving them.

The status of the Orthodox Church after the Kuntsevich episode remained so tragic that Job, the Orthodox metropolitan of Kiev, secretly appealed to the Tsar Michael of Russia in 1625 to annex Rus' parts of the Commonwealth to Muscovy. But the petition was turned down: Russia, still smarting from the Time of Troubles, could ill afford a war with Poland.

In 1633, however, on the eve of royal elections, the Russian Party threatened that it would oppose the candidacy of Prince Wladyslaw unless he promised to re-legalize the Orthodox Church. Wladyslaw gave his promise and kept his word after the election, by giving the Orthodox Church the same status she had had prior to 1596. As a compromise, however, he refused to recognize those bishops who were consecrated secretly by the Patriarch of Jerusalem, and in their place appointed individuals more acceptable from the Polish perspective. One of these royal appointees was the new Metropolitan of Kiev, Peter Mohyla. An offspring of a Moldavian princely family, Mohyla had been so latinized during his years in Roman Catholic universities, during which time he had to conceal his Orthodoxy and receive Roman communion as a condition for acceptance, that the catechism he authored was rejected by a Moldavian council of bishops for its "Latin heresies." Consequently, the theology and philosophy taught at the Kiev Slavonic-Greek-Latin Academy, i.e., university, into which Mohyla transformed a brotherhood school, was thoroughly impregnated with Latin scholasticism. Despite its name, all teaching at the Academy was in Latin; Greek and Slavonic were taught superficially; Russian was totally ignored; and students were penalized for talking in Russian or Slavonic among themselves. The Greek Church Fathers were better known in Oxford than in Kiev or Moscow, where another such academy was founded, chiefly by Kievan scholars, towards the end of the century. The Kievan model was adopted by all Russian seminaries, which may have had very high academic standards, but did little to train future priests for practical pastoral duties. A priest who had to celebrate in Church Slavonic, sermonize in Russian, and teach his flock the basics of Orthodox theology was never taught his native tongue or its literature, knew little Slavonic and not enough Greek to read Orthodox theology in the original. He could recite Latin poetry from memory, but had barely heard of St Gregory Palamas!

According to Kartashev, Mohyla's latinism was in reaction to the Calvinism of his contemporary, Ecumenical Patriarch Cyril (Loukaris), whose theology was condemned in 1638 by a council in Constantinople. In response, at a *sobor* convoked in Kiev in 1640, Mohyla tried to offer his own "Russian school of theology." But it proved to be so Latinized that it was rejected by the Moldavian council of Jassy in 1642. Historians suspect that Mohyla hoped to become Ecumenical Patriarch, and from that position strive towards Church union. No doubt, the Moldavian rejection of his theology was a blow to such ambitions, if indeed they existed. At the same time, Mohyla was a consistent fighter against Uniatism and published numerous polemical-apologetic tracts. However faulty Mohyla's theology may have been, he deserves to be credited with the re-establishment of the Orthodox theological educational system, which had collapsed after the Ottoman conquest of Constantinople.

Outside of Kiev and the area directly protected by the Dnieper Cossacks, the situation of the Orthodox did not improve much after 1633: the king's words and decrees meant little in the aristocratic anarchism that ruled over the Commonwealth. The response of the West Russians (Ukrainians and Belorussians) was an almost permanent state of civil war in the eastern part of the Commonwealth. The main fighting force in these rebellions was the Cossacks, who several times sent embassies to the Tsar asking him to take Ukraine under his "lofty hand," but Russia was still seeking to avoid direct confrontation with Poland. Only in 1654 did Russia finally agree to join forces with the Dnieper Cossacks against Poland. First, however, Russia issued an ultimatum to the Polish king to abolish the Unia, which he refused to do.

While the Cossacks and the common West-Russian population were looking towards Muscovy as liberators, the leadership of the Church had changed its mind: this was not 1625, and the position of the Orthodox Church was not that desperate. The Kievan Metropolitan, Sylvester (Kosov), feared that union with the less sophisticated but highly centralized Moscow Patriarchate might be detrimental to Ukrainian theological scholarship and its general education and publishing achievements.

Orthodoxy and Uniatism after the War

The war ended inconclusively in 1667. The east (left) bank of the Dnieper, including also Kiev and its suburbs on the right bank, became a part of Russia; the rest of the west or right bank, including Volynia, Galicia, and Podolia, remained under the Commonwealth; while the Zaporozhie ("beyond the rapids") free Cossack area chose to join the Ottoman Empire. As a result, more than half of the Kiev metropolitan's flock remained either in Poland-Lithuania or in the Sub-Carpathian Rus', under Hungarian control. One of the conditions in the final treaty with Poland, concluded in 1686, was that the Orthodox Church retain her status of 1633 and that there would be four Orthodox dioceses in the Commonwealth under Kiev. The Kiev *sobor* of 1685 therefore begged Moscow not to annex the Kievan Metropolitanate to the Moscow Patriarchate, as this would aggravate the condition of the Orthodox population in the Commonwealth; Moscow ignored these arguments. In 1686, the Kievan Metropolitanate became an integral part of the Moscow Patriarchate (a year later this was approved by Constantinople), and as a result the Orthodox population in the Commonwealth and Hungary became a "fifth column" of Moscow in the eyes of the Polish and Hungarian (later Austrian) authorities. Consequently, Orthodoxy was to be entirely wiped out in Galicia and Sub-Carpathia during the eighteenth century-areas which, throughout the seventeenth century, had defended their Orthodoxy more stubbornly than the areas to the east. In fact, in Sub-Carpathian Rus' the struggle for Orthodoxy continued through much of the eighteenth century. The prolonged survival of Orthodoxy was helped by the fact that Hungary was itself ecclesiastically split between Roman Catholics and strongly anti-Catholic Calvinists. In areas controlled by Calvinist princes, Orthodoxy was preferred to Catholicism. The annexation of Hungary by strongly Catholic Austria in the eighteenth century, and the granting by the Austrian government of freedom from serfdom to the Uniate, but not the Orthodox, clergy, however, militated against the survival of Orthodoxy in the area. The rest was completed by the Basilian Order and its schools.

In the West-Bank Ukraine, bishops and their priests began to defect to the Unia immediately after the subordination of the Kievan See to Moscow. Thus the Orthodox Archbishop of Lvov in 1700 became the Uniate Archbishop of Lvov. Two years later, the bishop of Lutsk, the largest Orthodox diocese of the Kievan Metropolitanate, with 1,000 parishes, followed the example of Lvov. The bishop of Sambor, in the Polish-Lemko Carpathian area, joined the Unia in 1692; but in the mountains the Lemkos held on to Orthodoxy through most of the eighteenth century, until 1791, when the Austrian government forcibly transferred the last Orthodox parish to the jurisdiction of the Uniate bishop.

The Uniate restoration in Volynia, Podolia and Western Belorussia was short-lived, however. Peter the Great, in restoring Poland after its complete destruction by the Swedes in the Great Northern War (1700-1721), forced the Polish Government once again to allow the re-establishment of a single Orthodox Diocese in Mohilev, Belorussia, responsible for all Orthodox parishes in the Commonwealth and to recognize Russia as the official protector of all Orthodox subjects under the Polish Crown, with the right of interference into Poland's internal affairs on behalf of the Orthodox. The Uniates, however, were left unprotected in the face of continuing latinizing policies, adopted by the Polish Government in 1715, which:

1. Excluded the hiring of Russian gentry into the civil service;

2. Stipulated that only polonizers would be appointed as Uniate bishops;

3. Banned the building of new Russian schools;

4. Stipulated that only semi-literate persons be ordained as Uniate priests, who are to be gradually placed under Polish bishops;

5. Ruled that the Russian urban population be gradually replaced with Jews.

These decisions, as well as the right of the Basilians to choose episcopal candidates, were approved by a Uniate Council of Zamoscie. This intensive latinization of the Uniate Church in Poland stimulated the mass return of entire parishes to Orthodoxy in Poland. The process became universal after the partitions of Poland under Catherine the Great. By 1795, over 2,000 Orthodox parishes of the Right-Bank Ukraine had returned to Orthodoxy. Uniatism still survived in Belorussia, where it competed with the Orthodox Church, and the Unia was the sole religion of the Russian (or Ruthenian) population in Galicia and Sub-Carpathia, under Austrian control, and in the Holm and Podliashie provinces of the River Bug area, which were annexed by Prussia.

The Austrian occupation of Galicia put an end to the polonization of the Uniate Church, because the Austrian Government, in order to strengthen its hold over the area, wanted to cut the Ruthenians off from both Polish and Russian influences. Under Austria, the Uniate Church was renamed the "Greek-Catholic Church"-a much better-sounding epithet. Two graduate theological Greek-Catholic academies were opened and financed by the Austrian Government, one in Lvov, the other in Vienna, where students were taught not only theology, but also local nationalism. By the end of the nineteenth century, this nationalism came to be designated as Ukrainian, a term which originally simply meant "frontier-land" and was applied to regions bordering on areas without stable governments, such as the Dnieper area bordering on the nomads of the Black Sea steppes, or to the frontier lands of Muscovy's south and east (the Siberian Ukraine, for instance). With the development of Ruthenian-Ukrainian nationalism in Galicia, the Uniate Church became transformed from an instrument of polonization into the champion of the new, Ukrainian nationalism.

Within the Russian Empire, the last remnants of Uniatism were liquidated under Nicholas I and Alexander II. The initiative to end the Unia in Belorussia came from the last Uniate bishop of Polotsk, Joseph (Semashko), who in 1827 appealed to his flock and clergy to reunite with the Orthodox Church. After the reorganization of Semashko's diocese in accordance with Orthodox administrative structures, numerous editions of popular educational Orthodox literature appeared in 1834. Five years later, in 1839, the Unia was officially liquidated in Belorussia and the Ukraine, not without considerable administrative pressure. Those who categorically refused to join the Orthodox Church could, with some difficulty, join the Latin Roman-Catholic Church. About 10 percent of the Belorussian population chose that route and soon lost their Belorussian identity, becoming wholly polonized.

This re-conversion also included Podliashie, which became a part of the Russian Empire after the Napoleonic wars. The Holm Province, however, fell under the Russian Crown as part of the autonomous Tsardom of Poland created by the Congress of Vienna in 1815, on the initiative of Alexander I of Russia. Russian Poland lost this autonomy in 1863 after two bloody national insurrections against Russia. As a result, the Unia was abolished in the Holm

Province in 1875 much along the lines of the 1839 liquidation in Belorussia. This time, the chief Orthodox agent was a Russophile Uniate priest from Galicia, Fr Markel Poppel. He began by de-latinizing the Uniate Rite both in Austrian Galicia and in the Russian Holm Province. After the Uniate services became practically identical to those of the Orthodox, he brought from Galicia one hundred Russophile Uniate priests who, after becoming Orthodox, completed the task of converting almost a quarter of a million people. Such conversion was not always voluntary, to say the least, as after the proclamation of religious freedom in Russia in 1905, one third of the Holm population joined the Latin Rite.

FOR FURTHER READING

Fedoriw, George, *History of the Church in Ukraine* (Toronto, 1983).

Fotiev, K.V., *Popytki ukrainskoi tserkovnoi avtokefalii v XX veke* (Munich: A-W [n.d.]).

Golubev, S.T., *Kievskii mitropolit Petr Mogila i ego spodvizhniki,* 2 vols. (Kiev, 1883-98).

Hrushevs'kyi, M., *Istoryia Ukrainy-Rusy,* 10 vols. (Kiev, 1913-36).

Isaevich, Ia.D., *Brats'tva ta yikh rol' v rozvytku ukrayins'koyi kul'tury VI-XVIII st.* (Kyiv, 1966).

Jablonowski, A., *Akademija Kijowsko-Mohilanska* (Krakow, 1900).

Kartashev, A., *Ocherki po istorii Russkoi Tserkvi,* 2 vols. (Paris: YMCA-Press, 1959).

Kelsiev, A.V., *Galichina i Moldavia: putevye pis'ma* (St Petersburg, 1868).

Khyzhniak, Z.I., *Kyivo-Mohylians'ka akademiia* (Kyiv, 1981).

Moroziuk, Russell, *Politics of a Church Union* (Montreal [n.d]).

Nichols, R. & T. Stavrou, eds. *Russian Orthodoxy under the Old Regime* (Minneapolis, 1976).

Oksiiuk, I.F., "Pervye stoletiia khristianstva na Rusi i latinskii Zapad," *Bogoslovskie trudy* 28 (Moscow, 1987).

Pekar, Athanasius B., OSBM, *The History of the Church in Carpathian Rus'* (New York: Columbia U. Press for East European Monographs, 1992).

Subtelny, Orest, *Ukraine, a History* (University of Toronto Press, 1988).

Sysyn, Frank, *Between Poland and the Ukraine: the Dilemma of Adam Kysil, 1600-1653* (Cambridge, MA, 1985).

Svitich, A. *Pravoslavnaia Tserkov' v Pol'she i ee avtokefaliia* (Buenos-Aires, 1959).

Tazbir, Janusz, *Piotr Skarga, Szermierz kontrreformacji* (Warszawa, 1985).

Vertogradov, V.S., "Pravoslavnaia Tserkov' v Galitsii v drevneishii period," *Bogoslovskie trudy* 30 (1990).

Vlasovs'kyj Ivan, *Outline History of the Ukrainian Orthodox Church* (New York, 1956).

Znosko, K., *Istoricheskii ocherk tserkovnoi unii* (Moscow, 1993).

CHAPTER 6

THE EIGHTEENTH CENTURY

Adrian, the last of the seventeenth-century patriarchs, died in 1700. Although he supported education in general, and the Moscow Slavic-Greek-Latin Academy opened in 1685 in particular, in all other matters he was an arch-conservative. Peter had supported the candidacy of the highly educated bishop Markell, who had held westerners in high esteem and had mastered several languages, but Peter's mother chose Adrian as patriarch in 1690, when the young Peter had entrusted the governance of the country to his arch-conservative mother and her brother. The highly authoritarian—or, more correctly, totalitarian—Peter was particularly irritated by Adrian's enthronement encyclical, in which he repeated Nikon's formula of the priority of the patriarch's power over that of royalty. Equating his voice to that of Jesus, Adrian stated that "whoever ... ignores my words, ignores the words ... of our Lord God." A few years later in 1698, during his prolonged European journey, Peter became acquainted with the situation in Lutheran Prussia and Anglican England, where the king was head of the Church. In England in particular, he had prolonged conversations with Anglican theologians and members of the royal family, from whom he assimilated the idea of a Church subordinated to the head of state. Hence, on Adrian's death, he prevented the immediate convocation of a council to elect a new patriarch. Had his friend Markell still been alive, Peter might have chosen him for the patriarchal throne; but Markell had died in 1690.

Peter possibly already considered the idea of abolishing the patriarchate. In fact, in 1700, the boyar Tikhon Streshnev, a mortal enemy of the late Patriarch Nikon, advised Peter to replace the patriarchal office with a permanent council consisting of several bishops, learned monks and lay state officials. For the first time, the fate of the Church was being decided by the tsar and his officials, with no clergy participation. But Peter shocked even these anti-patriarchal advisers, who had suggested the reform-minded and well-educated Archbishop Afanasi of Kholmogory and Archangelsky for chairmanship of the proposed mixed council. Instead, Peter chose Stephen (Stefan) Yavorskii, an unknown young professor from the Kiev Academy. He was consecrated as the youngest metropolitan in the Russian Church, with the unprecedented title of "Exarch, Keeper and Administrator of the Patriarchal

Throne." An "exarch" is a representative, typically of a patriarch; but since there was no patriarch in the Russian Church, then the exarch could be nothing else but the representative of the tsar. In this way the concept of the tsar as head of the Church crept in almost imperceptibly.[1]

In choosing a young Galician from Lvov who had received his education in the best Polish Jesuit academies, Peter took on not only Russia but the whole Orthodox East. The Patriarch of Jerusalem had warned Peter not to appoint any Ukrainians or Greeks to top positions in the Russian Church, as they were contaminated by Latinism, and he threatened Yavorskii that should he agree to become the Patriarch of Russia, the Eastern Patriarchs would not recognize him. Such doubts arose because the most talented graduates of the Kiev Academy received the blessing from their bishops to continue their graduate studies in Jesuit academies and Catholic universities, where they pretended to be Uniates and received communion. On their return to Kiev, they would be re-accepted into Orthodoxy. This religious hypocrisy made them and their bishops theologically and morally suspect in the eyes of their stricter co-religionists.

It would be wrong to think that Peter had no choice. There was the above-mentioned Afanasi of Kholmogory and Archangelsky, the saintly Mitrofan of Voronezh, and Iov (Job), Metropolitan of Novgorod. All were well-educated, supported Peter's westernization program, and donated large sums for the construction of his navy. Iov, in addition, had given refuge and protection to the learned Greek Likhudes brothers, whose Novgorod Greek-Slavic School was clearly superior to the Moscow Academy. He established a network of homes for homeless adults and children, as well as hospitals. But Peter did not want Great Russians in positions of church leadership, because he was not interested merely in reforms. He sought a revolution within the Church, and no Great Russian bishops would agree to that. He chose Ukrainians because they, as strangers to the Great Russian traditions, had to rely on the emperor's authority and support and would therefore support any of his actions. In addition, he felt that they, as westerners, would in general be more sympathetic to his imitation of things western.

Peter, the Totalitarian

The process of 'europeanizing' Russia began in the reign of Ivan III and gathered momentum under Peter's father, the Tsar Alexei. Peter's real

---

1 According to one contemporary source, when at the end of the first session of the newly created Synod in 1721 some bishops suggested that it would be good if a patriarch presided over the Synod, Peter pointed at himself and declared: "I am your patriarch!"

innovation then, consisted not in the europeanization of Russia, but in the introduction of totalitarianism and secularization. Totalitarianism, however, could not be fully realized prior to the invention of modern means of communication and mass media. Short of totalitarianism, Peter succeeded in building a secular police state (*Polizeistaat,* in German) with as many characteristics of totalitarian control over the population as was possible at the time. Thereafter, Russia remained a *Polizeistaat,* of varying degrees of severity, until the introduction of a semi-constitutional system in 1905.

As long as the patriarchal system remained, however weakened by the centralized autocracy, total secularization and near-total command over the population could not be achieved. On the difference between the Russo-Byzantine autocracy and the Western secular absolutism introduced by Peter, Fr Schmemann writes:

> However far the reality might have digressed from the symphony ideal, [the digressions] were always perceived as digressions...because the state [of the Byzantine-Roman autocratic tradition] recognized that above its authority stood the Church [as] the guardian of Christian Truth. Western absolutism, having developed from the duel between the state and the Church, left for the latter only the function of "serving the spiritual needs," as *defined*, however, *by the state* [emphasis supplied, D.P.], which also defined how these needs are to be served.

As far as the Church was concerned, Peter even "strengthened" her in a way, by expanding the network of seminaries and forcing the children of clergy to attend them, with the alternatives only of being inducted into the army for life or turned into serfs. But the Church as institution was deprived of her own voice. In the words of Peter himself the Church became "the religious team," i.e., her role from then on was to be an ideological tool used by the state to mobilize the nation.

From its very beginning, Peter's reign was marked by persecutions of independently minded clergy. Thus, in 1691, in contradiction to his westernism, Peter executed Sylvester Medvedev, one of Russia's best educated clerics and a founder of the Moscow Academy—allegedly for Latin heresy, although ten years later he appointed Yavorskii, a convinced and active latinizer, as the patriarchal locum tenens. Medvedev's "crime" was that he had been father-confessor to the Grand Duchess Sophia, regent during Peter's youth, and his half sister, whom Peter had to overthrow by force in order to regain his throne. Medvedev's real "crime" was either that he was intellectually too independent or that he knew too much, or both. Such was also the case with an outstanding Moscow educator the Abbot Avraami (Abraham) whose theological school at the Moscow Monastery of St Andrew was by far the best educational institution in the city. In 1697 Avraami was brutally tortured and then imprisoned in chains for life at a far-away monastery for writing a memorandum to Peter criticizing him for his contempt of human life and indifference to his subjects' material well-being. He advised Peter to stop his blasphemous and drunken orgies and endless travels, and instead to focus his energy on governing the country, to be consistent in his reforms, to pay particular attention to justice and fairness, and carefully to choose able, honest and popular administrators in both secular and ecclesiastical spheres, particularly in the case of bishops. Avraami was a loyal citizen who supported Peter's reforms in principle, but one word of criticism made him a criminal in Peter's eyes.[2]

In his attempts to weaken the Church and to squeeze as much money out of her as possible to pay for his costly wars, in 1701 Peter turned the Monastery Department over to civilian administration. Earlier, this department had been restored to the Church in 1675, in accordance with the advice of Eastern patriarchs at the 1666-1667 *sobor*. Later, Peter ordered monasteries to house army veterans and invalids with their families, and also to pay them stipends and feed them. However, in response to the complaint by the Church that after the expropriation of monastery estates by the state treasury the monasteries had become too poor for that burden, Peter abolished the Monastery Department and once again returned the lands to Church control.

Peter's treatment of the Church as a tool of the state is reflected in his 1708 order to Metropolitan Stephen (Yavorskii) to excommunicate Mazepa, the Ukrainian hetman and close friend of the metropolitan, for his support of King Charles XII of Sweden against Peter. Kartashev aptly compares Peter's behavior here to that of Ivan IV, who did not even consider requesting the excommunication of his leading general, Prince Kurbsky, after the latter's defection to the enemy during a war with the Polish-Lithuanian Commonwealth; and thus demonstrated an appreciation that there *is* a difference between rendering service to God and to Caesar.

2 Interestingly enough, Peter tolerated criticism from his close collaborators and drinking buddies, and occasionally even expressed gratitude to them for their honesty. It was from Church circles, particularly from the Muscovote clergy, that he tolerated no criticism, realizing and fearing the Church's potential power.

We have already discussed the reasons why Peter preferred Ukrainians, rather than Great Russians, as bishops. There were, however, two strains among the learned clergy from Kiev. Most had received their graduate education in Roman Catholic academies and universities. After the traumatic experience of religious deception while at these schools, some returned to Kiev as latinizers, intermingling their Orthodox theology with Roman Catholic concepts. Others, on the contrary, returned full of hatred and anger toward Roman Catholicism because of the humiliations they had endured. As Orthodox theology was still in the very early stages of its revival after the collapse of Byzantium, the Kievan scholars who turned against Roman Catholicism tended to adopt Lutheran ideas. Lutheranism declared that the population had to belong to the religious faith of the ruling monarch—this is the principle of a national state Church. Roman Catholicism, on the other hand, was based on the exterritoriality of the Church, i.e., of her priority over the local state. Obviously, the Lutheran principle was more acceptable to Peter than the Roman one.

In Peter's Russia the most famous Latinophile was Stephen Yavorskii, whose most important book, *The Rock of Faith*, an uncompromising defense of the patriarchal system and of the autonomy of the Church vis-à-vis the state, was banned during Peter's lifetime. The most influential pro-Lutheran clergyman was Feofan (Theophanes) Prokopovich, another young professor from the Kiev Academy. Peter first met Prokopovich in 1709 at a church service in a Kiev cathedral, when the young theologian was delivering a fiery sermon praising Peter's victory over the Swedes and Mazepa at Poltava. Seven years later, Peter brought Prokopovich to his new capital, St Petersburg, for a series of sermons. This indicated that Prokopovich would soon be made a bishop, causing an uproar at the Moscow Academy, which four years earlier had already protested to Peter that Feofan's theology was Lutheran and incompatible with Orthodoxy. This time, the Kievan professors at the Moscow Academy, archimandrites Feofilakt Lopatinskii and Gedeon Vishnevskii, together with Metropolitan Yavorskii, submitted a written protest to Peter, which delayed the consecration of Prokopovich for two years. In 1718, he was consecrated bishop of Pskov, and therefore also of St Petersburg, which had not yet been elevated into an episcopal city. In fairness, it ought to be said that Prokopovich did not seek the episcopacy. In a letter to his friend at the Kiev Academy, he wrote in 1716 that he hated the vestments, ritual and all the ceremonies associated with the episcopate.

Seventy-five percent of Prokopovich's library of 3,000 volumes consisted of Lutheran works; and all his publications, about seventy altogether, mostly polemical tracts, were based on Lutheran authors and concentrated on glorifying the power of the monarch, stressing the mystical qualities of the monarchy, while denigrating and demystifying the episcopate. Using the Old Testament and the Roman imperial tradition as points of reference, Prokopovich defended the Protestant concept of a single majesty—that of the king as head of both state and Church, totally ignoring the Orthodox doctrine of symphony.

Not surprisingly, Peter favored Feofan over Stephen (Yavorskii), who in distant Moscow even dared, however cautiously, to criticize Peter's extreme secularization of the state, particularly the fact that Peter had given the newly-created Senate full control over the Church in the tsar's absence, as well as his developing the institution of fiscals (i.e., "stool-pigeons") attached to the Senate. Yavorskii particularly attacked Peter's use of fiscals in Church affairs.

Little by little, Peter and Feofan deprived bishops of the last vestiges of independence. In 1716, all bishops, and not only the newly consecrated ones, were ordered to pledge an oath of personal loyalty to the tsar. This oath forbade bishops from interfering in state affairs. Even in extraordinary situations, bishops had to request an audience with the tsar, but could not act independently. Bishops were also obliged to keep a close watch over monastics, allowing them to travel only when absolutely necessary.

A near-mortal blow to Stephen's status was the secret defection to Austria of Peter's only son and heir, Alexei, in 1717. Alexei was very close to the metropolitan. A year later, Peter's agent practically forced his return to Russia, promising him Peter's full forgiveness on the condition that he abandon all claims to the throne. Alexei gladly complied, but Peter nevertheless ordered his arrest and torture. All the bishops with whom Alexei had communicated in any way were brought to Petersburg. Submitted to violent torture, they confessed having formed a plot with Alexei to restore the old traditions in Russia upon Peter's death. The Metropolitan of Rostov was broken on the wheel, the Metropolitan of Kiev died while being transported to Petersburg in chains, and several bishops were exiled in chains to distant monasteries. Alexei was soon dead: he was either executed on Peter's orders or died as a result of tortures, even though many bishops, including Metropolitan Stephen, signed a petition requesting Peter's mercy on him.

The Spiritual Regulation and the Synod

As we have seen, preparations to replace the patriarchate with a more direct imperial control of the Church were in the making since 1700. One of the steps in that direction was the granting of special powers over the Church to the Senate. In 1715-17 Peter introduced a system of state colleges, each responsible for one administrative program (e.g., foreign affairs, internal affairs, defense, etc.), based on the Swedish model. He was advised by Francis Lee, an English legal scholar, to charge one of the colleges with Church affairs. And, in 1718, Peter instructed Prokopovich to draft such a reform.

Two years later, Prokopovich produced his notorious *Spiritual Regulation*, on which basis a "College for Spiritual Affairs" was to be set up. In January, 1721, all bishops were forced to pledge their acceptance of the new system and give an oath of loyalty, not only to the tsar but to all members of the dynasty, blasphemously recognizing the tsar as their ultimate judge.[3] The College was to consist of the following members: the senior metropolitan by age of consecration was to be the president, with two archbishops as vice-presidents, three archimandrites as counselors, four married archpriests as assessors, and one Greek monastic priest. At the first session in February, 1721, the bishops protested that "college" is not an ecclesiastical term, and that since it had replaced the patriarchate, its status should be no lower than that of the patriarch, hence it could stand no lower than the Senate and could receive orders from no one but the tsar. Peter agreed. Thus, at its very first session on February 14, 1721, the college was eliminated and replaced by the Ruling Holy Synod, parallel to the Ruling Senate. With time, its membership came to consist of bishops only, although it never became the conciliar institution that Peter had claimed. To the last days of the monarchy, it remained a bureaucratic body fully subordinate to the tsar, administered by an overprocurator (the official term was *Oberprokuror*, a German word), a bureaucrat appointed by and responsible only to the tsar. But in Peter's time the overprocurator's position was still vague. The real head of the Synod was its creator, Archbishop Feofan Prokopovich.

As for the *Spiritual Regulation*, it was neither a regulation nor spiritual. It was an ideological manifesto of sorts, venomous and contemptuous of Church traditions, the Russian clergy and canon law, as Fr Florovsky states. Prokopovich certainly did not see the Church as the mystical body of Christ.

---

3 This oath was to be repeated by every bishop called to a term of service in the Synod until 1901, when the bishops protested to Tsar Nicholas II that even senators were not required to give such an oath, while the Final Judge for a Christian is God, not the monarch. Nicholas agreed and had that phrase eliminated

He defines the Church as "An association of the people of God into a society or republic of citizens for the purpose of knowing each other better, being of help to each other, and so that, with God's help, they might defend themselves better from their enemies." The abolition of the patriarchate is justified on the grounds that the ceremonial and vestments which make patriarch look so majestic create a danger that "simple souls might think that the Church order represents a state, and even a better one [than the secular state] ... and in some cases they might turn their eyes more to the Supreme Pastor than to the Emperor." Playing with the etymology of the Greek word *episkopos*, meaning a "supervisor," the *Regulation* calls the tsar the "supervisor over supervisors" and "supreme supervisor over the state," therefore he is the supreme bishop over the bishops of the state Church. With regards to the monarchy, Prokopovich is a defender of extreme absolutism. But when he turns to Church affairs, he becomes a republican, claiming that people more willingly submit themselves to the commands of a council than to those of a single person; therefore, he argues, a college is more legitimate than a patriarch.

In 1722, the clause in the bishop's oath obliging him to report all cases of seditious intent to the police is extended to the lower clergy, who had to pledge at their ordination to report to the police any person who confessed any intended or committed actions against the tsar or his government. This was a scandalous breach of the universal Church tradition of secrecy of the confession. This clause seems to have lapsed in the nineteenth century, as it is absent from the 15-volume *Code of Laws of the Russian Empire*, first published in 1835.

The *Regulation* was particularly harsh on monks, who were forbidden from keeping ink and paper in their cells, except when allowed to by the abbot for a particular purpose. While writing, the monk was obliged to keep the door of his cell open and then to submit his writing to the abbot for censorship. One would expect that unlettered persons would have made ideal monks, but, illogically, the *Regulation* forbade the tonsuring of illiterates and men under 30 years of age. Monasteries were now forbidden to accept tramps, deserters, former criminals, and persons of unspecified social status. These measures, as well as the drafting of novices and sometimes even young tonsured monks into the army, reduced the monastic population in the empire from 25,000 in 1724 to 14,000 in 1738.

Theological Education in the 18th Century

Peter supported all forms of education, but as a pragmatist he favored secular education with an applied and professional orientation. His favorite project was the creation of the so-called "cipher schools," which, along with most of the educational institutions established directly by him, proved a miserable failure. Most ceased to function even before he was dead in 1725. Paradoxically, only the ecclesiastic schools, which were instituted just before his enthronement but which mushroomed under Peter, continued subsequently to grow and became Russia's best educational establishments. The foundations for a three-tier secular educational system, laid only under Catherine II in the late eighteenth century, were turned into a regular network under her grandson, Alexander I; but they matched and surpassed the ecclesiastical schools only in the fourth decade of the nineteenth century. Several reasons explain the relative success of the ecclesiastic schools. First, Peter legislated that the sons of clergy who remained illiterate would either be inducted into the army or turned into serfs. Second, only in the Church did a tradition of schooling, however rudimentary, survive in pre-Petrine Muscovy. Significantly, it was the Church Sobor of 1551 that resolved to establish an educational system in Russia, although its realization was not to begin until the late seventeenth century. Third, the Kievan, and later Moscow's Slavonic-Greek-Latin academies produced cadres of potential teachers and scholars. No such source of instructors was readily available to Peter's secular schools.

Although Peter's reign brought about an unprecedented quantitative growth in ecclesiastical education, Peter himself dealt a deadly blow to the budding Muscovite school. Preferring teachers from the Ukraine and Belorussia because of their western links via the Polish schools, with their help he totally latinized the Moscow Academy. He also closed the excellent Novgorod College, which was just beginning to create a purer Greek-Russian educational system and to revive the study of patristics. Peter's closing of this school delayed the revival of Orthodox patristic theology by at least a century.

The west-Russian pedagogues latinized the fledgling Russian seminary education to such an extent that the Russian language, for instance, was not even taught as a subject until the last decades of the eighteenth century. Slavonic and Greek were taught superficially. Even less attention was paid to the Greek Church Fathers. But Latin—poetry, rhetoric, stylistics, oratory, and the Roman pagan classics—was studied by rote. Philosophy and the theology taught at these schools were a mixture of pagan classics and Thomism. The westernization and latinization of the Russian Church reached such proportions in the eighteenth century that Catherine the Great wrote to the French encyclopedists that the difference between the Orthodox and Lutheran Churches was only in their rituals. Because of Prokopovich, this westernization eventually took more of a Lutheran than a Roman Catholic turn.

The tragedy for the Russian clergy was that the education they received was mostly irrelevant to the Russian reality, as well as to their future pastorate. Graduating from these seminaries, the newly ordained priest was usually sent to a rural parish, with a very poor knowledge of the Church Slavonic in which he had to celebrate the services, lacking proper knowledge of the literary Russian in which he was to communicate with his parishioners and preach to them, and having only vague ideas about the Orthodox patristic theology on which his pastorate and sermons were supposed to be based. Moreover, most of his livelihood was to come from the patch of arable land attached to each rural parish, and which he had to cultivate like any peasant unless he could afford hired labor. This left little time for pastoral and educational activities beyond the prescribed church services. Moreover, as most seminary teachers in the eighteenth century came from the Ukraine, their legacy survived in the form of a peculiar "seminary Russian" with a Ukrainian pronunciation, full of ukrainianisms and latinisms, which sounded like a parody on the Russian language and became an object of jokes about the clergy. Linguistically, priests were therefore at home neither among the secular intellectuals, nor among the gentry, nor among the lower classes.

Prince Nikolai S. Trubetskoi, one of Russia's leading thinkers, remarked not without reason, although somewhat hyperbolically, that it was the Kievan-Ukrainian cultural heritage that prevailed in Russia from the time of Peter the Great, not the Muscovite one. Ukrainian-led seminaries and Ukrainian and Belorussian bishops—as hardly any Great Russian bishops were consecrated in the eighteenth century until the reign of Empress Elizabeth—were the breeding ground of that culture. Through the seminaries, that Ukrainian culture penetrated far beyond the church, because the seminaries also produced numerous Russian eighteenth- and early nineteenth-century statesmen and most secular school teachers. Seminaries were the educational springboards into university graduate studies: most medical doctors and university professors of the period were former seminarians. The nineteenth-century intelligentsia (mostly, but not exclusively, radicals) were also frequently ex-seminarians.

The eighteenth century also witnessed a gradual transformation of the clergy into "a caste," which could not happen in the Muscovite tradition, in which candidates for the priesthood were usually elected by parishioners. The final decision to ordain or to refuse ordination remained, of course, with the bishop. Although there were still plenty of cases in the eighteenth century when a parish would refuse to accept a newly-ordained seminarian sent by a bishop, with the numerical growth of seminaries a seminary degree came to be required as a condition for ordination. Consequently, the appointment of clergy by election gave way to the practice of centralized episcopal appointments. The problem of the parish farm also contributed to the development of the clergy "caste." A priest who had spent his lifetime improving the farm and his household wanted to retain them within his family. He therefore did his best to ensure that his son chose the same vocation, or, if he had no son, that his daughter married a seminarian who would then inherit the parish. Thus developed the clergy estate, with families passing on the priestly vocation from generation to generation, often with little or no spiritual dedication to ministry.

Feofan Prokopovich, the Dictator

Fr Georges Florovsky affirms that Prokopovich succeeded in raping the Church, but not in becoming her leader: his legacy was so alien to Orthodoxy that it could not become an organic part of the Orthodox Church. The legacy that he did leave, however, was, in Florovsky's words, a legacy of fear: the Russian clergy became an intimidated estate.

That intimidation was originally caused by the executions, tortures, and imprisonments of the clergy perpetrated in the era of Prokopovich, with his active participation and often on his initiative. Not that the victims were guilty of any crime. The intimidation was aimed at turning the clergy away from any form of independent thought, to force them to give up their dreams of some Byzantine symphony or dualism of power. The terror began under Peter, reached its extremes under Empress Anna (Peter's niece: 1730-40), and did not end even under Catherine II.

The status and powers of the Synod and its members were never clearly specified. Its chairman was formally the senior metropolitan, but his prerogatives were likewise never specified. The lay Overprocurator (*oberprokuror*) was defined in the *Spiritual Regulation* as the Tsar's Eye over the Synod, which could be and eventually was interpreted as the equivalent to being in charge. But the first overprocurator appointed by Peter was the insignificant Boltin, who was paid less than the Synod's bishops, and who apparently did not know what to do with his appointment. In charge, of course, was Prokopovich.

Upon Peter's death in 1725, the throne fell to his illiterate and fun-loving widow, Catherine I. The real power, from 1726, was in the hands of an aristocratic Supreme Privy Council, which, after her death in 1727, ruled in the name of Peter's infant grandson Peter II until the latter's death in 1730. During the administration of the Privy Council, the Synod's overprocurator was turned into an ordinary procurator (attorney), while the Synod itself was made accountable to the Senate (contrary to its title—"the *ruling* Synod"). This action by the Privy Council aroused Prokopovich's ire and led him to plot against it. He got his chance when, after the death of Peter II, the Privy Council decided to invite Anna, a niece of Peter the Great, to be crowned empress. The Council, however, imposed certain conditions (*Konditsii,* was the official term) which limited her powers and actually reduced her to the status of a constitutional monarch. A widow of the Duke of Kurland (the southwestern part of today's Latvia), she had reigned over that tiny and poverty-stricken principality, surviving on annual subsidies from the Russian crown. The *supremists* (*verkhovniki*), as the Privy Council's members were known, assumed that Anna would be happy to become an empress of Russia on any condition. And so she did. Before she arrived in Moscow, however, Prokopovich hurried to Kurland and advised her to tear up the *Konditsii* upon her arrival in the Kremlin Palace. Imperial guard regiments would then rush into the palace and pronounce her the autocrat of Russia.

The plot succeeded. A Russian constitution was not to be for another 175 years, and Anna's decade of mismanagement and terror began. For the rest of her reign, Anna remained insecure. She executed several thousand people, including the *supremists*, and sent over twenty thousand persons to Siberia. She surrounded herself with Baltic Germans and even formed a special guard regiment consisting exclusively of Baltic Germans. Even Prokopovich, now in charge of terrorizing the clergy, became merely the executor of the will of Anna's German Lutheran chancellor, Ostermann, who despised the Orthodox clergy and tried to force them to wear Lutheran clergy garb and to shave their beards. Under Anna, the supreme power over the state and the Church belonged to Anna's personal Cabinet, consisting of three persons. The Senate was reduced (both in numbers and in importance) to a small chancery reporting to that Cabinet. The Synod was forced to follow suit. At first, it was reduced to four bishops and five members of the lower clergy. By 1739, the

Synod was further reduced by terror to but one bishop and two priests. Prokopovich was intelligent enough to realize that he was destroying his own brain-child. Kartashev explains Prokopovich's actions by his venomous hatred for Russian ecclesiastical conservatism, which he identified with the Roman Catholicism he hated more than anything else in the world.

In his efforts to root out all traces of suspected Roman Catholicism, Prokopovich had hundreds of monks and priests tortured and imprisoned in chains in distant monastic jails. Six bishops, including two Synod members, were put through similar ordeals for such "crimes" as failing to celebrate special solemn thanksgiving *Te Deums* on the occasion of Anna's coronation, expressing a preference for the restoration of the patriarchate in intimate private conversations with fellow bishops, jokingly referring to a bishop as a worthy candidate for patriarch, or possessing some notes criticizing the Synodal system and Prokopovich, its architect. The most scandalous case was that of Feofilakt, the archbishop of Tver'. He was arrested, tortured almost to death, stripped of all his clerical and monastic titles, and condemned to life imprisonment in a Vyborg fortress tower for publishing, in 1728, with the government's permission, Stephen Yavorskii's *The Rock of Faith*, which had been banned under Peter the Great. The case was sensationalized and stories were fabricated that Feofilakt and his friends were the Pope's agents and Polish spies.

Only after Anna's death in 1740 were those imprisoned bishops who survived released and rehabilitated; but none returned to their episcopal functions, as all were invalids after the ordeal. Feofilakt, for instance, died four months after his release. In all these "trials" Feofan was not merely a participant on the side of the prosecution, but an activist. After the Senate had given relatively light sentences to the bishops, Prokopovich continued his own private investigations, finding excuses for additional torture and retrials, leading finally to those brutal sentences despite the lack of any conclusive evidence. In addition to direct persecutions, Anna's reign was marked by a mounting offensive against the Church. Monasteries were closed and their properties nationalized; clergy who were deemed useful to the state were forced out of their estate and mobilized; members of clergy families were often deprived of the right to follow in their fathers' or brothers' footsteps and were inducted into the army or some special schools, as deemed useful for the state.

From Empress Elizabeth to Catherine the Great

Anna willed the succession to the infant Ioann (John) Antonovich VI of Braunschweig,[4] a great-grandson of Peter's elder brother Ioann V (or Ivan), a half-wit who had been the nominal co-emperor with Peter during Sophia's regency. The regent for the infant tsar was to be Anna Leopol'dovna, his mother and Ivan V's granddaughter. Brought up in Germany, Anna Leopol'dovna, just as her predecessor, surrounded herself with Germans. This was more than the Russians could tolerate, and in 1741 another coup by the imperial guards placed the very Russian Elizabeth, Peter the Great's youngest daughter, on the throne. The 20-year reign of this extravagant, moody, rather lazy, not very intelligent, but pious and good-hearted woman was a respite for the Church and the clergy. The latter could also count on the support of Elizabeth's morganatic husband, Count Razumovskii, an orphaned former shepherd boy in the Ukraine who had been brought up by priests and always retained his love and respect for them.

No sooner had Elizabeth been crowned, than she released all of Anna's political prisoners, restored the Synod to its original status, turning it into a de facto synod of bishops consisting of six bishops and one archimandrite from the Trinity-St Sergius Monastery. For the first time since its creation, the Synod was chaired by a Great Russian, Dimitri (Sechenov), Archbishop of Novgorod. Elizabeth issued a decree that episcopal candidates be chosen from among both Great Russian and Little Russian clergy. The Synod and its individual members received the right to address the Empress directly. During her reign, the leading role of the overprocurator was also established once and for all. The first overprocurator of her time, Prince A. Shakhovskoi (1741-53), was an honest, hard working, and talented administrator. He fought a winning battle against corruption and moral transgressions by the clergy, introduced proper order in financial affairs, and discontinued the practice of dual salaries for members of the Synod (from their dioceses as well as from the Synod). He took measures to improve the clergy's education, excelled in publishing large editions of popular religious texts for the common man, and had these distributed regularly to distant parishes. As a professional bureaucrat, however, he initiated a network of lay bureaucrats on the diocesan level

---

4 Peter the Great changed the succession from the unwritten tradition of father to eldest son, to a written law which entitled the ruling monarch to choose any successor he liked. It was this law that caused so much misfortune, instability, and several coups in the 18th century, until a new law with the traditional dynastic succession was promulgated by Paul I.

answerable to the overprocurator, not to the local bishop. This system continued to develop during the next century, in practice stripping the bishops, both on the periphery and in the Synod, of all real power in the Church. But in Elizabeth's time, this system was only rudimentary.

The ill-fated Monastery Department, renamed the College of Economy under Peter, and nationalized under Anna in 1738, was again returned to the control of the Church by Elizabeth, following Shakhovskoi's advice. But this was only a short-term victory. In 1757, Elizabeth convened a joint conference of the Senate and the Synod and proposed that lands belonging to monasteries and diocesan administrations be placed under the control of retired military officers, while villages owned by monasteries should be turned over to landed gentry. Income from these properties would support war invalids, with a certain percentage going to the Church as compensation for the loss. The initiative for this conference must have come from the Senate, because in the heated debate between the Senate and the Synod that followed, Elizabeth took the side of the Synod and closed the subject for the rest of her reign.

The Metropolitan Arsenii (Matseyevich) Affair and Monastic Properties

Metropolitan Arsenii's problems began in 1740, when he agreed to pledge his allegiance to the infant-tsar Ioann, but not to his regent-mother, as she was a Lutheran. He avoided real trouble at the time by departing immediately for Tobol'sk in Siberia, his diocesan city, and then came the coup. In the meantime, his friend and fellow-Volynian, Ambrose (Amvrosii) of Novgorod, succeeded in having Arsenii reappointed to the metropolitanate of Rostov and Yaroslavl', some 250 km north of Moscow. The appointment was to take effect when Arsenii arrived in Moscow for Elizabeth's formal coronation in 1742, at which he would also have to pronounce the oath to Elizabeth. But this proved to be another stumbling block: he refused to read the section of the oath composed under Peter by Feofan, which named the monarch as the bishops' ultimate judge. Elizabeth agreed that there was an element of blasphemy in this formula and permitted him to omit these words. Arsenii, however, refused to read even a part of the oath as long as long as these words were not removed from the official text. The Empress allowed him to take up his new appointment without any oath. Such generosity may have stemmed from the fact that an alternative text of the oath, drafted by Arsenii, was submitted to the Empress by Archbishop Ambrose and two other bishops. In this version, Jesus Christ was called the ultimate Judge, not the monarch. In 1745, after the death of Arsenii's friend, Archbishop Ambrose, the more docile Great Russian members of the Synod once again raised the issue of the oath with Arsenii, who repeated his original objections and attached his alternative text to his written deposition. The Empress must have sympathized with Arsenii's argument, for she left him unharmed; but she probably did not dare to alter a document adopted by her father. She ordered Arsenii's memorandum and the text of his proposed oath burned. But it was evidently not destroyed, because it surfaced once again under Catherine the Great.

In the meanwhile, Arsenii was getting into trouble on another issue. Elizabeth died childless in 1761, having appointed her late sister's son Peter as heir to the throne. Peter was born and raised in Germany as a Lutheran. Brought to Russia as a 14-year old boy, he was made to convert to Orthodoxy and to learn Russian. He remained, however, a German at heart, admiring Frederick the Great and hating all things Russian. Rash, un-diplomatic, abrasive and not very bright, he antagonized everyone who surrounded him. Within a year, he was overthrown and killed in another coup by the imperial guards, who enthroned his brilliant widow, Catherine II, in his place.

During his short reign however, Peter III renationalized the College of Economy. The *economic peasants,*[5] who gained freedom from all control and who, clearly anticipating that this freedom would not last long, grabbed as much arable land per household as they could, savagely cut down forests, and cleaned out the former monastic fisheries. Arsenii protested this act to Peter, but again he was saved by a coup. Catherine abolished Peter's decree in order to win the sympathy of the clergy, but stated that the issue needed final resolution and would be discussed in the future. She appointed a mixed commission, consisting of senior civil servants and bishops, to study the matter. Most of the bishops appointed by her to the commission were the more compliant Great Russians, but even they were a minority compared to the lay civil servants. She silenced the bishops' grumbling by a brilliant if cynical reprimand, reminding them that the Church's Kingdom was not of this world, and that the clergy was supposed to imitate Christ's poverty. Therefore, she stated, the estates owned by monasteries and dioceses are state property by right. Accusing the bishops of having stolen that property from the state, she declared it was now being returned to its proper owner.

5 This was the official name of the serfs belonging to the monastic and episcopal estates after the Monastery Department was renamed the Economic Department.

Thus, after all the vagaries in the fate of that department over a period of 120 years, the Great Russian bishops were prepared to accept their final loss of control over the monastic estates. But they were probably not prepared for Catherine's statement that, although religion deserved respect, in no way should it influence state affairs. Finally, on February 26, 1764, the Commission resolved to transfer the College of Economy, with its almost one million peasants, under state control. During the 1780s, the net annual profit from these lands to the state amounted to approximately four million rubles, of which only 500,000, i.e., some 12-13 percent of the profits, was transferred to the Church as compensation.

Arsenii again raised his voice of protest against the act, as well as against the whole Synodal system, and proposed the restoration of the patriarchate. Other bishops secretly encouraged him, but kept silent themselves. The Synod, meanwhile found Arsenii's 1743 memorandum about the oath in its files, had him tried and sentenced to banishment in a monastery near the White Sea. He could not, however, be silenced and continued to send memoranda to the Empress criticizing the 1764 regulations. In 1767, he was put on trial once more, this time by Catherine's civil servants. Catherine personally devised a most sadistic punishment: Arsenii was immured in a tiny cell in a Talinn (Rehval at the time) tower for life, with only a hole in a wall through which food was thrown to him. No one in the prison was to know his real name. On Catherine's order he was renamed "Andrei the Liar." He died in 1772 and was buried anonymously. On imperial order the Synod defrocked and excommunicated him.

Kartashev reported that at both of his trials Arsenii was suddenly given prophetic gifts. At the first trial, in which his former colleagues and friends sat in judgment, turning to the Synod's chairman and the court's president, Metropolitan Sechenov, Arsenii predicted he would die of his own tongue. To the 36-year old Gedeon, bishop of Pskov, he foretold that he would never again see his diocese. And to Bishop Ambrose (not his friend Ambrose who had been dead since 1743), he prophesied death from a knife. Sechenov died three years later, choked by his tongue after a stroke; Gedeon died suddenly on his way back from the trial; Ambrose was knifed to death by a mob in the 1771 Moscow plague riot. At his last trial, a certain prosecutor Naryshkin was particularly aggressive. Arsenii ignored his attacks, retorting didactically rather than answering the accusations and questions. Finally, he pulled out a 5-kopeck coin and gave it to Naryshkin with the words: "You will need it one day." A few years

later, Naryshkin was tried for pilfering state property, deprived of his properties, and imprisoned—his prison food stipend was five kopecks per day.

Metropolitan Arsenii was fully rehabilitated by the Sobor of 1917-18.
His canonization as a martyr for the Church seems to be the next logical step
in his rehabilitation.

The Old Ritualists in the 18th Century

After the death of the last Old Ritualist bishop, Paul of Kolomna, sentenced
to monastic exile for life, splits began to develop among the Old Ritualists
over the problem of how to replenish the clergy ranks once they were left
without a bishop and their last canonically ordained priests died. Some proposed to accept those Nikonian priests who agreed to change sides. The more
rigorous Old Ritualists, however, rejected that solution, claiming that the
Nikonian clergy were uncanonical and lacked real charisma, since they had
bowed to the Antichrist. Hence, they concluded, Doomsday was imminent,
and they decided to await it without any priesthood. Thus arose the so-called
"Priestless Accords," which concluded that there were only two sacraments
which the laity could not perform, the eucharist and church marriage. Therefore, henceforward they lived without both sacraments. The icon screens in
their churches remained closed. Their spiritual leaders or instructors served a
partial liturgy before the closed icon screen, instructed their members in religion and literacy, baptized, buried and even heard confessions. The "Accord,"
however, suffered further splits, beginning in 1720 on the question of married life: some rejected any form of marriage and insisted on celibacy; others
accepted various forms of blessings and prayers for a God-protected cohabita-
tion as man and wife.

After most cruel persecution under the Regent Sophia, the secularistic
eighteenth century brought a certain respite to the Old Ritualists. Peter the
Great did not abolish Sophia's 1684 decree, according to which Old Ritualists
who persisted in their "schism" and refused to recognize the official Church
were subject to burning at the stake. Nevertheless, Peter's law of 1702, which
invited foreign experts to move to Russia and declared the principle of religious tolerance, could not but positively affect the status of the Old Ritualists
as well.

Under Peter the Great, the semi-monastic Vyg community of the *Pomorie*
(Maritime) Priestless Accord, established in the late seventeenth century in

the south-eastern corner of Karelia (north-east of St Petersburg), grew in size and achieved relative security and economic prosperity. It consisted of a feminine and a masculine communities, located about 18 km. apart from one another. Led by two Denisov brothers, Andrei and Semen, who proved to be gifted administrators, diplomats, entrepreneurs, and strict celibates, both communities observed a strict separation of the sexes. Married couples were not allowed to join the communities.

The religiously tolerant Peter the Great had nothing against the Old Ritualists in principle, but the latter persisted in waging a propaganda campaign against him, especially after his return from Western Europe, calling him the Antichrist. Nor could he forget or ignore that the *strel'tsy* (Muscovite Court infantry) rebellions, which Peter had so ruthlessly and bloodily suppressed, as well as the Bulavin rebellion in south Russia, had consisted mostly of Old Ritualists. It was these facts, rather than their rituals, which aroused Peter's hostility. However, he stopped short of any systematic persecutions; although there was a case when Peter ordered a certain Deacon Alexander decapitated for having gone over to the Old Ritualists from the official Orthodox Church and for disseminating his apologetic *Deacon's Responses*, which defended the old rituals. More typical of Peter, who always looked for ways to replenish his treasury, was the imposition of taxes on Old Ritualists at double the standard rate.

The Vyg communities were fortunate to reside in the area of the Olonets iron ore deposits, which the Vyg monks extracted in open pits and supplied to Peter's newly-established iron foundries. They therefore found a solid protector in the local provincial governor. As the "Vygovites" were useful to the state and did not participate in the anti-Petrine propaganda, Peter's attitude to them was expressed in the short phrase: "Let them live." Quite another matter was their active proselytism, which at least in one case led to a mass self-immolation. This resulted in the Synod's order to the Olonets Governor that he forbid the Vygovites to leave their area of settlement on the threat of execution.

In Russian religious history, the Vyg community is remembered for the so-called *Pomorie Responses* (*Pomorskie otvety*), composed by the community's leader Andrei Denisov for the 1723 debate with Neofit, an Orthodox missionary sent for this purpose to the Vygovites by the Synod. For his *Responses*, Denisov masterfully cited such writings of the Church Fathers as St John

Chrysostom's words that "The Church is not in the walls and roof, but in life and faith," as well as texts from the Hundred Chapter Sobor in defense of the two-fingered sign of the cross, and pointed to discrepancies between different editions of the Nikonian service books. The debate ended inconclusively, Neofit's arguments having failed to convince the Vygovites. After the debate, which lasted, with interruptions, for over seven months, the Vyg Community received an official certificate that the community had satisfactorily fulfilled its obligation to debate; and it was left more-or-less in peace. The 106 *Pomorie Responses* became, as it were, an Old Ritualist catechism. Eventually the importance of the Vyg community to the state declined, as the poor quality Olonets ores were superseded by the much higher quality ores mined in the Urals. But the community continued to be tolerated as a result of Semen Denisov's order to pray for the Tsar in all public worship.

The other major Priestless Accord is known as the Fedoseevites, founded by Feodosii (Theodosius) Vasiliev. They broke with the Vygovites in 1703 over the issue of marriage. The Vygovites rejected marriage completely, while Feodosii accepted into his community first those couples who had been married before the Schism. Later he accepted those who were married in the Nikonian Church but were baptized before the Schism. Those who had been both baptized and married in the Nikonian Church but who wanted to join the Old Ritualists, Feodosii accepted through second baptism but invalidated their marriage. This compromise underwent further evolution in 1728 in the teachings of Ivan Alekseev, a Fedoseevite preceptor (preacher and performer of the religious services), who taught that Old Ritualists who wanted to have families should marry in the official Orthodox churches as, according to the Church Fathers, marriage is a union of love and belongs to the realm of natural law. The marriage rite should therefore be viewed simply as an act of registering one's civil status and declaring to one's community the mutual responsibilities the man and wife take upon themselves. But the 1752 Sobor of the Fedoseevite Accord rejected Alekseev's position and imposed a long penance[6] on those members who were married in the official Orthodox Church. This gave rise to the common practice of Fedoseevites' being married in the State Church, followed by their repentance and a prolonged penance; whereupon the couple was received back into the community as man and wife. Later, at their *sobor* of 1883, which re-confirmed

---

6 Crummey gives 1728 as the date of Alekseev's statement, whereas according to Bolshakov the statement was made public a decade after the Fedoseevite Sobor of 1752.

the 1752 position, the Fedoseevites again split into those accepting marriage and those rejecting it.

The number of priestly Old Ritualists began to grow towards the end of the eighteenth century, while that of the priestless declined, because Doomsday failed to arrive and fanaticism subsided. The decline in the number of the priestless was also due to natural reasons, as a majority of them denied marriage and insisted on celibacy. The Old Ritual also attracted converts, especially among the peasants and other lower classes, because of the pitiful status of the official Church resulting from post-Petrine, Synodal-bureaucratic constraints. The priestly accords attracted priests from the state Church for the same reason; although disciplinary and economic factors must have also played a role. The Old Ritualists were very short of priests, so they accepted even those who had run afoul of their bishops on moral grounds. Because of the clergy shortage, Old Ritualist priests enjoyed much greater prosperity than did the "Nikonian" ones, especially as Old Ritualist industrial capitalism began to develop and grow towards the end of the eighteenth century.

At first priests were accepted through re-baptism by total immersion in full clergy vestments, as if to re-sanctify and purify them from the Nikonian "Spirit of Antichrist." Illogically, but no doubt out of practical necessity, their Nikonian priestly ordination was recognized. After undergoing this ceremony, they served as Old Ritualist priests. It was over the question of reception of Nikonian deserter-priests, and over the procedure of this acceptance, that further splits developed among the priestly Old Ritualists. Approximately in the middle of the eighteenth century, a certain Deacon Aleksandr, a former Nikonian who had joined the priestly Old Believers, declared that it was wrong to treat the Nikonian Church as heretical. Her errors were only in the realm of rituals, not of doctrine. Therefore, a convert from the Nikonian Church, whether clergy or lay, should be accepted by the Old Ritualists without re-baptism. Consequently, a priestly *sobor* of 1779 resolved to accept Nikonians only by chrismation.

This marked the first step towards *edinoverie*, i.e., the 1800 declaration by the Synod of the state Church inviting Old Believers to re-unite with the Russian Orthodox Church while keeping their ritual and all their traditions. This act was earlier preceded by the petition of a certain Old Ritualist hieromonk Nikodim to the Synod in 1783 to accept him and his 1,500 parishioners into the state Church on condition that they be allowed to keep their rituals. The

Synod agreed. Several similar groups of priestly Old Ritualists followed suit. The Synodal resolution of 1800 on *Edinoverie* resulted in a considerable proportion of the priestly Old Ritualists becoming a part of the official Orthodox Church in the course of the nineteenth century. As a result, among the Old Ritualists remaining in schism from the "Nekonian" Church, the *priestless* came to exceed the priestly ones in number, although only a minority of priestly Old Ritualists joined the state Church.

In conclusion, it ought to be stated that the otherwise very cruel reign of Anna Ioannovna did not worsen the status of the Old Ritualists. She was too religiously indifferent to be bothered by them. As to Catherine the Great, she prided herself on her religious tolerance. Only the double tax on the Old Ritualists remained unchanged from the time of Peter. Otherwise, they enjoyed religious freedom, and punishments for priests deserting the official Church for the Old Ritualists in the reign of Catherine II are unknown, at least to this author.

The Codification Commission and the Church

Although Catherine II abolished corporal punishment for the gentry and clergy, the clergy estate remained downtrodden and suspect. The Church was simply an anomaly in Catherine's externally scintillating and enlightened society of rationalism captivated by the French encyclopaedists. Consistent with that reign of rationalism, Catherine, seeing herself as the chief lawmaker, decided to convene a legislative commission to devise new laws for the empire and improve its infrastructure. Characteristically, the Russian Orthodox Church was given the right to send but a single representative, just as any single department of the state—i.e., the Church in Catherine's eyes was the Synod, and the Synod was equated to a state department. And since the Synod was governed by an overprocurator, therefore Ivan I. Melissino, the arrogant overprocurator at the time, took it for granted that he should represent the Church in the Commission and decide for the Church what she needed and what she should propose to the Commission. Consequently he submitted a thirteen-point program to the Synod, consisting of the following elements:

1. Complete religious freedom to all foreigners in Russia;

2. Complete freedom to the Old-Ritualists;

3. Shorter and less severe fasting periods;

4. The correction of errors and contradictions in Church canons;

5. The formation of a commission consisting "of people free from prejudices" in order to liberate the Church from superstition and false miracles, especially in connection with icons and relics;

6. The abolition of taking icons in procession to homes;

7. A reduction in the number of feast days and the abbreviation of services;

8. A step-by-step abolition of monasticism, on the grounds that it did not exist in the early Church; ... bishops should be chosen from among the ranks of married clergy, who may continue to live with their wives according to the teaching of St Paul;

10. Permission for priests to wear "more appropriate clothes";

11. The abolition of prayers for the dead as acts of extortion;

12. The simplification of divorce and the addition of other reasons, besides adultery, as valid causes for divorce;

13. The withholding of communion from children under ten years old.

Whatever the merits of these proposals, the point is that the overprocurator felt himself to be the head of the Church, which in his eyes was nothing more than a bureaucratic department in which things could be changed simply by the decision of its state overseer. There was no concern for canonical order, not to mention for conciliar decisions by the whole Church.

The Synod, however, had the wisdom to ignore Melissino's proposals and took steps successfully to have him retired by the Empress. Nevertheless, because of such high-handed treatment by the Crown and its officials, the Synod lost its sense of direction. Unclear about its own role and possibilities, it did nothing to present a program of its own to the Commission, as if the Church had no problems she needed to address. The Commission proved to have been still-born. It met without an agenda, and with no clear leadership, either from any of the elected members or from the officialdom. Having produced not a single piece of legislation in a year and a half of deliberations, the Commission was dissolved by Catherine in 1768.

Melissino, the free thinker, was replaced by Brigadier P. P. Chebyshev, who openly denied the existence of God, insulted bishops, and cursed them if they did not agree with him. Trying to indict a bishop by accusing him falsely of corruption, Chebyshev unexpectedly met with a stubborn defense of that bishop by the Synod, which in turn started to investigate Chebyshev and found him guilty of embezzling huge sums from the Synod's budget. This ended his career in 1774. The next overprocurator was S.V. Akchurin, a very decent and pious state counselor. In 1786, he was succeeded by another pious Orthodox Christian and very able administrator, A.I. Naumov. In general, the atmosphere began to change in Church's favor during these last decades of the century. The experiences of the bloody Pugachev Cossack rebellion in Russia, and the revolution in France, fundamentally undermined the whole rationalistic philosophical base of the eighteenth century.

The Beginnings of a Spiritual Reawakening

While the Synod was at loggerheads over how to become respectable in the new society and tried to solve the problem of the clergy's alienation from society by requesting the same honors as those granted the laity—medals, civil service ranks, the acquisition of gentry status through service—a genuine spiritual reawakening was beginning in distant areas, far removed from the centers.

The foundation for this revival was laid by the saintly elder, Paisii (Velichkovskii), who had left the Kiev Academy prior to graduation and went first to monasteries in Moldavia, and later to Mt Athos. There he gained a following of over 800 pupils, with whom he began the work of translating the *Philokalia* and other writings of the Greek Fathers into the Russo-Slavonic of his time. His disciples spread their master's teaching and revived Athonite *hesychastic* monasticism in Russia. The first and most important Russian hesychastic center was the Optina Pustyn', some 180 kilometers southwest of Moscow. It also became a center for translating and publishing patristic Orthodox theology, attracting such leading intellectuals of the time as Nikolai Gogol', the Slavophile Kireevskii brothers, Alexei Khomiakov, the Aksakovs, Samarin, and others to hesychasm and to the work of its dissemination. Thus the revival of Orthodox theology began not in the latinized and lutheranized seminaries, but on the periphery and through lay believers. However, things also began to change in the center, in the Church establishment. Among Paisii's admirers was the Metropolitan of Petersburg, Gabriel (Gavriil Petrov). He supported the monastic revival, corresponded with the Elder Paisii and helped publish his *Philokalia* (*Dobrotoliubie*, in Russian). Another famous and holy contemporary was St Tikhon of Zadonsk.

At Catherine's court itself, there was at least one defender of monasticism. This was the famous Platon (Levshin), a teacher of religion to the future Emperor Paul and to his German bride. He was a monk and archimandrite at the Trinity-St Sergius Monastery, then a bishop, and finally Metropolitan of Moscow. Yet it is quite typical of the Age of Enlightenment that when Catherine, on her visit to the monastery, was charmed by his oratory and his handsome looks and asked him why he had become a monk, he replied: "Out of love for enlightenment." The typical desire "to be with the times" was also reflected in his reaction to the move from Latin to Russian instruction at a seminary. On his arrival in Tver' in 1764 as the newly-appointed bishop, Platon discovered that the local seminary's former rector, a Serb Makari (Petrovich), had introduced Russian as the language of instruction. Platon ordered the restoration of Latin, declaring that high society considers the Russian clergy to be uncouth because they speak neither French nor German. If in addition, they did not know Latin either, they would be considered totally worthless.

And yet he was a genuine monk, preferring solitary monastic meditation to the hustle and bustle of the capitals. Very reluctantly, he accepted Catherine's order to move to Moscow as its Metropolitan. After holding that post for seven years, he reminisced that, on his arrival in Moscow, he found the clergy wearing birch-bark shoes but left them wearing leather boots; he found them in the gentry's entry ways, but left them in the gentry's living rooms. Indeed, Platon paid a great deal of attention to raising the cultural and material level of the clergy. At court, however, he had his antagonist, Catherine's father-confessor Pamfilov, who hated monastics and wanted to raise the status of the married clergy to that of the monastics. Pamfilov indeed managed to convince Catherine to reward married (or "white," in Russian usage) clergy with the miter, which by tradition belongs to bishops and archimandrites. Since then, the Russian Church is the only Orthodox Church to award the miter to the "white" clergy.

As we have mentioned, the traumatic effect of the French Revolution and of the Pugachev Rebellion undermined eighteenth-century rationalism. As a result, not only "some provincials," but even Petersburg's and Moscow's high society, turned toward meta-rational ideas and yearnings for mysticism. But the whole spirit and culture of the eighteenth century, as well as Peter's legacy, made it psychologically almost impossible for them to embrace the official Church and to accept the authority of its clergy, wearing their "indecent clothes," in Melissino's words. The search for the spiritual outside the Church led them to the mystical German branch of masonry. The most famous

Russian masons of the time were Shvarts and Novikov in Moscow. The latter led the Publishing House of the Moscow University and published *The Drone*, a testy journal of political satire. Catherine exchanged barbs with him through her own satirical publication, until she found his satires of her too transparent. She ordered both arrested and exiled to Siberia, and masonry was banned in Russia for the rest of Catherine's reign. Nevertheless, Metropolitan Platon, when Catherine asked him to examine Novikov's and Shvarts's Christianity, reported that he would be happy to have more such excellent Christians among his clergy as those two masons.

Somewhere between this mystical masonry and Orthodox Christianity stood (or more accurately, tramped across the country with little more than a Bible in his knapsack) the elder (as he liked to be called) Gregory Skovoroda. Nicknamed "the Russian Socrates" for his dialogues and his denial of material riches, this religious philosopher and graduate of the Kiev Academy undoubtedly had his base in Orthodox theology, but he was more of a free Christian thinker than a theologian. On his deathbed, he asked for the following inscription to be written on his grave: "The world had tried to catch me, but failed."

The closeness of the Orthodox revival and the masonic searches can be illustrated in the case of the Kireevsky brothers. Their father had been a Voltairian and a mason; and one of the brothers, the very Christian philosophical ideologue of the early Slavophiles and a disciple of the Optina monks, also began his spiritual searches as a mason.

The century which began with the confident steps of the proudly optimistic man firmly believing in the supremacy of the enlightened, rational mind, was ending in a state of intellectual and spiritual ferment and confusion. Once again, utopianism suffered a crushing defeat. Alas, this did not deter humanity from new and much bloodier attempts to create a utopian paradise on earth in times much closer to our own.

FOR FURTHER READING

Arkhangelsky, A.S., *Dukhovnoe obrazovanie i dukhovnaia literatura Rossii pri Petre Velikom* (Kazan', 1883).

Bagaliy I., *Ukrains'kyi mandrovanyi filosof Gr. Skovoroda* (Kiev, 1926).

Bogoliubov, V., *N.I. Novikov i ego vremia* (Moscow, 1916).

Bobrinsky, Gr. P., *Starchik Grigorii Skovoroda. Zhizn' i uchenie* (Paris, 1929).

Bolshakoff, Serge, *Russian Nonconformity* (Philadelphia: Westminster Press, 1950).

Chetverikov, S., *Moldavskii starets Paisii Velichkovskii* (Paris: YMCA Press, 1938).

Chistovich, I., *Feofan Prokopovich i ego vremia* (St Petersburg, 1908).

Cracraft, James, *The Church Reform of Peter the Great* (Stanford U. Press, 1971).

Crummey, R.O., *The Old Believers and the World of Antichrist* (Madison: University of Wisconsin Press, 1970).

Freeze, Gr., *The Russian Levites. Parish Clergy in the 18th Century* (Harvard U. Press, 1977).

Gorodetzki, N., *St. Tikhon Zadonsky* (London, 1951).

Kliuchevsky V., *Course of Russian History*, vol. 4.

Muller, Alexander V., *The Spiritual Regulation of Peter the Great* (Seattle, 1972).

Papmehl, K.A., *Metropolitan Platon of Moscow* (Newtonville, MA: Oriental Research Partners, 1983).

Pierling, P., *La Russie et le St Siège,* 5 vols (Paris, 1886).

Pypin, A.N., *Russkoe masonstvo XVIII i pervoi chetverti XIX vv.* (Moscow, 1916).

Raeff, Marc, ed., *Peter the Great Changes Russia* (Lexington, MA: D.C. Heath, 1972)

_____, *Origins of the Russian Intelligentsia: the Eighteenth Century Nobility* (New York, 1966).

Riasanovsky, Nicholas, V., *The Image of Peter the Great in Russian History and Thought* (Oxford University Press, 1985).

Smirnoff, E., *Russian Orthodox Missions* (London, 1903).

Smolitsch, I. *Geschichte der russischen Kirche, 1700-1917* (Leiden, 1964).

CHAPTER 7

CHURCH AND STATE IN PRE-REFORM
19TH CENTURY RUSSIA

The Reign of Paul I

Paul's unhappy reign (1796-1801) was transitional in more than one way. Chronologically and culturally, it marked the transition from the eighteenth to the nineteenth century. But his education, upbringing, and character also made him a transitional figure, a man "in-between." Fearing lest her son might legitimately claim the crown in her lifetime, Catherine, a usurper whose only "legitimacy" stemmed from the guards' coup, kept him under virtual house arrest at the suburban Gatchina Palace. But she did not dare to enact her plan of bypassing Paul and making her grandson, Alexander I, the immediate heir to the throne. Consequently Paul, although forty-two years old at his coronation, remained politically immature.

In contrast to his mother, who was a deist at best, Paul, who had grown up with Metropolitan Platon as his religious teacher and spiritual mentor, was a sincere believer. But like his son, Alexander, Paul inherited from the eighteenth century a non-confessional attitude to faith. Thus he gave asylum in Russia to the Jesuits, disbanded by the Pope under pressure from Napoleon, as well as to the Knights of Malta, whom Napoleon had expelled from their island. From the Knights of Malta he accepted the title of "Grand Master"—an Orthodox emperor became master of a Roman Catholic Order! He even invited the Pope to move to Russia. At the same time, he tried to emulate the Byzantine emperors when, during his coronation, he tried to enter the sanctuary through the Holy (Royal) Doors (reserved only for the clergy), wearing his sword, in order to receive communion together with the clergy. Metropolitan Platon stopped him, saying that here the clergy offers the bloodless sacrifice, and that no one with a sword may enter. Paul submitted and took off his sword.

Paul treated the clergy with great reverence, though he expressed this in terms of secular officialdom: he began to decorate the clergy with secular medals and distributed other such distinctions. Although Metropolitan Platon turned down Paul's offer of a decoration, from this time began the curious tradition of wearing secular medals on clergy cassocks. Subsequently, both

Russian and other Orthodox Churches began to create their own medals and decorations.

The extent of the overprocurator's power had not yet been fully established in Paul's time; much depended on the personality of the incumbent. The first overprocurator in Paul's reign was Prince V.A. Khovanskii, who watched almost every step of each bishop by extending his control over peripheral dioceses through diocesan clerks answerable to his office. But as a result of Paul's friendly disposition towards bishops, the Synod succeeded in having Khovanskii deposed and obtained Paul's permission to select the next overprocurator, Count Dmitri Khvostov, a mild and unambitious man who gave over control to the Synod's chairman, Metropolitan Ambrose. Khvostov's three-year tenure was the Synod's swan song before the long, despotic tenure of the sinister Prince A.N. Golitsyn under Alexander I. Paul's reign was also financially beneficial for the Church. The emperor doubled the size of the annual compensation to the Church for the nationalization of her estates, raising it to some 25 percent of the income they provided. In addition, the state subsidy for ecclesiastic educational establishments was considerably enlarged. Many new seminaries were established, and the seminaries of St Petersburg and Kazan' were raised to the status of graduate academies in 1797. Paul also enlarged the land holdings of bishops' residences and monasteries, and handed over numerous water mills, fisheries, and other income-producing facilities. One of the last acts of his reign was the invitation to the Old Ritualists to return to the established Church while being allowed to retain their rituals and traditions (*edinoverie*), as discussed in chapter 6.

The tragedy of Paul's reign lay in his unsuitability for the art of governing: he lacked flexibility, consistency, and an ability to compromise. He hated his mother's legacy and her courtiers, turning them against himself. He also reintroduced corporal punishment for the nobility, although not for the clergy. All these strictures, and finally his attempt to start a war against Britain, cost him his crown and his life.

The Spiritual "Climate" of the Alexandrine Era

For Russia, the nineteenth century really began with Alexander I's accession to the throne. Alexander was an enigmatic, controversial, often hypocritical, person, given to bursts of mysticism, swinging from millennerian dreams to pessimistic apprehensions of the dominance of evil, of the human inability to overcome it, and hence of the futility of attempts to improve things. Handsome, romantic, and amorous, he personified the new age about which the Russian Ivan Aksakov, the foremost publicist of the mid-nineteenth century, aptly remarked that it was a time when poetry appeared to be a special call of history, "becoming a religious rite," as it were. Florovsky calls this era "an awakening of the heart." But it was too impulsive, emotional, romantic, dreamy, too close to the eighteenth century's superficial Enlightenment, with its naive faith in the supreme rationality of man and the supreme power of the human reason, to be a true awakening of the intellect or of any deep theological speculations. The blood bath of the French Revolution and Napoleon's proto-totalitarianism had badly shaken the eighteenth-century dogmas, hence the new Romantic pessimism and certain inclinations to mysticism. But a replacement for the intellectual foundations of the previous era had not yet been found.

It was because of this eighteenth-century legacy that the gallicized and mostly Voltairian Russian high society could not reconcile itself to the idea that the Truth could be found in that "backward" and "oriental" Church of the "peasants." Instead, it sought to quench its spiritual thirst in the man-made mysticism of the pietists and masons. These teachings were much more trustworthy from the very fact that they were western imports. Both spoke of two churches: an outer church of external rituals and rites, canons and doctrines is necessary for the uneducated masses; but it also acts as the gate to an "Inner Church" within the person, through which one achieves direct contact with the Deity, the Creator. Having obtained that inner Church, the educated man does not need the traditional Church. In this scheme of things, communal worship is necessary only for the unenlightened masses, and the sacraments of the Church are treated simply as rituals. Interconfessional doctrinal differences lose their meaning. Indeed, the Alexandrine era was the most religiously tolerant time in the history of the Russian Empire. Paradoxically, however, this tolerance did not extend to the state Church. The Orthodox Church was treated with contempt for her doctrinal complexity, ritualism, and particularly for the importance of communal worship in her teachings. The Church was unable to defend herself, because apologetic literature involving criticism of (other) religions was banned.

Sects of different kinds, both imported and home-grown, as well as masons, all had their day. Alexander's brilliant chancellor, Michael Speranskii, was a mason, even though he had been a seminarian and a seminary professor. He even forced the St Petersburg Theological Academy to appoint Fessler, a

Lutheran pietistic theologian and simultaneously the grand master of the St Petersburg Masonic Lodge, as professor of philosophy and Hebrew. Its young but very influential rector, the Archimandrite Filaret, succeeded only with great difficulty to have the appointment withdrawn. But the Moscow Academy was powerless against Speranskii when he moved his friend there. Much more influential than the Orthodox Church were the Rosicrucians, who succeeded in removing Fessler from the Moscow Academy by protesting to the Tsar that Fessler, in denying the divinity of Jesus, was an enemy of Christianity.

Along with the Rosicrucians, Jesuits, and Masons, such extremist Russian sects as the Molokans, Dukhobors, "Shakers" (*khlysty*) with their living "god-birthgivers" and ecstatic dances leading to mass sexual orgies, were openly preaching to the common people. Selivanov, head of the officially banned sect of castrators, openly lived in St Petersburg and was several times invited by Alexander to the palace for chats. Being a sectarian was even profitable. Thus the Molokans, who refused to bear arms, to recognize any form of civil government, and to pay taxes, were granted, free of charge, very fertile farmland near the Black Sea in the amount of forty acres per male. Pacifist German Mennonite settlers were also freed from military duties and were even unofficially encouraged by Prince Golitsyn of the Holy Synod to convert their Russian peasant neighbors to their faith. But the law-abiding and pious Orthodox peasant remained in servitude, paid taxes, and spilled his blood in wars.

Nevertheless, in that general spiritual confusion a certain religious reawakening was taking place. On the one hand, there was a search for God taking place in society, however sentimentalist and unchurched. An illustration of that salad of mysticism is the case of Paul Pestel, the leader of the most radical wing of the Decembrists,[1] who wanted the whole ruling dynasty to be physically exterminated and a virtually totalitarian political system installed in Russia—he wrote in his diaries that, after establishing that "republican" government, he would retire to a monastery. But there are no other traces in Pestel's life and statements which even hint at a religious faith. Such a thought would never have occurred to Pestel's radical eighteenth-century predecessor, Radishchev, even though he had written a religious-philosophical tract testifying to his faith in a Godhead. On the other hand, the monastic revival, which had begun towards the end of the previous century, spilled over into

---

1 A secret officers' society which attempted a rebellion in the name of a radical social change in December 1825, taking advantage of the dynastic succession confusion after the death of the childless Alexander I.

the Alexandrine period and, by the 1840s, began to influence some circles within Russian high society.

"The Dual Ministry" and the Bible Society

The experience of the degeneration of the French Revolution into a blood bath, then into Napoleonic despotism and his bloody wars, shattered all the republican illusions inculcated into Alexander by his chief educator, the Swiss republican La Harpe. Returning from Paris and Vienna a pessimistic mystic, Alexander in 1817 amalgamated the Synod and the Department of Education into a Ministry of Spiritual Affairs, better known as the *Dual Ministry*, and placed it under Golitsyn, who was raised to that post from the synodal overprocuratorship. The Tsar was guided in this move by a desire to inculcate the educational process with a moral-religious content, in order to protect young generations from radical contamination. But his choice of leadership for this dual ministry left much to be desired. The mason Golitsyn considered himself to be a "universal Christian," recognizing only that religion, he said, which was based on the spiritual experience of the heart. He therefore sympathized with the pietistic sects. As far as the Orthodox Church was concerned, subordination of the Synod to the Dual Ministry meant further humiliation, especially with Golitysn in charge.

The semi-official organ of Golitsyn's quasi-theology was *The Messenger of Zion*, published by Labzin, chairman of the Rosicrucian Lodge and a disciple of Shvarts and Novikov. To protect himself from accusations of masonry, Golitsyn kept a certain Fotii, an obscurantist archimandrite, at his side. Both Alexander and Golitsyn, as well as Fotii, dreamt of creating a theocracy, though each understood it in his own way. The Golitsyn-Fotii cooperation meant an obscurantist censorship over the press and education. Their agent for the theocratic reconstruction of universities was another obscurantist, Magnitskii, who began by "reforming" the recently established University of Kazan'. He converted the students' dormitories into semi-monastic communes by dividing the dormitory floors in accordance with the morality of the students. The morally healthy floors prayed for the forgiveness of sins of the morally inferior floors. Every floor had a prison cell to hold students indicted for their transgressions by a student court. Professors were similarly punished if, in the opinion of Golitsyn and Magnitskii, their lectures contradicted the Bible. Lectures in philosophy had to be based on the Old

Testament, jurisprudence had to be based on the medieval *Russian Justice* (*Pravda russkaia*).

Magnitskii's "reforms" were eventually abolished by Nicholas I. The Golitsyn-Fotii friendship ended in 1824 when the latter at last realised that Golitsyn's masonic-pietistic theology was far removed from Orthodoxy. Even before that break, Fotii began to bombard the emperor with letters warning that the pietistic booklets published with Golitsyn's blessing were full of revolutionary spirit. Alexander decided to have a personal talk with Fotii, who failed to understand during the encounter that Alexander's ideas were very close to Golitsyn's. Believing that Alexander was on his side, Fotii anathematized Golitsyn and continued to bombard the tsar with letters requesting that he halt further editions of the Russian translation of the Bible, liquidate the Dual Ministry, sack Golitsyn, and expel Fessler and the leading Methodists from Russia. Fotii was supported by Serafim (Glagolevskii), the Metropolitan of St Petersburg. Golitsyn was indeed sacked, and the Dual Ministry was abolished.

Characteristic of Golitsyn's regime was the notorious episode of the publication in 1818 of a book entitled *A Conversation over the Coffin of an Infant on the Eternity of the Soul*. On Golitsyn's orders, the author of this work, a pious Orthodox Serb named Stanevich, was expelled from the Capital. The official censor, Archimandrite Innocent (Smirnov), was punished even more severely for having permitted its publication. The official explanation of Golitsyn's wrath was that it was immoral to write about the death of infants. But the real reason was that the book obliquely criticized Golitsyn's ministry and directly attacked *The Messenger of Zion*. But in 1824, soon after Golitsyn's retirement, both the author and the censor were vindicated and given back their jobs, and the book was republished with an endorsement by the Synod as a very useful moral reader. Both the ban and the approval of the book were signed by the same emperor!

Golitsyn's ministry, however, also deserves gratitude for having supported the first translation into Russian of the Scriptures, undertaken by the Bible Society, an affiliate of the British Bible Society. The translation, from Hebrew and Greek, was done by professors and graduate students of the St Petersburg Theological Academy. One of the translators was Filaret (Drozdov), the future Metropolitan of Moscow and a brilliant linguist. Filaret, the young rector of the Academy, was also striving to introduce Russian as the teaching language in the theological schools in place of Latin. He succeeded in achieving this goal only under Nicholas I. For the moment, he had to content himself with the several editions of the New Testament, the Psalter and the Pentateuch, which appeared during Alexander's reign, in a Russian language not too far removed from the spoken idiom.

Although the Synod was again separated from the Ministry of Education after Golitsyn's retirement, the newly-appointed Minister of Education, Admiral Shishkov, continued, quite illegally, to give orders to the Synod. He led a campaign against the Russian Bible, claiming that there was no distinct Russian language, but simply two variants of Russo-Slavonic—a lofty language used by the Church, and the vulgar, spoken dialect. He argued that translating the Holy Bible into that vulgar dialect was almost a blasphemy. And a mass edition of the Bible in the spoken language would debase the Book so much that people would use its pages for wrapping paper. Such an irreverent attitude to the Holy Writ could lead only to the proliferation of heresies and atheism. He and his ally, Metropolitan Serafim, were particularly incensed by the translation of the Pentateuch from the Hebrew original, pointing out that in some cases the translation did not agree with the Slavonic text. Their attack was so aggressive that the authorities decided to burn the entire first edition. Then they attacked Filaret's Catechism. Though written specifically for primary school pupils, it was attacked for being in a language too close to the spoken idiom. Eventually, the Catechism was salvaged, but only at the cost of replacing the Russian texts of the prayers with the Slavonic "originals" and by adding some archaisms into the text. As to the liquidation of the Bible Society and the discontinuation of the publication of the Russian texts, the unholy trinity of Fotii, Serafim, and Shishkov achieved this under Nicholas I. The tsar, however, prevented the destruction of those texts already published, and ordered their free distribution to prisoners in jails.

Three years after his enthronement, Nicholas appointed a new Minister of Education, Prince K.K. Lieven, a Baltic German and a member of the Moravian Brethren Sect. He had been one of the founding members of the Russian Bible Society, but he cared little for the religious enlightenment of the Russians, made no efforts to revive the Russian Bible Society. Instead, he restored the German Bible Society in the Baltic region, but not in the rest of the empire. Thus the spiritual needs of the Russian people were of little concern both to the Minister of Education and to the Emperor. Regarding the closing of the Russian Bible Society, Florovsky for one saw some justification of this act because of the concern at the time that it was evolving into a Russo-English sect, far removed from the Church, propagating interconfessionalism and pietism. Instead of liquidating it, however, a Church-oriented, Bible Society might well have been formed. And the publication of the Bible in Russian could have continued under the direct auspices of the Synod, as happened under Alexander II, when the full Russian Bible was finally published.

Characteristically, the publication of a Russian Bible was preceded by a Russian translation of the Quran, as well as translations of the Bible into the Mordovian, Tatar, and other languages of the Russian eastern minorities. Incomprehensibly, even Speranskii was against a Russian Bible. When his daughter wrote to him that she did not understand the Slavonic text, he advised her to read the Bible in English!

The School and the Clergy

As we have already mentioned, the best education in the eighteenth and early nineteenth century Russia was to be found in the ecclesiastical schools. These gave their students a solid grounding in classics, philosophy, Latin, historiography, and even in the natural sciences. The vast majority of leading Russian scholars and statesmen—from Lomonosov to Count P.V. Zavadovskii, the head of the 1782 commission establishing a regular three-tiered educational system, to such statesmen as Bezborod'ko and Speranskii—were seminary graduates. Indeed, after Zavadovskii's commission had founded the St Petersburg Pedagogical Seminary (which was soon transformed into two schools: a university and a pedagogical institute), it was found that the graduates of theological seminaries were about the only ones who could cope with the program of these educational establishments. The government solved the problem by establishing quotas on how many seminarians had to be transferred by the Synod each year to the secular schools of higher education. By 1801, consequently, over 300 of the 400 graduates of the Pedagogical Seminary came from the theological seminaries; of the sixty-six professors of the Moscow University, twenty-two were seminary graduates, thirty-three were foreigners, and only eleven were "other" Russians—mostly educated by private tutors (who in turn were either seminarians or foreigners) in wealthy homes. Similarly, of the 762 graduates of the St Petersburg Medical Academy, the best medical school in Russia, over 700 were seminary graduates. When, under Nicholas I, the academic training of Russia's best lawyers began, without whom the great law reform of the 1860s would have been impossible, 75 percent of the 1828-76 law students were former seminarians.

However, as long as the seminary served as the best general education school of the country, it could not develop into a truly professional, pastoral-theological school. Only after Alexander I had completed the development of the three-tiered system of secular education begun by his grandmother, could measures be taken to reform the seminary. With this purpose in mind, the 1808-14 reform of theological schools was undertaken. The result of this reform was a four-tiered ecclesiastical education system: the first tier consisted of the so-called "county schools" (*uezdnye uchilishcha*) which taught elementary literacy, with some basics in theology; these were followed by the diocesan schools (*eparkhial'nye uchilishcha*), which provided a partial secondary education, stressing theology; the third tier was a six-year seminary, which could be compared to an undergraduate theological school (although in Russia it was known as secondary theological education); atop the system stood the graduate theological academy of four years. Four such academies existed in the Empire from the time of Alexander I, when to the Moscow and Kiev Slavic-Greek-Latin academies, renamed into theological academies,[2] were added one in St Petersburg and another in Kazan'. The academies produced professors for the seminaries and for the academies, bishops, leading theologians, teachers of religion for high schools and universities, as well as the best-educated priests in the country, forming perhaps twelve percent of the total clergy.

Latin remained the language of instruction. However, the first step towards russianization was made when the Russian language, literature, and history were introduced as subjects, as well as more intensive study of Slavonic and Greek. More and more subjects began to be taught in Russian instead of Latin. Pagan classicism and some other secular subjects began to give way to a deeper study of theology, and particularly of the eastern Church Fathers. In short, although the reform was far from ideal, its implementation resulted in the gradual penetration of patristic theology into the seminary curriculum, stimulated in part by the rebirth of the hesychastic "elderhood" (*starchestvo*) in Russia. The reform was followed by the expulsion of the Jesuits from Russia in 1820, and the closing of their theological academy and spiritual center, which had existed in Polotsk (Belarus') since 1811. Nevertheless, Metropolitan Filaret's petition to publish all seminary textbooks in Russian instead of Latin was turned down. The characteristic pretext—obviously originating from Shishkov—was that textbooks published in Russian would then be accessible to the general public,

2 The verbatim translation of *dukhovnaia akademiia* is in fact "spiritual academy"; and *dukhovnaia seminaria*, "spiritual seminary."

who, because of their theological illiteracy, might be tempted into heresies. Nevertheless, Latin as the language of instruction was withering away even before the death blow brought about by the reorientation of the seminary in the 1830s to a more pragmatic curriculum, geared to the daily needs of a rural pastor. The reform introduced the teaching of elementary medicine and agriculture, at the cost of a further reduction of Latin. In the 1840s, Latin was finally replaced by Russian as the general language of instruction.

At the same time, seminaries were increasingly becoming the schools of the clergy estate. First, as we have already seen, ever since Peter's time the sons of clergy had to enter seminaries in order to avoid becoming serfs or army recruits. Second, after Catherine's confiscation of church lands, the Synod was for financial reasons forced to limit access to the theological schools almost exclusively to the scions of clergy families. Third, the clergy in general were too poor to afford tuition in secular schools, while at the seminaries clergy sons received scholarships, however meager they were.

Having lost a considerable part of her income after Catherine's secularization, the Church was also badly hurt by the inflation of the 1820s-30s. At the same time state and private schools were improving in quality and hiring the best teachers by paying them 30-100 percent higher salaries than those offered by the ecclesiastical schools. By the 1830s-40s, therefore, the quality of education in ecclesiastical institutions began to stagnate and to lag behind that of the secular schools.

The seminary system also produced certain tensions in the clergy estate. In the pre-seminary era episcopal candidates were often elected by diocesan gatherings of clergy and some laity.[3] The following criteria of a good bishop were generally applied in descending order: personal piety, high morals, administrative ability, intellect, and education. From the time of Peter the Great, formal education of the candidate becomes the first priority. This was one factor leading to the numerical dominance of graduates of the Kiev Academy in the eighteenth-century Russian episcopate, as the Moscow Academy was still inferior to the Kievan. There were, of course, also the political reasons discussed in the previous chapter. The result was an influx of Ukrainian bishops, many of whom came from the polonized Ukrainian nobility. These bishops imitated the life style of the Polish Roman Catholic episcopate, who were

---

3 E.g., the grand duke, the tsar, local princes and state officials, or, in the case of Novgorod, the city assembly of all adult males (the *veche*).

mostly scions of Polish aristocracy and lived in luxurious, palatial episcopal residences. Ukrainian bishops now brought these traditions to Great Russia, where bishops had mostly been of humble origins and continued to live modestly after being elevated to the episcopate. Now even Great Russian bishops began to emulate the life style of their Ukrainian colleagues, as well as their despotic manner in handling parish priests. This contributed to a certain amount of tension among the clergy. Much more serious, however, were the tensions aroused by the appearance of so-called academic monasticism. As bishops were chosen from among the ranks of academy-educated monks, career-minded academics often took monastic vows while still students. With no vocation for true monasticism, with no intention ever to be real monks, and never having resided in a monastery, after their consecration they would live in relative luxury, not denying themselves secular human pleasures. It was primarily these new bishops and academic "monks" who aroused serious tensions and antagonism between the white (married) and the black (monastic, unmarried) clergy in modern Russia. Married priests often felt they were being punished for their high moral standards when they saw their former seminary/academy colleagues assuming positions of leadership in the Church despite their rather unscrupulous moral behavior, such as living with "common law wives" while pretending to be celibate monks. During the more liberal era of Alexander II, the great reformer, this internal tension exploded in published attacks against these pseudo-monks by such figures as Belliustin, Rostislavov, and Askochenskii. The most vicious attack against bishops was contained in the *Description of the Clergy in Rural Russia*, which was anonymously published in Paris in 1858, but was later found to have been authored by I.S. Belliustin, a provincial parish priest. It was only thanks to the Tsar and his family and Count Dimitri Tolstoy, the anti-episcopal overprocurator of the Synod, that Belliustin was saved from defrocking. Belliustin attacked these pseudo-monastic bishops for their hypocrisy, amorality, and sexual perversion—which may have been true for the individual cases cited in his book—but he tended to generalize, thus wrongly indicting the whole episcopacy and even monasticism per se. To use a term coined by Florovsky, this "Protestantism of the Eastern Rite," was certainly a foretaste of the Renovationist Schism in the Russian Church in the early twentieth century.

The Synod and the Overprocurators.

In 1817, the Synod over-procuratorship passed from Golitsyn to Prince Meshcherskii, during whose tenure the Minister of Education, Shishkov, continued to interfere in Church affairs despite the fact that his ministry had been separated from the Synod. Both of Meshcherskii's successors, Nechaev and Count Protasov, showed their utter contempt for the bishops and did their utmost to belittle their role in the Synod.

Nechaev (1833-36), a mason, surrounded the bishops with police informers, whose duty it was to report to him every move, word or sermon made by bishops, who then had to justify their words and actions to the secular authorities. The bishops were once again terrorized, fearing to make any independent decision, to undertake any initiatives. Their authority was thus continually diminished until Metropolitan Filaret dared to raise his voice against the petty interference by the overprocurator and by Nicholas I himself, after the latter tried to appoint his son and heir to membership in the Synod. Reluctantly, the Tsar withdrew his order. The Metropolitan took advantage of this victory to protest against the petty police surveillance over the Church and the constant bureaucratic meddling into her affairs, which abased the Church in the eyes of her flock. He pointed out to the Tsar that the source of his authority is anointment by the Church, which does not, however, extend to tsar's civil servants.

Filaret's protest was supported by the entire Synod, and, in 1836, Nechaev was replaced by Count Protasov. In contrast to Nechaev, Protasov was a religious believer, educated at home by hired Jesuit instructors. Although he disliked Roman Catholicism, from his Catholic educators he inherited his authoritarian and centralist methods of administration. Protasov gave the Orthodox Church the bureaucratic appellation of *The Department of Orthodox Confession*. Appointed overprocurator, he wrote to his friend: "Now I am the commander-in-chief, the patriarch, the Devil alone knows what I am." A contemporary churchman said that only the latter was true: the Devil knew what he was. But Protasov was no fool. He had his program for the Church. He finalized and streamlined the system of secular diocesan consistory chancelleries, whose officials treated diocesan bishops as highhandedly as the overprocurator treated the members of the Synod. These consistory secretaries reported directly to the overprocurator, bypassing the Synod. The process of converting the Church into a state bureaucracy totally subordinate to the government, which had begun under Peter the Great, was completed under Nicholas I. The borders of episcopal sees were made coterminous with the borders of the provinces (*gubernii*); the clergy were awarded exactly the same decorations as those given members of the civil service; and the last traces of clergy elections disappeared. Bishops came to be appointed by the tsar on the Synod's recommendations. Part of this system was also the passing on of parishes from father to son or to son-in-law.

The chief achievement of Protasov's tenure was the mass return of the remaining Belorussian and Little Russian (Ukrainian) Uniates to the Orthodox Church (see ch 5). The conversion at first led to serious economic complications. The Uniates in the western part of the empire were almost exclusively peasants; while most members of the landed nobility were polonized Roman Catholics (urban craftsmen were predominantly Jews). Obviously, once their serfs had been converted to Orthodoxy, the noblemen stopped supporting the churches. Churches situated on their estates began to be taxed by the landowners, or else put up for sale together with the plots of land on which they were situated. But the peasants were poor, most often serfs of these Polish lords, and lacked the funds to buy out their churches. Rural priests, most with large families, became impoverished once they lost their subsidies from the landowners.

To solve the problem Protasov set up a special commission. After the commission presented its report, Nicholas ordered that an annual subsidy of half a million rubles be given to the Church for the support of the poorest parishes and their clergy, mostly in the former Uniate areas. The question of solving the financial problems of the clergy then arose. Should a system of fixed state salaries for the clergy be established, similar to that in most West-European states? Or should clergy welfare depend on the generosity of parishioners, a system which would have to include charges for private services, such as funerals, weddings, or baptisms? The priest's situation, especially that of the rural priest, was rather difficult. On the one hand, in accordance with Peter's *Spiritual Regulation,* the parish priest acted as a police official of sorts, reporting on local disorders, presenting lists of potential army recruits, etc. On the other hand, unlike the police and other state officials, the priest derived no income from the state and had to rely on donations from the very people on whom he was supposed to report. In addition, his social status was very ambiguous. Having received an excellent classical education, he had to spend most of his post-seminary life working in the fields like a peasant. Devoting most of his time to the farm, the priest had little time to carry out his proper pastoral and educational functions. Always short of money, he was forced to charge his parishioners for individual prayers, which made him appear greedy in the eyes of the peasantry. For despite his modest means, he still had a higher income than the average peasant, who ignored the fact that the priest also had higher expenditures than the peasant. The priest had to see his children through school and college, he had to buy books, and he was required to entertain visiting bishops and state officials. But the fact that the priest had to take money from the peasants naturally created much friction and distrust.

Yet, when the question of transferring the clergy to state salaries by the imposition of a small, additional tax on the population was discussed by state commissions and in the Synod, it was Metropolitan Filaret who protested against the scheme. He argued that eliminating the dependence of the clergy on the generosity of the parishioners would abolish their sense of alms giving and charity, about which Jesus had taught His disciples. Filaret's argument would have been stronger had it not been for the police services that the priests had to perform. As a result, the issue of priests' incomes was never resolved in the Russian Empire, although the state appropriation to the Synod for partially subsidizing the poorest parishes and clergy increased from year to year, surpassing 14 million rubles a year by 1914, some 40 million short of a minimum wage for all Orthodox clergy in the Empire.

Old-Ritualists and sectarians were severely persecuted under Nicholas I. Although a believer, he did not distinguish between religion and military service, where neither duality of command nor free choice was tolerable. Under Nicholas I, also, the formula for official petitions became: "I, Ivan Ivanov, a member of the Orthodox Church having recourse to the sacraments of confession and communion on an annual basis..." Such a strong emphasis on the State Church in the long run undermined her authority, especially among the educated segments of the population. At the same time, statistical surveys of the religious adherence of the population, conducted in detail for the first time under Nicholas I, shockingly revealed how numerous the Old Ritualists and sectarians were among the common peasants.

Neither Protasov nor the whole imperial bureaucracy was able to meet that challenge by any other means but administrative repression. As Golitsyn had done before him, Protasov found a convenient aide in the person of the obscurantist Archimandrite Afanasii (Athanasius), whom he appointed rector of the St Petersburg Theological Academy. Afanasii forbade the professors to read their lectures from their notes. Instead, they had to read word-for-word only from published textbooks approved by the censors. These textbooks, by Protasov's and Afanasii's order, consisted of Russian translations of seventeenth-century Latin texts; both gentlemen, therefore, saw the era of Peter Mohyla as the model of Orthodoxy! They succeeded in postponing the publication of the complete Bible in Russian by the three decades of Nicholas's reign. Characteristically, Afanasii, a learned man who mastered numerous languages, was contemptuous of Russian letters and read only foreign books in the original. Afanasii was almost the ecclesiastical double of Chaadaev, except that the latter was a true philosopher and a lover of freedom—both qualities which were absent in Afanasii.

The Fate of the Old Ritualists in the Era of Nicholas I

The soldier's mind of Nicholas I could not accept the existence in his empire of another Orthodoxy, a variant of the Orthodox Church that was not under his control. Of all the Old Ritualists, he saw the priestly accord as the most threatening to the state Church, and he used all possible means to force them into *edinoverie*. Persecutions alternated with visitations from *edinoverie* missionaries who, in their debates in which Old Ritualists were forced to participate, used the pre-Nikonian texts. When this happened, hard-line Old Ritualists would retort: "You used to torture and murder us for these books; and now suddenly they are acceptable?"

Alexander I, during the reactionary part of his reign, passed a decree forbidding the Old Ritualists to build new churches. In 1826, that decree was extended by Nicholas I, who forbade them also to repair the existing ones. Then came further orders to remove crosses and other distinguishing signs from their churches and forbidding the Old Ritualists from accepting clergy deserters from the state Church. A more effective blow to the acquisition of new priests through desertions than the official ban (which could be circumvented by appropriate bribes handed out generously by the many prosperous Old Ritualist entrepreneurs), however, was the previously described improvement in the material well-being of the Orthodox clergy. But even such an authoritarian ruler as Nicholas I could not be consistent in his repressive policies toward the Old Ritualists. For example, he could ill afford to persecute the Cossacks, among whom a very high proportion were Old Ritualists, as he needed their loyalty for his armed forces. Nor could he persecute Old Ritualist entrepreneurs, not only because they could buy their freedom—and corruption was prevalent among civil servants under Nicholas I—but even more so because their industries, based on hired labor, were the most advanced in the country. Gradually replacing the collapsing serf-based, gentry-owned factories, they were leading Russia into the industrial age. Thus his reign was marked, on the one hand, by mass arrests and forced exile of tens of thousands Old Ritualists to distant parts of the empire, as well as the closure and liquidation of all their known sketes and spiritual centers, including those of Vyg and Irgiz by 1853; on the other hand, decrees in 1827 and 1834 forbade the police from arbitrarily searching the Old Ritualists' private residences and closing home chapels.

In response to the attempt to force the priestly Old Ritualists to join the official Church while retaining their rituals (*edinoverie*), the majority of those who had refused to do so established their own hierarchy. Paradoxically, they received it from a bishop of the Greek Church, i.e., from that very Church which caused their ancestors to break with the "Nikonian" Church. Several representatives were sent to the Balkans and the Middle East to find a worthy bishop who would agree to consecrate a bishop for the Russian Old Ritualist Priestly Accord. In 1847, they found a certain Metropolitan Amvrosios, an ethnic Greek and a former bishop of Saraevo who had been forcefully retired by the Turks for pronouncing anti-Turkish sermons, and who was living in retirement in Constantinople. In the meanwhile, the Old Ritualists had established their monastery in the Bukovinian town of Belaia Krinitsa, with the permission of the Austrian authorities there. The Old Ritualist representatives managed to convince the Metropolitan to move to Belaia Krinitsa, where he consecrated the first two Russian Old Ritualist bishops, the first one being Archbishop Kirill. The consecration was somewhat irregular, as it was performed by a single bishop, whereas the Orthodox tradition requires that a bishop be consecrated by an assembly of bishops, i.e., at least by two. Then, under pressure from the Russian Government, the Austrian authorities closed the Belaia Krinitsa monastery. Metropolitan Amvrosios returned to Constantinople, where the Turkish Government forced the Ecumenical patriarch (probably also under Russian pressure) to defrock him. However, what was done was done: the Old Ritualists had at last obtained their own hierarchy and no longer needed to depend on clergy deserters. The staunchest priestly Old Ritualists, however, refused to accept a hierarchy stemming from the Greeks; thus a new schism arose among them, with the new schismatics continuing to rely on clergy deserters from the Russian state church. As to Belaia Krinitsa, a short while later the Austrian Government changed its mind, and the Old Ritualist monastery was revived as a spiritual center of the Belokrinitskoe Accord, beyond the reach of the tsarist police.

Although quite a few Old Ritualists did and continued to join *edinoverie*, the persecutions of those persisting in the "Schism" attracted the interest and sympathy of large portions of the population. Moreover, many aspects of Old

Ritualism made it attractive to new converts. The Old Ritualists retained the original, Orthodox *sobornost'* which had been eliminated in the official Orthodox Church by Peter I. The Old Ritualists continued to convene councils of laity and clergy. In the Priestless Accords, lay instructors and preachers were chosen by the communities of faithful; in the priestly Belokrinitskoe Accord, candidates for the priesthood were likewise chosen by the communities; while among the *priestly fugitive communities*, entire congregations decided whether or not to accept a given priest-deserter as their pastor. By contrast, all clergy appointments in the official Orthodox Church were made bureucratically from the top. Tightly controlled by the state, the official Church could not criticize any government acts, not even the institution of serfdom. Moreover, despite the new subsidies to the poorest priests introduced under Nicholas I, the clergy of the official Church remained on the whole very poor, and this made them vulnerable to corruption. Wealthy Old Ritualists offered them bribes not to report to the government how many "schismatics" there were in their parishes and who they were. Consequently, despite the persecutions, and perhaps even because of them, the Old Ritualists continued to attract new converts. Whether or not their proportion in the total population in fact grew substantially, as some authors have claimed, it certainly did not decline.[4]

The effect of the Old Ritualist phenomenon among the peasants, craftsmen, and artisans[5] could even be compared to the effect of some sectarian imports from the West on the aristocratic society of the time—an example is the one brought by Lord Redstock, known in Russia as *Redstockism* and described by the Russian writer Nikolai Leskov. In both cases, the departure from official Orthodoxy was motivated by a frustration with the bureaucratism of the official Church. Aristocratic sectarianism replaced masonic pseudo-mysticism, which apparently ceased to satisfy the spiritual thirst of high society. The Orthodox Church remained too Oriental for them, incompatible with their high-society westernism on the one hand, and too closely controlled by the state, too mute and unfree, on the other. As to the native Russian popular sects, the nineteenth century expert on the Old Ritualists and related sects, A. Shchapov, a historian and ethnographer, traced a line of continuity from the seventeenth-eighteenth-century impostors (from the series of False Dimitris to Pugachev) to the era of

---

4 It is known that persecutions achieve their aims only if they are total, consistent and prolonged. The tsarist persecutions conformed to none of these criteria.

5 We do not mention separately the merchants-industrialists, because they all sprang from any of the enumerated groups.

dissemination of diverse sects which, as a rule, grew out of the priestless accords, particularly those that rejected marriage. In both cases, there were impostors. For about a century and a half after the Time of Troubles, rebellious Cossack leaders adopted the name of one or another murdered crown prince or tsar who, they alleged, miraculously survived a murder attempt. In the name of such a monarch, whether he had in fact existed or was simply invented by the impostor, the rebel would proclaim an anarchist freedom from all obligations and state duties. The pretenders' epoch ended with the quashing of the Pugachev rebellion, when it became clear to the rebels that the state was too powerful to be taken over by a simple Cossack uprising. One could only run away. Hence the appearance of such sects as the Wanderers, Runners (or Fugitives—*beguny*, in Russian), whose founder, a certain Evfimii (Euthemius), was, perhaps not coincidentally, a younger contemporary of Pugachev.

Nicholas finally understood that persecution alone could not solve the problem, and that the official count of 910,000 "schismatics" in the whole empire, as well as the official claim that their number was declining from year to year, bore little semblance to reality.[6] And so, in the 1850s Nicholas ordered that special commissions be formed, composed of conscientious civil servants and scholars, to undertake an honest and thorough study of the real situation of sects and schisms and to obtain more reliable data on their numbers. The findings by the commissions were shocking indeed. Their data overturned all the traditional assumptions that the Russian people constituted an Orthodox monolith. Extrapolating from the 1852 Commissions' findings in several sample provinces, one finds roughly 10 million schismatics of numerous sects and Old Ritualist accords—i.e., almost 20 percent of the Empire's population were either Old Ritualists or belonged to popular sects derived from them. But if Muslim and other historically non-Orthodox elements are excluded, and the 10 million "schismatics" are compared only to the historically Orthodox sector of the population, then the "schismatics" and sectarians amount to a solid 25 percent of the East-Slavic population of the Empire. Even more shocking were the revelations about some trans-Volga provinces. Thus, although the figure obtained by the commission on the Yaroslavl' Province (a northern neighbor of the Moscow Province) was 278,000 sectarians and "schismatics," Ivan Aksakov, a member of the commission, a

---

6 As pointed out above, it was in the interest of the parish priest as well as of every state official, from the district police commander to the provincial governor, to report Orthodox missionary successes in converting the schismatics and in bringing about their numerical decline.

dedicated Orthodox Christian and a leading Slavophile, claimed that in reality practicing members of the official Orthodox Church constituted no more than 25 percent of the population of that province.

The Old Ritualists and their derivative sects were most numerous in the trans-Volga north and north-east, in Siberia, and in the areas of the Cossack hosts. These are regions where there were very few gentry landowners, and the peasants were either completely free from serfdom (e.g., Cossacks and certain national minorities), or those where the so-called "state" and "court" peasants predominated.[7] In addition, local self-government, introduced during the enlightened early period of Ivan the Terrible's reign, survived among the peasants and tradesmen in the north and north-east. Semi-free state and court peasants, residing on poor soils and in harsh climates, were forced to supplement their meager farming incomes by engaging in all sorts of crafts. Some became wealthy entrepreneurs, factory owners, millionaires; others either developed cottage industries or acted as middlemen between the rural and urban industries, or even owned wood and pulp, wool or food processing plants, hiring local peasant workers, and linked up with urban distribution agencies or factories producing finished consumer goods.[8] An additional incentive for the Old Ritualists to succeed in business was the need to bribe local state officials in order to keep their prayer houses and monastic *sketes* open and to conceal the Old Ritualists' existence in official reports. All these enterprises, as well as the requirement to participate in debates with Orthodox missionaries, made it essential for Old Ritualists to be literate. Many Old Ritualists, therefore could read and write and were rather well-read in Scriptures and related literature, while most "Nikonian" peasants remained illiterate and much poorer. These factors also raised the Old Ritualists' prestige in the eyes of the peasant masses. Moreover, the "Nikonian" peasant-craftsmen also depended on middlemen and other rural and urban entrepreneurs, most of whom were Old Ritualists. The peasant masses thus had very close ties to Old Ritualists of all types. Furthermore, the Old Ritual was seen by them as the true "peasant faith," in contrast to the official Orthodoxy associated with the ruling class, supported by the gentry serf-owners, and imposed by an authoritarian state. All this alienated the peasants from the official Church.

---

7 State peasants were legally bound to state land, allotted for their use in return for certain duties, obligations and taxes. Court peasants were bound to estates belonging to the imperial family. Both categories had much more freedom of action than private serfs, especially after the reforms of the 1830s.

8 Such rural entrepreneurs were known as the "thousanders," in contrast to the urban factory owners (also mostly of serf or state peasant background), who were known as the "millionaires."

Iosif Yuzov, a late nineteenth-century Russian specialist in Russian schisms and sects, estimated that there were some 13 million "schismatics" and sectarians of Old Ritualist origin in 1878: 2,640,000 belonged to the priestly accords; 7,150,000 to the priestless Old Ritualists; and 65,000 to the "shakers" and castrators. As he writes, "...no accurate data has been collected on the remaining 2,145,000 ... of [whom] ... at least 1 million are 'spiritual christians'," i.e., dukhobors, molokans, etc. But these estimates take us beyond the Nicolaevan era.

Chaadaev and the Birth of the Slavophile/Westernist Controversy

Characteristically, Chaadaev wrote almost exclusively in French, although the wealthy Russian aristocrat had lived almost his entire life in Russia, having visited France only as an officer in the victorious Russian occupational forces. In his most famous *First Philosophical Letter*, published in Moscow in the 1830s, he denied that Russia had or could make any original contribution to European civilization. He saw Russia as a parasite on world culture: this bothered him tremendously, because Chaadaev was a deeply religious person who believed that God had created each nation for a certain messianic purpose. Yet he failed to see Russia performing any such function, as if God has failed in His creation. As a child of his age, he had no idea about Byzantine civilization. Ignorant of the fact that, while western Europe was living through its "Dark Ages," the ninth-eleventh centuries were the era of Byzantine's cultural glory and of great missionary dynamism of her Church, Chaadaev wrote that Russia's tragedy had been that she adopted her Christianity from a stagnant and decaying civilization, thus failing to inherit the vigor and dynamism of the Roman Church. He later revised this thesis in his *Apology of a Madman*, saying that Russia, as a young culture without the heavy cultural baggage of western Europe, would inherit the best of European civilization while avoiding the errors of the West. Russia would, therefore, one day take over cultural leadership from an aging and degenerating western Europe. Never, however, did he reverse his original statement that Russia had no past, no cultural heritage of her own.

This was a challenge to the Russian public, which after Chaadaev's *Letter* split into the Westernist and the Slavophile currents. The former adopted the Chaadaev thesis uncritically; the latter began an in-depth study of Russian archives, *Chronicles*, pre-Petrine Russian literature and traditions, as well as the legacy of the Eastern Church Fathers, and whatever they could find in old Russian theological writings. In this way, the "slavophile" Russian intellectuals encountered Paisii Velichkovskii's hesychastic disciples in the Optina Pustyn'. Their cooperation resulted in the proliferation of Russian translations of Church Fathers, published by the Optina publishing house and, for the first time, widely available to the laity. Thus a small group of enlightened gentry landowners (the Kireevskii brothers, Alexei Khomiakov, Yurii Samarin, the Aksakovs, Koshelev, and several others), together with a community of monks in a little-known provincial monastery of Optina Pustyn', made a contribution of the greatest importance for the revival of Orthodox theology. That theological revival and rejuvenation was to reach the seminaries only at the end of the nineteenth century. Although eastern patristics was studied in Russian theological schools quite intensively at least from the time of the Alexandrine reforms, that teaching was dry, scholastic, detached; and the Palamite hesychastic theology was almost unknown. Its restoration, which took place through the cooperation of the Optina elders with Russian intellectuals, also brought a rediscovery of iconography as a part of the theology of Godmanhood, of the Palamite teaching on the uncreated, divine energies, given to man as God's co-creator. The Slavophile-Westernist controversy also led to the development of Byzantine studies as a scholarly discipline.

As to the *westernizers*, they soon lost the spiritual roots of Chaadaev's westernism. Accepting his thesis that Russia's fate was to copy the West, mechanically and uncritically they borrowed whatever was fashionable in western Europe at the time. As this was the era of positivism, radicalism, materialism, and socialism, these doctrines began to infest Russia beginning from the 1840s, via the predominantly atheist Russian westernizers. With regard to revolutionary radicalism, first came the French socialist ideas, which undoubtedly influenced the Russian populism of the 1860s-70s, then followed revolutionary Marxism. As far as popular religion was concerned, the westernizers and the Russian marxists adopted as a matter of faith Visarion Belinskii's statement, made in the 1840s, that the Russian peasant was an atheist at heart, irreverently speaking about God while scratching his bottom.

The Slavophiles preferred Konstantin Aksakov's words that the history of the Russian people is the history of the only Christian nation in the world. Orthodox Christianity is the only basis of the Russian people, and its history reads like the Lives of saints.

The twentieth century was to put both statements to the test.

Ecumenical Contacts and Hopes: From Alexander I to the 20th Century.

I. Anglican-Orthodox Relations.

Fr Florovsky attributes the birth of modern ecumenism to the Alexandrine Holy Alliance, which resulted from the Congress of Vienna. Alexander I hoped to create, on the ruins of Napoleon's empire, a pan-European confederation in which every nation and every Christian faith would be treated as branches of a single, confederal "holy nation," although with no formal unification of the religions into a single Church. Hence the Dual Ministry and the Russian branch of the Bible Society.

Even Metropolitan Filaret (Drozdov) of Moscow was an ecumenist of sorts, as reflected in his *Conversation of a Seeker and a Believer Concerning the Truth of the Eastern Greco-Russian Church,* in which he says he has no right to condemn as false any Church which believes that Jesus is the Christ. Wholly cut off from the one universal Church are only those religions, he writes, which deny that Jesus is the Son of God, the incarnate God and Savior. He asserts that the Church of the Ecumenical Councils has fully survived only in the Orthodox Church, yet he understood the one "Universal Church" (which he said was invisible and mystical) to be a mystical unity of all religions which recognize the divinity of Christ.

Close to Filaret's views and even closer to Alexander's notions of "the holy alliance" stood the so-called *Oxford Movement* in the Anglican Church, with its theory of a single Catholic Church with three branches: the Roman-Catholic; the Greek Orthodox (the Oxford Movement called it Greek-Catholic); and the Anglo-Catholic, i.e., Anglican. These High-Anglicans believed that, by breaking with the papacy, the Anglican Church had restored herself as a western branch of the undivided Orthodox-Catholic Church. And, since according to the apostolic canons there can be only one bishop in one city, therefore each of the above "branches" should offer eucharistic hospitality to members of the other branches when they find themselves in the geographical territories of another "branch." Naturally, this branch theory did not extend to those communions which lacked the historic episcopate. Such a position is, of course, tenable only if doctrinal differences are seen as unimportant, which is impossible for the Orthodox. It was with these attitudes that Anglicans began to establish close contacts with St Petersburg and Constantinople. Difficulties soon arose over the *filioque* and the question of whether the Anglican episcopate had retained apostolic succession, which the

Orthodox doubted. On the other hand, the Anglicans recognized only the first six ecumenical councils, but not the seventh, which restored the veneration of icons.

One Oxford Movement enthusiast, Deacon William Palmer, came to Russia in 1839 with the aim of being recognized by the Orthodox Church. As an Anglican, he said he belonged to the One Catholic Church, and as such he could receive communion in the Russian Church. He held that since the English Church had not been involved in the schism of 1054, she did not separate from the Orthodox Church. The Russian hierarchy responded that, although doctrinal differences between Anglicanism and Orthodoxy were *insignificant*, the Church of England, having been under Rome, was also encompassed by the schism, and that Palmer could therefore receive communion in the Orthodox Church only through chrismation. He was prepared to accept this condition, but decided first to obtain the views of the Greek Church. To his surprise, the Church of Greece demanded full re-baptism. Palmer was shocked by such a divergence of views on so fundamental a question. Doubting that the Eastern Churches constituted one Church, Palmer went to Rome and converted to Roman Catholicism; but to the end of his life he believed that the fullness of the apostolic Faith was contained only in the Orthodox Church.

Although Palmer was quite influential in certain Anglican circles, his visit to Russia was a private affair. Formal contacts between the two Churches began in 1842 with the appointment of Fr Eugene (Evgenii) Popov to the chaplaincy of the Russian embassy in London. Originally optimistic about the prospect of an Orthodox-Anglican union, Popov gradually cooled to that idea after gaining closer familiarity with Anglicanism. In 1851, a group of Anglicans composed a petition to the St Petersburg Synod to accept them into the Orthodox Church, but with permission to retain the Anglican Rite. Nothing came of that project. But British initiatives aimed at bringing the two Churches closer together continued. In 1857, an *Association for the Promotion of the Unity of Christendom* was founded in Britain, with the aim of achieving unity of worship between the three Churches. This rather sizable organization, which had some Orthodox members, fell apart in 1869, after Rome forbade any Roman Catholic participation.

By then, an *Eastern Church Association* had been in existence since 1863. Among its members were some of the most influential Anglican scholars and clergy, as well as Eugene Popov and a Greek Archimandrite, Constantine

(Stratoulas), on the Orthodox side. In 1866 a delegation from the Church of Scotland, headed by its Bishop-Primate, visited Russia in hopes of establishing intercommunion on the basis of the Anglican branch theory. A year later, a delegation of the Eastern Church Association went to Russia. Russian Orthodoxy left a deep impression on the delegates. One of them wrote: A "sense of God's presence ... seems to me to penetrate Russian life more completely than that of any of the Western nations." The Scots met the old Metropolitan Filaret, but no agreement on inter-communion was achieved. Palmer's original idea had been that the Scottish part of the Anglican Church should lead the way toward reunification with Orthodoxy, because, in contrast to the Church of England, she was not a part of the British government establishment, and therefore not subject to parliamentary legislation.

Later, leadership in the search for unity fell on the American Episcopalians, whose relations with the Orthodox began in the early 1850s when the early Episcopalian settlers on the Pacific, calling themselves The Church of California and basing themselves on the principle of one bishop in one city, addressed a petition to the Orthodox bishop of Alaska and the Aleutian Islands to accept them as a part of his diocese, as his jurisdiction included the whole West Coast. Nothing came of this attempt. By 1857, there was already an Episcopalian bishop of California. Then, after the transfer of the Russian Diocese from Alaska to California in 1872, the Episcopalians claimed that the Orthodox on the West Coast should instead become a part of the Episcopalian Diocese of the Pacific. Nothing came of this attempt either. However, in discussions between some Anglican leaders and the Russian embassy chaplains from Paris and London, American Episcopalians were advised that the Orthodox would agree to intercommunion only after certain changes were made in the Anglican-Epispopalian doctrines, and that the American Episcopalian Church, because it was independent of state control, would be best suited to lead such negotiations with the Orthodox. Should they succeed, that would be precedent-setting for the Anglicans. Consequently, an Episcopalian delegation went to Russia in 1864, where they found Metropolitan Filaret in principle open to intercommunion—although he said it would not be accepted by the masses of Orthodox laity and could lead to a major schism in the Church. Filaret, however, doubted the canonicity of the Anglican clergy and saw the road to inter-Church rapprochement as being reached only through careful study and the eventual resolution of the following issues: 1. the Anglican theological doctrines; 2. the *filioque*; 3. apostolic succession in the Anglican Church; 4. the role of tradition in Anglicanism; 5. the Anglican doctrine on the sacraments, especially on the Eucharist.

From the 1870s, periodic consultations between official delegations of Anglican and Orthodox theologians took place. Orthodox representation expanded to include not only the Russians, but also Greeks, Rumanians and Serbs. Hopes rose for a forthcoming union of Churches. Thus a resolution of the Third All-Anglican Conference of 1888 expresses "hope that the barriers to a fuller communion may be, in course of time, removed..." But the documents of the conference mention how difficult it is for the Anglicans to reject the *filioque* and "to enter into more intimate relations with that Church so long as it retains the use of icons, the invocation of the saints, and the cults of the Blessed Virgin, even if the Greeks disclaim the sin of idolatry." In 1902, the Bishop of Wandsworth nevertheless introduced a petition at the Convocation of Canterbury to exclude the *filioque* from the Creed. The same petition was submitted at the Convocation of 1904. The Fifth Lambeth Conference instructed the Archbishop of Canterbury to establish a permanent committee on Anglican-Orthodox relations, suggesting the immediate implementation of such aspects of intercommunion as the rendering of pastoral services to the members of each other's Churches in such extreme cases as death and dying, when no priest of the dying person's confession is available.

FOR FURTHER READING

Arseniev, N., *Holy Moscow: Chapters in the Religious and Spiritual Life of Russia in the 19th Century* (New York, 1940).

Belliustin, I.S., *Description of the Clergy in Rural Russia*, translated by Gregory L. Freeze (Cornell University Press, 1985).

Blagovidov, F.V., *Ober prokurory Sviateishego Sinoda v XVIII i pervoi polovine IX v.* (Kazan, 1900).

Bolshakoff, S., *The Foreign Missions of the Russian Orthodox Church* (London, 1943).

_____, *Russian Nonconformity* (Philadelphia: Westminster Press, 1950).

Chaadaev, P.Ya., *Polnoe sobranie sochinenii*, 2 vols (Moscow: Nauka, 1991).

Christoff, P.K., *An Introduction to Nineteenth-Century Russian Slavophilism*, 4 vols: Vol.1: A.S. Xomiakov (The Hague, 1961); vol. 2: I.V. Kireevskij (The Hague, 1972); vol. 3: K.S. Aksakov: a Study in Ideas (The Hague, 1982); vol. 4: Iu. F. Samarin (Boulder, Co, 1991).

Crummey, Robert C., *The Old Believers and the World of Antichrist* (Madison and London: University of Wisconsin Press, 1970).

Florovsky, Georges, "Orthodox Ecumenism in the Nineteenth Century," in *Aspects of Church History* (Belmont, Mass.: Nordland, 1975).

Freeze, Gr., *The Parish Clergy in Nineteenth-Century Russia: Crisis, Reform, Counter-Reform* (Princeton U.Press, 1983).

Gratieux, A.A.S., *Khomiakov et le mouvement slavophile*, 2 vols (Paris, 1939).

Khomiakov, A.S., Sochineniia (Moscow, 1900).

Lutteroth, Henri (Nikolai Ivanovich Turgenev*), La Russie et les Jesuites de 1770 à 1820 d'après de documents la plupart inedits* (Paris, 1845).

Macarius, *Letters of Direction, 1834-1860* (London, 1944).

Nadler, V.K., *Imperator Alexandr I i ideia Sviashchennogo soiuza*, 5 vols. (Kharkov, 1886-92).

Palmer, W., *Notes of a Visit to the Russian Church in the Years 1840, 1841* (London, 1882).

Pleyer, V., *Das russische Altglaubigentum* (Munich, 1961).

Pypin, A.N., *Obshchestvennoe dvizhenie v Rossii pri Alexandre I* (St Petersburg, 1915).

Piskanov, N. K., ed., *Religioznye dvizheniia pri Alexandre I* (St Petersburg, 1916).

Riasanovsky, N.V., *Russia and the West in the Teachings of the Slavophiles* (Cambridge, Mass., 1952).

_____, *Nicholas I and Official Nationality in Russia, 1825-1855* (University of California Press, 1967).

Shchapov, A.P., *Sochineniia v trekh tomakh, t. I: "Zemstvo i raskol"* (St Petersburg., 1906 / Reprint: Gregg International Publishers, England, 1971).

Stelletsky, N., *Kniaz' A.N. Golitsyn i ego tsarkovno-gosudarstvennaia deiatel'nost'* (Kiev, 1901).

Smolitsch, Igor *Geschichte der russischen Kirche*, 1700-1917 (Leiden: E.J. Brill, 1964).

Titlinov, B.V., *Dukhovnaia shkola v Rossii v XIX st* (Vil'na, 1908).

Yuzov, Iosif (Kablits), *Starovery i dukhovnye khristiane* (St Petersburg, 1881).

Zenkovsky, Vasili, *Istoriia russkoi filosofii*, 2 vols (Paris, 1948-1950).

_____, *Russkie mysliteli i Evropa* (Paris, 1965).

CHAPTER 8

THE CHURCH IN POST-REFORM RUSSIA
(1860s TO THE 20TH CENTURY)

To see the Synodal period in proper perspective, we should point out that canon law regarding the appointment of bishops had been violated long before the synodal system. Thus, even before the establishment of the patriarchate, metropolitans of Rus' were chosen, directly or indirectly, by the grand dukes, and in the patriarchal period, by the tsars. According to Orthodox canon law, however, a bishop appointed by civil authorities or on their order is to be defrocked and all his ordinations are deemed invalid. It was precisely on the basis of these canons that Serapion Mashkin, a radical Optina Monastery elder, who corresponded with Paul Florensky and St John of Kronstadt, claimed that the whole Russian clergy was uncanonical. In fact, most Russian patriarchs enjoyed not a great deal more independence from the tsars than did the Petrine and post-Petrine Synod. But, as both Kartashev and Florovsky have pointed out, the breaches of canons occurring in the pre-Petrine era were perceived as breaches—as can be seen, for example, in Patriarch Nikon's rebellion against the 1649 Code. But in the Synodal era these came to be perceived as a perfectly normal situation.

In all fairness, it should also be stated that, despite all irregularities, the two centuries of the synodal era witnessed some considerable achievements. We have already seen the major steps taken in the field of education. The other major achievement is in the area of Orthodox missionary activities in Siberia, the Far East, Alaska, Japan, China, and Korea, as well as among the Nestorian Assyrians in the Ottoman Empire (present-day Iraq). Let us discuss this in more detail.

Russian Orthodox Missions From the Volga-Ural Tribes to Altai

Various parts of the Volga-Ural area had been the object of Russian missions long before the Synodal era. Thus the Komi-Perm Finnic tribes of the northwestern Urals were christianized in the course of the fourteenth century by St Stephen who, following in the tradition of Cyril and Methodius, devised an alphabet and grammar for the Permiak language and translated the Scriptures and service books. Unfortunately, the rest of the Church establishment was not up to St Stephen's level. A few decades after his death, this alphabet was destroyed and books written in it were destroyed, and services in Church Slavonic imposed, making the church services incomprehensible to the Finnish-speaking tribe.

The Orthodox missions in the rest of the Volga-Ural area began with the conquest of Kazan' and Astrakhan' by Ivan the Terrible in the sixteenth century, as we have already seen. But due to the lack of an educational system and a shortage of adequately trained missionaries, christianization of that area prior to the late eighteenth century was elementary and unstable, with many people moving back and forth between Islam, Christianity and paganism.

Systematic missionary work in this area (and further east) received a solid foundation after 1842, when the Kazan' graduate Theological Academy began to specialize in Islam and other Oriental religions. One of its earliest graduates, Nikolai Il'minskii—who mastered Persian, Turkish, Tatar, Chuvash, Altaian and several other eastern languages, not to mention Greek, Hebrew and Latin which he knew as a matter of course—began to create the first schools in Tatar and in several other local languages. Prior to him, the Tatars and other Islamic peoples of the area had only Arabic-based, strictly Islamic, schools. Il'minskii created the Tatar, Chuvash, and other modern literary languages based on the Cyrillic alphabet (instead of the Arabic, which was unsuited for the Turkic languages). The educational programs were modeled on the Russian state schools of the time, using European principles of general secular education, but including also classes in basic Orthodox theology. Translations were prepared by Il'minskii, the real creator of the modern Tatar literary language, which stimulated the birth of a new Turkic secular intelligentsia and opened it to European culture and political concepts, including a nationalism which gave rise to pan-Turkism. The latter eventually influenced Ottoman Turkey in the form of the Young Turk movement of Atatturk.

Prior to Ilminskii's work, the Russian Government had tried to lure the Muslim Tatars into Christianity by granting converts free farm land, freedom from serfdom and from recruitment into the army. This led to the conversion of a quarter of a million Tatars in the eighteenth century. But having received all these grants, many Tatars began to return to Islam after the abolition of serfdom in 1861 and the introduction of a universal draft army which included the Tatars, both Christian and Muslim. Il'minskii's conversions through education proved much more stable. Thus, by the end of the nineteenth century, close to 99 percent of the former pagans of the Volga-Ural region (mostly Finnish tribes) and some 10 percent of the former Muslims were solidly Christian. By that time, the Translations Committee of the Kazan' Academy published Orthodox religious literature in twenty-two languages of the Russian Orient. Church services were likewise conducted in those same languages. The only people who continued to be deprived of services in its native tongue were the Russians, who had to make do with the poorly understood Church Slavonic. A Russian Church historian, Sergei Bolshakoff, posed a rhetorical question in that connection: were not the church services in the native tongues of the nations of the Volga-Ural region responsible for the fact that, according to him, these neo-Christian peoples defended the Church from the Bolshevik onslaught much more energetically than did the local Russians?

As to Altai (southwest Siberia), the pioneer there was the Archimandrite Makarii Glukhariov. He had created an Altaian alphabet, based on Cyrillic, in the 1830s and translated all the necessary Church service books, as well as the entire New and parts of the Old Testament. Glukhariov was a Christian ecumenist who dreamt of building a cathedral with three altars under one roof: an Orthodox, a Roman Catholic and a Lutheran. He could not comprehend why Nicholas I and the Synod, while welcoming his translations of the Scriptures into Altaian, banned the publication of the Russian Bible. For his persistent requests to permit a Russian edition of the Bible—he even wrote directly to the Tsar—Makarii was accused by the Synod of the sin of pride. He was ordered to return to St Petersburg and, in "punishment," commanded to serve a daily liturgy for six consecutive weeks. The pious monk was happy to have this opportunity to immerse himself in worship and could not fathom wherein was the punishment.

The complete Russian Bible was finally published in the 1860s. It was a translation from the Hebrew of those Old Testamental books which had survived in the original, and from the Greek of those which did not. That was the last achievement of the aging Metropolitan Filaret of Moscow, who had fought for it over four decades. The translation was done by professors of the theological academies under the editorial control of Filaret, whose linguistic expertise included six dead and four living languages, in addition to Russian. Some of the translations were in fact done by the Metropolitan himself.

Alaska

Orthodox missionary work in Alaska began in 1794 with the arrival of three Russian monks from the monastery of Valaam (on Lake Ladoga, northeast of

St Petersburg) in 1794. One, the Hieromonk Yuvenalii, was murdered by Indian tribes a short while later.[1] But the two best remembered Alaskan Russian
missionaries were: St Herman, one of the three original missionaries; and St
Innocent who arrived three decades later. St Herman built himself a monastic
cell on Spruce Island, working among the natives, enlightening them with
Christian teachings, teaching them how to grow vegetables. He also defended
them from unfair treatment and exploitation by the Russian colonial authorities, writing numerous complaints to the central government and to the
Synod in St Petersburg. But the Alaska mission received its real and systematic
development only with the arrival in 1824 of the priest Ivan Veniaminov-
Popov, the future bishop Innocent. He mastered several local dialects and created the Aleut and Tlingit written languages on the basis of the Cyrillic alphabet. Having translated the main service books and parts of the Bible into these
languages, he began to establish schools, which were open both to the native
population and the children of Russian administrators and businessmen, as
well as to the Creoles of mixed marriages. Having lost his wife in the late
1830s, he was consecrated Bishop of Kamchatka, the Kuriles and Alaska in
1840, with his diocesan seat in Novo-Arkhangel'sk, the administrative center
of Alaska, now known as Sitka.

In 1868, Bishop Innocent was appointed Metropolitan of Moscow. But
he never ignored the Alaskan mission. In a memorandum to the Synod, he
prophetically welcomed the sale of Alaska to the US as opening a new missionary field to the Orthodox Church—the whole North American conti-
nent. He therefore proposed that its diocesan center be moved to the "Lower
Forty-eight." The Metropolitan also established the Siberian Committee,
later transformed into The Russian Imperial Missionary Society, whose main
function became the dissemination of Orthodoxy among the natives of Siberia, the Far East, Alaska, and later the "Lower Forty-eight". The Society selected and trained Orthodox missionaries for America. Missionaries were
materially well provided for, and the American Mission did not suffer from a
lack of worthy candidates, among whom only the best were selected for the
mission. After the sale of Alaska therefore, the mission not only did not die,
but, on the contrary, continued to grow, bringing numerous Athabaskan In-
dians and Eskimos to Orthodoxy. The apostle to these tribes who, following

---

1 According to a popular legend, his murderer was an Indian chief who had offered Yuvenalii his daughter. Being ignorant of monastic vows, the chief took Yuvenalii's refusal as a personal insult and killed him.

the example of his teacher Innocent, created literary languages for them, was the recently canonized Priest Jacob Netsvetov, an Alaskan Creole.

Among Bishop Innocent's Alaskan educational facilities was a seminary, a teachers' college and a simplified medical school. Some native Alaskan graduates of these schools continued their higher education in Russia. Some became Russian naval officers, navigators, or naval geographers, who mapped the Alaskan coasts and islands. As already mentioned, Innocent's disciples continued his work quite successfully, so that an American Alaskan governor reported to President Theodore Roosevelt that, by the early twentieth century, the Americans had done nothing for the natives, while all the schools for Alaskan natives were Russian and belong to the Orthodox mission. In contrast to the Orthodox policies of nativizing the Orthodox Church, the American policy was to de-nativize the natives. Consequently, when American schools for Alaskan natives finally appeared, they were founded in the "Lower Forty-eight." Their graduates became a lost generation—fitting neither into their own native, nor into the white American milieu—giving rise to alcoholism, crime, suicides. With the sale of Alaska, the North-American Orthodox mission became the first mission of the Russian Orthodox Church beyond the borders of the Empire, except for the Peking Mission.

China

In contrast to the Alaskan Mission for the natives, the Peking mission was originally meant to serve the spiritual needs of the Russian Cossacks captured by the Chinese when they seized the Russian Fort Albazin in 1685. The Cossacks and their priest, Maxim Leontiev, were forcefully settled in Peking, where they were treated very kindly by the Chinese emperor, who turned them into a special detachment of imperial guards with a status roughly equivalent to that of Russian service gentry. The Cossacks married Chinese women and assimilated in all but their faith, thanks to the priest's presence. The emperor gave them a Buddhist temple, which they transformed into an Orthodox chapel. Ten years later, Fr Maxim received a letter of moral support and blessing from the Metropolitan of Tobolsk and Siberia, Ignatii (Rimskii-Korsakov), who encouraged him to engage in missionary work among the natives. Peter the Great issued a decree in 1700 naming it "the Russian Spiritual Mission of Peking" and materially subsidizing it so that it could "preach the word of the Holy Gospel among the pagan population and bring them into the fold of the Orthodox faith."

In 1711, the Chinese emperor agreed to legitimize the mission as specified by Peter the Great, on condition that it be accompanied by a Russian medical doctor. As the mission's flock, consisting of Cossacks, were Chinese subjects, the Imperial Court took upon itself the material upkeep and the payment of salaries to the mission personnel. This was formally confirmed in 1727 in the terms of the Russo-Chinese Peace of Kiakhta, which also allowed the Mission to build a large Orthodox church, to keep several priests, and to bring young men for the study of the Chinese language. All of them received Chinese salaries which, however, were so modest by Russian standards that, in periods when no financial subsidies came from Russia, the Mission would mortgage or even sell its property in order to keep its members from starving to death. Such, for instance, was its plight during the Napoleonic wars. Its head at the time, the uniquely erudite sinologist, Archimandrite Iakinf Bichurin, was even recalled to Russia and tried for making such sales. He was unjustly sentenced to five years of forced residence in a monastery and the deprivation of his clergy ranks, despite his colossal scholarly contributions to sinology: he had composed several Russian-Chinese scholarly dictionaries, translated numerous Chinese philosophical and historiographic works into Russian, and Orthodox service books into Chinese.

The Mission produced some of the world's greatest sinologists, experts in the languages and cultures of China, Korea, and Mongolia. But in missionary endeavors its achievements were very modest. In the early eighteenth century, when China was ruled by emperors sympathetic to Christianity, the Mission was led by unscrupulous Ukrainian clergy. Then came the anti-Christian emperors of the last six decades of the eighteenth century, who banned conversions of the Chinese, actively persecuted Roman Catholic missionaries for such actions, and killed many Chinese converts. The official attitude toward Christians, particularly toward Chinese converts, remained very negative, with periods of active and cruel persecutions, until the opening up of China to Europe in 1864. In terms of purely religious activities, the Russian Mission's main preoccupation was with preventing the Cossacks' descendants from reverting to Chinese paganism. As to the number of conversions, the Mission's statistics vary from 200 native Chinese in the early nineteenth century, to several dozen later in the century. After 1864, the Mission was officially split into the Mission proper and the secular-diplomatic Russian embassy: prior to that, the archimandrite in charge of the mission had also acted as the de facto Russian ambassador. Only after that split did the Mission begin to pay more attention to enhancing Christianity in China, and by 1900 the number of Chinese Orthodox converts grew to 1,000 in Peking, with small groups of converts on the periphery. But the nationalist Boxer Rebellion of 1900 led to the massacre, in Peking alone, of 300 Cossack descendants and over 100 native Chinese converts,which dealt a serious blow to the Mission's efforts.

After the rebellion was suppressed the Mission renewed its work, which was markedly intensified with the arrival after the Russian Civil War (1917-1920) of several hundred thousand Russian emigres, including numerous priests and bishops. In Kharbin (Manchuria), with its Russian population of well over 100,000, a seminary and a theological institute were founded, as well as numerous other Russian educational institutions. As a result, the number of Orthodox Manchurians grew to 5,000 by 1940, mostly through mixed marriages. The figures for the rest of China remained very modest. This contrasted markedly with the very rich collection of Chinese translations of Orthodox theological works, not to mention church service books and Scriptures—all done by the Mission's sinologists over two centuries. The missionary failure cannot be explained by persecutions alone. Roman Catholics were persecuted even more severely, and they never enjoyed the imperial privileges of the Russian Mission; and yet there are several million Roman Catholic Chinese. The weakness and spiritual passivity of the Russian Mission ought to be blamed on the Synodal system and on the administration of the Mission. In the final analysis, the imperial bureaucracy was more interested in diplomatic and scholarly work than in the religious aspect. For the first 170 years of its existence, it had to act also as a Russian embassy; hence conversion to Orthodoxy for the Chinese was confused with the notion of changing one's nationality or national allegiance in some way.

The Orthodox Missions in America and Japan

In 1868, after the sale of Alaska to the United States, the Orthodox diocesan center was transferred to San Francisco. A decade or so later, the economic migration from eastern Europe, the Balkans, and the Middle East—with a large proportion of Orthodox migrants—changed the profile and even geography of the Orthodox Church in America. One of the larger groups of immigrants consisted of poor peasants from the Austro-Hungarian Empire, namely the Galicians and the Carpatho-Ruthenians, most of them Uniates (Roman Catholics of the Byzantine Rite and with married clergy). The Latin Rite American bishops, mostly of Irish background, however, refused to recognize married clergy and the Eastern Rite, and ordered Latin-Rite Polish priests to minister to the Galicians and Carpatho-Ruthenians. The Uniates refused to accept this. In 1890, one of their leading priests, Alexis Toth, after obtaining the approval and support of his flock, decided to petition the San Francisco Russian Bishop, Vladimir (Ziorov), to accept him and his parish into Orthodoxy. The acceptance of the Uniates of Minneapolis into the Orthodox Church in 1891 brought two large waves of ex-Uniates into the Orthodox Church in America. The first wave came in the last decade of the nineteenth and the early years of the twentieth centuries, the second in the 1930s. As most of these migrants settled in the industrial and mining belts of the east and mid-west, the center of gravity of the Orthodox Church moved in the same direction. Thus Archbishop Tikhon (the future Russian Patriarch), who ruled the American Missionary Diocese from 1898 to 1907, moved the diocesan center in 1905 from San Francisco to the newly-constructed St Nicholas Cathedral in New York. In 1906, Archbishop Tikhon submitted a memorandum to the Holy Synod in St Petersburg in which he argued that Orthodoxy in America has sufficiently matured to be granted either autocephaly or at least autonomy. He planned, under the ruling Archbishop or Metropolitan of America, to have a titular bishop for each of the major Orthodox ethnic groups—Greek, Serbian, Arabic...—as well as a bishop of Alaska. During his American tenure, the diocese was elevated to an archdiocese. And it was in this archdiocese that the conciliar principle was restored ten years prior to its restoration in its Russian mother-Church. Prior to his departure for Russia in 1907, Archbishop Tikhon called a representative council of clergy and laity in Mayfield, Pennsylvania, at which, among other decisions, a model parish statute was adopted. This parish statute then served as the model for the Russian parish statute adopted at the 1917-18 *Sobor* in Moscow. It could safely be said that the future patriarch of Russia placed the Orthodox Church in America on her feet, giving her a thoroughly Orthodox conciliar structure which helped her to survive the turbulent and trying post-revolutionary years, when all financial aid from Russia was cut off and the Church in America was torn apart by ethnic religious conflicts, as well as by the Renovationist schism, imported from revolutionary Russia and supported in America by pro-Bolsheviks.

Japan

The Japanese Orthodox mission was partly inspired by the Alaskan mission. In 1850, the diocese of the Aleuts and Alaska was raised to the status of an Archdiocese and expanded to include Yakutia and Chukotka in the Siberian northeast. Archbishop Innocent now split his time between Alaska and Yakutia, learning Yakut, creating a Cyrillic-based alphabet, and translating church literature for the Yakuts as he had done for the Alaskan natives. It was in 1860, shortly before his departure for Japan, that Archimandrite Nicholas, the future apostle to Japan, met and consulted with the Archbishop. Following Innocent's example, Nicholas studied the Japanese language, did all the necessary translations into Japanese, preached and served in that language. During his near-fifty years of missionary work in Japan, he succeeded in converting some 30,000 Japanese to Orthodox Christianity. He commanded such love and popularity that the Japanese still call Holy Resurrection cathedral, which he constructed in Tokyo, *Nikolai-do*, i.e., the "House of Nicholas." The Japanese Orthodox Church canonized him in 1970.

There has been criticism, however, that the language St Nicholas of Japan had learned from his samurai teachers was archaic already in his time, and it is now poorly understood by the average Japanese. This may be one of the reasons why the Orthodox Church in Japan ceased to grow after his death. If this criticism is accurate, then this is but a part of the general problem of modern Orthodoxy holding on to archaic languages no longer generally understood, e.g.: Old Greek, Old Slavonic, Old Georgian, etc.

But let us look at the story of Japanese Christianity more closely. Until 1859, Japan was closed to foreigners. The first Christians appeared in Japan in the twelfth century, apparently by way of the Nestorian missions in China. But they left no trace. Southern Japan had a very active Portuguese Roman Catholic mission in the sixteenth century. Conversions were numerous because at that time the Japanese government sought to reduce Buddhist influence; and the conversion of a *samurai* meant the conversion of his whole extended family and all his numerous serfs. In the following century, Japan became isolationist and expelled all missionaries; and in 1639 Christianity was banned. Nevertheless, when foreigners were allowed back into Japan in 1859, remnants of the original Japanese Roman Catholics were found to have survived in the area of Nagasaki, without priests or churches.

In the same year, Russia signed a consular agreement with Japan. The city assigned for the first Russian diplomatic mission was Hakodate, on the northern island of Hokkaido, where there had never been any Christians. Officially, the seventeenth-century death penalty for conversion to Christianity was still in force, and Christian clergy were tolerated only as chaplains of the foreign diplomatic missions. This was the situation when a young Russian hieromonk, Nicholas (Kasatkin), joined the Russian embassy staff in Japan to serve in the embassy chapel. He began a thorough study of the language, culture, history, and traditions of the country. He hired a private tutor, a samurai by the name of Savabe, who had been brought up in Japanese isolationism and hatred of all foreigners and their Christian Church, of which he knew nothing. After meeting the young monk, however, he agreed not only to teach him Japanese, but also to hear from him about Christianity. Later, Savabe became his first convert and the first Japanese Orthodox priest.

In 1869, Nicholas convinced the Synod to permit the opening of an official Orthodox mission in Japan, although this was still in violation of Japanese laws. At first, he was the only missionary, but he had twelve Japanese converts whom he had trained as catechists and who were actively educating interested Japanese in the basics of Christianity and Orthodox doctrine—even in Fr Nicholas' absence, when he had to travel to Russia for several years of medical treatment.

Returning in 1872, Fr Nicholas established the first Orthodox school for the Japanese in Hakodate. By that time, the Japanese central government had become rather tolerant of the Christians, but the local authorities, making use of the above law, which was still on the books, imprisoned Savabe and eight other catechists in 1872 and released their 120 converts on bail. This was followed by mass arrests of all the other catechists and their converts during Holy Week of that year. Under pressure from the Russian government, the Japanese ordered their release, and, in 1875, the law banning conversion to Christianity under threat of death was abolished.

In 1874, three more priests from Russia came to help Nicholas. An Orthodox school and another mission were opened in the city of Yeddo. In 1875, Savabe and another Japanese catechist were ordained deacons, and the center of the mission was transferred to Tokyo. In 1880, Nicholas was consecrated titular bishop of Revel (presently Tallinn, the capital of Estonia), with his de facto seat in Tokyo. The construction of the Tokyo Cathedral was begun. In 1890, Bishop Nicholas received another assistant, hieromonk Sergii (Stragorodsii), the future Russian patriarch. By that time, the Japanese mission already included several Japanese priests. Sergii, in his book on the Japanese mission, describes Bishop Nicholas' efforts to acculturate the

Orthodox Church by adopting some Japanese traditions, just as Archbishop Innocent had done with Alaskan customs and traditions. On Bishop Nicholas' insistence, Japanese Orthodox priests wore their traditional national costumes, and the Church celebrated the official Japanese state holy days. The seminary established in Tokyo taught Russian only inasmuch as it was necessary for the Japanese clergy to be able to read Russian theological works and to translate them into Japanese. By 1917, at least 100 Japanese Orthodox catechists were engaged in active missionary work.

Although Bishop Nicholas remained in Japan during the Russo-Japanese war and, on his instruction, the Church prayed for victory by the Japanese, conditions became more difficult for the Orthodox Church there after the end of the war. The rate of conversions decreased markedly because of growing anti-Russian sentiments. But the real stagnation in the growth of the Orthodox Church in Japan occurred only after the victory of the Bolsheviks in Russia, and especially in the thirties and during World War II.

Bishop Nicholas, elevated to the rank of metropolitan in 1907, died in 1912. After his elevation, he was assisted by a vicar bishop, Sergii of Kyoto, who was appointed ruling archbishop of Japan after Nicholas' death. Sergii remained faithful to the Moscow Patriarchate, and this greatly worsened his situation in Japan during World War II. According to a 1939 law, Christianity, together with Shintoism and Buddhism, was declared an official religion under state control, and the state demanded that all these religions be headed by Japanese nationals. Under pressure and facing accusations of russophilism, Archbishop Sergii retired in 1940, transferring all the properties of the Russian Mission to the newly-established "Japanese Orthodox Church." The first primate of that Church was a Japanese archpriest, Ioann Ono, whose wife, a daughter of the late archpriest Savabe, agreed to take the veil in a Russian convent in Harbin, Manchuria. In 1941, Ioann Ono was consecrated bishop and metropolitan of Japan, with the monastic name of Nicholas. Both bishops, the Russian Sergii and the Japanese Nicholas, died in 1945.

After the war, the Japanese Church was temporarily administered by the Orthodox Church in America (the Russian Metropolia, as it was then commonly known). The Japanese Orthodox seminary was reopened in 1954. In 1970, after the Orthodox Church in America had received autocephaly from the Moscow Patriarchate, the Church in Japan voted to return under the Moscow Patriarchate as an autonomous or self-ruling local Church.

Currently the Church holds her own but shows signs of only very modest growth, as Japanese society has become overwhelmingly secular and nonreligious. Only some 7.5 percent of men and 13 percent of women acknowledge belief in any kind of God or gods. Christians comprise less than 1 percent of Japan's population, and the Orthodox constitute only one to three percent of this small group. But while being only 1 percent of the Japanese population, Christians constitute a much higher proportion of Japanese religious believers. Thus 3 percent of the University of Tokyo male students and 8.5 percent of the females declared themselves practicing Christians. The sociologist Basabe maintains that contemporary Japanese society is predominantly religiously indifferent, which can probably be explained by the irrelevance of the spiritually primitive Shintoism to the sophistication of the Japanese secular culture, which then reflects negatively on population's attitude to any religion.

The Russian Far East and Korea

Missionary work in the Russian Far East expanded after the sale of Alaska and the creation of the separate Diocese of Kamchatka. During the last three decades of the nineteenth century, over 17,500 natives were brought into the Church. By 1900, the Kamchatka Diocese had twenty-four missionary stations, seventeen priests, seventeen catechists, and twenty-three schools with 500 pupils. In 1899 alone, 626 Kamchatka natives were baptized. In 1900, the seat of the Far Eastern diocese was transferred from Petropavlovsk-Kamchtaskii to Blagoveshchensk, on the Amur River, just opposite the Chinese border; and another diocese was established in Vladivostok. The Diocese of Kamchatka was reorganized as the third diocese in the area on the eve of World War I. Its first bishop, Nestor (Anisimov), emigrated with the White Armies to Manchuria, and later went as a very active and successful missionary to India. After World War II, he returned to the Soviet Union and, after spending some eight years in Stalin's concentration camps, served until his death as the Metropolitan of Kishinev and Moldavia. The Kamchatka Diocese was not restored until 1993, by which time not a single church building remained, and the diocese began by building its first church in Petropavlovsk.

As a result of the 1858 Russo-Chinese peace treaty, Russia gained the Ussuri Region, bordering on China to the west and on North Korea to the south. The population in this area consisted of Koreans, Goldians, Manchurians, and Chinese. The first missionary among them was the tireless St Innocent, who in 1862 moved his diocesan center from Yakutsk, where he had baptized almost the whole Yakut population of 300,000, to Blagoveshchensk. In the Ussuri Region, he baptized some 10,000 Koreans, many of whom moved to Korea at the end of the century. With them began the Orthodox Korean mission, theoretically from 1897, but in practice much later, because the Korean Government took a generally negative view of foreign Christian missions. This was especially the case in regard to their Russian neighbors, as they feared that Russian political penetration into Korea would come on the heels of the religious mission. Only on the eve of the Russo-Japanese War did a zealous Russian archimandrite, Khrizanf (Stsetkovskii) succeed in establishing a permanent mission in Seoul. He built a large Orthodox church, a school, and several other buildings, and began the systematic catechization and conversion of Koreans. The war temporarily halted his work. But in 1906 it was renewed by another missionary, Archimandrite Pavel (Ivanovskii). He translated service books and some Orthodox theological works into Korean, ordained the first Korean priest, Father Ioann Kan, and built several Orthodox churches in provincial towns. In 1912, he was consecrated bishop and continued his missionary work in Korea until his death in 1920. In 1923, Patriarch Tikhon attached the Korean Mission to the Japanese Diocese. It is not clear what happened to the 10,000 Orthodox Koreans baptized by St Innocent in the nineteenth century. According to church statistics, there were only 820 Orthodox Koreans in 1934, although the mission, in addition to its Seoul church, continued to run a school in the city and six missionary stations in the countryside. The Seoul church was destroyed during the Korean War in the 1950s. The mission has since been renewed and a new church was built by the Ecumenical Patriarchate, in which jurisdiction it remains to this day. There are currently over 1,000 Korean converts in the Seoul parish, plus additional members in several provincial missionary stations.

Missions in the Caucasus and the Middle East

After the voluntary annexation of Georgia[2] and in the course of the military conquest of the remaining parts of the Caucasus, it was discovered that during the centuries of Muslim aggression and repression of Christianity, several tribes which had formerly been part of the ancient Christian Kingdom of Georgia had fallen away, some into Islam and some into their pre-Christian, tribal pagan cults. Among the largest of these tribes were the Ossetians and the Abkhazians. Russian missionaries started a program of voluntary re-

---

2 The last Georgian king willed his country to the Russian tsar, but the Russians simply annexed the country to the empire between 1801-1805.

Christianization. By 1860, some 100,000 people returned to Christianity. The progress of Christianity among the Caucasian mountain people was one of the causes for the fanatical Muslim rebellion, or "Holy War" led by Shamil, head of the secret militant order of *miurids*. Lasting some twenty-five years, the rebellion was finally suppressed by Russian forces in 1859.[3] After the end of the war, conversions to Christianity continued at the rate of some 8,000 per annum for the first ten years, decreasing thereafter to several hundred a year.

Massive pilgrimages to the Holy Land from Russia led to the formation of the Imperial Palestinian Society in 1882, which contributed significantly to the Orthodox revival in the Middle East, where the ancient Patriarchates of Jerusalem and Antioch, totally impoverished during centuries of repression by Arab and Ottoman Muslim overlords, were unable to hold their own in the face of Roman-Catholic proselytism financed by the Vatican. In 1840, for example, the Orthodox constituted 90 percent of all Christians in Palestine; by 1880 their proportion declined to 67 percent, while the number of Roman Catholics grew from 3,000 to 13,000. Another difficulty was created by the fact that, whereas the vast majority of the laity and parish priests were Arabs, the patriarchs were all Greeks. It was under direct Russian pressure that, in 1899, an Arab, Meletius, assumed the patriarchal throne of Antioch for the first time since the Middle Ages. The Imperial Society provided scholarships for Arab men to attend Russian theological schools and created a network of elementary and secondary Russo-Arabic Christian schools in Syria and Palestine. There were 101 such schools by 1906, with 5,750 male and 4,700 female students.

The last pre-revolutionary missionary achievement of the Russian Orthodox Church was the creation, in 1898, of a mission among the Nestorian Christians in Persia, which resulted in the conversion to Orthodoxy of 50,000 Nestorians of the Urmian Diocese. Despite her isolation from the rest of Christendom after the final confirmation of Nestorius' excommunication by the Council of Chalcedon (451 AD), the Nestorian Church remained very active, spreading its missions by the tenth century throughout Central Asia, with a flourishing metropolitanate in Samarkand, as well as to India, China, Mongolia, and even Japan, as we saw above. Faced with the militant offensive of Islam in the Middle East, Central Asia, Afghanistan, and India, and with

---

3 Shamil was captured, enrolled into the Russian nobility, and granted an estate in central Russia by the tsar. Forbidden ever to return to the Caucasus, he was eventually granted permission to emigrate to Mecca. He died in Medina in 1871. But his sons stayed in Russia and studied in Russian military cadet schools. The best book on the Shamil rebellion is Leo Tolstoy's novel *Hadji-Murat*.

the anti-Christian pagan reaction in China and Japan, the Nestorian Church was reduced to several small eparchies in Persia (modern Iran) and the eastern part of the Ottoman Empire (now Iraq). Some Nestorians joined Rome as another version of "Uniatism." Some remained independent under the name of the "Assyrian" or Aisoran Church.

In 1898, the bishop heading the Urmian Diocese of the Aisoran Church visited St Petersburg, where he rejected Nestorianism and was accepted into the Orthodox Church. On his return to the diocese, he brought a Russian mission, which began opening Orthodox schools to help with the conversion process. The mission was headed by the remarkable Archimandrite Kirill (the future Metropolitan of Kazan', a martyr of Soviet persecutions). By 1905, there were eighty Orthodox parishes and excellent Orthodox schools in the Urmian diocese. When World War I and the Turkish offensive began, the mission, its schools, and most of the Orthodox flock were evacuated to Russia. The Turks forced the remaining Urmian Orthodox to convert to Islam. Those who refused were murdered. The remaining 100,000 Nestorian Aisorians were expelled by the Turks in 1918 to the inner areas of the Ottoman Empire. Some settled near Baghdad, where about 30,000 are to be found to the present day.

Thus it must be affirmed that the Synodal period in Russian Church history does have considerable missionary and educational achievements to its credit. Nevertheless, the achievements were uneven and the successes, as we have seen, depended in most cases on the charisma, talents, and colossal energy of certain individuals (such as Sts Innocent and Nicholas), while most of the failures were caused by the clumsiness and bureaucratism of the Synodal system and excessive interference by the state (as in China and Korea, as well as in post-1905 Japan). These systemic defects were even more visible in the Church's contacts with the Christian confessions of the West.

Ecumenical Contacts in the Twentieth Century

In 1871, a group of Roman Catholic clergy and theologians, rejecting the newly-formulated doctrine on papal infallibility, broke with Rome and established the so-called "Old Catholic" Church. In contrast to the rather vague theology of the Anglicans, the Old Catholics had a much clearer and theologically more orthodox profile once they had rejected the papacy. But Orthodox theologians never achieved any consensus on the Old Catholics. Some theologians, such as the priests Ianyshev and Osinin, and the lay theologians Kireiev and Bolotov (one of the most authoritative Orthodox theologians of the time), were in favor of immediate intercommunion with the Old Catholics, as a faith which had fully preserved apostolic succession and a basically orthodox theology. All that was necessary for their reunification with the Orthodox Church, they argued, was a declaration by the Synod. As to the *filioque*, Professor Bolotov argued that it could be retained in the Old Catholic Church merely as a theologoumenon, i.e., as a private, non-binding opinion. In addition, in Switzerland and the Netherlands the Old Catholics had excluded the *filioque* from their Creed, while the Germans and Austrians retained it in parentheses. The more conservative theologians, represented by such outstanding figures as Alexii Maltsev, a chaplain at the Russian Embassy in Berlin, and Bishop Sergii (Stragorodskii), argued that, since the Old Catholics had been within the Roman Church at the time of the 1054 schism, they were a part of the legacy of the Roman Schism and could therefore be received into Orthodoxy only by officially accepting the complete contemporary theological system of the Orthodox Church. Thus the Old Catholic issue remained unresolved.

Contacts with the Anglicans were once again renewed shortly before World War I. In 1912, an Association of Friends of the Anglican Church was formed in Russia, chaired by Archbishop Evlogii (Georgievskii) of Volynia, the future head of the West European Russian Exarchate of the Ecumenical Patriarchate. The parallel organization in England time was The Anglican and Eastern-Orthodox Churches Union, which had an American branch, organized in 1908. In 1914, the Union was merged with the Eastern Church Association to form The Anglican and Eastern Churches Association. Not much happened in those years other than mutual visits and the parallel English and Russian publications in 1912 of F. W. Puller's *The Continuity of the Church of England*, "an impressive vindication of the Catholic claims of the Anglican Communion," in the words of Florovsky, who then adds that on "the Filioque ... there was in principle no disagreement between the two Churches." But the war interrupted further contacts. Nevertheless, the Great Moscow Sobor, in its resolution on ecumenism adopted just before its forced dissolution on September 20, 1918, declared that it "authorizes the Sacred Synod to organize a Permanent Commission with departments in Russia and abroad for the further study of Old Catholic and Anglican obstacles in the way of union, and for the furtherance ...of the speedy attainment of the final aim."

Orthodox caution on the Anglican issue was caused by their discovery in the course of the mutual discussions that there was no unity in the Anglican

Communion on some fundamental doctrinal questions. Answering the request of Ecumenical Patriarch Joachim III in 1902, who was seeking the views of local Orthodox Churches regarding Anglicanism, the Russian Synod pointed to the lack of unity among Anglicans on the issue of amalgamation with the Orthodox Church. A part of the Anglican Church, the Synod continued, is saturated with Calvinism and rejects the Orthodox doctrine of the Church. The union must be with the whole Church, not just with a part. The Orthodox Church, conversely, did not agree on the question of the validity of Anglican orders. Professor V. A. Sokolov of the Moscow Theological Academy, in his doctoral dissertation, argued in favor of the apostolic succession of the Anglican clergy; he was supported by Professor Afanasii Bulgakov[4] of the Kiev Academy. But the Russian Church eventually decided to laicise all Anglicans on their acceptance into Orthodoxy. Professor Andrutsos of the Athens Theological Faculty, agreeing with the Russians that the Anglican understanding of orders is too ambiguous from the Orthodox point of view, nevertheless allowed the acceptance of individual Anglican clergymen into Orthodoxy without laicization, by *oikonomia*. Fr Florovsky points out that this was the first application of the term to ecumenical relations.

The problem of the conversion of clergy arose from certain precedents. In the early 1860s, a French Roman Catholic theologian, Abbot Guettée, joined the Orthodox Church. He was soon followed by a German Roman Catholic priest, Josef Overbeck, a professor of the Bonn University's theological faculty. In 1865, Overbeck moved to Britain, joined the Russian Embassy parish, and began to propose the creation of an Orthodox Church of the Western Rite. Around 1870, he submitted a draft of such a liturgy based on the Latin mass, but with additions from the Mozarabic liturgy, an ancient Western Rite that presumably survived in those parts of Spain which had been under prolonged Moorish occupation. The draft was approved in principle by Fr Popov and by the Synod in St Petersburg. The final decision on the issue was put aside because of the dialogue with the Old Catholics which, it was hoped, would result in an Old Catholic Western Rite Orthodoxy. Overbeck's project, however, was approved by the Ecumenical Patriarchate in 1882; but it was rejected by the Church of Greece, and in 1884 it was rejected by the Russian Synod as well, on the advice of the new Russian Embassy chaplain, Eugene Smirnov. This rejection was at least partly a result of pressure from the Church of England, which argued that a western Rite Orthodoxy would be

---

4 He was the father of the famous novelist and playwright Mikhail Bulgakov.

an uncanonical intrusion into the territory of the Anglican Church, on a par with similar uncanonical acts by the Roman Church. That the Anglican Church was unhappy about the conversions was amply demonstrated in the case of Father Timothy Hartley, who had converted in Constantinople through re-baptism in 1856 and started an English Orthodox community in London. But then, bowing to direct Anglican pressure, the Ecumenical Patriarch forbade Hartley to proselytize under the pretext that this was undermining efforts to-wards Church union. This led Hartley to transfer to the Russian Church.

The belief in an Orthodox-Anglican union was dying hard. Even the con-temporary Metropolitan of Sourozh, Anthony (Bloom) of London, until a decade or two ago, accepted converts from Anglicanism very reluctantly, be-lieving that one day the whole Anglican Church would become a Western branch of Orthodoxy. Only after having become convinced that the Anglican Church has tread along the false road of modernism, that she has abdicated the role of a firm spiritual and moral leader of her flock, Metropolitan An-thony has become more open to proselytism.

Overprocurator Dimitri Tolstoy and His Time

The great reforms of Alexander II, it must be said, had little effect on the Church. Like Golitsyn under Alexander I, the despotic Dimitri Tolstoy was both Synod overprocurator and Minister of Education. The only difference was that the two departments were not amalgamated. Tolstoy simply held two separate portfolios; but as Minister of Education he was also a member of the Committee of Ministers, to which overprocurators did not belong. Thus his power over the Church was greater than that of all his predecessors, except Golitsyn. As Minister of Education, he was an extreme conservative who froze and even curtailed the liberal educational reforms of Golovnin, his predecessor. And later, as Minister of the Interior, he was remembered as an extreme reac-tionary. But in Church affairs, he was a radical, in fact almost a revolutionary. He particularly disliked monastics, and therefore also bishops—probably be-cause he sensed in them a spirit of opposition to his aggressive secularism and against state control of the Church. Because of his dislike of the bishops, he car-ried out several reforms favoring the "white" clergy and protected priests who criticized bishops—including, for example, the priest Belliustin, author of the anti-episcopal and anti-monastic *Description of the Clergy in Rural Russia*.

Tolstoy broadened the parish clergy's participation in the administration of local church affairs, simplified the procedure for resigning from clergy ranks, and removed the traumatic consequences that haunted former priests in their subsequent secular life. Tolstoy expanded the network of parochial schools and raised the academic standards of the seminaries, restoring the seminarian's automatic right to continue his education in secular universities. But his motives were as remote from political liberalism as they could be. Although an atheist or, at best, an agnostic, Tolstoy feared the dissemination of atheism, which he considered to be forerunner of revolutions. By inviting seminarians to study at universities, Tolstoy hoped to strengthen the conservative element in the student body. By strengthening and enlarging the parochial school network, Tolstoy hoped to retard the growth of secular schools run by *zemstvos*,[5] where most of the teachers were radical populists. His attempt to obtain financial support for parochial schools from the *zemstvos'* self-imposed school taxes failed, because members of the *zemstvos* preferred to spend those taxes on their own rather than on parochial schools. Tolstoy's expansion of the prerogatives of the parish clergy was a part of his struggle against the bishops whom, as an aristocrat, he disliked. He did not mind peasant-like parish priests, but could not bear to see peasants' sons as princes of the Church. His handling of the Synod was crude, condescending and despotic. He appointed Synod commissions to draft ecclesiastical school reforms, but then canceled them when their proposals differed from his ideas, though their plans were wiser than his. For instance, the first such commission proposed to turn the seminaries into *ecclesiastical* liberal arts colleges,[6] with a somewhat greater stress on theology than in the regular *gimnazii*. According to this plan, the schools would continue to serve predominantly the children of clergy, but entailing no obligation for them to pursue further theological studies upon graduation. These schools, according to the proposal, would be under the Ministry of Education, with the local bishop serving simply as a guardian of the school. Those intending to train for the priesthood would continue their education at theological institutes for four additional years. These theological institutes would be open both to seminarians and to secular gimnazii graduates who passed exams in basic theology. Similarly, seminary graduates could continue their studies in secular universities.

---

5 This was the name of the elected local governments introduced by Alexander II.

6 The term was *gimnazii*, i.e., high schools, but their programs, as well as those of the regular seminaries, were much more advanced and sophisticated that what is found in contemporary American secondary schools. In sophistication and knowledge, they were much closer to a BA from a good liberal arts college.

Tolstoy rejected the proposal, dissolved the commission, and, with no explanation, enacted his reform of 1869, which retained the old seminaries, slightly expanding their theological subjects, especially in their three senior years. Seminary graduates could then enroll at a university without problems; and a young man from a non-clergy family could study at a seminary. But the reform did not provide for the secular school graduate who felt a calling to the priesthood. The institutes proposed by the Church commission, however, would have solved that problem and would have effectively ended the isolation of the clergy estate from the rest of society.

One positive byproduct of Tolstoy's reform was the appearance of annual diocesan clergy congresses, which became necessary because of the need to raise additional funds to finance the increased cost of the reformed ecclesiastical schools. These congresses helped to identify the more prosperous parishes which could contribute more generously. This led to an expansion of the ecclesiastical school network, particularly for girls, as well as to an increase in teachers' salaries, and subsequently improved both the quality of life and education for the students.

Tolstoy's expectations of a conservative body of seminarians were not met. In fact, seminarians proved to be more radical than regular university students and contributed to even greater student radicalization. Another side effect of seminarians' entering secular universities was a marked drop in educated candidates for ordination. Finally, as a result of the opening of seminaries to young people from outside the clergy estate and the availability of stipends and tuition-free education, young people with no intention to become priests enrolled at the seminaries in large numbers, overtaxing the very limited Church budget. Consequently, in 1879, Tolstoy implemented a counter-reform. He ended the automatic availability of university education to seminarians, and restricted the right of entry to the seminaries for children of secular parents. Seminarians who sought to enroll at a university now had to pass very strenuous entrance exams; while candidates from non-clergy families could enroll at the seminaries only after submitting a written pledge of their intent to be ordained upon graduation. This element of compulsion had a strongly negative effect on the moral atmosphere of the seminaries, as we can see, for example, in Metropolitan Evlogii's (Georgievskii) memoirs about his years as rector of a seminary in Russia around the year 1900.

He writes how saddened he felt at the obligatory, communal prayers, because he knew and could easily detect that, for a majority of the students, the prayers were just a formality, because they were either atheists or very superficial believers who had no intention ever to become priests. Their fathers, poor rural priests in most cases, simply lacked the money to pay for their education at a secular school. If they had the choice, writes Evlogii, most of them would not be there, and their places would have been taken by those children from secular families who loved God and wanted to become priests. The atmosphere in the seminaries would have been much healthier. In Evlogii's opinion, the seminarians' rebelliousness and ugly alcoholism was bred precisely by their spiritual frustration at having to put on a false show of piety. Evlogii explains the roots of the seminarians' sociopolitical radicalism by citing his own childhood. Like most seminarians, he was born into a rural clergy family, poor but with many children. His father began with a genuine priestly vocation. In his sermons, he criticized the village usurers and called his flock to charity and clean, moral living. But as his numerous children grew and had to be sent to a city for education, he was obliged to appeal for help to these same usurers (*kulaki*) for financial help. He had to stop the sermons of old, was forced to invite these rich peasants to his home and offer them hospitality, to flatter them. The children felt ashamed because of their father's behavior; while Christian upbringing had made them very sensitive to social injustice. Evlogii concludes that a young person brought up in such conditions, having absorbed the Christian concepts of justice and morals but lacking a deep faith in God which would exclude the use of force and terror, easily becomes a revolutionary. This is why a majority of the radical and revolutionary intelligentsia of the nineteenth century were former seminarians or ex-seminarians, and in most cases came from clergy families.

It was concern over seminary radicalism that caused so many reforms and counter-reforms of the theological schools during the last six pre-revolutionary decades. The reforms were begun by Dimitri Tolstoy and continued by his most sinister and reactionary successor, Konstantin Pobedonostsev, whose reactionism, however, differed greatly from that of Tolstoy. Tolstoy was an activist who tried to stem the revolution by finding new ways to impose conservatism—for instance, he supported religious education in order to produce a better educated clergy, so that it could influence society. He supported religious periodicals and religious discussion circles. Thus, with his blessing, a Society of Lovers of Spiritual Enlightenment was established in 1863. It held regular meetings, organized public lectures and debates, which were the published in the society's serial, *Readings* (*Chteniia*).

Pobedonostsev and His Time

In contrast to Tolstoy, Konstantin Pobedonostsev tried to prevent the revolution he felt was coming by trying to put Russian society, the Church and the whole empire on hold. Tolstoy lacked all appreciation of the Church per se and closed over 2,000 of the poorest parishes, which depended on subsidies for their survival, as if Church were a profit-making business. He was convinced that by closing them he improved the economic well-being of the Church, failing to realize that it is often precisely the poorest parishes, those which are not properly supported by the local population, that are most needed in a missionary sense, to evangelize the people and bring them to the Church. Pobedonostsev was a church-going, religious believer, and, in contrast to Tolstoy, he built and opened thousands of new churches during his tenure as overprocurator (1880-1905). He feared theological sophistication of any kind. Preferring priests with undergraduate seminary education, he reduced enrollment at the four graduate theological academies, introduced very difficult entrance exams for seminary graduates, and practically closed the academies' doors to graduates of secular schools. He also closed the above Society of Lovers of Spiritual Enlightenment and its *Readings*. In the apt words of Florovsky, Pobedonostsev distrusted the intellect because it harbors doubts. He favored the instinctive faith of the common people and disliked theology and theologians. He valued only the "unsophisticated pastors of a naive flock." He favored general literacy of the common people, but only of a very basic kind. The rural parochial school, which he fostered most actively, was to be tangential, leading nowhere. By no means must these schools be the first step towards any further education. To satisfy the curiosity aroused by this simple education, and at the same time to cap it at that level, he published huge quantities of primitive, pious literature for peasants.

He was leery of the religious revival that began in the early twentieth century among the formerly Marxist and radical intellectuals, the so-called "God-seeking" movement. Under much pressure from the secular public as well as from the clergy, in 1901 he reluctantly permitted the famous St Petersburg Religio-Philosophic meetings, which were chaired by the brilliant young rector of the St Petersburg Theological Academy, Bishop Sergii (Stragorodskii), the future patriarch. The proceedings of the meetings were published in the society's philosophical journal, *The New Way* (*Novyi put'*), and drew much public attention and discussion—all this Pobedonostsev loathed, and two years later he ordered the society and its meetings closed.

He also tried to eradicate Dimitri Tolstoy's reforms, even in their truncated 1879 version. But the rectors of all the theological academies except the Kievan, which was the most conservative, protested so energetically that, in his 1884 counter-reform, Pobedonostsev was able to make only minor changes. He sought to abolish the diocesan assemblies, but most bishops, and even the Synod, defended these most vehemently, seeing in them the beginnings of the renewal of *sobornost'* (conciliarity or catholicity). In practice, assembly discussions were not limited to financial matters alone. Diocesan and parish problems were raised and often solved, and the bishop became more directly acquainted with his diocesan clergy, with their strengths and weaknesses. Further, the assemblies fostered clergy solidarity, which became an effective foil against episcopal despotism and arbitrary rule, from which parish priests had suffered a great deal. Under pressure from all sides, Pobedonostsev failed to ban the assemblies altogether, but eliminated the stipulation that they meet annually; this enabled the most despotic bishops to resume their arbitrary rule by indefinitely delaying the convocation of diocesan assemblies. Failing to eradicate the professorial corporations in the seminaries and academies, with their right to elect administrators and teachers (introduced by Tolstoy), Pobedonostsev placed the process under the supervision of the Synod, i.e., of the overprocurator, which was granted the right to veto the corporations' appointments.

Not everything, however, was negative in the reform of 1884. For one, the theological program in the seminaries was expanded, while the classics, ancient Greek and some purely secular subjects, were reduced. Some of these non-theological subjects were made optional, thus giving the student some say in shaping his program. However, Pobedonostsev further isolated the clergy from the society around them by reducing general culture courses, i.e., elements that could be shared by both cultures. In this way, therefore, he pursued his goal of freezing the process of cultural integration.

Pobedonostsev succeeded in his pre-1905 struggle against the current partly because his position in the bureaucratic, tsarist establishment was unprecedentedly solid. Not only did he hold the overprocuratorship longer than anyone in the history of the Synod, not only was he the chief educator of both Alexander III and Nicholas II, but he was also the first overprocurator to be appointed a member of the Council of Ministers *ex officio*, rather than by combining the overprocuratorship with a ministerial portfolio, as had been the case with his two predecessors. He set the precedent, and after him all the overprocurators until the abolition of the office in 1917 were members of the Council of Ministers. And yet, even he could not stop the process of liberalization that was occurring in society. Failing to achieve his goal in society at large, he focused on the Church and the clergy alone. He turned both into a static anachronism, fatally marginalizing the Church at the very time when the intelligentsia was searching for religious truth, when society was destabilized, when the need for an enlightened and authoritative clergy was greater than ever. The best educated priests and most bishops were unhappy with the reformed theological schools. Academically, the schools were of a very high caliber. But their concern was with the moral climate in the theological schools, as reflected in the 1905 bishops' responses to the questionnaire on the need for Church reforms. In these responses, published in three huge folio volumes plus a volume of addenda, the bishops criticized the seminaries for their failure to prepare students properly for ministry. They saw too much routine, brutality, and bureaucratism in seminary life and in student-teacher relations. The seminaries, in the bishops' words, had become cradles and hot houses of revolution, anarchism, and nihilism. Some bishops, including Archbishop Antonii (Khrapovitskii) of Volynia, proposed to eliminate all existing seminaries and to replace them with new pastoral schools, which would be established in rural monasteries, as far from the morally corrupt and atheistic cities as possible. Theological schools, they insisted, should be open to all young people willing to serve God, no matter what their social background. They should cease being schools of the clergy estate. The emphasis in those schools should be on worship, asceticism, and active love.

This section could be concluded with the late Professor Nicholas Zernov's comparison of the Church of the Synodal era with the Russian double-headed eagle: one head, in his words, represented the Church bureaucracy with the Synod, the other stood for the dedicated parish priests and the faithful laity.

Old Ritualists in the Last Decades of the Russian Empire

The end of serfdom in 1861 resulted, at least statistically, in an increase in the number of Old Ritualists. As serfs, peasants had been registered as members of the parish in whose jurisdiction was the estate to which the given serf community belonged. Now that the peasants were free, they could choose to join an Old Ritualist community. Thus the real increase in the number of Old Ritualists was probably more modest than the figures suggested. In previous counts, many Old Ritualists had simply appeared as members of the State Church. However, the Old Ritualists attracted new converts as well, especially among peasants, who preferred a Church which had retained the *sobornal* tradition of elected clergy, of periodic councils of clergy and laity, and where the laity participated directly in the life and governance of the parishes. In contrast, the State Church of the post-Petrine era was administered entirely from above, and the laity, particularly in the lower classes, had no say in the choice of parish priests, who were simply appointed by the diocesan bishop. Reacting to the revelation of such large numbers of Old Ritualists, the Government issued decrees in 1864 and 1874 granting them the right to register their marriages and baptisms at state offices. These acts de facto recognized the legal status of the Old Ritualists.

Conflicts and schisms, however, were developing among the Old Ritualists. Old Ritualist peasants remained mostly steadfast in their isolation from ordinary Orthodox Christians, treating them almost as "Antichrists" and refusing to send their children to state schools or to read any books except those written either by their own or prior to the Great Schism. Their urban co-religionists, however—chiefly craftsmen and merchants—were speedily being assimilated by the secular culture. That process began as early as the 1840s and gathered momentum in the1860s. These city-dwellers, especially the Old Ritualist industrial magnates, began to send their children to the best schools and even universities, began to wear fashionable European-style clothes, attended theaters and balls, collected secular art and financed artists, musicians, composers. Most famous among such patrons and connoisseurs were the Morozovs, Mamontovs, Tretiakovs, Shchukins, and many others. It was out of that milieu of enlightened Old Ritualists that the *Circular Epistle* of the Belokrinitskoe Accord appeared in 1862. Addressed to all Old Ritualist communities, it rejected the Priestless doctrine, that there was no more Orthodox clergy in the world and that the Antichrist reigned over the post-Great Schism era. The *Epistle* recognized the Nikonians as genuine Orthodox Christians, appealed to the Old Ritualists to associate with them as co-religionists and proposed a complete reconciliation with the official Orthodox Church, criticizing the latter only for persecuting the Old Ritualists.

The *Epistle* caused great commotion in Old Ritualist circles and led to a split within the *Belokrinitskoe Accord* into *circularists* and *dissenters*. Many circularists, including one of the *Epistle's* authors, Bishop Onutril, two other old ritualist bishops and several scores of priests, joined the *edinoverie* branch of the official Orthodox Church. The dissenters were now destined to intellectual petrification; their education was limited to the level of literate peasants and their home-bred preachers. Although most of the merchants and entrepreneurs remained Old Ritualists—65 percent of all Russian merchants and industrialists were Old Ritualists on the eve of World War I—their most enlightened representatives intermarried with the gentry and the intelligentsia, integrated in the national culture, in many cases joining *edinoverie*, and lost their influence on the rural Old Ritualist masses.

Although there was no active persecution of the Old Ritualists under Alexander II, and his attitude to them was much more tolerant than his father's, he did not abolish his father's anti-Old Ritualist decrees, nor did he re-open the Old Ritualist sketes and chapels, whose altars had been sealed by Nicholas I. Moreover, the altars of the *Rogozhskoe* Cemetery churches in Moscow, the main shrine of the Belokrinitskoe Accord, had already been sealed under Alexander II, in 1856. Thus Alexander III's return to an actively repressive policy against the Old Ritualists was not a revolutionary reversal. However, Pobedonostsev understood that continuing the oppression could be painful. The new legislation on the "schismatics" issued in 1883 permitted the Old Ritualists to receive passports, which made them legally equal to all other subjects of the Empire, to own businesses in their own name, to trade, to hire workers and employees, to own icon painting shops and to hire iconographers. Moreover, they received the right to hold their religious services and to bury the dead according to their traditions, as long as the burials did not become public demonstrations. The same legislation banned Old Ritualist processions outside their church yard, the singing of the Old Ritualist hymns in the streets, and any form of public procession with icons and religious banners. They were at last granted the right to unseal their altars, but on condition that, in each individual case, permission was granted by the local state authorities and that there would be no external signs on the church buildings indicating their religious character. These rights did not extend to the Old Ritualist monasteries and sketes which had been sealed since 1853. That ban was revoked only under Nicholas II, by his *Ukaz* of April 17, 1905.

The reign of Nicholas II, however, began with the last repressive measures against the Old Ritualists of the tsarist era, issued in 1900. The new decree required the Old Ritualist clergy to pledge that they would not use their clerical titles or perform public religious services. Those refusing to give a written pledge were exiled to distant areas of the Empire under police surveillance.

Among those exiled was Archbishop Ioann (Kartushin), the head of the Belokrinitskoe Archdiocese of Russia, along with several of his diocesan bishops. Other clergy continued to circulate in the underground. These last tsarist repressions were likely triggered by the census of 1897, which registered 2,143,340 Old Ritualists in the Empire. Russian scholars, however, consider that the real figure was at least double the official one. On the one hand, many Old Ritualists preferred to conceal their religious affiliation; and on the other, the census takers likely presented an artificially lower figure because of government pressure to conceal such a large presence of dissenters. The Government was obviously aware that the real figure was much higher; hence its concern and the subsequent repressive legislation.

The *Ukaz* of April 17,1905, which appeared after numerous petitions to the Tsar signed by tens of thousands of Old Believers, including numerous leading millionaire-industrialists, at last legitimized the Old Ritualists under their proper name, instead of their former official designation as "schismatics." They were granted the right to build churches and prayer houses, as well as to establish new parishes. Their rights were further expanded under the *Ukaz* on Religious Tolerance, issued on October 17, 1906, after Pobedonostev's retirement, and by laws on religious tolerance passed by the Duma in 1913. The above *Ukaz* and the laws granted state recognition to Old Ritualist clergy. Even priestless lay preachers were recognized as ministers of religion. All Old Ritualist accords received the right to build churches, to open sketes and monasteries, as well as schools, both general and theological. The only right not given the Old Ritualists, as was the case for all non-Orthodox faiths to the last day of the Empire, was the right to proselytize.

The Romanov dynasty paid a very high price for its persecutions of the Old Ritualists. By its very nature, the old Ritualist phenomenon was conservative, deeply patriotic, and traditionalist—the very stuff of which monarchies are made. Thus the policies of repression and persecution deprived the monarchy in Russia of its potentially most reliable base of support and turned a force of national stability into an antagonized and destabilizing agent. Members of such leading Old Ritualist, industrialist families as the Morozovs, Riabushinskiis, Guchkovs either participated in plots against Nicholas II or subsidized revolutionary parties (including the Bolsheviks). Even more fatal was the fact that the persecutions radicalized the lower masses of Old Ritualists, and that the radicalization was not only political but also religious, giving birth to numerous extremist and radical sects with rebellious moods and even actions against lords and tsars. Their fanatical radicalism and anar-chistic rejection of the state undoubtedly influenced the mood of the lower classes in general, and thus had a direct impact on the revolutionary events of the twentieth century and on the destructive behavior of the masses during the Russian revolutions and the Civil War.

The God-Seekers Movement and Its Sources

The outside world and the secular intelligentsia mistook the unattractive state-Church officialdom for the real Church. Nineteenth-century positiv-ism, however, with its *a priori* negative attitude towards anything that could not be experimentally demonstrated, was losing its intellectual grip. The su-perficiality and the moral dead-end of materialistic socialism also failed to sat-isfy truly questing minds. Undoubtedly, this frustration with materialism and positivism contributed to the great creativity of the arts of the Russian "Silver Age." The unfulfilled quest for spiritual food expressed itself in a revival of poetry after the realistic prose of the previous half-century, as well as in un-precedented achievements in drama, ballet, opera, instrumental music, and painting, the latter inspired by the rediscovery of the icon and the beauty of medieval Russian church architecture.

This new path, however, was blazed first by the early Slavophiles, Dosto-evsky and Vladimir Soloviev. Through the Optina elders and Patristic writ-ings, the Slavophiles found their way to the Church, not to the official, Synodical Church, which they treated as a temporary aberration, but to the ideal Church of the Fathers. But the twentieth-century Russian intelligentsia, with its openness to the West, could not "digest" the Slavophile point of view completely, with its categorical anti-westernism. Dostoevsky and Soloviev acted as "middle men," as it were, delivering the Slavophile Orthodox ideal to the twentieth-century Russian intellectuals. Dostoevsky's tortuous return to the Church from Fourierist socialism, paid for by years of hard labor in the company of common criminals, witnessing the common folk's mercy towards them as "the unfortunate ones," so brilliantly reflected in his novels, opened to the Russian intelligentsia a new vision of the unfathomed spiritual wealth of Christianity. His nativism (*pochvennichestvo*) proved to be much broader and universal in its appeal, more attractive to the traditional populist intelli-gentsia, than the nationalist isolationism of the early Slavophiles.

His younger contemporary, Vladimir Soloviev, travelled a similar jour-ney, though purely on the intellectual plane—from socialist leftist

Hegelianism, through liberalism and a critique of Slavophilism in which he had been raised, to the Church, though with an ecumenical, inter-faith leaning, thus offering a new interpretation of the Slavophile ideas of unity-in-diversity (*vseiedinstvo*). He made Orthodoxy "respectable" in the eyes of the secular intelligentsia by his decision, unprecedented at the time, to enroll at the Moscow Theological Academy after graduating from the university, and by his lifelong philosophic *apologia* of Christianity, and in particular of Orthodoxy as the theologically unblemished carrier of patristic Christianity, and finally by his *apologia* of Dostoevsky, branded by nineteenth-century populist critics as a reactionary obscurantist. Soloviev thus brought the God-seeking intelligentsia along the path leading to the Church, and not the least by his tolerance towards western Christianity. He justified the papacy as historically best adapted to disseminate Christianity across the globe. In Lutheranism, on the other hand, he saw freedom and an emphasis on the intellect, which were also God's gifts.

According to Florovsky, the intelligentsia began to shed the extreme forms of positivism and nihilism in the late 1870s, although most of them continued to consider themselves atheists. He points to expressions of unconscious religiousness, such as the habitual asceticism of many Russian populists. Some, for instance, gave pledges to abstain from all sexual relations and from other carnal sins. A majority of those who went "among the people" in the 1870s carried a New Testament in their backpacks and read it, even though they saw Christ primarily as a social revolutionary. Nevertheless, some unbaptized populists, mostly Jews, converted to Orthodox Christianity towards the end of the century, after having encountered the religion of the peasants. Others were attracted by Russian sectarianism—usually various branches of priestless Old Ritualism. A certain Mal'kov, whose preaching of non-resistance to evil had influenced Leo Tolstoy, formed his own sect of Godmen, took his followers to the United States, where he established a commune. After its failure, he returned to Russia and to Orthodoxy.

Sergei Bulgakov called those ascetic, sentimental popular socialists, "atheistic monks." Nicholas Berdiaev and Peter Struve wrote that it was necessary for Russian radicals to pass through the school of Marxism in order to return to God. The encounter with Marxism had a sobering effect on those Russian socialists who were able to reflect and who were intellectually honest. The reason for this lies in the fact that, in contrast with earlier brands of socialism, Marxism demanded intellectual discipline, perseverance, and a serious study of philosophy and history. And those who did abide by these Marxist requirements soon discovered inconsistencies, as well as the moral and intellectual dead-end of materialism. They saw that the moral issues raised by Marxism could not be solved through materialism or the Marxist class-determined ethics.

Soloviev's pioneering critique of Marxism was very influential. He argued that the ethical questions raised by Marxism are simply mechanistic borrowings from Christianity. Marx's protest against the exploitation of man by man makes no sense in terms of class ethics, with its rejection of universal human moral principles. If man is but a part of matter, then exploiting him is no different from the exploiting of a lathe. If only class ethics exist, then there are no criteria for placing the interests of one class above those of another. Thus, if the bourgeoisie is in power, then from that power class' point of view there is nothing morally wrong with oppressing other classes, as long as it serves the interests of the bourgeoisie. Hence, argued Soloviev, the notions of injustice, exploitation, and alienation are Christian notions *per se*, which can be solved only within the framework of Christian ethics.

Such a critical analysis of Marxism led the most perceptive members of the Russian intelligentsia to the so-called "idealistic" philosophy and to the search for God, bringing many of them to the bosom of the Church. That movement, known as the "Russian Religio-Philosophic Renaissance," was associated with such great names as: Sergei Bulgakov, who began as a Marxist economist and ended up as a priest, one of the twentieth century's greatest religious philosophers and a co-founder and dean of the St Serge Orthodox Theological Institute in Paris; Peter B. Struve, likewise a Marxist economist and author of the first Russian communist social-democratic manifesto of 1898, who later became a noted Christian thinker; Semen Frank, who moved from Marxism to become perhaps Russia's greatest Christian social philosopher; Paul Florensky, professor and priest, theologian, physicist, astronomer and musicologist, murdered by the Bolsheviks in a concentration camp. The list could be expanded to include Nicholas Lossky, Nicholas Berdiaev, and many others.

All of them were inspired by the Orthodox Church in her pure and uncompromised form, as taught by the Church Fathers, and not by the official Synodal Church, to which Dostoevsky referred as being in a state of paralysis. The voices of such notable public figures as the above, however, made the movement toward church reform and renewal louder. Perhaps for the first time since the suppression of the Church by Peter the Great, the voice of the

Church received support from an influential sector of the public opinion, and with its help the struggle for *sobornost'* gathered momentum at the beginning of in the twentieth century, leading to pre-conciliar conferences and eventually to the Great Sobor of 1917-18.

FOR FURTHER READING

Basabe, Fernando M., *Japanese Religious Attitudes* (Maryknoll, NY: Orbis Books, 1972).

Bazil, John, "Konstantin Petrovich Pobedonostsev: an Argument for a Russian State Church," *Church History* 64, No. 1 (1995) 44-61.

Belliustin, I.S., *Description of Clergy in Rural Russia*. Translated with an interpretive essay by Gregory L. Freeze (Ithaca: Cornell U. Press, 1985).

Blagorazumnov, N., *K voprosu o vozrozhdenii pravoslavnogo prikhoda* (Moscow, 1904).

Bolshakoff, Serge, *Russian Nonconformity* (see ch. 7).

Byrnes, R.F., Pobedonostsev: *His Life and Thought* (Bloomington, IN: University Press, 1968).

Copleston, Frederick C., *Russian Religious Philosophy* (University of Notre Dame Press, 1988).

Edi James, James Scanlon, Mary-Barbara Zeldin, eds., *Russian Philosophy, An Anthology*, 3 vols (Chicago: Quadrangle Books, 1965).

Florovsky, Georges, *Aspects of Church History*, vol. 4 in *the Collected works of Georges Florovsky* (Belmont, MA: Nordland, 1975).

_____, Puti russkogo bogosloviia (Paris: YMCA Press, 1988).

Frank, S.L., ed., *Iz istorii russkoi filosofskoi mysli kontsa XIX i nachala XX veka. Antologiia* (Washington, D.C.: Inter-Language Literary Asssociates, 1965).

Hale, C.R., *Russian Missions in China and Japan* (Willits, CA: Eastern Orthodox Books, 1875, rep.: 1975).

Kuznetsov, N.D., *Tserkov', dukhovenstvo i obshchestvo* (Moscow, 1905).

Lossky, N. O., *A History of Russian Philosophy* (New York, 1951).

Milovidov, V.F., *Staroobriadchestvo v proshlom i nastoiashchem* (Moscow: "Mysl'," 1969).

Nichols, L. and T. Stavrou, eds., *Russian Orthodoxy under the Old Regime* (Minneapolis: University of Minnesota Press, 1978).

Papkov, A.A., *Nachalo vozrozhdeniia tserkovno-prikhodskoi zhizni v Rossii* (Moscow, 1900).

_____, *Tserkovno-obshchestvennye voprosy v epokhu Tsariaosvoboditelia* (1855-1870) (St Petersburg, 1902).

Petrov, V. *Rossiiskaia dukhovnaia missiia v Kitae* (Washington, D.C., 1968).

Pleyer, V., *Das russische Altglaubigertum* (Munich: O. Sagner, 1961).

Putnam, G.F., *Russian Alternatives to Marxism: Christian Socialism and Idealistic Liberalism in Twentieth-Century Russia* (Knoxville, TN, 1977).

Raeff, Marc, ed., *Russian Intellectual History. An Anthology* (New Jersey: Humanities Press, 1988).

Runkevich, S.G., *Russkaia Tserkov' v XIX veke* (St Petersburg, 1901).

Schmemann, A., *Historical Road of Eastern Orthodoxy* (Crestwood, NY: St Vladimir's Seminary Press, 1977).

_____, ed., *Ultimate Questions: an Anthology of Modern Russian Religious Thought* (New York, 1965).

Sergii, arkhimandrit, *Na Dal'nem vostoke: pis'ma iaponskogo missionera* (Arzamas: Dobrokhotov Publishers, 1897).

Smolitsch, I., *Geschichte der russischen Kirche*, 1700-1917, 3 vols (Leiden, 1959-61)

Soloviev, V.S., *Sochineniia v dvukh tomakh* (Moscow, 1988).

Zernov, N., *The Russian Religious Renaissance in the 20th Century* (London, 1963).

_____, *The Russians and Their Church* (London: SPCK, 1978).

Zenkovsky, V.V., *Russian Thinkers and Europe* (Ann Arbor, MI, 1953).

CHAPTER 9

THE EARLY TWENTIETH CENTURY: THE STRUGGLE FOR THE FREEDOM OF THE CHURCH

An imperial manifesto of December 12, 1904, declared that there would soon be a law on religious tolerance. The Metropolitan of St Petersburg Antonii (Vadkovskii) reacted to the Manifesto with a memorandum warning the Tsar that such a law would place the Orthodox Church into an underprivileged position: other religions, free of government control, would enjoy freedom; while the Orthodox Church, as the state religion and remaining under government's control, would continue to be constrained in her actions. His memorandum therefore asked the Tsar for permission to convoke a conference of Orthodox clergy and laity, but *without state officials*, in order to devise a system of autonomy for the Church that would free her from "direct state or political functions." It further proposed that the parish be granted the status of an autonomous person-in-law, that clergy be given the right to participate in the local self-government *zemstva*, that several places be provided in the State Council for representatives of the episcopate, who would thus receive the right to address the Council of Ministers directly.

This memorandum led to the convocation by Sergei Witte, Chairman of the Council of Ministers, of a consultation on Church matters, to which Bishop Sergii (Stragorodskii) and several theology professors were invited. The Consultation produced the so-called "Witte's First Memorandum" on Church reform, authored predominantly by Bishop Sergii (rector of the St Petersburg Theological Academy at the time). It categorically condemned the Synodal-overprocuratorial system and called for the immediate convocation of a local council of clergy and laity to renew the Church by freeing her from state control.

The aging Pobedonostsev protested that these issues ought to be discussed by the Synod, rather than by state ministers. He must have been absolutely sure of the Synod's loyalty, for he did not even bother to attend the session discussing Church reforms. To his great surprise, the Synod proposed to the Tsar an even more radical solution than Witte's consultation had: the Synod called for the immediate convocation of a local council and the election of a patriarch. Nicholas II at first agreed, but his old mentor, Pobedonostsev, convinced the Tsar to retract his permission. Pobedonostsev then sent questionnaires on the matter of Church reform to all the diocesan bishops of the Russian Church in the hope, no doubt, that the provincial bishops would be more conservative than the Synod. On the first point the overprocurator succeeded, and the Tsar's final word to the Synod was that, though he agreed in principle with the idea of holding a council, it would have to be postponed until social peace had been fully secured. As to the bishops' views on reform, here the results were so radical that Pobedonostsev decided to retire. He died a year later.

Published in three large folio volumes, plus a volume of addenda, the bishops' responses were a clarion call for major reforms, including: the restoration of the patriarchate; regular *sobors*; the elimination of the overpocuratorial system; the autonomy of the Church from the state and independence from the state bureaucracy; decentralization of Church structure through the creation of autonomous metropolitan districts; lifelong tenure for bishops in the dioceses for which they had been consecrated; the restoration of the autonomous, self-ruling parish; more active participation by the Church in society; a change to a liturgical language to bring it closer to spoken Russian, so as to make the church services more comprehensible to the average parishioner. Numerous bishops requested the restoration of the old tradition of electing parish priests by the parish.

One of the supporters of this principle was Archbishop Tikhon (Bellavin, the future Patriarch), although he stated that this reform could not be implemented immediately and uniformly, as it required appropriate preparation of both clergy and laity. He was more categorical in proposing to cut out or abbreviate repetitive litanies, to eliminate some unimportant parts of the liturgy, and to russify the Church Slavonic. He had no objection to abbreviating or simplifying the fasts. As head of the missionary North American Diocese—located in a pluralist society where in addition, many local Orthodox traditions existed side by side and were creating obstacles to Orthodox unity—the Archbishop suggested that the hoped-for All-Russian local council be followed by a Pan-Orthodox Council, which would reduce the differences among local traditions, so as to convince the outside world that there was indeed one Orthodox Church ready to welcome new converts into her bosom. Archbishop Tikhon also wanted to lift the anathemas against the Old Ritualists, and he stressed the need for a theological clarification on the issue of Western clergy, particularly the Anglican. Finally, he favored clergy participation in central and local legislative bodies in order to Christianize politics.

The most controversial issue was the proposed make-up of the future local *sobor*: would the council consist of bishops alone, or bishops with other clergy, or bishops, clergy and laity? And if so, should the parish clergy and the laity have voting rights, or only consultative ones? On these issues, the respondents split in the following way: six bishops, including Antonii (Khrapovitskii), the future head of the émigré Karlovci Synod, favored a council of bishops, where priests and laity could be present only as observers, perhaps with a consultative voice, but without voting rights; twenty-three bishops, including Antonii (Vadkovskii) of St Petersburg, Tikhon (Bellavin) of America, and Sergii (Stragorodskii) supported active participation of clergy and laity. The third volume of the Responses, summing up the episcopal attitudes on the *sobor*'s configuration, indicates that a majority of bishops favored granting decisive voting rights only to bishops and their representatives. It points out, however, that some bishops, including Sergii of Finland (Stragorodskii), referring to the precedents of the Ecumenical and local Russian *sobor*s, indicate that bishops often took with them or even sent in their place monks, parish priests, or even lay persons as representatives with full voting rights. As to those who favored full participation with voting rights for parish clergy and laity, the volume names six bishops, including Antonii of St Petersburg, Sergii of Finland, Evlogii of Kholm (the future head of the émigré West European Diocese). Archbishop Tikhon also favored this, as indicated by his establishment of a system of mixed councils in America ten years prior to the Great Moscow *Sobor*. Although the volume names Archbishop Sergii as one of the six, his position was in fact half-way between those of the two Antoniis. He wrote that ideally the episcopate represents the whole Church by a mandate and authority of love from the clergy and the laity, and therefore its decisions do not need any additional representation to be binding on the Church. With the bureaucratic Russian system of bishops' appointments, he continues, the latter command neither love nor authority. Therefore, in order that the decisions of the forthcoming council have sufficient authority to unify and strengthen, rather than split the Church, it is imperative that representatives of the lower clergy and the laity be elected to the *sobor* with full voting rights. Sergii proposed a two-chamber *sobor*: the assembly of the whole house, where all issues on the agenda are discussed and voted on; and a chamber of bishops, where the decisions are reviewed from the doctrinal perspective, after which they are either ratified by the bishops or sent back to the whole assembly with comments and/or corrections. This principle was in fact adopted by the Great Moscow Sobor of 1917-18.

The Radicalism of the Clergy and the Reaction

Roughly at the same time, a "Union of Church Renovation" was born in St Petersburg out of two memoranda on Church reforms submitted by a "Group of Thirty-two St Petersburg Priests" to Metropolitan Antonii in 1905. These, along with numerous articles and further studies emanating from individual members of the "Group of Thirty-Two" and their sympathizers, were collected in a single book under the title *Toward a Church Council,* and published in 1906. Their demands included the following: the abolition of all decorations and awards in the Church; the participation of parish clergy and laity in Church administration, to purge the Church of clericalism; the electoral principle to prevail at all levels of the clergy; the separation of Church from state; the development of a social Christianity—the participation of the Church in all spheres of social life as well as in the struggle for social justice.

This was a period in which Christian socialism was rather widespread among clergy of all ranks. Thus Archimandrite Mikhail (Semenov), a professor at the St Petersburg Theological Academy, even published a *Program of Christian Socialism.* Thus the relative radicalism of the "Renovationists" shocked nobody, although a few churchmen, particularly the extreme rightist Antonii (Khrapovitskii) of Volynia, attacked them, mainly for their anti-monastic stance. To be sure, the focus of their attack was not monasticism, but the monastic monopoly over the episcopate. A well-known lay theologian, Nikolai Aksakov, in an article commissioned by the "Thirty-Two," pointed to the married episcopate of the early Church. Further, basing himself strictly on documentary evidence, he pointed out that the reluctance to appoint monastics as bishops in the early Church sprang from the Church's view of monasticism as a loftier form of service than the episcopate; hence the episcopal consecration of a monk was for him a step down. Aksakov argued that the monastic calling is that of contemplation and prayer, while a bishop has to be a politician, an administrator, a compromiser, a diplomat, who has to function in the turmoil of national life. He wrote that a monk could be called to episcopal service at a time when a holy elder was needed to calm human passions and conquer evil. But the problem with Russian bishops, he continued, is that in most cases they are monks in name only, having accepted tonsure in their seminary days only to enhance their career prospects. This attack on "academic monasticism" and the call for "white" (married) bishops was the only thing that distinguished the "Thirty-Two" from some of the more radical suggestions in the bishops' Responses. The very fact that

Metropolitan Antonii accepted the memoranda as a proposal for the future Sobor's agenda and encouraged authors to continue to work on them indicates that the ideas were not treated as heretical.

The radicalism of the clergy came as a shock to the tsarist government of the Duma era. All six priests elected to the First Duma joined the leftist and centrist Duma factions; while the two elected bishops joined rightist factions. Of the eleven priests elected to the Second Duma, four joined the social-revolutionaries, three, the left-liberal "Kadets"; the remaining four and the two bishops (Platon, later of America, and Evlogii) spread among the liberal-conservative Octoberists and the rightist factions. In 1907, under pressure from the Government and its right-wing members, the Synod forbade clergy-deputies to support socialist factions in the Duma, under threat of laicization. Those who persisted, including the popular pamphleteer Father Gregory Petrov, were indeed defrocked (though they were later reinstated by the 1917-18 Sobor). After this, only loyal clergy (or at least those outwardly so) were eligible for election to the Duma. In 1912, the Government attempted to create a clergy party in the forthcoming Fourth Duma. Archbishop Evlogii received a personal visit from Sabler, the overprocurator of the Synod, who suggested this to the Archbishop. Evlogii categorically refused, stating that such a party would create an unhealthy clericalism and would cause a tragic split between the clergy and the laity. After Evlogii's refusal, the Synod advised him to withdraw his electoral candidacy. He complied. Yet no clerical party was formed. Forty-six members of the clergy, however, were elected to the Fourth Duma, and only six of them joined the moderate centrists, all the others being to the right of center. This artificial selectivity did not save the Church from internal tensions and schisms after the collapse of tsarism.

The Struggle for the Sobor

As the first revolution subsided, Nicholas II permitted a pre-Sobor consultation to convene. This came just after the publication of the final text of the April 1905 Decree on Religious Tolerance, which—as Metropolitan Antonii had prophesied—placed the state-controlled Orthodox Church in a very disadvantageous situation. The position of the Church was further aggravated by the fact that, ever since the introduction of the Duma, the State Church depended not only on the Tsar (who, after all, was a practicing Orthodox), but also on the Duma, which included representatives of all religions, as well as many members, especially among its leaders, who were either atheists or totally indifferent to religious matters. In fact, the First Duma was led by the left-liberal Kadets with a party program that contained not a word about the Church. When this was mentioned to its leader, Professor Paul Miliukov, he replied: "Oh, we have completely forgotten about the Church!" The Kadets were most representative of the liberal Russian intelligentsia of the time, hence Milukov's remark tells a tale...

The proceedings of the Pre-Sobor Consultation, in which leading Russian theologians participated, as well as other authoritative public figures active in the Church, were published in four large volumes. The Consultation addressed the question of setting the Church apart from state institutions in twelve clear points, and defined her prerogatives in relation to those of the State. The proposal to restore the patriarchate met with some opposition, especially from the white clergy, who feared a further escalation of episcopal despotism; but those supporting the patriarchate prevailed by a fourteen-to-eight majority. The draft document recognized the tsar as the only state authority with whom the leadership of the Church would have to coordinate decisions of national significance, such as the convocation of a *sobor,* the election of the patriarch, etc. As permanent liaison between himself and the Church leadership, the tsar could appoint a procurator (but by no means an overprocurator), who would not be permitted to participate in meetings of the administrative organs of the Church. His main prerogatives would be to verify that decisions by the Church leadership did not contradict state law. If they did, he was to inform both the Church leadership and the tsar. As a liaison officer between Church and State, the procurator would have the right to attend meetings of the highest government organs without being a member of the Council of Ministers; in this way the procurators would not have to be changed with every cabinet reshuffle. The twelfth point of the draft defined the head of state's relations with the Church: "The Emperor, being of the Orthodox faith, is the supreme patron of the Orthodox Church and the guardian of her well-being."

The Tsar's response, in 1907, was disappointingly negative: no *sobor* for the time being. Hoping that he would agree to convene the council for the Tercentennial of the Romanov dynasty in 1913, the Synod called a Pre-Sobor Conference in 1912. Its proceedings were published in five volumes, but its appeal to the Tsar to call the *sobor* again fell on deaf ears. It seems that the Tsar, deprived of full political control over his country with the establishment of the Duma but remaining faithful to the Byzantine doctrine of divine right, now saw his role as temporal head of the Church as his last line of communication with and mystical leadership over his nation. The Tsar's great statesman, Peter Stolypin, had also opposed the restoration of the patriarchate, though chiefly for practical, political reasons of control and use by the State of such a "handy" institution. But Stolypin was now dead, killed by a revolutionary terrorist in 1911. The Tsar's relations with him, moreover, had become very cool for some time before the murder. So the Tsar's reluctance must have been his own, probably stimulated by his mystically inclined wife.

Thus the reforms of 1905-06, which radically changed the face of the Russian state, seemed once again to have passed the Church by. Yet the mood in the Church was now different: there was now a general expectation that things would soon change, that the old structure would not last long. The existence of the Duma and the clergy's participation in it also influenced the very atmosphere and life of the Church.

Multiple religio-philosophical discussion groups and circles again appeared. Many of them appealed to the Church and to Christians in general to take an active part in public life. Brotherhoods and sisterhoods appeared in parishes, especially in the factory and port city districts, engaging in charity and moral and religious education. There was a strong revival of preaching, which continued after the revolution until the physical liquidation of the most popular clergy by the Bolsheviks in the 20s and 30s.

The growing flow of intelligentsia returning to the Church brought some of them into clergy ranks. Among these could be mentioned Paul Florensky, Prince and later Bishop, Andrei Ukhtomskii, Professor and then priest S. Bulgakov, Father Valentin Sventsitskii, a former leftist publicist, and many others. The publication in 1909 of the *Landmarks* (or *Signposts*) collection, was a manifesto of sorts, composed by Orthodox neophytes—all former Marxists. Its seven authors—some of them, such as S. Frank, S. Bulgakov, N. Berdiaev, P. Struve, were among Russia's greatest twentieth century thinkers—submitted the Russian radical intelligentsia to scathing criticism for its rootless and irresponsible radicalism. They argued that the radicals' Westernist points of reference and nihilism were incomprehensible to the almost instinctively religious common people. The propaganda of the radical intelligentsia, they wrote, was capable only of depriving common Russians of the positive values by which they had lived, unleashing the worst destructive instincts and bringing down the whole state structure, burying under its rubble the culture and the very intelligentsia which had brought the catastrophe to fruition. The *Landmarks* appealed to the intelligentsia to put an end to its suicidal activities and instead to work constructively within the system for a better future.

To a considerable extent, thanks to the return of some leading members of the intelligentsia to the Church, the latter was freed from the artificial ghetto into which she had been pushed by the government, by the Synodal bureaucracy, and by the revolutionary radicals. The socially influential neophytes made it impossible for the government to continue gagging the Church. These changes were, however, merely "atmospheric." The legal position of the Church remained the same as before 1906. Why is it then that the Church could not achieve the same freedom obtained by secular society? To begin with, the educated liberal public, being on the whole quite distant from the life of the Church and failing to appreciate the complexity of her problems, did not include the Church in its struggle for freedom, erroneously identifying the Church with the state apparatus. Secondly, the most radical elements did not want a vibrant and authoritative Church, for she would become an influential barrier against violent revolution. Third, the Church herself, her faithful members, brought up on the principles of church-state symphony, could not consider using the methods of struggle employed by secular society, let alone terrorism.

Nevertheless, despite the post-1907 right-wing Synodal policies, which became even more reactionary after the death of Metropolitan Antonii of St Petersburg in 1912, Church leaders never abandoned the hope to distance the Church from the State, to free her from responsibility for the policies of the state, which caused increasingly negative attitudes in the general population, particularly in connection to an unpopular war. In 1916, at the eleventh hour, as it were, the clergy members of the Duma presented their last address to the Tsar, requesting the immediate convocation of a *sobor* and the election of a patriarch. The address stressed the need for an immediate restoration of conciliarity in the administration of the Church in order to put an end to the Government's use of the Orthodox clergy as a tool of the Government's internal policy. This final appeal, as well, was not heeded.

The Revolution and the Church

Statistically, the Church on the eve of the revolutions of 1917 appeared to be a mighty institution. In 1914, there were officially 117 million Orthodox Christians in the Empire served by 48,000 parish churches and some 25,000 chapels, with about 51,000 parish clergy of all ranks divided into sixty-seven dioceses headed by 130 bishops. The Church ran 35,000 parochial schools, several hundred junior ecclesiastical high schools, fifty-eight seminaries and four graduate theological academies. But beneath these positive externals, parish and diocesan reports spoke of declining faith, especially in industrial and mining districts, such as the Urals, for instance, and of the success of revolutionary propaganda among industrial workers under the slogan: "There is no God, down with the Church!" Some reports said that most seminarians, university students, and high-school pupils supported the revolutionaries, while the clergy was too lazy to teach in parochial schools, which were therefore in decline, giving way to secular primary schools "in which the teachers engage in revolutionary propaganda."

There is little wonder then that at the 1917-18 Sobor one delegate declared: "We say we have 110 million Orthodox Christians; but what if [in reality] we have as few as 10 million!" And indeed, according to reports from military chaplains, the proportion of soldiers receiving communion fell from nearly 100 percent in 1916, when it had been obligatory, to less than 10 percent in 1917, after the Provisional Government made the observance of religious rites voluntary. This came as no surprise to such perceptive officers as General Denikin, a White Army leader, who wrote in his memoirs that the clergy had failed, during World War I, to evoke any deep religious commitment in either soldiers or officers. On one occasion, for instance, no sooner had the soldiers built a makeshift church, than a young officer turned it into a soldiers' bivouac, ordering soldiers to build a latrine in the sanctuary of the church. What amazed Denikin was that "two to three-thousand Russian Orthodox soldiers ...showed complete indifference to...such blasphemy."

On the eve of the Bolshevik coup, the prestige of the Church fell very low for several reasons. First, there was the unpopular war, which appeared to be endless and was unprecedentedly bloody. The brunt of its fury was borne by the peasantry, because industrial workers in war-related industries were often spared military service, while practically all able-bodied peasant males of appropriate age were drafted. At first the war was greeted enthusiastically in the cities by diverse groups: liberals and moderate socialists welcomed the war because Russia was allied with the two chief democracies of Europe, France and Britain, and they thought the war would bring the imminent destruction of autocratic and militaristic Germany and Austria; the Slavophiles and other conservatives, as well as the Church, welcomed it as an act of solidarity with Orthodox Serbia, and saw in it a prospect for liberating Slavs from Austrian domination, as well as of gaining the Straits of Bosphorus and the Dardanelles for Russia. But no one asked the opinion of the peasants, who comprised 80 percent of the population; nor was there any political indoctrination of the peasant-soldiers, who had no reason to hate the Germans. Many of them were familiar with German farming settlements in Russia and knew the Germans as solid, hard-working neighbors. In the countryside, the main supporters of the war were the village priests. As the war dragged on, therefore, anti-war feeling focused on the priests and the Church. These sentiments were fomented by leftist propagandists, often in the persons of local school teachers. A second important irritant was the Rasputin affair. Because of the control Rasputin exercised through the Empress, his opponents among the higher clergy were either retired to monasteries or appointed to far-away dioceses, while the bishops in Petersburg, Moscow, and in several other major cities, as well as the Synod Overprocurator Sabler, were either Rasputin's "appointees" or persons who played up to him. As a result, and again with the help of leftist propaganda, the Church was associated with Rasputin and his scandals.

Consequently, irritation with the whole tsarist establishment reached such proportions, that even the generally conservative clergy deputies in the last Duma joined the "Progressive Bloc," which was plotting to overthrow the Tsar. On the eve of the February (March, according to the Gregorian Calendar) Revolution, even the conservative Synod rejected Overprocurator Raev's plea to issue an appeal to the nation to support the crumbling monarchy. The Synod advised the Tsar's brother, Michael, appointed successor by Nicholas in his abdication manifesto, to refuse the crown. And on March 4/17 the Synod, which included in its membership such conservatives as Metropolitan Antonii (Khrapovitskii), signed a declaration appealing to the nation to give full support to the Provisional Government and to the new democracy. Although the declaration was issued under direct pressure from the Synod's new overprocurator, the signature of such a stubborn and principled person as Antonii must have been more than just a show of political obedience to secular authorities. Shortly before the revolution, he had tried to prevent the consecration of a Rasputinite as bishop. Told that this was the wish of Tsarskoe Selo (the Tsar's suburban residence), he replied: "Oh, on Tsarskoe Selo's whim we will consecrate even a grey gelding!"

As a result of the Tsar's repeated refusals to allow a local council, his abdication decapitated the Church, as he had been the official head of the Church in the Synodal system. Moreover, because this system lacked a proper infrastructure, the Church entered the revolution not only without a temporal head but in a state of chaos. The Church had no internal structure: parishes were not organized as autonomous primary Church units, and dioceses lacked autonomy. Thus, having irresponsibly abdicated without giving a thought to what was to follow, and how the Church was to function, the Tsar betrayed both his country and his Church.

Such was the inglorious end of the "Constantinian" epoch of the Church-State symphony. Many people, both lay and clergy, however, did not fathom that this was indeed the end of the Constantinian epoch; elements of this incomprehension are reflected in some decisions of the 1917-18 Sobor.

The Sobor, the Church, and the 1917 Revolutions

Although the second millennium of the Russian Church began in 1988, one could make the case that the new millennium actually began with the dramatic changes in 1917-18: technically with the Tsar's abdication and the end of the Constantinian era, essentially with the momentous decisions and reforms initiated by the Sobor.

The Provisional Government, a coalition of liberals and moderate socialists, abolished all privileges based on religion, ethnic identity or class. But it had no intention to impose any structural changes on the religious communities of the country, as such changes were to be left to the communities themselves. As to the Orthodox Church, therefore, the new regime simply replaced the last tsarist overprocurator Raev by Vladimir L'vov, a member of the constitutional-monarchist "Octoberist" Party who later moved to the left and joined the Renovationists in the 1920s. Of rather despotic inclination, L'vov purged the Synod of its old members, retaining only Archbishop Sergii (Stragorodskii). Its new members included: Metropolitan Platon (Rozhdestvenskii) as its chairman,[1] Archbishop Agafangel of Yaroslavl', who was to play a pivotal role in the Church events of the1920s, Bishop Andrei (Prince Ukhtomsky, who would later join the Old Ritualists and die a martyr's death), Bishop Mikhail of Samara, and four parish priests. The inclusion of priests was a "democratic" innovation, although in the eighteenth century the Synod had contained one or two priests.

---

1 A former exarch of Georgia, Platon had also been the Archbishop of the North American Archdiocese (after Tikhon's departure for Russia in 1907). After the end of the Civil War, he returned to the USA and headed the Russian Orthodox Metropolitan District of America and Canada until his death in 1934.

The new Synod forcefully retired twelve Rasputinite bishops and appealed to the Church to conduct popular elections of bishops at diocesan assemblies. The electoral principle proved a success. Thus Tikhon, the future Patriarch, was elected Metropolitan of Moscow; Veniamin, a very popular young bishop, was elected Metropolitan of Petrograd; and Germogen, an uncompromising critic of Rasputin, was elected Archbishop of Tobol'sk. All three later joined the ranks of the new martyrs, Patriarch Tikhon indirectly, the last two directly.

The Synod also adopted a temporary regulation on the autonomous parish as a legal entity and the primary unit of the Church. On May 8, the Synod announced the convocation of a preconciliar committee, which was to begin meeting on June 11/24. The committee was made up as follows: all members of the Synod; seven additional bishops chosen by the college of bishops; eight delegates from the All-Russian Congress of the Clergy and Laity, which was taking place at the time in Moscow; four delegates from theological schools; eight delegates chosen by the councils of the graduate theological academies; two elected monastic delegates; one representative of the Georgian Church; one representative of the *edinovertsy* (see ch. 7); and eighteen appointed by the Synod. By July 10/23, the preparatory work was completed, including the electoral procedures for the forthcoming Sobor. The Committee announced the beginning of the elections and the Sobor's opening day, August 15/28, 1917. Bowing to pressure from the Church, the Provisional Government abolished the Synodal system on August 5/18, replacing it with a governmental Department of Confessions. Anton V. Kartashev, a young theology professor, was named as Russia's first and only Minister of Confessions.[2] The only serious conflict between the Church and the Provisional Government occurred over the nationalization of parochial and other general education schools under the control of the Synod. Otherwise, relations were good. Paradoxically, the Church had to wait for the fall of her "supreme protector," the emperor, and the arrival of a secular republic to obtain freedom from state shackles.

That newly gained freedom, however, also allowed internal tensions in the Church to rise to the surface. The first issue had to do with the Church of Georgia. The abolition of Georgian autocephaly by the Imperial Government in 1811 had already been recognized as unfair by the Pre-Conciliar Conference of 1906. Now the Georgians rebelled, arrested their Russian

2 Later, in the diaspora, he was professor of Church history and Hebrew at the St Sergius Orthodox Theological Institute in Paris.

exarch, Metropolitan Platon, expelled him to Russia, and proclaimed the restoration of the Georgian Patriarchate. The Georgian question was placed on the Sobor's agenda. L'vov cabled to Georgia that the Provisional Government had recognized the autocephaly of her Church in principle, subject to its approval by the Sobor. The Georgians, however, went ahead with the election of their own patriarch and did not bother to send delegates to the Sobor.

Society, including the faithful of the Orthodox Church, was seething. The "Group of Thirty-two Priests" resurfaced. To the left of it appeared such groups as: "The Petrograd Union of Progressive Clergy," which called on the clergy to go to the factories and join the workers in their struggle for social justice; "The All-Russian Union of Democratic Orthodox Clergy," which preached Christian socialism and was led by the priest Alexander Vvedenskii, the future leader of the Renovationists. Similar groups appeared in Kiev and other cities.

The Moscow Sobor was the most representative in Russian history. Each of its dioceses (except Georgia) was represented by the diocesan bishop, two clerics, and three laymen elected by diocesan conferences. In addition full voting rights at the Sobor were given to ten vicar-bishops representing the seventy-odd titular bishops, twenty representatives of the monasteries, twenty-six representatives of the military chaplains and of the armed forces, twenty-two representatives of the *edinovertsy* vicariates, twelve representatives of the theological academies, fifteen representatives of the Academy of Sciences and the universities, twenty representatives of the Duma and the State Council. All in all, the Sobor included 564 delegates: eighty bishops, 149 priests, nine deacons, fifteen sextons, and 299 laymen. The Sobor laid the foundations for the life of the Church in totally new conditions. Its principles, agenda, and programs were based on proposals worked out at the various consultations and conferences beginning in 1906, as well as at the above mentioned Moscow Congress of Clergy and Laity, and finalized at the pre-Sobor Conference of 1917. The Sobor's decisions, therefore, were an organic product of the Church, not some sort of a radical outburst, as often claimed by extreme rightists in today's Russia, as well as among right-wing émigré monarchists. The fact is that the implementation of the prerevolutionary *sobor*nal project became possible only with the fall of the monarchy. As Kartashev wrote:

When the 1917 revolution broke out and placed the convocation of the Sobor on the agenda, the Russian Church proved to be up to the challenge, both technically and in principle...

On the one hand, Kartashev continued,

there was elation that the Church had at last achieved freedom after two centuries of shackles, and the long awaited possibility to act had finally arrived. On the other hand, with the Tsar's abdication "the juridical base linking the Church with the state disappeared." The new government was based no longer "on God's mercy," but on "the will of the people."

This, according to Kartashev, was felt immediately, and society began to act, to act from below. The formerly debated question about lay and parish clergy representation at the Sobor ceased to be an issue. Moreover, as we have seen, the Sobor was preceded by numerous assemblies of the lower clergy, which often adopted democratic resolutions and proposals for the Sobor's agenda.

The Sobor, the Patriarch and the Civil War

The main sources of Sobor's agenda were: 1. The pre-*sobor* consultation of 1906 and the pre-*sobor* conference of 1912; 2. The 1917 Moscow congress of 1200 representatives of leftist-populist clergy and laity groups, which proclaimed the abolition of large landed estates, freedom of speech and of religion, but proposed the retention of religious instruction as a part of the school curriculum and, while seeking a distancing of the Orthodox Church from the Government, but not total separation, nevertheless requested a status of "first among equals" for the Orthodox Church and the retention of Church-run schools by the Church; 3. The 1917 pre-*sobor* committee, which finalized the agenda, accepted those resolutions of the above Congress of Democratic Clergy and Laity which related to the status of the Church in society, including its formula of distancing without separation.

The most important act of the Sobor was the restoration of the patriarchate, the election of the first patriarch since 1700, and the restructuring of the whole administrative structure of the Church in connection with the restoration of the patriarchate. At first, a majority of the pre-*sobor* committee, including Metropolitan Sergii, favored a collegial system of Church administration, although without the overprocurator. Opinions shifted in favor of a patriarchate when the threat of Bolshevik victory became obvious. They believed that the leadership of the Church must be personified in order to face an atheistic onslaught. Any unmarried or widowed member of the Sobor was eligible for election, including laymen (many, for example, voted for Samarin, a layman). After several rounds of voting, in the course of which those with smaller numbers of votes were gradually eliminated, the following three candidates remained, in declining order of votes: Metropolitan Antonii (Khrapovitskii), Archbishop Arsenii (Stadnitskii) of Novgorod, and Metropolitan Tikhon (Bellavin) of Moscow. The three names were placed in a container under the Miraculous Icon of Our Lady of Vladimir, an *akathist* was served to the Mother of God, after which a 90-year-old monk, Alexii, pulled out the ballot bearing Tikhon's name. Thus was elected Patriarch Tikhon.

The statutes adopted by the Sobor restored a true conciliarity (*sobornost*) The Church was to be decentralized by being divided into five autonomous metropolitan districts, each covering an extensive area. An archbishop would be at the head of each province, and a bishop in each county, thus making bishops much more accessible to both clergy and laity and bringing them closer to the daily life and needs of individual parishes. The metropolitan districts were to have their local *sobors*, and the archdioceses would hold archdiocesan and diocesan assemblies or conferences. In this system, the patriarch was merely chairman of the Synod and of the Higher Church Council, as well as presiding over *sobors*, with two votes in case of a tie. Sobors of the whole Church were to meet once every three years. Each *sobor* was to elect, for a three-year term, one monk, five parish priests and six lay persons for the Higher Church Council. Three bishops for this Council were to be elected by the Synod, which was itself to consist of thirteen bishops: the patriarch and the metropolitan of Kiev *ex officio*, six bishops elected by the *sobor* for a three-year term, plus five bishops elected by rota by the Synod for one calendar year, one from each of the metropolitan districts. Juridical procedures for a conciliar trial of the patriarch and for other ecclesiastical courts were likewise worked out.

But the main and basic source of conciliarity was to be the autonomous parish, which was to have the status of a legal person (person-in-law), with the right to own real estate, to elect its administration, and even its priest or candidate for the priesthood. All this was found in the model statute adopted at the Sobor and based on the statute of the American Missionary Diocese, adopted during Tikhon's tenure as its head. After long debates, the principle of an elected episcopate was likewise adopted, although with some canonical and disciplinary limitations, leaving the final and decisive word to the metro-politan, the Synod, or the patriarch (depending on the situation).

The following decisions were also made: 1.) That a fraternity of learned monasticism be created, allowing learned monks to form special monastic communities, instead of living outside monasteries—the Sobor forbade monks to live outside monasteries; 2.) That sermons be delivered at every church service, not only at Sunday liturgies, and that the institution of lay preachers be formed for that purpose;[3] 3.) That seminaries and other theo-logical schools be established in monasteries (apparently in the ones with fra-ternities of learned monks).

Unsolved Issues

The Sobor ended on September 7/20, 1918, without completing its work be-cause the Bolsheviks confiscated the Moscow Seminary building in which most of the Sobor delegates resided and where some of the sessions took place. Moreo-ver, Lenin's Decree on the Separation of the Church from the State and of the School from the Church, issued on January 23/February 5, 1918,[4] deprived the Church of all her income-producing enterprises and of her bank accounts; this made it impossible for the Church to finance further Sobor expenses.

The following issues were to be debated at the planned spring 1919 ses-sion of the Sobor, which never took place because of chaos during the Civil War and the material bankruptcy of the Church, caused by the nationaliza-tion of all her properties and bank deposits.

1. The establishment of a Patriarchal Office of Church Art;

2. Rules for the establishment of a Bible Council, attached to the Higher Church Administration;

3. Canonical structures for the Church in Finland;

4. The problem of the Georgian Church;

5. The establishment of the Patriarchal Publishing Department;

6. A statute for an Ecclesiastic Court of Justice;

3 The term used was *blagovestniki*, i.e., messengers of theGood News.

4 In fact, it was issued on 20 January (Julian), but later became known as the Decree of 23 January. Probably that was the date of its physical publication in the mass media.

7. Questions of divorce procedures;

8. Statutes for theological academies and the higher theological schools in general;

9. The issue of the Church calendar: Julian or Gregorian;

10. The issue of extra-mural religious education of the laity;

11. The question of the legal status of the clergy in the Russian state;

12. Educational requirements for ordination;

13. The restoration of the order of deaconesses.

The issue of restoring deaconesses was raised just before the Sobor closed, when Professor Gromoglasov of the Moscow Theological Academy delivered a report on that institution in the Early Church. He explained that deaconesses were equal to male deacons and performed the same functions, including serving at the altar. They were, he pointed out, full members of the lower clergy, but so were singers and church readers. Thus, he argued, the *sobor's* granting women the right to act as church readers, choir directors, and wardens, not to mention the diaconate, means their inclusion in the ranks of clergy. This notion was so revolutionary that the Sobor, inconsistently in Gromoglasov's opinion, allowed women to assume all the above functions except the diaconate. Regarding the issue of deaconesses, the Sobor decided to postpone it to the spring session, obviously because it could be solved only after a decision on what constitutes membership in the clergy—and the inclusion of women in the clergy would certainly arouse a great deal of controversy and debate.

Altogether, the planned future session was supposed to study the reports of twenty-three *sobor* departments, including such subjects as liturgical reforms and the issue of liturgical language.

The Political Posture of the Sobor and the Patriarch

Sensing worse things to come, the Sobor ruled, shortly before ending its sessions that the Patriarch should make a will naming three successors in case he died or was deprived of the possibility to continue in office, and the convocation of a *sobor* to elect a new patriarch was made impossible. The will was to be kept sealed in a safe place. Such an appointment of successors by a bishop violated Orthodox canon law, but it was the only realistic decision under the circumstances. Moreover, of necessity, in contradiction with the conciliar structure of the patriarchate which the Sobor had devised, the Patriarch was authorized to rule the Church autocratically in the event it became impossible to do so collegially.

At least at the beginning, the Sobor apparently did not think the Soviet regime would last. Hence the somewhat unrealistic decisions on the position of the Church in the state, which were authored mainly by such an outstanding mind as Professor Sergei Bulgakov, who was ordained priest by the Patriarch at the end of the Sobor. Bulgakov's report and the subsequent decisions of the Sobor described the Orthodox Church as first among equals and stipulated that the head of state be a member of the Orthodox Church.

As far as the Civil War was concerned, the Sobor and the Patriarch tried their best to maintain political neutrality, recognizing the new Soviet power as the government with which they had to deal. Beginning with the rebellion of the Moscow military cadets, which started November 2/15, 1917, and throughout the Civil War, the Sobor repeatedly appealed to both warring sides to be merciful to the vanquished and to prisoners, and to stop the bloodshed altogether. On November 11/24, the Sobor ordered the Church to give Christian burials to the casualties on both sides. Though deciding to hold a memorial service for the murdered Tsar as a baptized Christian and member of the Church, the Patriarch at the same time categorically refused to transmit his blessings, even in secret, to the White Army and its leaders, who had sent their courier, the Prince Gregory Trubetskoi: the Church cannot bless fratricide, especially when members of her flock are to be found on both sides. In his encyclical of September 25/October 8, 1919, the Patriarch and his Synod declared the civic loyalty of the Church to the Soviet Government. The encyclical categorically forbade the clergy to greet the Whites by ringing church bells or by holding services of thanksgiving. Although pointing out that, since the Church has been separated from the state as an institution, she bears no responsibility for the political choices of her flock or even of her priests as citizens, the Patriarch, nevertheless, stated that "there is no power but that from God" (Rom 13:1) and warned against the pointlessness of the struggle against the new power, for "Nothing will save Russia... until the nation ... is born again spiritually into the new man." That encyclical was issued at the height of the White offensive, when they were less than 200 km. south of Moscow, and their entry into the capital was expected from day to day. Hence, had the Church leadership really adopted an opportunist stance, as was often claimed by official Soviet historians and their imitators in the West (e.g., John Curtiss), it would have issued the above declaration in January 1918, and a pro-White, sycophantic one in the early fall of 1919.

Instead, on January 19/February 1, 1918, the Patriarch issued his so-called "anathema encyclical," which condemned in no uncertain words all those who were shedding the blood of innocents, blaspheming churches, and killing the clergy. He did not mention the Soviet Government by name, but excommunicated all those guilty of these crimes who had been baptized in the Orthodox Church. The encyclical appealed to the faithful to form Christian alliances and brotherhoods to defend the Church, opposing their spiritual strength and faith to the physical power of the persecutors. He advised them to organize church processions to morally strengthen the faithful. In response, in each of the capitals, 60-70,000 people joined "Unions of Believers," which, together with city and regional parish alliances, protected and preserved the disfranchised Church and saved the clergy from starvation. The Bolsheviks had categorized the clergy as a parasitic class (*lishentsy*) and either deprived them of ration cards or provided starvation rations. Similar associations to defend the Church and clergy were formed in most towns. They also provided unarmed bodyguards for the clergy.

The first bishop to be murdered was Metropolitan Vladimir of Kiev. The murderers were a roving group of bolshevized sailors. They raided the Kiev Monastery of the Caves, where he lived, and murdered him on January 26, 1918, almost before the very eyes of the monks. Their hostility to Vladimir was caused by his demonstrative anti-Ukrainianism and his refusal to recognize the validity of all Church institutions established after the 1917 revolutions. Vladimir was only the first. In the year that followed his murder (until January 1919), at least nineteen bishops were murdered, as well as 102 parish priests, 154 deacons, ninety-five monks and nuns. By the end of the Civil War, at least 12,000 members of the laity, several thousand parish priests and monastics, and twenty-eight bishops were martyred for their faith. Among them was Archbishop Germogen of Tobolsk, who had been persecuted by Nicholas II for his staunch opposition to Rasputin—ironically, he was killed for stopping with a church procession in front of the house where members of the Tsar's family were imprisoned, and for making a sign of the cross in the direction of that house.

The Sobor served public requiems for the murdered churchmen and declared the day of Metropolitan Vladimir's murder as the Day of the New

Martyrs (mistakenly designating the 25th rather than the 26th January). But the Sobor and the Patriarch remained aloof from politics and from turning the commemoration of the new martyrs into a political event. Only once did the Patriarch and the Sobor criticize the new regime's official policies. That was the Patriarch's condemnation of the separate peace treaty of Brest-Litovsk in March 1918, which he called a betrayal of national interests. But he was not alone. Almost the entire Bolshevik Central Committee at first refused to accept the treaty; and only after Lenin's threat to resign was it reluctantly accepted.

There was also the Patriarch's letter to Lenin on the occasion of the first anniversary of his taking power, which condemned the regime's unnecessary cruelties in the following terms:

> ...you have divided the whole nation into confrontational camps and forced it into unprecedentedly cruel fratricide. You have replaced Christ's love with hatred...people live in constant fear of house searches, robbery, deportation, arrest, execution...At first you robbed the rich, then under the name of dekulakization you began to rob...hard-working peasants, multiplying paupers;...by ruining vast numbers...of citizens you are destroying the national wealth and bringing the country to ruin. Having tempted...the ignorant people by the promise of easy fortunes, you...have suppressed in them the sense of sin...You promised freedom...but instead you have mercilessly repressed all expressions of the civic as well as the spiritual freedom of mankind. What kind of freedom is it, when one is not allowed to provide oneself with food without special permission?...when no one dares to speak one's mind? Where is the freedom of speech, the freedom of the press, the freedom of the church sermon?...Many daring preachers have paid with their lives for their sermons.

The letter then speaks about the mocking at the faith and the believers, public blasphemy, lies and slander to which the Church has been subjected by the Soviet press; and it concludes thus:

> It is not our business to judge the terrestrial power...We merely address to you...these words of admonition: do celebrate your first anniversary...by the liberation of the prisoners, by ending the bloodletting, violence, plundering, oppression of the faith;...give rest to the nation...from the fratricidal war. Otherwise you will be made to pay for the blood of the righteous...and you "who take the sword will perish by the sword."

This was the Patriarch's letter to Lenin, not an address to the nation, as the former two had been. His third address or encyclical, issued on July 21, 1919, was clearly aimed at all the fighting forces. After once again criticizing the Bolshevik use of hostages and their leaving "mountains of corpses," the encyclical attacks the pogroms against Jews perpetrated on territories controlled by the Whites, and particularly in areas in the hands of the Petliura forces in the Ukraine. In that encyclical, the Patriarch calls the pogroms

> the horror...of genocide...[when] embittered man...transfers to all the blame for the misfortunes suffered at the hands of a few. Orthodox Russia! Do not allow the Devil, the enemy of Christ, to seduce you by the passion for revenge!

In all these addresses, the Patriarch recognizes Soviet power, explicitly or implicitly, as "our government," and merely applies the traditional right of patriarchs to admonish and appeal for mercy and justice.

The Ukrainian Church Issue

As the Ukrainian National Council (*Rada* or UNC) declared the autonomy of the Ukraine within the democratic Russia in the spring of 1917, and full independence after Lenin's coup in Petrograd, two currents appeared within the Ukrainian Church: one favored a self-ruling, autonomous Ukrainian Church within the Moscow Patriarchate, the other sought complete autocephaly. Under the UNC's pressure, a Ukrainian Church Committee (UCC) was formed in the spring of 1917, aiming at the separation of the Ukrainian Church from the Russian. In November 1917, the UCC renamed itself the Ukrainian Ecclesiastical Council (UEC) which, with Patriarch Tikhon's blessing, convoked an All-Ukrainian Church *Sobor* for January 7/20, 1918.

In contrast with Patriarch Tikhon, Metropolitan Vladimir of Kiev adopted a confrontational attitude towards the Ukrainophile church party, refusing to recognize any church organs which had appeared in the Ukraine after the February Revolution. He prophetically declared that he would rather die than recognize the UEC, and he criticized Archbishop Evlogii of Volynia and other bishops for their recognition of the UEC as a competent church organ.

On February 9/22, the *sobor* sessions were temporarily halted when the Bolsheviks entered Kiev. After the occupation of Kiev by Austro-German forces and their installation of Pavlo Skoropadskii as Hetman of the Ukraine (he had declared that Ukraine would be autonomous in federation with Russia), the Ukrainian Sobor resumed on June 7/20. After the murder of Metropolitan Vladimir, the Moscow Sobor appointed and the Kievan diocesan conference elected Antonii (Khrapovitskii) as the new Metropolitan of Kiev, and he now chaired the Sobor. Despite heavy pressure from the pro-autocephalist UEC, the Sobor voted for autonomous status within the Moscow Patriarchate, by a vote of 250 to 80. And on July 9/22, it adopted a Statute to that effect. The Moscow Sobor ratified the Ukrainian Statute at its last session. It also adopted its own statute on relations with the Ukrainian Church fully in accord with the Ukrainian document. Both documents, however, contained contradictions. For instance, on the one had it was stated that the Moscow Patriarch's control over the Ukrainian Church was limited to approving the metropolitan of the Ukraine after his election by a Ukrainian Sobor, and to the role of judge of final appeal over the metropolitan and other bishops on petitions from the Ukrainian episcopate. On the other, there is a stipulation that "All decisions of the All-Russian Sobor and of the Holy Patriarch unconditionally apply to all the dioceses of the Ukraine."

Be that as it may, it is beyond doubt that the Ukrainian Sobor's decisions and the Autonomy Act reflected the absolute majority opinion of the Ukrainians. But, like all totalitarian revolutionaries, the radical national socialist Petliura and his Directory, who took power in Kiev on December 19, 1918, cared little about majority opinions. The new government openly supported the autocephalists, and on January 1, 1919, issued a law on the autocephalous structure of the Orthodox Church in the Ukraine and her independence from Moscow. Metropolitan Antonii and Archbishop Evlogii were arrested and sent to Lvov (Lviv) under the supervision of Metropolitan Andrei Sheptitskyi, head of the Ukrainian Uniate Church there. They were later transferred to a monastic Polish prison in Cracow.

Meanwhile, not one Orthodox bishop in the Ukraine agreed to break with the Moscow Patriarchate. This placed the autocephalists outside the Orthodox hierarchical structure. The Petliurovites were soon ousted by the Bolsheviks, who also recognized and supported the autocephalists, although for other reasons, namely, to break up the unity of the national Church. Leading autocephalists were three archpriests: Vasyl' Lypkivskyi, P. Tarnvaskyi and Nestor Sharayivskyi and a lay preacher, Volodymyr Chekhivskyi. Concerned by the absence of bishops in their camp, they were at first ready to put off the question of autocephaly, provided that the *locum tenens* of the Kievan metropolitanate, Bishop Nazarii, allowed them to establish a parish in Kiev which would use only the Ukrainian language in services. Nazarii rejected that plea, thereby contradicting the decisions of the Moscow Sobor. The autocephalist leaders then turned to the Bolshevik authorities with a plea to obtain St Michael's Cathedral, which was particularly dear to the Ukrainian nationalists because it had been built by Mazepa, the Ukrainian Cossack leader who had rebelled against Peter the Great by joining forces with the Swedes against Russia in 1709. The Soviets agreed. This led Nazarii to take his words back and to permit the Lypkivsky group to read the Scriptures at that cathedral in two languages: Slavonic and Ukrainian. But Lypkivsky hurriedly translated the entire liturgy into Ukrainian. The Bolsheviks gave the autocephalists two more churches: the eleventh-century St Sophia and the eighteenth century St Andrew's Cathedrals. The first-ever liturgy in the Ukrainian language was celebrated in St Sophia Cathedral on July 29, 1919. As this service was conducted without episcopal blessing, this date marks the real beginning of the autocephalist schism.

Less than a month later, Kiev was liberated by the White Armies. This was soon followed by the return of Metropolitan Antonii, recently released from Polish captivity because of Allied pressure. He outlawed the autocephalists but gave the "Little Sophia" church to the Ukrainophile party for services in Ukrainian. In December 1919, the returning Bolsheviks again gave the main St Sophia cathedral to the autocephalists. Bishop Nazarii, once again the Kievan *locum-tenens*, because Metropolitan Antonii evacuated with the White Armies from Russia, banned the whole Ukrainian autocephalist clergy. The autocephalist UEC responded with a statement of May 5, 1920, branding all bishops as "pharisees" and calling Patriarch Tikhon "a prince of this world." Their Statement declared the Ukrainian Church "fully autocephalous," with all services in Ukrainian, a married episcopate, and the right for widowed clergy to re-marry.

The Patriarchal (Autonomous) Church established an Episcopal Council of the Ukraine (ECU) which, on February 21, 1921, declared the whole autocephalous clergy to be defrocked, and excommunicated the laity who had joined them. The autocephalists responded with a resolution issued by a "Committee on the Ukrainization of the Church," which also called itself the "Pre-Conciliar Assembly of the Representatives of the Parishes of the Kievan District." This resolution welcomed the Soviet regime, thanking it for having granted religious freedom, and condemned the bishops of Kiev as "black-hundreders... suspended" from their sees. But realizing that not a single Ukrainian bishop had agreed to act without the Patriarch's blessing, the Committee began a frantic search for a bishop who would agree to participate in the autocephalist *sobor*. They failed to find one, and the first sobor of the autocephalists, which opened on October 14, 1921, consisted only of parish clergy and laity. They laid hands on one another and on their first episcopal candidate, the married priest Lypkivskyi (using also the arm of a saint's relic from the Kievan Caves monastery), proclaiming him the first bishop-metropolitan of the Ukrainian Autocephalous Orthodox Church (UAOC), who would then consecrate additional bishops for the Church, which became known as the "self-consecrators." Having violated the rules of episcopal apostolic succession, that Church failed to achieve recognition by any other Orthodox Church until 1995, when her diaspora branch was accepted into the Ecumenical Patriarchate.

The late Leontii, Bishop of Chile, formerly a monk of the Monastery of the Caves in Kiev and a bishop in the Ukrainian Autonomous Orthodox Church under German occupation, reminisced on the autocephalists' methods of obtaining churches:

> First came the "missionaries," i.e., propagandists. The local authorities would be informed about their arrival by the GPU in advance and were advised to render them secret support. The propagandists would be surrounded by a group of young activists...in many cases members of the Communist Youth League (Komsomol). The chief propagandist would make a speech on the Tsarist regime and on the bishops who did not allow the Ukrainians to pray in their native tongue; then he would praise the Soviet power for granting...religious freedom...The mob is then invited to enact this freedom here and now; whereupon the mob, headed by the propagandist, marches towards the local church. Unless believers rang the church bells and called together an impressive crowd to defend the church,...the mob would expel the priest, should he refuse to join the Autocephaly, from the rectory, often throwing him, with his family and belongings, straight out into the snow, if the attack happened in winter.

But the Soviet regime's flirtation with the UAOC was rather brief. As early as 1922, the GPU, in its secret instructions, decided to shift its support from the autocephalists to the Ukrainian Renovationists. This instruction was made evident in the decision of the 1923 Moscow Renovationist Sobor to grant autocephaly to the Ukrainian Renovationist Church. From then on, short-term arrests of the Lypkivskyite bishops, including Lypkivsky himself, began to occur. Yet, in comparison with the terror unfurled against the "Patriarchists," the treatment of the Lypkivskyites continued to be quite mild, at least until late 1928. Nevertheless, at its peak, reached by the mid-twenties, the UAOC consisted of over 2,000 clergy and some 1,500 parishes—i.e., under 20 percent of the functioning Orthodox parishes in the Ukraine at that time.

With Stalin's attack on "bourgeois nationalism" in 1929, the GPU ordered Lypkivskyi to liquidate his Church. Lypkivskyi complied by convoking a

UAOC *sobor* in 1930 which declared the Autocephalous Church null and void, and advised the priests to continue their parish pastorate independently, without expecting any further directives from the bishops. Thereafter, almost all the bishops of the UAOC perished in Soviet concentration camps or were executed. The only known exceptions were Lypkivskyi himself, who was allowed to live quietly in Kharkov until his natural death, and Bishop Fotii (Topiro), who was consecrated by the Lypkivskyites in 1928, but then joined the Patriarchal Church in 1934 and served as a diocesan bishop into the 1950s. According to archival records, he was never imprisoned; was he a plant?

After its formal abolition, the original Lypkivskyite autocephaly survived only in North America, where a UAOC bishop, Ioann (Teodorovych) was sent in 1924 in response to a petition of local Galician immigrants who had converted from the Uniate to the Orthodox Church and wanted a bishop of a Ukrainian Church. There, Teodorovych assembled a diocese of some 300 churches and chapels in the United States and Canada, served by sixty priests. Her leader, Mstyslav (Skrypnyk), declared patriarch by the renewed UAOC in the Ukraine in 1990, died in 1993. But the diaspora Church he had headed was finally granted canonical status by the Ecumenical Patriarchate in 1995, when she was accepted as a an autonomous metropolitanate within the Patriarchate's jurisdiction. The pretext for that move was that by then all priests ordained by Teodorovych had died, while Mstyslav's ordinations were canonically regular, as he himself had been consecrated by bishops of the canonically valid Polish Orthodox Church.

FOR FURTHER READING

Aivazov, I.G., *Obnovlentsy i starotserkovniki* (Moscow, 1909)

Aksakov, N.P., "Chto govoriat kanony o sostave sobora," *Tserkovnyi golos* (St Petersburg, 1906).

Antonii, Metropolitan (Khrapovitskii), *Khristos Spasitel' i evreiskaia revolutsiia* (Berlin, 1922).

Armstrong, John, *Ukrainian Nationalism* (New York, 1963).

Bogolepov, Alexander, *Church Reforms in Russia, 1905-1918* (New York: Russian Orthodox Church in America, 1966).

_____, "Ot sviateishego sinoda k sviashchennomu soboru," *Sbornik v chest' N.S. Timasheva: Na temy russkie i obshchie* (New York, 1965).

Bulgakov, S., *Intelligentsia i religia* (Moscow, 1908)).

Byrnes, Robert, *Pobedonostsev: His Life and Thought* (see ch. 8)

Cunningham, James, *A Vanquished Hope* (Crestwood, NY: St Vladimir's Seminary Press, 1982).

Curtiss, John, *Church and State in Russia, 1900-1917* (New York: Octagon Books, 1965).

Dublians'ky, A, *Ternystym shliakhom* (London, 1962).

Evlogii, Mitropolit (Georgievskii), *Put' moei zhizni* (Paris: YMCA Press, 1947).

Fotiev, K., *Popytki ukrainskoi tserkovnoi avtokefalii v XX veke* (Munich, n.d.).

Fülop-Miller, René, *Rasputin, the Holy Devil* (New York: Viking, 1929).

Heyer, Friedrich, *Die orthodoxe Kirche in der Ukraine von 1917 bis 1945* (Koln, 1945).

Iz Glubiny (De Profundis). A Miscellany on the Russian Revolution (Moscow, 1967 [Reprint: Paris: YMCA-Press, 1967]).

Kartashev, A.V., "Revolutsiia i sobor 1917-18," *Bogoslovskaia mysl'* (Paris: Institut theologique orthodoxe St Serge, 1942).

K tserkovnomu soboru. Sbornik gruppy peterburgskikh sviashchennikov (St Petersburg, 1906).

Lypkivs'kyi, metrop. Vasyl', *Vidrodzhennia tserkvy v Ukraini* (Toronto, 1959).

Marcynkovsky, V.F., *Zapiski veruiushchego* (Prague, 1929).

Mikhail, arkhimandrit (Semenov) *Svoboda i khristianstvo* (St Petersburg, 1907).

Nichols, R. & Th. Stavrou, eds., *Russian Orthodoxy under the Old Regime* (Minneapolis: U. of Minnesota Press, 1978).

Poltoratsky, N.P., *Russian Religious-Philosophical Thought of the 20th Century* (University of Pittsburgh Press, 1972).

Pospielovsky, D., *The Russian Church under the Soviet Regime* (Crestwood: St Vladimir's Seminary Press, 1984).

_____, *Russkaia Pravoslavnaia Tserkov' v XX veke.* (Moscow: Respublika, 1995).

Robson, Roy R., *Old Believers in Modern Russia* (De Kalb: Northern Illinois University Press, 1995).

Shavelsky, G.I., *Vospominaniia poslednego protopresvitera Russkoi armii i flota*, 2 vv. (New York: The Chekhov Publishing House., 1954).

Schulz, Günther, "Der Beschluss des Konzils der Orthodoxen Kirche in Russland 'Über die Vereinigung der Kirchen' vom 7/20.9, 1918," *Geist und Kirche, Festschrift für Eckhard Lessing* (Frankfurt/M.: Peter Lang, 1995), pp. 249-265.

_____, *Das Landeskonzil der Orthodoxen Kirche in Russland 1917/18-ein unbekanntes Reformpotential* (Göttingen: Vanderkoeck & Ruprecht, 1995).

Simon, Gerhard., *Church, State and Opposition in the USSR* (London, 1974).

_____, *Pobedonostsev und die Kirchenpolitik des Heiligen Sinod, 1880 bis 1905* (Göttingen, 1969).

Smolitsch, I. *Geschichte der russischen Kirche, 1700-1917* (See ch. 8).

Spinka, M., *The Church and the Russian Revolution* (New York, 1927).

Stavrou, Th., ed., *Russia under the Last Tsar* (University of Minnesota Press, 1969).

Sventsitskii, V., *Khristianskoe bratstvo bor'by* (Moscow, 1906).

Sviateishii pravitel'stvuiushchii Sinod. *Otzyvy eparkhial'nykh arkhiereev po voprosu o tserkovnoi reforme*, 3 vols + a volume of addenda (St Petersburg, 1906).

_____, *Zhurnaly i protokoly zasedanii Vysochaishe uchrezhdennogo Predsobornogo prisutstviia*, 4 vols. (St Petersburg, 1906-1907).

_____, *Predsobornoe soveshchanie*, 2 vols. (St Petersburg, 1912-1916).

Trubetskoi, kniaz' G.N., *Krasnaia Rossiia i sviataia Rus'* (Paris, 1931).

Valentinov, A., *Black Book: the Storming of Heavens* (London, 1924).

Valliere, Paul. "The Problem of Liberal Orthodoxy in Russia, 1905," *St Vladimir's Theological Quarterly* 22, 3 (1976).

Vekhi. A Miscellany on the Russian Intelligentsia (Moscow, 1909).

Zenkovsky, V.V., *A History of Russian Philosophy*, 2 vols. (New York, 1953).

Zernov, N., *The Russian Religious Renaissance of the Twentieth Century* (New York: Harper and Row, 1963).

CHAPTER 10

THE CHURCH, THE STATE, AND SCHISMS
1920-1925

The Church and the White Emigration

On November 20, 1920, the Patriarch issued an encyclical permitting local groups of dioceses, should contact with the Patriarchate become impossible, to jointly form temporary autocephalies. On the pretext that on this very date the last ships containing remnants of General Wrangel's White forces had evacuated from Crimea and gone to the vicinity of Constantinople (Istanbul), the émigré church administration, formed in Karlovci (Serbia) in 1921, would claim that Tikhon's encyclical legitimized their existence. This claim to canonicity is very dubious, however, as Patriarch Tikhon could not possibly have meant the establishment of an independent Russian Church structure on the canonical territories of other legitimate autocephalous Churches (in this case Constantinople and the Patriarchates of Serbia, Bulgaria, and Rumania).[1] Canonically, the encyclical could apply only to dioceses on the historical territories of the Russian Patriarchate, including newly independent states on the territories of the former Russian Empire, such as Poland, the Baltic states, and Finland. Moreover, according to canon law, bishops deserting their dioceses and priests leaving their parishes without canonical release are subject to automatic suspension. The Karlovci Church administration, which in 1922 renamed itself the "Episcopal Synod of the Russian Orthodox Church Abroad," also justified its existence on the basis of Canon 39 of the Sixth Ecumenical Council, which allowed the Archbishop of Cyprus to continue in his functions after he escaped to the Galleopontian province. But in that case the bishop had escaped from an invasion with almost his entire flock; here in the Russian case it was the desertion by the clergy of their flocks. The relationship of the bishops and clergy to the army of one million or so, and the civilians accompanying it, who escaped to the shores of Bosphorus, was accidental. Thus Canon 39 is not relevant in this case.

Another claim to legitimacy was the claim to continuity with temporary church administrations that arose on territories occupied by the White

---

1 Patriarch Tikhon strongly respected the canons, as illustrated in his letter to the Ecumenical Patriarch, reproaching him for interference into Russian Church affairs by giving a *tomos* of autonomy to the Russian émigré bishops in Constantinople under the name of "Temporary Higher Russian Émigré Church Administration," without a canonical release by their own patriarchate.

Armies during the Civil War, when regular contacts with the Patriarchate in Moscow were impossible. One such was the *Temporary Higher Church Administration of South Russia*, formed by the Stavropol inter-provincial *sobor* of May 1919, and attended by all locally available former deputies of the Moscow Sobor. This, and similar church administrations in other White-controlled territories, ceased to exist when the Whites evacuated. As long as these administrations existed on Russian soil, no émigré Church group could claim to be the continuation of any of them. The last to cease existence in Russia was the Crimean Church Administration; but no émigré church group could claim to be the continuity of the Crimean Administration, because the archbishop who had headed it did not emigrate.

The Karlovci Church consisted primarily of those members of the clergy who had directly served in the White Army as its chaplains (or even as combatants: several regiments, made up of clergy volunteers, were called "Jesus Regiments") or demonstrated their enthusiasm for the Whites publicly. This included Bishop Veniamin, the chief chaplain of Wrangel's forces in the Crimea. Emotionally, the White emigration bore a grudge against Patriarch Tikhon—the warriors for his refusal to bless their military exploits, the clergy for his ban on their pro-White activities. Much of the future behavior of the so-called "Karlovci Synod" or "Karlovcians" can be explained by this original, even if subconscious, hostility. Metropolitan Antonii (Khrapovitskii), who had gained the greatest number of votes for patriarch at the Moscow Sobor (and lost only in subsequent balloting), and who had been the candidate of the right wing of the Sobor, was among the refugees in Constantinople, among whom the right-wingers constituted a high proportion. Also among the Russian refugee bishops were Metropolitan Platon (Rozhdestvenskii) of Odessa, Archbishop Evlogii (Georgievskii) of Volynia, and the above-mentioned Bishop Veniamin (Fedchenkov)—all of whom would play a crucial role in future émigré Church splits.

As we have already seen, the Karlovcians' later claim of continuity from the Higher Church Administrations was invalid. Nor could Metropolitan Antonii claim any personal continuity, because during the Stavropol Sobor he and Archbishop Evlogii were still in a Polish jail. Released only in August 1919, they arrived in south Russia at the end of the month. Metropolitan Antonii proceeded straight to Kiev, his see; while Evlogii, because the Whites never reached his Volynian Diocese, joined the South Russian Higher Church Administration. With the crushing advance of the Reds, Evlogii left Russia for Serbia in January 1920, at the invitation of the Serbian Government. With the fall of

Kiev to the Reds in December 1919, Antonii fled to the Caucasus. There he functioned as the temporary head of the Ekaterinodar (Krasnodar) Diocese for several weeks, before emigrating to Constantinople.

The idea of founding a higher Church administration for the Russian *diaspora* belonged to Veniamin (Fedchenkov), the very bishop who was later the first to sever his ties with all émigré Church administrations and to remain faithful to the Moscow Patriarchate. But in December 1920, it was he, fresh from Crimea, who headed an émigré delegation to Metropolitan Antonii begging him to petition the Ecumenical Patriarchate for permission to organize a Russian ecclesiastical administration for the Russian diaspora. At first, Antonii replied bluntly and rudely: "Only a hopeless fool can dream of a separate Church administration on the canonical territory of the Ecumenical Patriarchate." Eventually, however, being a very emotional man, he consented to the idea. Two days later, the Ecumenical Patriarchate responded to his and Bishop Veniamin's petition with a *tomos* permitting the organization of an autonomous "Temporary Higher Russian Orthodox Church Administration Abroad" (HROCAA), *under the Patriarchate's omophorion*. The Patriarchate, however, retained all judicial functions over the HROCAA, its clergy and laity, including divorce settlements. This unilateral acceptance of the émigré clergy by the Ecumenical Patriarchate, without a release from the Moscow Patriarchate, was uncanonical, as would be later pointed out by Patriarch Tikhon in his correspondence with Constantinople.

The Monarchists and the Karlovci Church Conference

In 1921, the Serbian Patriarchate invited the Constantinople-based Higher Russian Church Administration Abroad to move to Serbia with residence in Karlovci. The HROCAA accepted this invitation without obtaining a canonical release from the Ecumenical Patriarchate. Out of their extreme hospitality, the Serbian Church leadership also twice violated the canons: when they invited the HROCAA without requesting a canonical release from the Ecumenical Patriarchate; and then by tolerating that group's virtual autocephaly on the canonical territory of their own, Serbian, Patriarchate. But the question of the prerogatives of a foreign church organization on the territory of the Serbian Patriarchate is that Patriarchate's own business. What the Serbs could not do, however, and never did, was to extend the HROCAA's prerogatives beyond the Patriarchate's canonical territory. Nevertheless, the Russian Karlovcian Church group continued to call itself the HROCAA, although permission from the Ecumenical Patriarchate to administer émigré Church affairs could last only so long as it remained under that Patriarchate. In July 1921, ignoring these facts, it adopted a statute affirming that the HROCAA was a part of the Moscow Patriarchate. This action constituted a blatant disregard of canon law and proper order: a self-declared branch of a foreign Church appropriated for itself the prerogatives of a de-facto autocephalous Church on the canonical territory of a legitimate local autocephalous Church, with claims of administrative rights of a geographically almost global character. According to S. Troitsky, the late professor of canon law at the Belgrade Theological Faculty, the Serbian Church tolerated that canonical scandal because of the HROCAA's assurances that it existed "by the approval of the Russian and Ecumenical Patriarchates." The Serbs had such high regard for Metropolitan Antonii and his collaborators, that they did not bother to investigate. But on April 30, 1924, Ecumenical Patriarch Gregory VII stated:

> ...the existence and activities of the Russian Synod [as the "Karlovcians" renamed themselves in 1922] on foreign ecclesiastical territory...cannot have any canonical basis and...[it] ought to disband itself immediately in accordance...with Patriarch Tikhon's order.

That there was no legitimization of the Karlovcians by Patriarch Tikhon can be ascertained from an undated letter (but written no later than April 1922) by Metropolitan Antonii to Archbishop Evlogii of Paris, in which Antonii complained that rumors were spreading "that our HCA and the Karlovci *Sobor*[2] have not been recognized by the Patriarch." He begs Evlogii to use his connections "to obtain a decree from the [Moscow] Patriarchal Synod recognizing the HCA....The Act on...the reconstruction of the HCA in Serbia,...the HCA...has forwarded to His Holiness, Tikhon.... No answer has even been received." In the same letter, Antonii argues that, by confirming Evlogii, a member of the HROCAA, as the head of all Russian Orthodox churches in Western Europe, the Patriarch of Moscow has indirectly recognized the Karlovcian HCA; thus Antonii recognizes that the source of the Karlovcians' legitimacy is Archbishop Evlogii, without whom the HCA, ecclesiastically speaking, could not operate.[3]

2 The émigré Church conference of November-December 1921, which pretentiously renamed itself a *sobor*.

3 This did not prevent the aging Metropolitan, or some secretary writing in his name, to write two years later to the Archbishop of Canterbury that Metropolitan Evlogii was not a representative of Patriarch Tikhon, but simply a bishop subordinate to the Karlovici Synod. The letter conceals Patriarch Tikhon's May 5, 1922 appointment of Evlogii as head of all Russian parishes in Europe and raising him to the title of Metropolitan. (See GARF, F. 6343/1, dd. 269 and 252, 11. 117 and 55-56.)

The only sustainable Karlovcian claim to recognition by Patriarch Tikhon is the Patriarchal Synod's order of March 26/April 8, 1921, confirming Evlogii's appointment as head of all Russian parishes in Western Europe "including...Sofia in Bulgaria and Bucharest," which states that this decision was made "Because of the same [earlier] appointment made by the Higher Russian Church Administration Abroad..." But the HROCAA's appointment was made on April 2/15, 1921, i.e., later than the Moscow confirmation; thus the Moscow Synod's order obviously referred to Evlogii's appointment by the Constantinople-based HROCAA of November 1920 which, as the April 2/15, HROCAA Decree stated, was a mere confirmation of his appointment to that position by the Crimean HCA of October 2, 1920, of which Evlogii was not aware. Be that as it may, having unilaterally broken with the Ecumenical Patriarchate, the Karlovci HROCAA lost its claim to being a legitimate successor of its Constantinopolitan predecessor, and therefore Moscow's reference to the Constantinopolitan HROCAA did not imply any recognition of its Karlovcian namesake. The Karlovcian HRCAA was based on its statute of July 1921, and on the First All-Émigré Russian Church Conference, which gathered in Karlovci on November 21, 1921, and later renamed itself *Sobor.* The conference consisted of eighty-six participants: twelve bishops, twenty-one priests, and fifty-three laymen. The real organizer of the Karlovci conference or *sobor* was the Higher Monarchist Council (HMC), formed a few months earlier at a congress in Bad Reichenhal, Bavaria. Both Metropolitan Antonii and Archbishop Evlogii were guests-of-honor at the monarchist congress, at which the Council's Chairman, Krupenskii, declared that the Moscow Sobor and its decisions were not valid because they had not been ratified by an emperor. Although the Council officially asked Archbishop Evlogii to form the steering committee for the projected Karlovci conference, the Monarchist Congress gave him no chance to speak, ostracized him, and tried to convince him to go to America to put church life there in order, rather than come to Karlovci. At that time, Evlogii's primary residence was in Berlin. The monarchists had strong connections in official circles both in Berlin and in Belgrade; and, "mysteriously," Evlogii was the only delegate to the Karlovci conference whose visa was delayed. Consequently, he arrived in Karlovci after the sessions had already begun and was therefore not in the conference presidium.

In the course of preparations for the Karlovci conference, the HMC established contact with Hitler via Alfred Rosenberg, a Baltic German who had been a Russian officer during World War I, but who was won over to Nazism after the revolution. The HMC partially funded the purchase of the newspaper *Völkischer Beobachter* for the Nazi Party, and its members subsequently published numerous anti-Semitic articles in that newspaper. In their negotiations with Hitler, an agreement was reached that should Hitler come to power he would support the training of Orthodox clergy in Germany for their future missionary work in the liberated, post-Communist Russia.

At the Karlovci "Sobor" Metropolitan Antonii, who in the 1905-06 discussions had opposed lay participation in Church councils, unilaterally appointed delegates from the HMC and gave them full voting rights, even though they represented no parishes. At the very first session, the monarchists requested the expulsion of Mikhail Rodzianko, who, as the chairman of the last Duma, had participated in the decision to convince the tsar to abdicate. Although Rodzianko had been a delegate at the Moscow Sobor, which ruled that its delegates had the right to participate in all Church conferences until elections were held for the next Sobor, Rodzianko departed for the sake of calming passions. Owing also to the voices of the HMC, the conference adopted a resolution seeking the restoration of the Romanovs as autocratic monarchs (only six of the twelve bishops and seven of twenty-one priests voted for this resolution). Metropolitan Evlogii writes: "I begged the most influential monarchists: spare the Patriarch...his situation is difficult enough without the resolution." Thirty-four delegates, including Evlogii and Anastasii, the future head of the Karlovcian Synod, and two other bishops abstained, submitting a statement that "the issue of monarchy and...the dynasty is political in nature...and is not a subject for discussion at a Church conference...," but all their efforts were in vain.[4]

The conference closed on December 3, 1921. Then, on January 22, 1922 an announcement appeared in the media about an international conference in Genoa the following April; there appeared also a statement, allegedly adopted by the Karlovci Sobor, appealing to the Genoa Conference to organize a crusade against Soviet Russia. This was a fabrication by Karlovci bureaucrats from the HMC, as, at the time of the conference, nothing was heard about any conference in Genoa, and no resolutions supporting a crusade were adopted.

The Karlovcians, the Moscow Patriarchate, and Church Schisms

All the Karlovci resolutions, including also the appeal to the Genoa Conference, appeared in the Moscow Soviet Government's political weekly, *The New*

4 Evlogii, *Put' moei zhizni*, p. 397.

Time. On learning about these resolutions, the Patriarch sought the opinions of diocesan bishops, who sent back condemnatory responses. A joint session of his Synod and the Higher Church Council then "categorically resolved to liquidate the HROCAA." A decree to this effect, signed and dated May 5, 1922, ordered its immediate dissolution and handing over of all power to Evlogii, who had recently been granted the title of Metropolitan by the Moscow Patriarchate.

Metropolitan Evlogii, however, out of his personal respect for and devotion to Metropolitan Antonii, did not carry out the Patriarch's order—even though Antonii had offered his resignation, and his closest adviser, Archbishop Anastasii, insisted at the time that the Patriarch's will had to be carried out exactly. Instead, Evlogii suggested its fulfillment in form, but not in content: namely, that the HROCAA be replaced by a *Synod of Bishops of the Russian Orthodox Church Outside Russia,* ROCOR). In contrast to the former body, which included two priests and two laymen, the Synod consisted of bishops only. Moreover, Evlogii suggested the splitting of the Russian Church abroad into four autonomous metropolitan districts—Western Europe headed by himself, the Balkans headed by Metropolitan Antonii, Manchuria and the Far East headed by Metropolitan Meletii, and North America headed by Metropolitan Platon (Rozhdestvensky). In this structure the Karlovci Synod was to be merely a liaison center; and once a year the heads of all Metropolitan districts would gather in Karlovci for episcopal *sobors* under the chairmanship of Metropolitan Antonii. This proposal was accepted, and Evlogii left for Paris, authorized by Antonii and Anastasii to draft a new statute reflecting this confederal church structure. But the Karlovci lay bureaucracy from the HMC, which ran the Synod's business, thought otherwise. Frictions between Evlogii and Platon, on the one hand, and Karlovci on the other, began almost immediately, at first because Evlogii's protests against the political resolutions at the Karlovci Sobor were neither forgotten, nor forgiven. Tensions reached their high point in 1924, when the Karlovcians adopted a resolution stating that because the Patriarch was under the GPU control, only those of his orders would be accepted by the Karlovci Synod which did not contradict the latter's interests. Then in 1925, taking advantage of the fact that no episcopal *sobor* had taken place in that year, the Karlovcians declared Antonii "...Deputy Patriarch with the right to represent the Russian Church...and to administer church life and the Church not only abroad, but also inside Russia." Moreover, after the death of Patriarch Tikhon, the Karlovcians at first refused to recognize Metropolitan Peter as his *locum tenens,* although he was universally recognized by the bishops in Russia. Metropolitan Evlogii protested against both of these Karlovcian acts, arguing on the latter issue that the real question was whether Metropolitan Peter recognized the émigré churchmen, and not the reverse. The Karlovcians referred to the canons which banned the appointment of successors by a ruling bishop. But the real reason for their reluctance to recognize Peter was that, on several occasions, he had expressed his negative attitude toward the Karlovcians and admitted his virtual authorship of Patriarch Tikhon's last encyclical, which became known as his Testament, owing to his sudden death and that it was first published after his death. That Testament called the Karlovcian activities "harmful to the cause of our Church...," and added: "we have no contacts with them, they are alien to us ...but they act arbitrarily in our name. The Karlovci Sobor...did not bring any good to the Church." The Testament threatened the émigré bishops with an ecclesiastical trial, "especially Metropolitans Antonii...Platon..."

But why Platon, whom the Patriarch had only three years earlier confirmed as Metropolitan of the Russian Orthodox Archdiocese of America, and who kept himself as aloof from politics as Evlogii in Europe? The story goes back to Odessa in 1919. The French forces occupying the city at the time suggested to the Metropolitan that he form voluntary Russian anti-Bolshevik "Holy fighting squads." He announced their formation, and thousands of young people enlisted. But then, in the face of a swift Bolshevik offensive, the French fleet fled Odessa in panic, taking Metropolitan Platon and Archbishop Anastasii (Gribanovskii, the future head of the Karlovci Synod after Antony's death) with them. Platon had no time to destroy the lists of volunteers, and thousands were executed by the Bolsheviks in the next few days. On that basis Tuchkov, the head of the GPU's Sixth Department in charge of Church affairs, made Patriarch Tikhon sign a decree banning Metropolitan Platon and removing him from the leadership of the Church in America. Tuchkov's purpose was obviously to clear the way for the pro-Soviet Renovationists in America, against whom Platon had led a decisive and quite effective struggle. According to the Patriarch's secretary, Archpriest and Professor Vasilii Vinogradov, Tikhon at first signed the decree, but after learning what was behind it, had it removed and hidden in his files. Tuchkov, however, without the Patriarch's knowledge, published it in *Izvestiia*. But because in those days *Izvestiia* and other communist newspapers published many lies and slanders, no one noticed that article. Metropolitan Platon later stated he was not aware of this "decree" until 1926 when, after his break with the

Karlovcians at the episcopal *sobor* in Karlovci, the US State Department received a cable from Karlovci declaring that Platon was a usurper removed from his post by Patriarch Tikhon. "Coincidentally," on almost the same date in 1926, the State Department also received a virtually identical cable from the Renovationists. Be that as it may, the appearance of Platon's name under the threat of an ecclesiastical trial should be seen in the context of the Renovationist issue. If Fr Vinogradov's version is correct, according to which the "Testament" was merely the latest draft of the Patriarch's declaration of loyalty demanded by the Soviets as a condition for legalizing the Patriarchate, and that the text had been circulating between the Patriarch, Metropolitan Peter, and Tuchkov in the process of its final editing when the Patriarch died, then it is likely that Platon's name was inserted by Tuchkov.[5]

The 1926 conflict which led to the émigré church splits was caused by the Karlovci's ultimatum to Metropolitans Evlogii and Platon to recognize the Karlovci Synod as their highest authority. The metropolitans refused, arguing that since they had been appointed by Patriarch of Moscow, Karlovci had no authority over them. Moreover, because they were the only émigré bishops with canonically valid appointments, the Karlovci Synod's only link to the Orthodox *oikumene* was through these two bishops, and without them the Synod would lose all claims to validity as a church structure. The conflict arose because the Karlovci Synod refused to accept Evlogii's draft statute on the confederal Church structure. In protest, both metropolitans left the 1926 episcopal *sobor*, and the Karlovci Synod issued bans against both of them, condemnations which were never recognized by either Metropolitan or by any of the local Orthodox Churches.

Lenin and the Church

In his Decree of January 23, 1918, Lenin was obviously guided by the classic Marxist thesis that religion is a superstructure over the material base. Should that base be removed, religion would simply wither away. But by 1921-22 even the Soviet media began to recognize that religion had not only not withered away, it was beginning to show signs of growth, especially in the cities.

---

5 It is worth noting that, whereas Metropolitan Antonii in Karlovci claimed that the "Testament" was a GPU fraud (and that became the official Karlovcian version later on), his chief deputy and heir, Anastasii, maintained that it was genuine, because: it did not contradict his earlier declarations of loyalty to the Soviet Regime; its concern was with the survival of the Church and the retention of her inner spiritual freedom while accepting full subordination to the state in civic matters—there would have been no such concern had it been composed by the GPU.

The narrow stream of leftist intelligentsia returning to the Church in the last decade before the war had turned into a river, as disappointment in the revolution and its results began to express itself in disappointment over the materialist doctrine of a godless perfectibility of society and man.

As the method of killing religion by its complete legal and material disfranchisement had failed, Lenin switched to a differentiated approach: sympathetic neutrality (and even direct support in some cases) toward Protestant groups, Muslims and Jews to some extent,[6] while directly attacking the national, i.e., the Orthodox, Church. The onslaught by the central government on the Orthodox Church began with the Decree of March 1, 1919, on the compulsory opening and destruction of relics. This decree was reiterated in August 1920, despite the Patriarch's appeals to Lenin to abolish it, warning that its implementation would lead to bloody clashes with believers, as actually happened. This, as well as the whole Soviet religious policy, made a mockery of the claim to separation of Church from State in Lenin's Decree of January 23, 1918. Officially, Soviet propaganda claimed that the government's attack on the Orthodox Church was not a religious persecution, but a struggle against the reactionary legacy of the tsarist past. The Karlovci political resolutions were useful for this propaganda. Because they all began by the phrase: "With the blessing of his Holiness the Patriarch of Moscow...," they made it easy for the Soviets to accuse the Patriarchate of participation in an anti-Soviet plot with the Karlovcian group. The Patriarch's ban on the Karlovci HCA was interpreted by the Bolshevik media as being merely a ploy, and not the genuine policy of the Church.

In order to demonstrate that the Orthodox Church was being persecuted for non-religious reasons, the Soviets needed another Orthodox Church which would be strongly pro-Soviet. Thus the GPU, on the Politburo's instructions, launched the so-called "Renovationist movement" in May 1922 as such an alternative Orthodox Church. The campaign was synchronized with Patriarch

---

6 Jewish affairs were subordinated to the so-called "Jewish sections" of the Communist Party on each administrative level. Their function was to secularize the Jews by banning Hebrew as a "reactionary language," stimulating Yiddish, setting up schools, theaters, publishing in that language. Only the Jewish sections could (and did!) liquidate the synagogues; whereas any group of anti-religious activists (especially after 1928, when mass destruction of prayer houses of all religions began), of Jewish, Muslim or any other background, could close an Orthodox church. Thereby the Communist rulers achieved two aims: on the one hand, it fomented anti-Semitism, as Jews were very prominent in the *Alliance of Militant Godless*, and it appeared to the average Russian that the restriction of the right to destroy synagogues to the Jewish sections alone was a pro-Jewish privilege; on the other, it demoralized the Jewish community from within, as all the destruction of Jewish religious life was carried out by fellow Jews.

Tikhon's arrest, under the pretext that he allegedly opposed the campaign to confiscate church treasures destined to preserve the famine-stricken population of the Volga area from mass starvation. In fact, the Patriarch was the first to appeal for help to Western Church leaders and to his own clergy and laity in August 1921.[7] By his order, a Church Fund was created for that purpose. But later in the year the Soviet Government ordered the Patriarch to turn all donations over to the State Fund for the Famine-Stricken and to close the separate Church Fund. The Patriarch complied and appealed to the clergy and the faithful to donate all church treasures, except those directly used in the Eucharist (chalices, etc.). At this point a mad campaign against the Patriarch and the Church was launched in the press, condemning them as selfish, heartless, and indifferent to human suffering. The State sought a confrontation with the Church at all cost, as can be seen from Lenin's letter to Molotov, dated March 19, 1922, in connection with resistance to the confiscation by believers in the textile town of Shuia.[8] On the Volga famine he writes:

> ...for us this...is the only moment when we can count on a 99 percent chance of...annihilating the enemy.... When cannibalism is taking place and there are hundreds or even thousands of corpses lying about on roadsides, we must...carry out the confiscation of church treasures in the most merciless way...only now a vast majority of peasants will either support us, or...would not be able to render any support to the groups of reactionary clergy and the urban bourgeoisie if they dared...to try out a policy of resistance...to the decree [on confiscations].

> We must...confiscate the treasures in order to gain a fund of several million or billion gold rubles ...Without it...any defense of our positions in Genoa...would be unthinkable...we must precisely now undertake a most decisive and merciless attack on the blackhundredist clergy and suppress its resistance with such cruelty which will force them to remember it for several decades.

Then follow technical instructions on how to achieve these aims and an order that all the instructions and reports be given only orally. Then Lenin gives an order to the court "that the trial against the Shuia mutineers be concluded...with the execution of a very large number of the most dangerous and influential blackhundreders in Shuia...Moscow and...other spiritual centers."

As can be seen from this document, the fate of the famine-stricken hardly bothered Lenin. The Politburo documents (published in the *Novyi mir*

7 As pointed out by Veniamin, Metropolitan of Petersburg, in a letter to Lenin on March 5, 1922.

8 The complete text of that letter and of the subsequent Politburo meeting appeared in *Isvestiia TseKa KPSS*, No. 4 (April 1990), pp. 191-197.

monthly in August 1994) indicate that Lenin was completely off the mark when he spoke of "millions and billions." The total collected was a mere 4,650,810 gold rubles plus 964 precious stones of poor quality. As to how those sums were spent, one clue was found in the archives: the cost of sustaining the Commission for the Confiscation of Church Valuables plus the costs of fomenting the split in the Church amounted to 1,559,592 gold rubles just for the month of April 1922; i.e., the overhead far exceeded the income, and not a penny went to save the famine-stricken!

The Revival of Radicalism in the Orthodox Church

Lenin's letter also contained the following significant words:

> [It is also necessary] ...to introduce a schism into the ranks of the clergy. [We] must take decisive initiative in that matter, providing state protection to those priests who openly speak up in favor of the confiscation [of church treasures].

Here Lenin had in mind radical clergy elements, which had been suppressed and repressed during the post-1906 reaction, and who came to the fore after the February 1917 Revolution. In Petrograd the Group of Thirty-Two Priests re-emerged under the name of the "Union of the Progressive Petrograd Clergy." Further to the left appeared an "All-Russian Union of Democratic Orthodox Clergy," led by the Archpriest Alexander Vvedenskii, the future leader of the Renovationist Schism. In Kiev, there appeared a "Union of New Christian Socialists." On the national scale arose an "Alliance of the Democratic Clergy and Laity," with chapters in numerous cities and regions.

In Moscow, F.I. Zhilkin, a textile worker and former activist in Fr Gapon's workers' movement of 1904-05, registered with the state authorities a "Social-Christian Workers' Party" in June 1917. The Party enjoyed Patriarch Tikhon's patronage, and he appointed the priest S. Kalinovskii (a future "renovationist") as its chaplain. Another prominent member of the party was N.D. Kuznetsov, a professor of canon law and a very active participant in the pre-Conciliar conferences of 1906-1917 and in the Moscow *Sobor*. Its socialist program was quite radical, except that instead of the socialist principle of class war, the party preached social harmony and called for an end to the fratricidal civil war which, the party appeals prophesied, would cost millions of human lives. Consequently, the party program was in fact closer to solidarism and to Pope Leo XIII's *Rerum novarum* encyclical than to Marxism. In March 1919, the leadership of the party appealed to the Patriarch to allow the party to operate within the Church, to recruit clergy and to distribute its literature in churches. The Patriarchal administration turned down this request, as "the Orthodox Church does not pursue any political goals," but it added that the Church's attitude to the party was sympathetic, as the aims set by the party served "the good of the Holy Orthodox Church." Appealing on behalf of the party Zhilkin and Kuznetsov succeeded in gaining the Bolshevik commissars' agreement to open the Kremlin for church services for the three Easter days of 1919. Also on behalf of the party, Kuznetsov delivered numerous protests to the Soviet Government against the persecutions and assaults on the rights of believers. Bolshevik "patience" was broken, however, by his memorandum condemning Lenin's January 23, 1918, Decree, calling it "an anti-pedagogical and anti-national act." This direct critique of the LEADER led to Kuznetsov's arrest, a ban on the party, and the conditional detention of Zhilkin.

These radical movements, arising from within the Church, were quite sincere, motivated by a mistaken, but in those days quite common, identification of Christianity with socialism (although most Christian socialists, similarly to Zhilkin's Party, rejected the class war idea). The only schismatic developments in these early days, known to this author, were the already mentioned Lypkivskyite Church schism and the mutiny of the former bishop Vladimir Putiata. That strikingly handsome son of a Jewish mother and of a scion of the medieval Prince Putiata, remembered for his bloody suppression of a pagan anti-Christian revolt in Novgorod in the eleventh century. Vladimir Putiata began his career as an officer in the imperial guards and a personal friend of Nicholas II. Then, suddenly, he retired from the army, went to the Kazan' theological academy, took monastic vows upon graduation, and was soon consecrated bishop. With no ascetic inclinations and possessing strikingly attractive features, he soon succumbed to carnal temptations. The Church constantly relocated him from one diocese to another because of scandals with women, but was unable to retire him because he enjoyed the personal protection of the Tsar. The post-revolutionary Moscow Sobor ordered him defrocked and moved to a monastery in Penza (on the Volga). In that city, however, he declared himself the archbishop of a new "Free Peoples' Church," whereupon the Sobor excommunicated him. Later he joined the Renovationist Schism; but at this point the Renovationists were still within the Church.

It was Lenin, in the 1922 letter cited above, who was looking for ways to foment a split in the Patriarchal Church. The idea went back to 1919, when Zinoviev, the party boss of Petersburg, held discussions with Vvedenskii, at the end of which he concluded that the Soviet Government would be willing to conclude a "concordat" with Vvedenskii's church group. According to recently discovered Politburo documents, by 1922 there were two schools of thought in the Party leadership regarding the Church. Lenin at first favored the physical destruction of the Church in a single stroke. Trotsky, on the other hand, wanted first to split the Church over the issue of confiscating Church valuables, supporting the pro-confiscationists and persecuting the patriarchists. His line prevailed. In a memorandum on March 30, he warned that in the long run the "Renovationists" should also be liquidated, because as modernists they would be more likely to influence "those advanced strata of toilers, which are or should become our support base," but in the short run the "Renovationists" should be actively supported by the Soviet leadership, officially registered, given funds and facilities to publish periodicals, to have congresses and *sobors*, with their agendas orchestrated and implemented by appropriate State agencies under the Politburo's and the GPU's close supervision.

The Renovationist Mutiny, the Patriarch, and Metropolitan Veniamin

A GPU report of March 1922 claimed that there were numerous Orthodox hierarchs and priests who were unhappy with the Patriarch's policy concerning the Church treasures issue, but their obedience to the canons did not permit them to act against him. The report therefore suggested that the Patriarch and his Synod be arrested; whereupon the "change-of-signposts clergy"[9] could carry out a pro-Soviet coup. On March 22, Trotsky responded positively to that idea, but warned the GPU to wait another "ten to fifteen days." And indeed, exactly fifteen days later, on May 6, 1922, Patriarch Tikhon was arrested and charged with instigating bloodshed, allegedly through his orders regulating what the churches could donate to the famine relief fund and what they should keep. Six days later, he was visited by a group of future Renovationist leaders, including the Petersburg priests Vvedenskii, Krasnitskii, and Belkov, as well as a Moscow bishop, Antonin (Granovskii). They convinced the Patriarch to hand the chancery over to them temporarily, arguing that, since people were being executed for having fulfilled the Patriarch's order, there was little chance he would be released from prison. Unaware of their rebellious intent, the Patriarch agreed, on

9 A movement of non-communist intelligentsia who believed that the NEP meant the end of the Communist ideology in Russia and the beginning of a pragmatic bureaucracy which would evolve into a more liberal political system as the country was pacified after years of the Civil War chaos. It was therefore now possible to cooperate with Lenin's government for the restoration of Russia. Trotsky applied this term also to the renovationist clergy.

the condition that they would turn the chancery over to his *locum tenens*, Agafangel, Metropolitan of Yaroslavl', as soon as he arrived in Moscow. But Agafangel never arrived. Tuchkov of the GPU delayed his departure for Moscow by initiating talks with him on various points of his future Church administration. Meanwhile, the above rebels issued a declaration to the effect that they were the provisional governing body of the Church, calling themselves the Temporary Higher Church Administration (THCA, or VVTsU in Russian). Agafangel, as Patriarchal Locum Tenens, responded to their declaration with an encyclical condemning the THCA as a mutiny having no ecclesiastic validity whatsoever, and repeating the Patriarchal encyclical of November 20, 1920, which instructed dioceses to group themselves into temporary autocephalies, should the central Church administration collapse or contact with it become impossible. This angered the Soviet leadership, as it undermined their original plans. Agafangel was arrested and exiled to the Arctic northeast.

A similar attitude towards the Renovationists was also adopted by the otherwise very mild and accommodating Metropolitan Veniamin. He excommunicated Vvedenskii, his former friend, and all the other Renovationist rebels in his diocese. Veniamin's arrest, however, was made difficult by his readiness to cooperate on the issue of the confiscation treasures. He had told the Petrograd Soviet that handing chalices over to them was out of the question because, as the eucharistic containers, they could not be touched by laypersons. Instead, he offered to melt them down and donate them in the form of gold (or silver) ingots. He then suggested that a priest or bishop should accompany the confiscation commissions in his diocese in order to avoid physical resistance and clashes. The Petrograd Soviet accepted his terms, and even its daily newspaper praised Veniamin for his cooperation. But Moscow wanted confrontation, not cooperation, and a fortnight after the above accommodation, on May 28, the Metropolitan was arrested. Veniamin had simply been too popular in the city, particularly among the working class youth, to be tolerated. Moreover, he refused to retract his excommunication of Vvedenskii's group, even when warned by the GPU that the alternative would be his arrest.[10] Along with him were arrested over a dozen of the most influential priests and lay religious activists in the city.

A show trial was staged in a hall with room for over 3,000, which remained packed throughout the trial. From the very first day, the defendant charmed the

10 So much for the separation of the Church from the State!

audience, despite the fact that a good proportion of them consisted of communist and Komsomol activists brought in to demonstrate "the masses'" resentment of the Church. The entire audience rose for the Metropolitan's blessing each time he entered or left the hall. His lawyer, Gurevich, declared that as a Jew his duty was to express Russian Jewry's gratefulness to the Russian Orthodox Church for defending and obtaining the release of the Jewish worker, Beilis, at the infamous Kiev trial of 1911-13, staged by Black-Hundreders seeking to prove that Jews used Christian blood for the preparation of *matzos* and accusing Beilis of ritual murder. At the same time, Gurevich forced the Renovationist Priest Krasnitskii, a prosecution witness, to depart in shame by revealing the latter's pre-revolutionary role as a Black-Hundreders' chaplain and ideologist, who had published numerous anti-Semitic tracts. Then the lawyer proved Veniamin's and his colleagues' absolute innocence of all charges presented by the prosecution, including his alleged cooperation with the Karlovci monarchists' anti-Soviet "plot." After the court, nevertheless, condemned Veniamin and most of his co-defendants to death, Gurevich declared that the Soviet State's cooperation with the Renovationists was doomed to failure, because "the nation can forgive a Saul changing into Paul, who replaced his former wealth with persecutions and martyrdom. But the reverse metamorphoses... receive quite a different and appropriate notoriety." If executed, Gurevich added, the Metropolitan would become more dangerous to the Soviet Government than the living one, for "the faith grows, becomes strong and rises to greatness by the blood of its martyrs."

As soon as the Bishop Alexii (Simanskii), the future patriarch but then the senior vicar-bishop of the Petersburg diocese, took over the diocesan administration after the Metropolitan's arrest, he was called to the GPU office and told that Veniamin would be executed unless he, Alexii, lifted the excommunication off Vvedenskii and his collaborators. Alexii reported this to the Diocesan Council, which resolved that any measures to save the Metropolitan's life would be justified. Thereupon Bishop Alexii, in an "Address to the Petrograd Flock," declared that Veniamin had not been aware of the Patriarch's approval of the THCA, and that, the bans on Vvedenskii and his HCA collaborators were invalidated, with their reinstatement to active priesthood. To avoid subordination to the Renovationists, Alexii and his assistant, Bishop Nikolai (Yarushevich), the future Metropolitan of Krutitsy and the Patriarchate's head of foreign affairs, declared the temporary autocephaly of the diocese while they negotiated with the Renovationist HCA, by correspondence to be on the safe side. In June, Alexii discovered that the GPU had cheated him by executing the Metropolitan nevertheless. He retired from his post; and two months later he was arrested and exiled to Central Asia.

The Roles of the Politburo and the GPU in the Renovationist Schism

No sooner had the Renovationists appeared on the scene than they were legitimized (registered) by the State, while the direct persecution of the Patriarchal Orthodox Church was accelerated. Some bishops sat quietly in their dioceses without officially committing themselves to either side, others were arrested, others actively joined the Schism, but the majority, in order to run their dioceses as before, formally recognized the THCA. Among these was the Metropolitan of Vladimir, Sergii (Stragorodskii), who declared his recognition of the HCA in June, but already in August signed a letter with two other bishops expressing their disagreement with its leadership and requesting complete independence from the HCA. Instead of receiving independence, he was imprisoned and kept in jail during the Renovationist "Sobor" that began on April 29, 1923. His signature is therefore absent from the Sobor's decree "defrocking" Patriarch Tikhon.

The "Sobor" opened with the singing of "Many Years" to the Soviet Government and a declaration that Lenin was the liberator of mankind. Then it resolved to russify the liturgical language (nothing was done by the Renovationists in practice to implement this reform), to use the Gregorian Calendar instead of the Julian, to allow the promotion of married priests to the episcopate, as well as to permit priests to divorce and re-marry. Ignoring Church canons, the "Sobor" tried the Patriarch in absentia, accusing him of shedding innocent blood by his decrees regarding Church treasures, and deprived him of all his clerical ranks and even of his monastic tonsure. Patriarch Tikhon, however, demonstrated exceptional courage: when visited in jail by a delegation from the "Sobor," he refused to recognize the validity of the "Sobor" or to sign its verdict against himself. No sooner had the "Sobor" ended than the Patriarch was unexpectedly released, mainly because of an ultimatum from the British Government, which threatened to break off moves towards full diplomatic relations with the Soviet Union unless the Patriarch was released.[11]

11 The signals to moderate the antireligious campaign first came from Chicherin, the Soviet foreign commissar, who reported that the onslaught was dangerously complicating Soviet interests abroad. His advice, however, was ignored by the Politburo until a similar warning came from Dzerzhinskii, the head of the GPU. It was after the Politburo meeting at which Dzerzhinskii's memorandum was read that the Patriarch was released. Britain was at the time in the process of negotiating full diplomatic recognition of the USSR, which was granted a year later.

Let us now return to the Politburo and GPU Church documents. On Trotsky's suggestion in his March 1922 memorandum, the Politburo appointed Kalinin, the "president" of the Soviet Union, to foment Church schism by giving public assurances that the state was not persecuting religion, but merely fulfilling the wishes of the starving masses to remove from public life the most reactionary bishops and other members of the bourgeoisie. Trotsky also suggested that, in order to make the campaign more credible, Kalinin needed a pro-confiscations bishop as a collaborator. He proposed Bishop Antonin (Granovskii), an old church dissident and one of the future leaders of the Renovationists. By May 30, the RCP(b) Central Committee's Organizational Bureau (Orgburo) assigned the responsibility for splitting the Church (in accordance with the above memorandum) to the GPU, which reacted to this decision with the following protest addressed to the Central Committee:

> ...The colossal historical responsibility of *creating* [emphasis: D.P.] a schism in the ranks of the clergy...demands not only much energy, but also great financial expenditures.
>
> Setting financial limits on those ecclesiastics who collaborate with us, limits on their publication activities, not to mention the costs of financing a whole staff of priests and of their travel and residence, would be equivalent to killing the whole project....[These expenses] are a heavy burden on the GPU budget.
>
> Causing of the schism cannot be included in the routine work of the GPU, neither can the costs be absorbed by its regular budget, which is very frugal....The GPU begs the Central Committee to revise the decision of the Orgburo of May 10, 1922.

On June 13, the CC Secretariat replied that the funding issue had to be resolved by the "All-Russian Executive Committee's Commission on the Confiscation of the Church Valuables."

As we have already seen, the funds obtained from robbing the Church were used for covering the expenses of the Confiscation Commission and for subsidizing Renovationist ventures, including the preparation of the constituent conference in Moscow of May 29, 1922, at which the "Living Church," the largest faction of the future Renovationist Church, officially came into being. Thus it can be safely assumed that, as the Confiscation Commission functioned for about one year, while the GPU's activities to foment schisms continued until approximately 1928 (followed thereafter by the wholesale destruction of all religion), it can be safely concluded that not a penny of the valuables confiscated from the Church went to alleviate the famine, as all these costs far exceeded the total pillaged from the Church.

The roles of the Politburo and the GPU in the creation of the schism are now beyond doubt. But did not the numerous letters by such Renovationist leaders as Vvedenskii, Krasnitskii, Kalinovskii, and Belkov, begging the Soviet Government to pardon Metropolitan Veniamin and other members of the clergy and laity condemned to death in the course of 1922, at least indicate an element of sincerity in the movement? Yes and no. The fact is that most these letters were orchestrated in advance by Trotsky! Archival materials include data on votes taken within the Politburo concerning the death sentences resulting from the trials of Church officials. Invariably, Lenin, Stalin, Trotsky, Molotov, and Zinoviev approved all executions, while Tomsky, Rykov and Kamenev, as well as Kalinin tried to reduce the number of executions. But then on May 12, Trotsky suddenly changed his mind and suggested that some leading Renovationist priests should be instructed to write public letters to the Soviet authorities seeking clemency for the condemned Tikhonites. That, Trotsky argues, will deepen the schism and weaken the positions of the Tikhonite Church, as well as contradict the popular belief that the Renovationists were the GPU's agents plain and simple. The Politburo should not pardon all of the accused or even the majority, but just a few. The fact that the pleas for pardon were only partly effective would, presumably, strengthen the impression that they were not simply agents of the GPU.

Indeed, such Renovationist figures as Vvedenskii and Granovskii, for instance, were not simply GPU agents. Thus, even on his own initiative, Vvedenskii desperately tried to reverse the death sentence meted out to Metropolitan Veniamin. As a Christian socialist, Vvedenskii may have believed in the sincerity of the Soviet leadership's support for the schism, and in his appeals on Veniamin's behalf he tried to convince the Communist leadership

> that the whole cause of Church renewal, the attempt...morally and ethically, depends on the final verdict. If there will be executions,...the Living Church (and I personally) will be murderers in the eyes of the crowd... The attempt at Church renewal will be killed.

Vvedenskii, of course, could not be aware of Trotsky's secret memorandum of March 30, in which number 10 said: "By the time of the convocation of the Sobor, we must put into motion a theoretical and propaganda campaign against the Renewed Church."

Trotsky, however, underestimated the difficulties and the time needed to destroy the Tikhonite Church: as long as she existed and enjoyed mass support, the Soviet leadership needed the Renovationists. All efforts focused on crushing the Patriarchists, as demonstrated in the following documents.

On October 30, 1922, Evgenii Tuchkov reported to the Central Committee:

[For the current]...five-months' attack on the Tikhonites...a group called "Living Church" has been formed, mostly of white priests, which gave us the opportunity to embroil the priests with the episcopate.

Along with numerous articles and appeals condemning the Tikhonites and their policies, the priests, having appropriated supreme power in the church, began to expel the Tikhonite and generally reactionary bishops. In the course of the last five months, about one hundred Tikhonite bishops...have been [forcefully] retired...ten Tikhonite bishops loyal to the Soviet Government were moved to other dioceses, twenty of similar views have remained in their dioceses. Five fanatical Tikhonites still remain in their dioceses...

Tikhonites are being expelled from parish councils by instigating quarrels in the councils through the formation of "lay groups of supporters of Renovationism."

[The next aim]...is firstly, to crush and discredit Tikhonism, which to the present day enjoys the greatest number of supporters; [and secondly]...to permit [the convocation of a *sobor*, at which a paralysis of the unity of the church will be achieved, as groups will quarrel with each other, resulting in a schism.

This is followed by minutes of an undated meeting of the Commission for the Enactment of the Separation of Church from the State (CESCS), which approved GPU activities aimed at eliminating the Tikhonites' influence on the renovationist Higher Church Administration by fomenting active confusion among the three groups [of Renovationists]: the Renaissance, the Living Church, and the leftists.[12]

The Commission for the Enactment of the Separation of the Church from the State, meeting on October 31, decided to place its bets on the "Living Church," forcing it into coalition with Vvedenskii's "leftist group." Antonin Granovskii was too independent for the Soviet Government, and his defense of monasticism went against the whole current of the Renovationist schism. The meeting, among other things, resolved: "To request...of the Procuracy to offer the GPU all possible help in its struggle by administrative

12 "The Union of the Regeneration of the Church" (*Soiuz tserkovnogo vozrozhdeniia*), led by Bishop Antonin (Granovskii).

methods against Tikhonism," i.e., by imprisonment and exile without trial. In other words, even in terms of Soviet law the Tikhonite clergy was legally innocent and could not be legally tried and sentenced once the confiscation campaign had concluded.

The New Policy of Re-Unifying the Renovationists with the Patriarchists and the 1925 Sobor

By 1923, the CESCS (under the chairmanship of Gubelman-Iaroslavskii, the future leader of the "League of the Militant Godless," with the GPU's Tuchkov as the secretary) was busily preparing the agenda for the first Renovationist Sobor. Aware of the nation's negative reaction to ecclesiastical radicalism, the Commission amended the *sobor's* original program (presumably authored by the Renovationist leadership), giving it a more conservative flavor. The Commission thus eliminated paragraphs declaring the Renovationists' "approval...of the social revolution and the unification of the toiling classes." This was clearly in accordance with Trotsky's warning against any attempts at identifying the Renovationists with the Soviet State. The Commission stipulated: "Any decisions on the issue of Church reform should not be permitted at the *sobor*, as the HCA has not prepared the laity to accept them." Instead, after the *sobor*, separate conferences of all the different renovationist factions should be convoked, at which issues of church reforms should be raised in order "to deepen the schisms between the different factions,...locally." The structure of the Church was to remain a coalition; Krasnitskii was to be the de facto chairman of the Sobor.

How ironic, in the light of the above documents, is Lenin's Decree on the Separation of the Church from the State, especially in view of the fact that the above decisions were taken by the Commission on the Separation of the Church from the State!

After Tikhon's release, GPU documents contain numerous reports of a progressive decline of all branches of Renovationists, their almost total desertion by the laity. This leads the Soviets to lose interest in the Renovationists: GPU informers with no one on whom to inform are of little use to the secret police. And so, as early as September 1923, the Government forces the Renovationists to initiate talks with the Patriarchate about a possible reunion. The first plan was to convoke a joint Patriarchal-Renovationist Sobor under the chairmanship of Tikhon, at which the latter would resign and the Sobor would elect another patriarch. But a conference of twenty-seven patriarchal bishops rejected that plan by an absolute majority. The enraged Tuchkov begins, in November 1923, to threaten the Patriarch with further imprisonment if he refuses to accept the Renovationists as a movement within the Church, with representatives in her various administrative bodies—obviously, the GPU wanted them there as faithful informants. The Patriarch and his advisers refused to budge. Renovationist clergy could be accepted into the Church only as individuals, by public repentance.

The following figures illustrate the collapse of the Renovationists. By the end of 1922, the Patriarchal Church had only four parishes in Moscow, with 400 belonging to the Renovationists. In Petrograd all the churches were controlled by Renovationists after the exile of Bishop Alexii and the imprisonment of Bishop Nikolai. 66 percent of the parishes across the country were held by the Renovationists. But by November 1924, Renovationist parishes declined to 30 percent of the total (14,000 parishes, against almost 30,000 held by the Patriarchate), although cases of Renovationist seizure of parishes by force, with the help of Soviet authorities, continued until the early 1930s. By 1926, the Renovationists had only 6,345 parishes and 10,815 clergy; the Patriarchal Church had well over 30,000 parishes with roughly an equal number of priests. Thus the decline of Renovationism continued after Patriarch Tikhon's death. No documents of the kind we now possess were available to the Orthodox faithful of the 1920s and 30s, yet they rightly sensed that Renovationism was a GPU "fifth column." The ordinary faithful, often illiterate or semi-literate, proved to have a much better intuition about the workings of the Soviet regime than most Western sovietologists, including such past "authorities" as the American fellow-traveler John Curtiss, who denied, against all implicit evidence, that the GPU administered the Renovationists.

The Communist totalitarian mentality could not accept defeat on such an ideologically critical front as religion. When the regime either launched or approved a "Second" sobor for 1925, it obviously hoped to carry out Trotsky's plan of March 1922, to conclude its alliance with the Renovationists by turning all sides against one another. Both the regime and the Renovationists believed that the generally mild Metropolitan Peter, locum tenens after Tikhon's death, would be more amenable to the convocation of a joint "re-unification" sobor announced for late 1925. But Peter, though very loyal to the Soviet state and completely apolitical, was absolutely intolerant of the Renovationists; he considered them to be an internal foe, and therefore subversive and much more dangerous than the external, communist attack against the Church. He refused to take part in the Sobor and strictly forbade his clergy to attend. His order was obeyed. The regime never forgave Peter for foiling their long-term plans—hence the arrest and particularly cruel treatment meted out to Peter, ending in his execution in 1937.

The Long-Term Effect of the Renovationist Schism

The Renovationist collapse was mainly due to their rejection by the Orthodox laity, more so than by the clergy. For whereas the clergy had on the whole remained the same as before the revolution, i.e., with a sizable minority of left-wingers,[13] the laity had moved far to the right. This was for two reasons: first, all the nominal Christians abandoned the Church once she was separated from the state, and particularly after the persecutions began; second, those who remained in the Church, and particularly the neophytes, mostly abandoned their leftist illusions after the experiences of the Civil War and of the Bolshevik rule. As a result, a Church that actively cooperated with the regime and praised its socialist ideology was unacceptable to the faithful in the post-revolutionary context.

A *samizdat* biographical novel called *Ostraia luka*, written apparently by the daughter of a martyr-priest, well describes the long-term problems created by the schism. The hero of the novel is an enlightened priest, a supporter of major reforms in the Church, including services in Russian and the use of the Gregorian calendar. But when these reforms are announced by the Renovationists, he prophesies with much pain that they have destroyed the chances of any reforms in the Church for many years to come. All attempts at reforms will henceforth be opposed as smacking of Renovationism, and the Church will be doomed to a long period of stagnation. His prophecies, alas, have proved correct. The Orthodox Church is conservative by virtue of her historicism. Reforms in the Church are always difficult, and are possible only when carried out by very authoritative or authoritarian kings, or when the bishops enacting them enjoy the popularity, love, and trust of the whole Church.[14] In the case of the Renovationists, however, the reformists turned out to be GPU agents (and the nation understood this), who participated in persecutions of the most popular priests, bishops, and monastics. Thus the very idea of reform was compromised for decades to come.

13 Their proportion must have declined, however, after the experience of the Civil War and the Bolshevik terror.

14 Hence Patriarch Sergeii's suggestions to return to the principle of elected bishops and the 1917-18 Sobor's enactment to that effect.

FOR FURTHER READING

Agursky, M., *Ideologiia natsional-bol'shevizma* (Paris: YMCA-Press, 1980)

Antonii (Khrapovitskii), Metropolitan, *Sbornik izbrannykh statei* (Jordanville, 1961).

Bociurkiw, Bohdan, "The Renovationist Church in the Soviet Ukraine, 1922-1939," *Annals of the Ukrainian Academy of Sciences in the US*. Vol. 9, No.1-2 (1961).

Bogolepov, Alexander C., *Church Reforms in Russia, 1905-1918* (Bridgeport, Conn.: Committee of the Metropolitan Council of the Russian Orthodox Church of America, 1966).

Bullock, Alen, *Hitler: a Study in Tyranny* (London: Penguin, 1975).

Chrysostomus, J., *Kirchengeschichte Russlands der neusten Zeit*, 3 vols. (Munich-Salzburg, 1965-1968).

Curtiss, John, *Church and State in Russia, 1900-1917* (New York: Octagon Books, 1940).

_____, *The Russian Church and the Soviet State, 1917-1950*. (Boston, 1953).

d'Herbigny, Monseigneur, *Tserkovnaia zhizn' v Moskve* (Paris, 1926).

Evlogii (Georgievskii), Metropolitan, *Put' moei zhizni* (Paris: YMCA Press, 1947).

Fletcher, William, *The Russian Church Underground, 1917-1970* (Oxford University Press, 1971).

Gubonin, M.E., ed. *Akty sviateishego Patriarkha Tikhona, pozdneishie dokumenty i perepiska o preemstve vysshei tserkovnoi vlasti, 1917-1943* (Moscow: Sviato-Tikhonovskii Bogoslovskii Institut, 1994).

Hecker, Julius, *Religion and Communism* (New York, 1934).

Kartashev, A., *"Revolutsiia i sobor 1917-1918 gg."* (Paris: *Bogoslovskaia mysl'*, 1942).

Kurov, M.N., "Khristiansko-sotsialisticheskaia raboche-krestianskaia partiia v Rossii (1917-1920)," *Voprosy nauchnogo ateizma*, vol.10 (Moscow, 1970).

Levitin-Krasnov, A., *Likhie gody* (Paris: YMCA Press, 1977).

_____, and Vadim Shavrov, *Ocherki po istorii Russkoi tserkovnoi smuty*, 3 vols. (Küsnacht, Switzerland: Glaube in der 2 Welt, 1978).

Pokrovskii, N.N. "Politburo i Tserkov' 1922-1923," *Novyi mir*, No. 8 (August, 1994).

Pospielovsky, D., A *History of Soviet Atheism in Theory and Practice, and the Believer*, 3 vols. (London: Macmillan/ N.Y.: St Martins, 1987-88).

_____, *Russkaia pravoslavnaia Tserkov' v XX veke* (Moscow: "Respublika", 1995).

_____, *The Russian Church under the Soviet Regime: 1917-1982* (Crestwood, NY: St Vladimir's Seminary Press, 1984).

Prokhanov, Ivan, *In the Cauldron of Russia, 1869-1933* (New York, 1933).

Seide, Gernot, *Geschichte der russischen Orthodoxen Kirche im Ausland von der Gründung bis in die Gegenwart* (Wiesbaden, 1983).

Sheinman, M.N., *Khristianskii sotsializm* (Moscow, 1969).

Spinka, Matthew., *The Church and the Russian Revolution* (New York: Macmillan, 1927).

Szczesniak, Boleslaw, ed., *The Russian Revolution and Religion. Documents on the Communist Persecution of Religion, 1917-1925* (Notre Dame, IN: University Press, 1959).

Vinogradov, V., "Krestnyi put' russkoi ierarkhii," *Vestnik Russkogo kristianskogo dvizheniia,* No. 150 (Paris-Moscow, 1987).

Zatko, James, *Descent into Hell: the Destruction of the Roman Catholic Church in Russia, 1917-1923* (Notre Dame: University Press, 1965).

CHAPTER 11

LOCUM TENENTES, THEIR DEPUTIES, AND FURTHER SCHISMS

Patriarch Tikhon's Succession

On April 12, 1925, at an unofficial *sobor* consisting of bishops who had assembled in Moscow for the Patriarch's funeral, Metropolitan Peter opened the sealed envelope containing Tikhon's will concerning his succession. The will contained the names of three metropolitans whom the deceased Patriarch preferred as his successors, in descending order: Kirill (Smirnov) of Kazan', Agafangel of Yaroslavl', and Peter (Polianskii) of Krutitsy and Kolomna. The first two were in internal exile. Only Peter was at liberty. Hence the *ad hoc* meeting of bishops confirmed him as the patriarchal *locum tenens,* until the time when a local *sobor* could be convened and a patriarch properly elected.

But before the year had ended, Metropolitan Peter had already been jailed on false charges of participating in an émigré plot to restore the monarchy. In reality, the imprisonment was an act of vengeance for banning his clergy from participating in the second Renovationist Sobor, the official aim of which was the reunification of the two branches of the Orthodox Church. Although the Renovationists may have been sincere in their desire to reunite, as their cause was spent, it is more likely that the Politburo and the GPU saw this council as a delayed implementation of Trotsky's plan (described in the previous chapter) to deepen splits by instigating the factions against each other. Peter was therefore a stumbling block to the fulfillment of that plan. According to Hieromonk Damaskin (Orlovskii), a present-day researcher on Metropolitan Peter, the Commission on Religious Cults resolved on November, 11, 1925: "To instruct Tuchkov to hasten in creating a split among the Tikhonites."[1] After twelve years of virtual torture in one of the harshest climatic zones in Arctic Siberia—in the last few years he never saw daylight, as his "fresh air" strolls were conducted at night in a tiny yard surrounded by foul-smelling outhouses—Metropolitan Peter was executed on October 10, 1937. He had never been tried. Among his "crimes" was his refusal to abdicate the title of patriarchal *locum tenens*; because in the absence of a *sobor*-elected patriarch,

1 Damaskin, *Mucheniki, ispovedniki,* Book 2, n.p. 350.

Peter's abdication would have deprived his appointed deputy of legitimacy as the temporary administrator of the Church in Peter's name. His other "crimes" were his refusal to act as a secret informer for the GPU and making public his letter of December 1929 to Metropolitan Sergii, in which he expressed his concern over the developing splits in the Church caused "by Metropolitan Sergii's exceeding his authority" as the deputy *locum tenens*. In that letter, he recommended that church leaders avoid any form of political activities, and neither praise nor criticize the Soviet Government. The fourth "crime" was his refusal to ask the Soviet Government for pardon for participating in anti-Soviet organizations, because, as he pointed out, he had never participated in any such organizations. The final "reason" for his execution was that, in August 1937, he confided to the deputy-commandant of the prison that he was the *locum tenens,* and that the only reason for his imprisonment was his refusal to abdicate his post. This was interpreted as anti-Soviet agitation worthy of execution! For the GPU, however, he was a dead man long before his execution, as can be seen from their "informing" Metropolitan Sergii of Peter's death already in 1936. After receiving this false information, over twenty bishops gathered in Moscow for a solemn service at the Patriarchal cathedral at which Sergii was proclaimed the [patriarchal] *locum tenens*; although in the early 1930s Sergii wrote in the *Journal of the Moscow Patriarchate* that his prerogatives depended entirely on the living *locum tenens*. The moment Metropolitan Peter died, he wrote, his deputy would lose his right to govern the Church, as the source of Peter's authority was the local sobor's instruction to the Patriarch, while Peter's appointment of a deputy had had no such conciliar legitimacy.

The "Grigorian" Schism

During the early years of Metropolitan Peter's detention, the GPU tried to use the isolated and uninformed Metropolitan, as well as the other candidates listed in the late Patriarch Tikhon's will, to foment confusion and splits in the Church.

Having come to the conclusion that the Renovationists were a spent force, the OGPU now decided to cause a split in the Patriarchal Church by launching a competing conservative Church group. That group consisted of nine bishops assembled for a conference in Moscow on December 25, 1925, and chaired by Archbishop Grigorii (Yatskovskii) of Ekaterinburg (renamed Sverdlovsk). Using the false pretext that Peter had allegedly participated in counter-revolutionary activities and that with his arrest the Church had been deprived of leadership, the group named itself the Temporary Higher Church Council (THCC), but became popularly known as the Grigorians, after its chairman's name. It immediately received official registration from the Soviet Government, something that both Patriarch Tikhon and Metropolitan Peter had been trying to obtain in vain since 1919.

The Grigorians' claim that the Church had no leadership was unfounded, as Peter had left a will with three names of deputy *locum tenentes* in case of his arrest. Metropolitan Sergii (Stragorodskii) of Nizhnii Novgorod was first on the list. After becoming deputy *locum tenens*, Sergii refused to recognize the Grigorians. But Tuchkov arranged for Grigorii to meet with Metropolitan Peter in jail, and Grigorii misinformed Peter that Sergii could not lead the Church, as he was in Nizhnii Novgorod, and the Soviets would not allow him to move to Moscow. As to the other two candidates named in Peter's will, Mikhail, Metropolitan of Kiev and Exarch of the Ukraine, allegedly refused to accept the post, while Iosif (Petrovykh) was an unknown entity and would thus not be accepted by the Church. Unaware of the real situation, Peter believed Grigorii, signed a document validating the THCC, but replaced three members of that Council with other bishops, and obtained Tuchkov's promise to inform Peter's candidates of their appointment. This promise, however, was never fulfilled. In order to sow further confusion and splits, Tuchkov also met with Metropolitan Agafangel, who was on his way back from a three-year detention. He convinced the aging Metropolitan, who had been the second choice on Patriarch Tikhon's list of *locum tenentes* to declare his acceptance of the post, allegedly in order to put an end to the struggle for power between Grigorii and Sergii (sic!).

The naive old man took Tuchkov at his word and, on April 18,1926, sent a message to Metropolitan Sergii proclaiming himself the *locum tenens*. Also sending copies of the message to other dioceses, Agafangel unwittingly laid the foundations for splits within the "Tikhonite" Church. The abovementioned Damaskin cites another document of the Commission on Cults:

> ...the OGPU line on demoralizing the Tikhonite part of the Church is commendable...Concentrate on fomenting a split between Sergii...and Agafangel,...at the same time strengthening...the THCC...as an independent unit. Agafangel's address to the believers on accepting the responsibilities of locum tenens is most timely.[2]

2 Damaskin, *op. cit.,* 389, n.

Despite Metropolitan Sergii's advice to the contrary, Peter agreed to surrender his title of *locum tenens* to Agafangel (although with the following proviso: "In case of Metropolitan Agafangel's refusal, the prerogatives of *locum
tenens* return to me, and of deputy *locum tenens* to Metropolitan Sergii."[3] In
the meanwhile Sergii succeeded in convincing Agafangel that his claims were
uncanonical, and the brief schism was mended. Sergii also declared a church
ban on the Grigorievites.

Peace between Agafangel and Sergii clearly wrecked the GPU's plans,
which were further frustrated by Metropolitan Peter. Having finally understood what was happening, Peter issued from prison an address to the Church
on January 1, 1927, declaring the Grigorian group ecclesiastically invalid,
and approving Metropolitan Sergii's bans on the Grigorians and Metropolitan Agafangel's surrender of claims to Church leadership. Now Tuchkov tried
to get rid of Sergii by attempting to convince Peter to appoint Sergii to the Siberian see of Krasnoiarsk. Fr Damaskin cites Metropolitan Peter's letters to
OGPU Chairman Menzhinsky from 1928-33, in which the imprisoned Metropolitan complained about Tuchkov's attempts in 1926 to prevent Sergii's
participation in the Synod. Peter praised Sergii in those letters as one of the
best and most authoritative bishops in the Russian Church, deeply loved by
his flock.

In the meanwhile, the Grigorian schism remained rather weak and unstable. At first Grigorii had about ten bishops. Some would leave Grigorii, return
to Sergii through public repentance, but then return again to Grigorii. The
schism peaked in 1932 with twenty-seven bishops, of whom twelve had been
consecrated in the canonical (Tikhonite) Church. But the number of bishops
was out of proportion to the small size of their flock. To raise the THCC's
prestige, in June 1927 Tuchkov brought the very respected Bishop Ilarion
(Troitskii), one-time chief adviser to Patriarch Tikhon, back from imprisonment in the Arctic Solovki Islands to Moscow for negotiations with Grigorii.
The perceptive Ilarion refused to have anything to do with the THCC and
was sent back to the Solovki (and to his early death three years later). After
that, Grigorii realized the hopelessness of his situation, and at the group's conference of bishops in November 1927 resigned from the chairmanship, remaining only as the Bishop of Sverdlovsk. In 1937 this schism was subjected
to the same brutal destruction as all other religions, but having no roots in the

---

3 *Ibid.* 356-7.). In the meanwhile Sergii succeeded in convincing Agafangel that his claims were uncanonical,
and the brief schism was mended. Sergii also declared a church ban on the Grigorievites.

nation, it disappeared virtually without trace. The four surviving Grigorian bishops returned via repentance to the Church headed by Metropolitan Sergii in 1943 and were restored to the ranks they had held prior to their abandonment of the "Tikhonite" Church. The Grigorian venture was even less successful than that of the Renovationists. The latter, after all, had something to offer to those unhappy with the conservatism of the Patriarchal Church, as well as to ideologically left-wing Christians. Had they not compromised themselves by too close a collaboration with the atheistic regime and the hated secret police, they might well have had a future. The Grigorians offered only one alternative to the Church led by Metropolitan Sergii: their unconditional support and recognition by the Soviet State. They were similar to the Renovationists in precisely that feature which turned the believers away from the Renovationists, and offered no alternative in theology and ecclesiology to the Church led by Sergii. Moreover, their ranks contained not a single outstanding theologian or popular, respected bishop.

Metropolitan Sergii and the "Declaration of Loyalty"

While Tuchkov was spinning his crafty designs regarding the Grigorians and Metropolitan Peter, Sergii, unaware of them, was continuing his legalization attempts, submitting draft declarations of loyalty to the Soviets. Simultaneously, in 1926, he agreed to a secret election of a patriarch by soliciting written votes from all bishops via couriers. By the time a majority of bishops had been contacted, with almost all of them favoring Metropolitan Kirill of Kazan', the three couriers were apprehended by the GPU. Two of them were executed, while the third, Tavrion Batozsky was to spend his next twenty-eight years in prisons and concentration camps, and in the 1960s-70s became a revered *starets*. Living and actively catechizing in a small monastic community near Riga, he brought thousands (particularly young intellectuals) to the Church. But GPU vengeance was not limited to the three couriers. All the bishops who had participated in the "election," including Metropolitan Sergii, were imprisoned.

While Sergii was in jail, Tuchkov conducted negotiations about the future leadership of the Church with Metropolitan Peter, Bishop Ilarion, and Metropolitan Kirill. Tuchkov was willing to allow Kirill's elevation to the Patriarchate, but on condition that he would remove bishops at the OGPU's demand. Kirill agreed, on condition that in such cases he could say to the victim: "Brother, I have nothing against you. But it is the order of the GPU." When Tuchkov protested that the removal would have to be presented as if it had originated from Church authorities, Kirill pronounced his famous words: "You are not a cannon and I am not a projectile by which you can wreck the Church." He, as well as Ilarion and Peter, were sent back to their arctic exile. Their perseverance wrecked the GPU's hopes of fatally splitting the Church. Splits there were, as we have seen, but they would have been much more serious had such authoritative figures as Peter, Kirill or Ilarion been involved in them. A revengeful Soviet regime turned these three hierarchs into martyrs.

Unaware of Tuchkov's latest initiatives, the imprisoned Sergii was bargaining with the OGPU over the final text of his Declaration of Loyalty. The final text of July 1927 was preceded by three drafts in 1926. The first draft, in May 1926, was composed by bishops held prisoner in the Solovki, with Bishop Ilarion as the main author. Metropolitan Sergii composed the other two drafts in June 1926. Sergii's first text was a petition to the Commissar of Internal Affairs, asking him to grant legal registration to the Patriarchal Chancery, as well as to the Synod and other Church governing bodies, and, once they were legalized, to permit the publication of a monthly journal and the re-opening of theological schools to train clergy candidates. Sergii's second document was an address to bishops, pastors, and the flock, which in its essence was almost identical to the Solovki text. Both spoke of the incompatibility between Marxism and Christianity, the unacceptability to Christians of the Marxist materialistic interpretation of history and, most importantly, of the Bolsheviks' aim "to fight God and His power in the hearts of people." Yet, "one of the achievements of the October revolution is the liberation of the Church from all political and state missions." The Church would hold to these principles while teaching and practicing civic loyalty to the Soviet State and encouraging all citizens to fulfill their civic obligations. The Church, however, "cannot take upon herself such functions as watching over the political preferences of her members...even if that amounted to dividing our parishioners into those politically reliable or unreliable..." Obviously, neither the Solovki text nor Sergii's draft satisfied the Bolsheviks. Hence the 1927 version...

On March 30, 1927, Sergii was released from prison. In May, he submitted a petition to the Commissariat of Internal Affairs to register his Synod. The registration was granted on May 20. The infamous declaration was published on July 29. It differed radically from the 1926 draft. It vehemently denied any persecutions of the Church and even thanked the Government for its concern for the Church. All this, however, could already be found in diverse published statements by the late Patriarch after his release from prison in 1923. Some statements, however, give this text a different emphasis. Thus: "We want to be Orthodox and at the same time recognize the Soviet Union as our civic motherland. *Her*[4] joys and successes are our joys and successes, her misfortunes are our misfortunes." But essentially similar ideas were also expressed by Patriarch Tikhon, when in his "Testament" he called on all those who were unable to serve the Soviet State conscientiously to remove themselves from any active role in Church organs. What was new in the Declaration was the demand that émigré clergy sign a statement of loyalty to the Soviet Union. Although this was much tougher than Sergii's 1926 statement, where he had said that unless the émigré clergy stopped participating in anti-Soviet politics the Moscow Patriarchate would have to break all contacts with them, and they would have to go under the jurisdictions of local Orthodox Patriarchates. Yet even the 1927 loyalty demand followed logically from Patriarch Tikhon's "Testament," with its threat to subject émigré bishops to an ecclesiastical trial for their political activities. The Soviet stranglehold on the Church was getting stronger, hence the terminology in Church declarations were likewise becoming less flexible. Moreover, the need for the 1927 declaration was caused by the obvious insufficiency, in the eyes of the Bolsheviks, of the Patriarch's statement of April 1925.

Metropolitan Sergii managed to achieve legal registration only for his Synod. Individual parishes were registered with local soviets as lay religious associations. The Church as an entity, however, as well as individual dioceses, were never registered. Moreover, as M. Odintsov, a contemporary Russian archivist, points out, that registration never received any legal tender. The Church remained as legally disfranchised as before.

In Western Europe, Metropolitan Evlogii, appreciating Sergii's extremely difficult situation, produced a formula of declaration of loyalty for his clergy to sign, which simply required from the signatory to abstain from using the pulpit for any political statements. Metropolitan Sergii agreed to this formula. As to the Karlovcians, they decided in September 1927 to break all administrative contacts with the Moscow Patriarchate. Their allegedly canonical right to continue as an independent Church they based on Patriarch Tikhon's encyclical of November 20, 1920, which, we have seen above, did not apply to their case.

---

4 Emphasis supplied by me to make it clear that in Russian "Soviet Union" is masculine, while "motherland" is feminine. As Sergii would later confirm confidentially, the distinction was made to make it clear that he was speaking of loyalty to the native land, not to the communist-ruled political system.

The arrangement between Evlogii and Sergii did not last long, however. In 1929, at the invitation of the Archbishop of Canterbury, Evlogii participated in ecumenical prayers in England on behalf of the persecuted Christians in the Soviet Union. Metropolitan Sergii interpreted those prayers (or rather was forced to do so by the OGPU) as a political act and requested from Evlogii a promise never to do so again. Evlogii argued that it was his pastoral duty to participate in such prayers, and that he could not therefore promise to abstain from such acts in future. In response, Sergii ordered Evlogii to resign and to hand his functions over to his vicar, Archbishop Vladimir (Tikhonitskii). The latter refused. Evlogii called a conference of laity and clergy representatives of all his parishes, which ruled that he should retain the leadership of the diocese and appealed to the Ecumenical Patriarch to accept it under his omophorion. The Patriarch agreed, granting the Russian diocese virtual autonomy in 1931; but Sergii refused to recognize the legitimacy of this act and placed ecclesiastical bans on Evlogii and his whole clergy. The only bishop in Western Europe to remain under the Moscow Patriarchate at that time was Veniamin (Fedchenkov), with a single parish in Paris. In 1933, Metropolitan Sergii sent him to the United States, where about a score of parishes remained under the Moscow Patriarchate, later joined by those parishes which had joined the Renovationists in the 1920s. After Veniamin's departure from Europe, Sergii appointed Elevferii, Archbishop of Lithuania, the only other bishop outside of the USSR remaining faithful to the Moscow Patriarchate, to head all the Moscow Patriarchate's parishes in Europe.

Schisms on the Right

The 1927 Declaration in itself did not cause any immediate splits. A propensity for schisms had been evident long before the Declaration. As we have seen the first stimulus in that direction was Metropolitan Agafangel's 1926 declaration, in which he claimed for himself the prerogatives of *locum tenens*. He justified his decision by the following factors: that he had been appointed *locum tenens* by the imprisoned Patriarch Tikhon in May 1922; that in the Patriarch's Will he was listed second, ahead of Peter; that Peter was currently in prison and could not thus administer the Church; moreover, having handed over his prerogatives to the Grigorian impostors, Peter had lost his right to administer the Church. Agafangel even forbade the mentioning of Peter's name in the liturgical prayers in his diocese. But before the end of June 1926, Metropolitan Sergii succeeded in convincing Agafangel that: his status as *locum tenens* had ended with Tikhon's resumption of his duties in 1923; Metropolitan Peter had rescinded his recognition of the Grigorians after having been properly informed; when Peter assumed the functions of locum tenens, the two other candidates mentioned in the Will lost their claims to the title, while Peter, as the only legitimate *locum tenens*, appointed Sergii as his deputy. Agafangel agreed with Sergii's arguments and renounced his claim. But this brief schism, caused by one of the most respected hierarchs of the Church, sowed seeds of doubts and distrust towards the hierarchs in church circles, seeds of suspicion.

Naturally, Sergii's 1927 Declaration could not but enhance suspicions and distrust. No believer could accept it lightly. The Solovki prisoners sharply criticized the document for betraying the martyrs by its expression of gratitude to the Soviet regime and for stating that no one was imprisoned in the Soviet Union for his religious beliefs. Yet they saw no cause for breaking canonical relations with Sergii, as the Declaration contained no theological heresy. This view was shared by Metropolitan Peter, who transmitted an oral message to Sergii through Bishop Vasilii (Beliaev) just released from exile in September 1927, in which Peter expressed general satisfaction with the Declaration, although disagreeing with some details "on which he preferred not to state his opinion, whether negative or positive." Even in his 1930 letter to Sergii, full of concern over new splits in the Church and advising Sergii to return the Church onto the direction "in which you were leading her during the first part of your tenure,"[5] Peter asks Sergii not even to think of retirement and assures him of his deep confidence and respect.

The largest, most extreme and persistent schism-on-the-right was fomented by Metropolitan Iosif (Petrovykh). But even this split was not directly caused by the Declaration. In 1926, Sergii appointed Iosif Metropolitan of Leningrad. Iosif accepted the appointment, but the GPU refused to give him a Leningrad residence permit. Then, in 1927, Sergii appointed him to another vacant see, that of Odessa. Iosif then accused Sergii of being a toy in the hands of the GPU and issued an appeal to the faithful of Leningrad to break with Sergii. The Josephite (Iosif = Joseph) split went so far as to deny the validity of the sacraments in the churches of the Moscow Patriarchate (this is reminiscent of the third-century Donatist heresy, also shared by the post-war Karlovcians). Yet, had the GPU not rejected Iosif's appointment to Leningrad, the split probably would not have taken place.

5 I.e., prior to Sergii's arrest.

Other groups of so-called "non-commemorators," i.e., those who did not commemorate Sergii's name at the liturgy, did not deny the validity of the "Sergians'" sacraments; their quarrel was over the extent of Sergii's legitimate powers as *deputy locum tenens*. Thus the two other most influential leaders of anti-Sergiite splits, Metropolitan Kirill of Kazan' and Bishop Afanasii (Sakharov) of Kovrov, argued that Sergii, as a mere deputy, had the duty to preserve the Church and to administer her by himself, but had no right unilaterally to create a Synod or any other collective administrative organs. Hence, they argued, his Synod and the decrees issued in its name had no validity. Sergii himself aggravated tensions by issuing bans against Kirill and other bishops who refused to remain under his administration; and, of course, they did not recognize the validity of these bans. In his correspondence with Kirill, Sergii argued that with his appointment as Peter's deputy he inherited all the rights of the *locum tenens*. As stated above, these prerogatives, argued Sergii, were valid only as long as the *locum tenens* was alive.

Metropolitan Iosif was executed in 1937, Kirill apparently died in exile in Kazakhstan in 1941. Bishop Afanasii survived the longest and thus became the widely recognized leader of the "noncommemorators" or the "Catacomb Orthodox." To the end of Sergii's life, he refused to recognize him. But his quarrel with Sergii had nothing to do with the 1927 Declaration or the general subservience to the Soviet regime, as can be seen from the following: first, he broke with Sergii in 1933 over the issue of his prerogatives, six years after the Declaration; second, as soon as Alexii I was elected Patriarch in 1945, Afanasii ended his schism, returned to the Moscow Patriarchate, and sent an appeal to all the "catacombers" to return to the Patriarchal Church. Yet that period was the worst in terms of the sycophancy of the Church leadership, with its sickening praise of Stalin. Yet even this was not sufficient reason for schism in the eyes of this confessor, who had spent a total of thirty-three years in prisons, camps, and exile.

There has also been a curious transformation of names. Today, the émigré Karlovcians and the former real or false "catacombers" claim to be the true successors of Patriarch Tikhon ("Tikhonites"), and disdainfully label as "Sergiites" those belonging to the Moscow Patriarchate, accusing Sergii of betraying Tikhon's legacy. But in the 1930s, the "Josephites" called those loyal to Metropolitan Sergii "Tikhonites," and they used the term with a pejorative connotation. Karlovcian authors of the 1930s, such as Talberg and Olsufiev, also pointed to that continuity and severely criticized Patriarch Tikhon for surrendering to the

Bolsheviks. Those authors lacked compassion and understanding of the situation, but at least they were honest, logical and consistent: Sergii's policies were indeed a direct continuation (under worsening conditions!) of Tikhon's policies, partly from as far back as 1919, and fully so from 1923.

Agreeing to such extreme compromises with the Soviet Government, Sergii, as he wrote and stated to his critics, hoped to achieve the release of all imprisoned clergy, to restore theological schools, the church press, church-related organizations, such as brotherhoods, sisterhoods, and youth groups—on a par with the Baptists, for instance. According to information from people who were close to Sergii, the GPU threatened him that, should he refuse to write a submissive declaration, all the imprisoned bishops (numbering 117) would be shot.

In practice, the gains were very modest and temporary: a small proportion of detained bishops and priests was released, a theological institute was opened in Leningrad but shut by the government three years later, and, between 1931-35, the *Journal of the Moscow Patriarchate*, edited by Metropolitan Sergii, appeared more-or-less monthly, with a circulation of 3,000 copies.

The All-out Offensive and Metropolitan Sergii

In 1927, the relatively liberal New Economic Policy was still in force, with its rather tolerant policies towards most religions; and Sergii thought he could, by his capitulation, win similar privileges for the Orthodox Church. Can he be criticized for lacking a prophetic vision of worse things to come, such as the April 1929 "laws" forbidding all forms of religious "propaganda" and allowing only "the performance of the cult" inside church walls? With the abolition of the NEP by the end of 1928, prohibitively high taxes were levied on all forms of private enterprise, and the Church was treated as a private enterprise—with no consideration that she was not a for-profit business and that her funds were made up entirely of voluntary donations.

Taxes often exceeded a priest's real income. The basic tax on private enterprise could be as high as 81 percent of its income. To this could be added a tax for failing to vote, whereas as social "deprivees" the clergy was deprived of the right to vote. A tax was also imposed for not serving in the armed forces. Again, "deprivees" were not allowed to serve in the army; instead, they were called randomly into the so-called "labor army," where they were made to do the hardest work possible, such as felling trees, in conditions that differed from a concentration camp only in the absence of armed prison guards and in the relative shortness of such tours of duty. The minimum tax for not serving in the army was up to 50 percent of one's income tax, though not exceeding 20 percent of one's total income. Thus the total tax demanded from a priest could be 101 percent of his income, not including the tax for not voting and other levies. In 1929, the clergy also began to be taxed for every piece of land surrounding their houses which they may have used productively, such as a kitchen garden. They also had to pay for the dwelling in which they lived, even if it was an old rectory; this amounted to 10 percent annually of the assessed total value of the house or apartment, whereas "the toiling classes" had to pay only 1 percent if the house was made of brick and 2 percent, if it was wooden. The archives contain numerous cases where they had to pay taxes far in excess of their total income. For instance, Bishop Sinezii of Izhevsk, whose income was 120 rubles per month, was given two days to pay a tax of 10,703 rubles for the year 1930.

A 1929 decree forbade the clergy to reside in nationalized or municipal urban housing if their income exceeded 3,000 rubles a year. If it did, they were forced to vacate such dwellings immediately. As private housing was very scarce in the post-NEP cities, and few people dared to offer housing to the besieged clergy, the latter were often forced fictitiously to divorce their wives to save them and their children from losing the roof over their heads. Another decree, in August 1929, deprived the clergy and their families of state insurance, including free medical care.

Rural taxes were mostly levied in kind. Since the post-revolutionary rural clergy had at best a meager kitchen garden, that tax was usually paid for them by well-to-do peasants. After *dekulakization* and collectivization, no such farmers remained. Unable to meet the tax demands, priests were accused of deliberately sabotaging the industrialization drive and sentenced to long terms in concentration camps, or even executed as "enemies of the people."

According to numerous archival documents, Metropolitan Sergii, even as he was being forced to make mendacious public statements about freedom of religion, bombarded the Cult Commission with complaints about those unfair and impossible taxes and about persecutions of the clergy. Thus, in 1930, the OGPU forced him to read a statement before foreign journalists about freedom of religion in the USSR (he read it without comment, bowed and left without entertaining any questions). But in February of that same year, he submitted a memorandum to Smidovich, chairman of the Cult Commission, protesting against persecutions which took such forms as:

> Insurance premiums on churches [which] especially in the rural areas,...are so high as to deprive the believers of the possibility to use them... authors' honoraria for church singing,...which should be levied only for singing works...composed by definite authors...not for choral singing and even clergy chanting... which is treated as an "artistic performance"

subjecting the clergy to an additional five percent tax on their income. The Metropolitan also complained that, although the State had ceased to provide insurance to church choir singers from June 1929, it continued to collect insurance premiums from them. He demanded also an end to the practice of expelling singers from the Artists Union for singing in church choirs. Sergii protested against taxes in kind, and against the special industrialization taxes levied on parishes. As parishes had no independent income, these taxes had to be paid by parishioners, and thus amounted to a veiled form of "special tax on faith." He protested against equating the Church and her servants with *kulaks* for taxation purposes, and demanded that their taxation levels be made level with those of the free professions. When a priest's property is confiscated for unpaid taxes, wrote Sergii, a basic minimum of furniture, household goods and clothes must be left to the family; and assigned labor duties should correspond to the age and health of the clergy. He requested the restoration of the priest's right to live close to the church in which he served, as well as the right of the clergy's children to attend state schools and universities. He requested that the opinions of believers, rather than of unbelievers, be sought when the question of closing a church arose; and he complained that the registration of religious associations was being used as a pretext to dissolve them and thus to close churches. In many cases, the associations' application forms were ignored, while the final date for registration was May 30, 1930. Religious associations unregistered by that date were simply dissolved. In conclusion, he reminded Smidovich of his 1929 petition requesting the reopening of the Leningrad Theological Institute.

From that list of complaints alone, the reader can form a realistic picture of the conditions under which the Church and believers had to live. One important factor leading to such concerted oppression was the "alarming" growth of the Church in the latter part of the 1920s. The number of Orthodox churches in the Russian Republic alone grew from 27,126 in 1926 to 29,584 in 1927. From the point of view of state atheism, this was a major scandal, a catastrophe which could be stopped and reversed only through the application of blanket terror, as all other methods (including selective terror) tried in the previous decade had failed.

As to Sergii's requests, they did not fall entirely on deaf ears because of the famous *Pravda* article by Stalin in March 1930, "Dizziness from Success," which represented a temporary, tactical retreat from the use of terror and brutal force in collectivization. And indeed, beginning in June 1930, there appeared numerous secret All-Union Central Executive Committee (AUCEC) and Commissariat of Finance circulars regulating taxes on the clergy. A secret AUCEC circular of August 30, signed by Kalinin, limits the tax on a priest's agrarian income from his garden plot to no more than twice a peasant's tax from a plot of equal size. The tax on a priest's financial remuneration may be increased by no more than 75 percent from the 1928-29 level, even if his income has remained absolutely static since 1928. And yet, these marked an improvement from the arbitrariness of 1929, a "respite" of sorts before the all-out attack of 1937-39. The orders were kept secret to prevent the possibility for those concerned to protest violations of laws, as they did not know or see them.

1929-30 also brought a cruel purge of the so-called "idealists" from the Academy of Sciences, when it was transferred from Leningrad to Moscow. The "idealists" were scholars who refused to accept Marxist dialectical materialism as the absolute truth and foundation of all learning. Some one hundred leading scholars, most of them practicing members of the Orthodox Church and including some former theology professors (clergy and lay) who were expert in ancient languages, Byzantine history, Slavonic linguistics, etc., were either condemned to long prison terms or even executed. The victims included such prominent figures as Platonov, the great historian, and Egorov, a leading mathematician.

In the religious persecutions of 1929 and the subsequent decade, all religions were attacked, prayer houses closed, and often dynamited. As far as the Orthodox Church was concerned, by 1940 only some 200-300 churches remained open for worship in the entire Soviet Union, not including the 4,000 or so Orthodox churches gained with the annexation of Moldavia, western Ukraine, western Belorussia, the Baltic states, and parts of Finnish Karelia in 1939-40. At least 40,000 members of the Orthodox clergy, a similar number of monks and nuns, and unknown millions of lay believers perished for their faith in the pre-war decades.[6]

6 The figure of 200,000 clergy annihilated by the Bolsheviks, recently announced in an official Russian Government release for the media is based on a confusion between two Russian terms: *sdviashchennosluzhiteli* (literally: servants of the sacred), i.e., clergy *per se*, and *tserkovnosluzhiteli*, i.e., sextons, choir directors, psalmists, etc. Monks and nuns were obviously also counted as clergy. That could easily add to and even surpass the total of 200,000.

On the other hand, the Communist slaughter reduced the number of functioning churches to the extent that people stopped differentiating between "Tikhonites" and "Grigoriites," "Josephites" and Old Ritualists, Noncommemorators and Renovationists. Believers simply went to the only open church in the area, and this helped to achieve church unity during the post-1943 recovery. Where no open churches survived, "catacomb" priests and tiny communities kept the faith. They were a mixed lot. Many "catacombers" were non-commemorators of various shades, but at least as many were unregistered "Tikhonite" (or "Sergiite") wandering priests, secretly visiting and ministering to the faithful, serving liturgies in their homes, as well as performing baptisms and marriages. As Natalia Kiter, a former active member of the Tikhonite/Sergiite Church in Leningrad remarked, all church life in the 1930s was in the catacombs, including even the officially open one:

> Underground brotherhoods grew. Their purpose was the fulfillment of the basic Commandments: the love of God and the neighbor ...there was much selfless charity work...aimed particularly at helping those persecuted by the Godless state...much running around to jails, hospitals, camps and places of internal exile...

> The life of the Church was moving underground...Not the Church herself, but her real life and activity.

Kiter denies the common misconception that Sergii banned public prayers for the victims of terror:

> On the dates of the death of Patriarch Tikhon, the execution of Metropolitan Veniamin [etc.] ...special memorial services were conducted during which long lists of the newly martyred and murdered were read;...and prayers were said in liturgies for the health of the imprisoned ones.

The Renovationists, she writes, to her last day in Leningrad (1941) continued to collaborate with the Soviets by denouncing the Tikhonites as counterrevolutionaries in sermons and public lectures. The Josephites, whose last church in Leningrad was closed in 1939, attacked the Tikhonites just as bitterly. The Josephites, she writes, lacked in Christian charity; they were proud in their self-righteous belief that they alone were the true Orthodox Christians, and had only contempt for everybody else. In the final analysis, however we may sympathize with Sergii's tragic plight, it is evident that his 1927 Declaration did not at all protect the Church from the near-total destruction of the 1930s. The Metropolitan himself, on the eve of the German attack, apparently thought that the Russian Church would go the way of the Church of Carthage. When Archpriest-

Professor Vasilii Vinogradov, just released from a concentration camp, visited Metropolitan Sergii in the spring of 1941, the Metropolitan said to him sadly: "Our Church is living through her last days of existence."

Phases in Soviet Antireligious Policy

The different phases of Soviet antireligious policies partly follow each other in sequence and partly overlap, coexisting and contradicting one another. On the whole, they correspond to the phases in general Soviet internal polices, and particularly the ideological party line.

The first phase accompanied the so-called "War Communism" of the Civil War period, which could be seen as an attempt to follow Marx's ideological precepts in the most orthodox way. In economics, it expressed itself in the abolition of the market and money economy, of private property and private enterprise. In religious affairs, Lenin hoped to kill the Church by depriving her of a material and legal base, according to Marx's doctrine that religion as a superstructure would simply wither away if deprived of its material basis. The Eighth Department of the Commissariat of Justice (in the early 1920s renamed the Fifth Department), whose task was to nationalize all Church properties, was quite symptomatically referred to as the "Liquidation Department," expressing a confident belief in the imminent liquidation of the Church. As much of the fighting in the Civil War was done by autonomous Bolshevik "war lords," the physical terror against the Church, the clergy and believers, although unleashed by the policies of Lenin and the Politburo, can conveniently be written off as arising from local initiatives.

The second phase began with the introduction of the New Economic Policy in 1921. The relatively relaxed climate of the NEP did not permit a head-on attack on the Church; while the end of the Civil War and the centralization of the state precluded the possibility of the central government's washing its hands of any local attacks on religion. So, Lenin adopted a policy of divide and conquer, as we have seen, attempting to single out the main national Church for attack while demonstrating a tolerant attitude towards other religions, claiming that the Orthodox Church was persecuted as a reactionary remnant of tsarism and for its alleged subversive policies against the Soviet state—and the Renovationist Church was launched as an Orthodox substitute and to provide an alibi. Archival Party documents indicate that party bosses saw this selective policy as a temporary situation, and that they believed a frontal attack on all religions was inevitable in the future. Trotsky even wrote that, in the future, after the Patriarchal Church was destroyed, the regime would have to liquidate the Renovationists who, because of their modernism, constituted a greater danger to the victory of communist atheism than did the traditional Church.

But while the divide-and-conquer policy was in effect, the various aspects of the antireligious struggle were relegated to several departments. The fabrication of "criminal" cases and other terroristic measures against the Church became the responsibility of the GPU's Sixth Department, headed by Tuchkov. In the autumn of 1922, a special Antireligious Commission of the RCP(b) Politburo was established to coordinate all aspects of antireligious policy. For the next eight years, this commission remained in charge not only of the whole Party's, but also the State's, antireligious front, as can be seen from such facts as that its meetings took place in the office of Kalinin, nominal "president" of the Soviet Union, and that Lenin, in his "On the Significance of Militant Materialism," hailed as his "philosophical testament," called the struggle against religion "a task for our state." Chairman of this Commission from the beginning to its closure was Emelian Yaroslavskii (real name: Minei Gubelman).

Also in 1922, or somewhat earlier, a "Commission on the Separation of the Church from the State" was created, at first chaired by the same Krasikov who headed the Eighth (later the Fifth) Department of the People's Commissariat of Justice. The Commission changed its name and status in relation to other state departments several times. In April 1929, it became the "Permanent Commission on Cults," headed by Smidovich and attached to the Presidium of the All-Union Central Executive Committee (AUCEC). In the latter part of 1930, Smidovich, a decent and somewhat legalistically inclined lawyer, resigned; and its head once again became the much less scrupulous Peter Krasikov. The Commission ceased to exist sometime in 1938. In this era of the total assault on religion, there was no longer any need for a body that had any pretense to legalism. Apparently, by then all religious matters were dealt with by the GPU/NKVD Sixth Department, or its equivalent.

Thus we have come to the Third Phase, marked by a total assault on all religions, which began with the liquidation of the NEP in 1928 and continued, with some minor respites, until the autumn of 1939. In that year the Soviet Union annexed western Ukraine and western Belorussia, with their well-organized and intensive religious life (predominantly Orthodox, but with large minorities of Byzantine-Rite Ukrainian Catholics, Jews and pockets of Polish Roman Catholics); and this forced the Soviets to moderate their physical attack on religion, at least in the western regions.

Documents on the number of functioning churches by 1940 on the original Soviet territories (before the annexation) have not yet been found. But even the Cult Commission figures for 1936, found in an internal memo, are quite telling. The following are some of its data on the Orthodox Church: where "there had been 72,936 [Orthodox] places of worship before the revolution...20,665 are functioning now." 41,868 had been closed officially, 9,878, unofficially. The "administrative" (i.e., arbitrary) methods of closure are spelled out as follows:

1. [The church] is temporarily used as a granary, but then never returned to the believers;

2. Believers are told to repair the church much more extensively than necessary and given an unrealistically short deadline;

3. Refusal [by the local soviet] to register new members of the religious association in place of those who had left;

4. Closing the church on the pretext of a quarantine [on the grounds of some epidemic in the area, although schools and other institutions remain open], which is then never lifted;

5. Refusal to register a [new] priest;

6. Subjecting a church to over inflated taxes, and then closing it on the pretext of tax default.

The memo also reports an annual growth of messages from local religious societies—from 1,094 in 1934 to 2,945 in 1936—and written complaints—from 8,229 in 1934 to 9,646 in 1936, most of them reporting on compulsory closures of churches and requesting their reopening.

According to its 1931 Statute (it is not clear whether that Statute was ever adopted or remained merely a draft), the Commission, if it discovered an illegal action by a local soviet regarding a religion, could only report the case to the AUCEC Presidium. But this body—in 1936 it became the USSR Supreme Soviet Presidium—and its chairman, Mikhail Kalinin, were powerless against the NKVD (the GPU's successor), which was implementing the Communist Party's policy of liquidating religion. Thus, in the Volga town of

Arzamas, where before the revolution there had been thirty-six churches and five monasteries for the population of 14,000, the county soviet closed the last two Orthodox churches in town and another in a suburban village. It acted illegally, not awaiting the Commission's conclusion, and based its decision on a vote taken at a local club in which only forty-seven persons out of 173 voted in favor of the closures (even though religious believers avoided the club!). The Commission's protest proved futile, as the chairman of the Arzamas soviet justified the closures on the ground that "there are still about 1,000 priests and monks living in the town," and the reopening of a church would lead to religious re-activation.[7]

While allegedly defending the "legal " rights of believers, the Commission's documents at the same time justify the enhanced persecutions of the late thirties on the grounds that religious activists were trying to use to their advantage Stalin's Constitution (of 1936), which had removed the stigma of "deprivees" from the clergy, as well as "the population census" of 1937, which was the last to ask whether the respondents' believed in God and to which confession they belonged. The census had revealed that over 50 percent of the population were still believers: 44 percent among literates and 74 percent among illiterates; 35 percent of 16-19-year-olds identified themselves as believers; almost 40 percent among 20-29-year-olds, etc. On the basis of that census—suppressed at the time—Yaroslavsky, leader of the League of the Militant Godless, suddenly began to state in his speeches and articles that fifty percent of the population were still believers: two-thirds among village dwellers and one-third in the urban population. This contradicted his earlier claims that up to 90 percent among the younger Soviet generations were atheists. Regarding references to the Stalin Constitution, Soviet reports of the time claim that its paragraph on the rights of social organizations to propose candidates for elections to the Supreme Soviet was being abused by the "clericalists," who claimed that the Constitution gave such rights to religious associations. Soviet ideologues responded that only societies upholding class-oriented, socialist ideas could be considered as proper social organizations in a socialist state. Religion, being a class enemy, could not enjoy the rights of a social organization in the USSR. These alleged attempts of believers were interpreted in Soviet propaganda publications as deliberate subversion against the construction of a socialist society and used for more mass arrests of the clergy in the final storm of 1937-39, in the course of which up to 20,500 Orthodox churches

---

7 By that strange "dialectical" logic, churches could function where there was no demand for them, but had to be closed where demand was particularly high!

must have been liquidated or closed, as by the end of 1939 the total number of still functioning churches was somewhere between 100 and 300, not counting the newly annexed territories.

The League of Militant Godless

The mass closure of churches, especially after 1928, and the public burning of icons, Scriptures, and other religious books were mostly brought about by the League's activists. In 1922 the movement began as "The Society of Friends of *The Godless* Newspaper." In 1924, the Antireligious Commission decided to change its name to the *League of the Godless*, which it officially adopted at its First Congress in 1925. From its beginning to its end during World War II, it was chaired by Yaroslavsky.

In 1929, at its second and last congress, the League added the adjective *Militant* to its name. Antireligious hooliganism became its main function: *pogroms* against churches and other houses of worship, blasphemous antireligious parades, equally blasphemous "Easters" and "Christmases," the torching of masses of icons, closing churches—all allegedly on behalf of the general public. These actions by an allegedly autonomous social movement fit well with the NEP system of tolerating some pluralism. In this way, the Government could pretend to bear no responsibility for such actions. However, this "closely allied" organization enjoyed the right to establish cells in schools, the armed forces, factories, and collective farms. As a "representative of the vanguard of society," the League demanded ideological accountability even from state institutions, such as schools or the Commissariat of Education, which the League took to task at its Second Congress for what it claimed was its insufficiently active antireligious struggle. The Commissariat of Education tried to justify itself by boasting that it had reduced the list of "cult structures" protected by the state for their artistic value (a euphemism for churches and monasteries) from 7,000 to a mere 1,000—i.e., 6,000 artistically unique churches and monasteries were doomed to destruction.

A Congress resolution demanded that schools be converted from areligious to antireligious, and that teachers be turned into propagandists of atheism, while teachers who believed in God should lose their jobs. Another resolution pledged to turn Moscow into a godless capital within five years, while raising the League's membership to 17 million by 1931. In fact, the LMG's maximum size was reached in 1932, with 5,670,000 members. During that year, the League adopted a five-year plan to eradicate all traces of religion in the USSR, coinciding chronologically with the Second Five-Year Plan. Between 1930-32, its publishing activity also reached its peak: in 1931 *The Godless* newspaper reached a circulation of 500,000, and its namesake illustrated magazine, 200,000 copies per issue; the total circulation of antireligious books and brochures grew from 12,000,000 signatures in 1927 to 800,000,000 in 1930. After 1932, the League's membership, as well as its publications, begin to decline. Even *The Godless* ceased publication for over two years between 1936-39. As neither the number of publications nor the volume of inductions into an organization supported by the Party and the State was determined by supply and demand, this decline could only be the result of a change in policy at the very top. Namely, with the abolition of the NEP, and especially with the adoption of a policy of total annihilation of all religions, the necessity for quasi-independent organizations on the antireligious front disappeared, just as did the need for the Cult Commission.

September 1939-June 1941

The period between the beginning of World War II and the Soviet Union's entry into the war with the surprise German attack of June 1941 could be considered either as Phase Four or as a brief interlude between Phases Three and Four. In the latter case, Phase Four began with the German attack and continued until Stalin's death in 1953 or, perhaps more accurately, until Khrushchev's new assault on religion beginning in 1957.

The Soviet annexation of the western territories in 1939-40 (eastern Poland, the Baltic republics, Moldavia and parts of Finnish Karelia) in 1939-40, presented by propaganda as the liberation of the toiling masses from their bourgeois exploiters, obliged the regime to moderate its anti-religious attack somewhat, not only in the newly annexed territories, but to some extent even in the original Soviet territories. The importance Stalin attached to his religious policies in the annexed areas is evident in the fact that, of the remaining four bishops of the Moscow Patriarchate (all the others had been either shot, imprisoned, or forced to live in retirement in disguise), two were sent to these territories: Metropolitan Nikolai (Yarushevich) to the Ukraine as Metropolitan of Kiev, spending most of his time in Western Ukraine; and Metropolitan Sergii (Voskresenskii) to Riga as Moscow's exarch for the Baltic republics.

In these twenty-odd months prior to the German attack, articles in the Soviet press again began to distinguish between, on the one hand, ordinary religious believers, many of whom—stated numerous articles—were decent

Soviet patriots and honest workers, and, on the other, religious ideologies and ideologues. Religion, they said, remained a class enemy, but not individual believers, whose religious feelings, however unenlightened, should not be insulted. In the annexed territories, high taxes on clergy income were introduced; but arrests of the clergy, both Orthodox and Uniate (Byzantine Rite Roman Catholic), were relatively rare; and the forced closure of churches was there virtually unknown. A normal seven-day week, with Sunday as the day off, was reintroduced in 1939 after ten years of experiments with a five day week. The five-day week had been greeted in 1929 by *The Godless* as a crucially important step towards the building of Godless socialism, as, with the abolition of Sunday as the day of rest, most people lost the possibility to attend church regularly. There were only a few cases when closed churches in the Soviet Union proper were reopened during this interlude; but the smell of war was in the air, and Stalin realized that he had at least to pay lip service to national traditions, beliefs and patriotism if he wanted to win the war.

FOR FURTHER READING

Aikman, David B., *The Role of Atheism in the Marxist Tradition* (Doctoral dissertation, U. of Washington, 1979).

Bennigsen, Alexandre and Wimbush, Enders S., *Muslim National Communism in the Soviet Union* (University of Chicago Press, 1979).

Constitution of 1936 (Moscow: Foreign Languages Publishing House, 1962).

Bociurkiw, Bohdan, "Lenin and Religion," in *Lenin: the Man, the Theorist, the Leader*, Leonard Schapiro and P. Reddaway, eds. (London: Pall Mall Press, 1967).

Bogolepov, A., *Tserkov' pod vlast'iu kommunizma* (Munich, 1958).

Chrysostomus, J., *Kirchengeschichte Russlands der neusten Zeit*, 3 vols. (Munich-Salzburg, 1965-68).

Curtiss, J., *The Russian Church under the Soviet State, 1917-1950* (Boston: Little Brown, 1953).

Damaskin, Hieromonk (Oklovskii), *Mucheniki, ispovedniki...*, vol. 2 (see previous chapter),

Dunn, Denis J., *The Catholic Church and the Soviet Government, 1919-1949* (New York: Columbia University Press, Monogr. No. XXX).

Elevferii, Metropolitan, *Nedelia v Patriarkhii* (Paris, 1933).

Fletcher, *The Russian Orthodox Church Underground, 1917-1970* (London: Oxford University Press, 1971).

Kiter, N., "Ispovedniki i mucheniki 30h gg." *Vestnik RKhD, NO.* 150 (1987), 235-48.

Manuil, M., *Die russische orthodoxen Bischofe von 1893 bis 1965. Bio-Bibliographie* (Erlangen: Oikonomia, 1981).

Marshall, Richard H. Jr., ed., *Aspects of Religion in the Soviet Union, 1917-1967* (University of Chicago Press, 1971).

Marx, Karl, *On Religion*, Saul Padover trans. & ed. (New York: McGraw-Hill, 1974).

Odintsov, M., archivist and ed, "Deklaratsiia mitr. Sergiia: dokumenty i svidetel'stva sovremennikov," *Disput*, Nos. 1 and 2, pp. 182-197 and 174-203, respectively (Moscow, 1992).

Olsufiev, Count D., *Mysli soborianina o nashei tserkovnoi smute* (Paris, 1928).

Ostraia luka. Samizdat Archives, Keston College (now "Keston Research," Oxford)

Patriarkh Sergii i ego dukhovnoe nasledstvo (Moscow: the Patriarchate, 1947).

Polskii, priest Mikhail, *Polozhenie Tserkvi v Sovetskoi Rossii: ocherk bezhavshego iz Rossii sviashchennika* (Jerusalem, 1931).

Pospielovsky, D., "Mitropolit Sergii i raskoly sprava," *Vestnik RKhD*, No. 158 (1991).

_____, "Ot patriarkha Tikhona k mitropolitu (patriarkhu) Sergiiu: preemstvennost' ili predatel'stvo?" *Tserkov' i vremia*," No. 3 (The Moscow Patriarchate, 1992)

_____, *A History of Soviet Atheism in Theory and Practice, and the Believer*, 3 vols. (1987-88).

_____, *The Russian Church under the Soviet Regime: 1917-1982*, vol. 1 (Crestwood, NY: St.Vladimir's Seminary Press, 1984.

_____, *Russkaia Pravoslavnaia Tserkov' v XX veke* (see previous chapter).

Prokhanov, Ivan, *In the Cauldron of Russia, 1869-1933* (New York, 1933).

Smolensk Archives (Cambridge, MA: Harvard U., Widener Library).

Shishkin, A.A., *Sushchnost' i kriticheskaia otsenka obnovlencheskogo raskola v Russkoi pravoslavnoi tserkvi* (Kazan', 1970).

Talberg, N.D., *Tserkovnyi raskol* (Paris, 1927).

Thrower, James, *Marxist-Leninist 'Scientific Atheism' and the Study of Religion and Atheism in the USSR* (Berlin: Mouton, 1983).

Vestnik RKhD, the "Sud'by Rossii" (Destiny of Russia) Section in issues Nos.: 150, 151, 152, 157, 158.

Yaroslavskii, Emelian, *Religion in the USSR* (New York: International Publishers, 1934).

_____, *Protiv religii i tserkvi: sobranie sochinenii,* 5 vols. (Moscow, 1935).

Zakonodatel'stvo o religioznykh kul'takh (Legislation on Religion: "restricted to state officials' use only"), 2nd ed. (Moscow: Iuridicheskaia literatura, 1971). (Smuggled out and reprinted: New York: Chalitdze Press, 1981).

CHAPTER 12

THE CHURCH DURING THE WAR

The German Attack

Possibilities for the Church changed radically after the German attack, as Sergii, the *locum tenens*, on Sunday, June 22, 1941, the very day of the attack, opted unequivocally to take a patriotic stand. Stalin, meanwhile, panicked, hid himself at his suburban dacha in Kuntsevo, and dared for the first time to appeal to the nation over the radio only on July 3. In a trembling voice, he spoke words more appropriate for a preacher than for the "leader of the world proletariat": "Dear countrymen, Brothers and Sisters! I address myself, to you, my friends..."

On June 22, Soviet newspapers reported nothing on the war: *Pravda* appeared with an editorial on teachers' summer holidays. Molotov, Chairman of the Council of Peoples' Commissars, made the first official announcement of the war only in the late afternoon, although the attack had begun at 4 a.m. In contrast, Metropolitan Sergii addressed a patriotic sermon to his flock at the end of that Sunday morning service.

For believers the day of the attack had a mystical significance, for it took place on the Sunday commemorating all Russian saints. The Metropolitan was informed about the attack by one of his assistants as he was about to begin the special intercessory service to Russian saints, after having completed the Sunday liturgy. At the end of the service he pronounced his momentous sermon. "The Orthodox Church," he said, "has always shared with her people their trials, as well as their joys. Neither will she abandon her people today, blessing...the coming exploit of the whole nation." He must have been aware that Hitler claimed to be defending Christian civilization, that the buckles worn by the German soldiers bore the words, "God is with us," when he warned the clergy not to ponder over "possible benefits on the other side of the front." He ordered that the sermon be mimeographed and distributed to all surviving parishes. This practice he continued throughout the war; even though the law forbade the Church from getting involved in state and social issues.

Four days later, after a special *Te Deum* service for victory, he delivered another fiery sermon: "Let the storm break out. We know that it will bring not only sorrow, but also relief. It will clear the air and remove poisonous fumes..." In October, when the Germans were reaching Moscow's suburbs, Sergii's sermon censured members of the clergy who, having found themselves on the other side of the front, were actively cooperating with the Germans. Among these was Metropolitan Sergii's closest friend, Metropolitan Sergii (Voskresenskii), the exarch of the Baltic Republics, who had chosen to remain in Riga and publicly declared his loyalty to the Germans, calling their offensive a liberation from Godless Bolshevism, but remaining faithful to the *locum tenens*. Despite the latter's loyalty, the paranoidally distrustful Stalin forced him out of Moscow to the Volga city of Ulianovsk on the very day of the publication of his condemnation of the collaborators. He was allowed to return to Moscow only in late August 1943.

In Ulianovsk, Sergii continued to issue patriotic appeals. One of the most notable, released on November 11, 1941, contained the following words: "Progressive humanity has declared a *holy war against Hitler, in defense of Christian civilization, in defense of the freedom of conscience and religion*" (emphasis mine, D.P.). These words had at least two aims: first, to deprive Hitler of the right to pretend that he was defending Christian civilization; second, emphatically to identify Christianity with progressiveness, civilization, and freedom, hinting to Stalin, as it were, to adopt a new propaganda line which would eventually force him to change his religious policies as well. But Stalin did not take this hint. The defense of Christian civilization never became an explicit theme of his propaganda. During the first two war years, he made only tiny concessions to the Church. Thus, in response to Metropolitan Sergii's 1942 telegram to Stalin reporting that collections were being taken for the war effort in all churches and that the Church needed a bank account for them, Stalin cabled back a message of thanks to the Church, granting the Patriarchate's permission to open a bank account. This amounted to a *de facto* restoration of legal person status to the Church. In the same year, the curfew was lifted for the Easter midnight services, and a handful of churches were reopened as a partial and highly inadequate response to the mass reopening of churches on German-occupied territories. The same year saw the publication of *The Truth on Religion in Russia*. It contained very little truth, but it was a signal that the Church was still alive.

The chief lieutenants of the *locum tenens* in these first two war years were Metropolitan Alexii (Simanskii) of Leningrad, who was also very active in issuing patriotic appeals and collecting donations for the war effort, and Metropolitan Nikolai (Yarushevich) of Kiev who, in contrast to his confrere in

Riga, retreated eastward with the Soviet troops all the way to Moscow. Nikolai, in contrast to Sergii, was allowed to stay in Moscow. In Sergii's absence, Nikolai began to collaborate with Soviet organs dealing with foreign affairs, even becoming a member of the *Extraordinary Commission for the Investigation of German Crimes on Occupied Territories*. As its member, he signed the false statement blaming Germans for the execution of thousands of Polish military officers in the Katyn' Forest by the NKVD.

Nazi Policy Toward the Orthodox Church

As we have mentioned before, the Russian émigré Higher Monarchist Council, the *de facto* creator of the Karlovcian Church body, conducted negotiations with Hitler in 1921 seeking his cooperation and support for the building up of Orthodox clergy cadres for the future Russia, should he come to power. Such leading members of the HMC as the last tsarist Don Cossack Ataman, Count Grabbe, his son Yurii (later ordained as Priest George and then the now late Bishop Gregory), Makharoblidze, Rklitskii (the future and now late Karlovcian Bishop of Washington), Talberg, Krupenskii, and others were the Karlovcian policy makers. The first three ran the Karlovci Higher Church Council's and later the Synod's chancery at different times.

Hitler fulfilled his promise of supporting the Karlovcians. Despite all their intrigues against Metropolitan Evlogii and their setting up of a separate Diocese, they had only two parishes (one in Berlin and another in Hamburg), while the Orthodox deanery in Germany under Metropolitan Evlogii had nine parishes, as well as numerous chapels built in German health spas before World War I. But in 1938, Hitler issued a decree transferring all the real estate owned by the Orthodox Church in Germany to the German Department of Cults, which in turn, after confiscating the "Evlogian" properties with the help of the Gestapo, handed them over to the Karlovcian Diocese of Berlin and Germany. Only three "Evlogian" parishes (in Berlin, Danzig and East Prussia[1]) survived the war. Additionally, Hitler built a beautiful Orthodox Cathedral in Berlin in 1938 at German Government expense as a gift to the Karlovcian German Diocese. Hitler's only condition was that the diocese be headed by a German. The Karlovcian Synod appointed Bishop Serafim (Lade), a German national and convert to Orthodoxy, who had been

---

1 Their Evlogian administrator, Archimandrite John (Shahovskoi, the future and now late Archbishop of San Francisco in the Orthodox Church in America), however, was forced by the Gestapo to formally recognize Karlovician Metropolitan Serafim as his superior.

consecrated bishop by the Ukrainian Renovationists in the Soviet Ukraine. In this case, the rigorous Karlovcians did not even bother to re-consecrate him (which was the rule for receiving of Renovationist clergy into the Moscow Patriarchate). The Nazis granted Serafim the title of "Führer of all the Orthodox in the Third Reich and in all territories controlled by the Reich." Serafim, however, was a decent man, and he did not insist on enforcing his "rights" over territories beyond Germany and Austria.

In June 1938, Metropolitan Anastasii (Gribanovskii), head of the Karlovci Synod after Antonii's death, sent a telegram to Hitler in which, beside the normal polite words of gratitude, he called Hitler a God-chosen leader, expressed the hope that the Lord would mercifully send a similar leader to Russia, and claimed that "the faithful Russian people...constantly raise to God prayers for...you." In 1939, again at German Government expense, an Orthodox seminary was opened in Breslau (now Wroclaw). A year or two later, however, it was closed for lack of students. Nevertheless, after the Germans had occupied parts of the USSR, they did not permit the Karlovci Synod to move from Karlovci. Their intention may have been to place all Orthodox churches in the *Ostland* (the official Nazi name for all Soviet territories under their control) directly under Serafim (who, under German pressure, had been elevated to Metropolitan by the Karlovcians), and gradually to make him independent of the émigré Church.

Such a plan, if indeed it existed, would have contradicted the official Church policy of Alfred Rosenberg, head of the *Ostministerium*, ostensibly in charge of *Ostland*. Rosenberg was a convinced enemy of Christianity. In particular, he hated Roman Catholicism as a force capable of standing up to Nazi totalitarianism. As to Orthodoxy, he saw it as little more than an ethnic ritualism; and its emphasis on humility and meekness, he claimed, even gave an advantage to the occupiers. According to his instructions, the formation of any national ecclesiastical center unifying all the Orthodox dioceses of a country should not be allowed. But the restoration of individual parishes and parish life should be tolerated. If that policy was carried out, there would obviously be no place for a supreme leader of the whole *Ostland* Church, even for a German national.

Rosenberg's power over *Ostland*, however, existed only on paper. First, Leningrad/St Petersburg, his future "capital," remained under Soviet control. Second, in Nazi Germany, just as under Communism, the real power lay with the Party, not the Government. Local Nazi administrators in occupied territories were under Rosenberg only administratively; but politically and ideologically, as party members, they were subordinate to Bormann, the Nazi Party secretary and directly under Hitler's control; while territories within approximately 100 km. of the front were under military administration, completely independent from Rosenberg. Third, Hitler never accepted Rosenberg's *Ostpolitik* concepts. Rosenberg's plan was to turn all the nationalities of the area (including those invented by him, such as Cossackia, Idel-Ural, etc.), except the Great Russians, into nominally independent states under German control. Then he wanted to instigate them all against the Great Russians, pushing the latter somewhere east of the Ural Mountains. Hitler, on the other hand, had no use for any Slavic or other states in the area. He saw the whole population of the Soviet Union, or rather of its European part, as slaves for the Arian Race.

In 1942, Rosenberg drafted an edict on religious tolerance and its application in *Ostland*; but because of Bormann's disapproval it was never published. Koch, the Commissar for the Ukraine, and Loose, the Commissar for Belorussia and the Baltic territories, although officially subordinate to Rosenberg, ignored the edict and issued their own instructions. The Koch instruction warned against allowing the revival of a single Russian Orthodox Church administration over the whole Ukraine. Instead, he advised support for the Ukrainian autocephalists, who must conduct services in the Ukrainian language, not in the Slavonic, common to all Orthodox Slavs. A similar policy was to be pursued in Belorussia and the Baltics. But in practice the situation was quite different. Thus, Loose did not oppose a single, unified Orthodox Church under the Moscow Patriarchate in the Baltics, where Orthodoxy was a minority religion; but he insisted on separation from Moscow for the Orthodox Church in Belorussia, where the absolute majority of the population was Orthodox. In the Ukraine, when Koch realized that, although the separatist Autocephalous Church had failed to win much support among believers, she had indeed become the hotbed of Ukrainian nationalism, he began to favor the autonomous, apolitical Church under the Moscow Patriarchate.

Church Revival under the Occupation

On the occupied territories there arose four independent ecclesiastic "provinces" and five Church structures. In the north, there were the three Baltic countries constituting a single "province," bordering on the Leningrad and Pskov regions of Russia proper. To the south-east lay Belorussia, bordering on the Smolensk and Briansk regions of Russia. Still further south was the Ukraine, bordering on numerous Russian regions to its east. The Odessa region, the Black Sea littoral around it and to some extent the Crimea formed another Church structure, under the Romanian Patriarchate.

Let us begin with the North, where Sergii (Voskresenskii) was the exarch of the Baltic republics. Several days after the arrival of the German troops, he came out of his hiding place in the crypt of the Riga Orthodox Cathedral and surrendered to the Germans. A few days later, he regained his freedom after convincing his German captors of the following: first, the Moscow Patriarchate, headed by Metropolitan Sergii (Stragorodskii), was not a voluntary collaborator of the communists but their captive; second, it was in the German interest that the Orthodox Church on their side of the front remain under the jurisdiction of the Moscow Patriarchate, as this would convince the population that the Germans were enemies of Communism, not of the Russian people, that they distinguished between the two and appreciated the predicament of the Church under the Communist yoke.

Let us now briefly digress to explain the situation of the Orthodox Church in the three Baltic republics. In Estonia in 1924, and some ten years later in Latvia, the nationalistic governments forced the Orthodox Churches to sever their allegiance to the Moscow Patriarchate (which had granted them internal autonomy) and to go under the Ecumenical Patriarchate, retaining their autonomous status. In contrast to the Orthodox Churches of Estonia and Latvia, each of which had sizable numbers of native Estonians and Latvians, the Orthodox Church of Lithuania consisted almost entirely of Belorussians and Russians. Consequently, a strongly Roman Catholic Lithuania was not interested in nationalizing the Orthodox Church, which was allowed to remain under the Moscow Patriarchate. The head of the Lithuanian Orthodox Church was Metropolitan Elevferii, whom the *locum tenens* had also appointed as his Exarch for the Moscow Patriarchate's parishes in Europe after the break with Evlogii in 1931. Sergii (Voskresenskii) was sent to Riga in 1940 to bring the separated Orthodox Churches back under the Moscow Patriarchate. As Metropolitan Elevferii had died in January 1941, Sergii (Voskresenskii) was made the Exarch for the Baltics.

The Latvian and Estonian metropolitans (both of autochtonous nationality), forced to return under the Moscow Patriarchate in 1940, tried to restore their allegiance to the Patriarch of Constantinople. But the exarch Sergii advised the Germans to prevent such a move. In addition to the above arguments in favor of the Moscow Patriarchate, he also maintained that the

Ecumenical exarch for Europe, residing in London, had close connections with British governmental circles and was Germany's enemy.

Consequently, the German authorities recognized Sergii (Voskresenskii) as the leader of the Orthodox Churches of all three Baltic lands, allowing him to commemorate the name of Sergii, the Moscow *locum tenens* and to engage in missionary work in the neighboring Russian areas. The Estonian Metropolitan, Alexander, and the Latvian, Augustin, were allowed, however, to keep the titles of metropolitans of Rehval (German for Tallinn) and of Riga respectively. Ethnic Estonian and Latvian parishes were allowed, if they chose, to remain under one of the above or to go under Metropolitan Sergii. All the other Baltic Orthodox bishops and most parishes (including many which were ethnically Estonian and Latvian) remained under Sergii, i.e., under Moscow.

Taking advantage of the permission granted by the German military command, Metropolitan Sergii (Voskresenskii) prepared and sent his first Orthodox mission to Pskov in August 1941, consisting of fifteen dedicated, energetic, young priests from Latvia and Estonia. On their arrival, they encountered a religious wasteland: only two functioning churches remained in the whole Pskov Province—in Pskov and Gdov. But the population met them as apostles and enlighteners. With German permission, and in some cases even unofficially receiving necessary supplies from the German army, churches were restored everywhere. At every service, churches were packed to bursting. One of those missionaries later reminisced: "At the very first service I held, all the worshipers went to confession...it was not we who were strengthening the faith of the people, but they were strengthening ours." An illustration of these words was the 1942 Epiphany procession to bless the waters in the river (19 January, Julian Calendar) in which 40 percent of the population participated (10,000 of the remaining population of 25,000). Public and private services (requiems, weddings, etc.) were conducted on a daily basis from 6 a.m. to 10 p.m., whenever and wherever a priest was available. The cited source baptized 3,500 children within four months in 1941. Almost all the school teachers, who had been made since 1929 to double as propagandists of atheism, returned to the Church.

German counterintelligence reported that virtually the entire population attended church services and concluded that the German authorities could gain the loyalty of the Russian people by active support of the Church alone (which did not, of course, happen, as it violated the German policy described above).

The mission published a regular bulletin, led catechetical courses for adults, restored religious education in all general education schools, organized intensive pastoral and theological courses; but the majority of priestly candidates were sent to the Riga Seminary. By the end of the German occupation in 1944, the number of churches in the Pskov Province, as well as in the German-occupied parts of the Leningrad and Novgorod Provinces, rose to 200, served by 175 priests. 10 percent of parish income went to the mission headquarters in Pskov for administrative and missionary expenses, of which one half was forwarded to Riga to cover the costs of seminary education. The clergy received no fixed salaries: they were supported by the faithful, while all church-related income was tax-free under the Germans.

As the territories were at the time part of the Diocese of Leningrad, the name of Alexii, Metropolitan of Leningrad, was commemorated at each service—until the day when Soviet airplanes dropped anti-German leaflets signed by Alexii. Thereafter, the German Command forbade the commemoration of Alexii's name; but Sergii (Stragorodskii's) name continued to be commemorated both as *locum tenens* and as Patriarch, after his election in 1943, although in his encyclical of October 14, 1941, he had threatened to submit all the clergy who collaborated with the enemy to ecclesiastical trial. Characteristically, the encyclical added that its author did not want to believe the rumors about such collaboration, and he named no names at that stage, probably to spare his friend Sergii (Voskresenskii) for as long as he could.

The situation of the Exarch was greatly exacerbated after the elevation of his Moscow superior to the patriarchate in September 1943. The Berlin Government responded to this event by moving the whole Karlovci synod to Vienna. Then, after augmenting the Karlovcian contingent with Metropolitan Serafim of Berlin, the "Evlogian" Bishop Sergii of Prague, and the Bishop of Belostok (which was now a part of the enlarged East Prussia), staged the so-called "Episcopal Conference of the Russian Orthodox Church" on November 8-13, 1943. The Conference condemned Patriarch Sergii for his collaboration with the Bolsheviks and claimed that his election was illegitimate because it involved only nineteen bishops (they wrongly cited 13 as the number), whereas there were over thirty Russian bishops on the German-occupied territories, not counting those in Soviet prisons and concentration camps. The Conference resolved that, because the majority of Russian bishops were not present at the electoral *sobor*, and because, according to the Moscow Sobor of 1917-18, the patriarch had to be elected by a full *sobor* of bishops, clergy and lay representatives, therefore Sergii's election was canonically invalid. Without such representation, according to the Conference,[2] the *sobor* was merely a political act. The Conference called Patriarch Sergii and his bishops "puppets of the Godless power," accepting "rewards from Satan." While attacking the Moscow Patriarchate, the Vienna Conference was also guilty of lies in its resolution declaring that, in contrast to the Moscow *sobor*, the Vienna Conference represented the free voice "of the freest part of the Russian Church," submitting to no external dictates whatsoever. In fact, the Conference and its agenda were directed from Berlin. Further, the Karlovci Synod remained totally passive in the Karlovci backwater, while the Moscow Patriarchate's Exarchate in the Baltics, as well as the clergy of the Polish and Romanian Churches, were actively missionizing on the occupied territories of the USSR.

While patriotic Russian lay émigrés and their offspring were busy finding ways to help their nation, getting into Russia by all possible legal and illegal ways (and often losing their freedom and even life at the hands of both the Gestapo and the NKVD's secret operators in occupied Russia), the Karlovci Synod obediently followed orders from Berlin, stayed put and did nothing until November 1943, and then went to Vienna and did what Berlin had told them to do. The Vienna Conference was in virtually the same position as the bishops in the Soviet Union: both had to wend their way between their duty to the Church and subordination to their terrestrial and totalitarian masters.[3] Having made these compromising statements, the Conference adopted a number of resolutions, which, if read between the lines, betrayed that the alleged "freedom of the Church" under the Nazis was not so sweet after all. Among other things, the resolutions demanded the following:

1. That there be free development of Orthodoxy in all occupied territories and that they be unified under the leadership of the Karlovcian Synod;[4]

2. That the clergy activate its struggle against Communism;

2 This view was apparently also shared by the catacomb bishop Afanasii, who, after the death of Metropolitan Kirill, was generally recognized as the leader of the Catacomb Church. He refused to accept the validity of Sergii's election, but recognized as valid the election of Alexii in 1945, appealing thereafter from his place of detention to all the catacombers to return to the Patriarchal Church.

3 The sole difference between them is that now, after the fall of communism, the Russian Church has admitted its former compromises, collaboration and lies, whereas the Karlovicians have not denounced any of their past acts as wrong, or even admitted that the Vienna Conference was forced upon them by the Nazis.

4 It could be asked on which grounds? The missionary work had been done by others but its glory to be reaped by the Synod which did nothing?

3. That Russian workers deported to Germany have free access "to the fulfillment of their spiritual needs";

4. That all Russian military units attached to the German Army be supplied with chaplains under the jurisdiction of the Karlovci Synod;

7. That religious literature be published in mass editions for people who "had been subjected to the demoralizing influence of Bolshevism";

9. That there be [Russian] broadcasts of religious apologetics;

13. That the Church receive the right to establish theological schools, seminaries, pastoral courses.

Of all these demands only the following were met: a.) chaplains were appointed to the units of the Vlasov Army;[5] b.) Russian slave laborers in Germany received the right to frequent Russian Orthodox churches. That was an important gain for them. Not only could they now worship in churches of their faith and meet resident Russian émigrés, but the latter organized soup kitchens for them at the churches, collected clothes, and gave them books to read, including religious literature.

Back in the Baltics, Metropolitan Sergii was now faced with an official German request, obviously coming from Berlin, to approve the Vienna Conference and its resolutions regarding the Moscow Patriarchate. Sergii refused and continued his attempts to convince the Germans that the Viennese enterprise was a serious strategic error. He thus dared to criticize policy decisions by the *Führer's* Office, and that in the face of Patriarch Sergii's threat of excommunicating clergy-collaborators. In an unpublished memorandum found in German military documents, Sergii (Voskresenskii) tried to convince the Germans officially to recognize the election of the Patriarch, and to make use of that in their anti-communist propaganda. They should argue that the Soviet permission to elect a patriarch proved the total bankruptcy of Communism and indicated its coming collapse, because of the incompatibility of Communism with Christianity.

5　Units of Russians wanting to fight against Communism began to be formed in 1942; in fact the so-called "Russian Corps" made up of Russian émigrés was formed by the Germans in 1941. But most units were formed out of Russian POWs, and after the publication of General Vlasov's Smolensk Manifesto in the autumn of 1942, many of these units received a sleeve stripe with the words "POA" (acronym for "Russian Liberation Army"), in accordance with the Manifesto's relation to General Vlasov, who was virtually under house arrest in a suburban Berlin villa until the autumn of 1944, when he finally got Himmler's oral agreement that an army be formed under Vlasov's direct command, which would be an ally of the Germans, not their subordinate. Between then and the end of the war, Vlasov succeeded to form two and a half divisions and a small air force unit.

This line of defense cost Sergii his life.

On April 28, 1944, the Exarch and his chauffeur, as they traveled from Vilnius to Riga, were gunned down by a motorized death squad dressed in German uniforms. The Germans claimed the murders were committed by Soviet partisans dressed as Germans. According to the late Fr Nikolai Trubetskoy of Riga, who spent ten years in Soviet concentration camps for having participated in the Pskov mission, a dying co-prisoner in his last confession to the priest confirmed that the murder had indeed been an act perpetrated by Soviet partisans on orders from Moscow, and that he had been one of the murderers. The details were so graphic that Trubetskoy did not doubt that the story was true. But according to a deposition made by a local Russian landowner, Bachmanov, a Russian high school girl student in the Metropolitan's car managed to hide in a roadside ditch during the shoot-out. She later claimed she recognized the head of the killers as Dr Aschach, the head of the local German counterintelligence, by his characteristic facial scar. Bachmanov added that Aschach was executed by a German court-martial shortly after the affair. Both versions are plausible: the Metropolitan was obviously inconvenient for the Bolsheviks, but after the Vienna Conference he became unacceptable for the Germans as well. Yet, the two versions are totally incompatible.

In conclusion, we should add that all the participants of the Pskov Mission who did not escape to the West with the Germans automatically received ten-year terms in Stalin's concentration camps, mostly in the deadly camp of the Kolyma gold mines in the Arctic Far East.

In Belorussia

The Rosenbergian idea of religious "divide and conquer" expressed itself in strong German pressure on the clergy to form a Belorussian Autocephalous Church and to sever all ties with the Moscow Patriarchate. That policy was dictated by the following factors: first, in contrast to the Baltics, the Exarch for Ukraine and Belorussia, Metropolitan Nikolai, left with the Soviet forces; second, Belorussia had a large Roman Catholic minority, which identified with Poland and supported Belorussian separatism from Russia; third, Belorussian national identity was very weak, as Orthodox Belorussians identified themselves mostly with Russia. A Church under the Moscow Patriarchate could only strengthen that association. By creating a separate autocephalous Belorussian Church, the Nazis hoped to strengthen Belorussian separatism from Russia and, at the same time, deprive the Catholic minority of the aura of being the sole champions of Belorussian nationalism. To strengthen the separatist party, the Germans repatriated ideologists of Belorussian nationalism from Poland and Prague.

The Belorussian Orthodox episcopate resisted autocephaly as best they could. Panteleimon, elected Metropolitan of the Belorussian Church at her local *sobor* in March 1942, rejected autocephaly and continued to commemorate the name of Metropolitan Sergii of Moscow. He particularly irritated the nationalists by refusing to give sermons in Belorussian, arguing that Russian was the spoken language of the cities. Although the nationalists did not dare depose him, they convinced the Germans to place Panteleimon under arrest in a monastery. Panteleimon's assistant, Archbishop Filofei (Narko), took over day-to-day control. He at first also resisted the separatists, arguing that as long as there was an elected metropolitan, his assistant had no right to make changes in Church structure. But Panteleimon gave him the blessing to call another local *sobor* to decide these matters. The German authorities physically prevented vocal anti-separatists from attending the *sobor*, which opened on August 30, 1942. The *sobor* proclaimed autocephaly with a proviso, however, that it would become valid only after its approval by all the patriarchs (i.e., including also the Patriarch of Moscow!).[6] The autocephaly issue thus remained a dead letter; and a May 1944 *sobor* of Belorussian bishops annulled it altogether, stating that it lacked validity because of the absence of the two most senior Belorussian bishops at the *sobor* of August 1942.

As to the actual situation of the Church in Belorussia at the moment of its occupation, the western part, which until September 1939 was under Poland, had a well-organized and relatively dense network of churches and monasteries served by the Vilno (Vilnius) Orthodox Seminary. Soviet Belorussia, as other parts of the Soviet Union, was a religious wasteland: for instance, not a single functioning church had survived in Minsk, its capital. By 1942, however, there were seven working churches in the city and 120 in the diocese, compared with the pre-revolutionary 400. Forty percent of the city's population participated in the procession of the January 1944 Epiphany blessing of waters. Smolensk, which the Germans attached to Belorussia and where only one church

---

6 The author of that ingenious formula was a young graduate of the Warsaw Orthodox Theological Academy, Vitalii Borovoi, who was imprisoned by the Bolsheviks in late 1944, tortured for several weeks, then freed through the intervention of the local NKVD boss, who happened to have been a village neighbor of the newly appointed Metropolitan of Belorussia, a former Renovationist Vasilii (Ratmirov). Ordained priest by that bishop, Borovoi became a theology professor in Leningrad and the virtual architect of the Moscow Patriarchate's ecumenical policies in the era of that Church's participation in the World Council of Churches.

still functioned in 1939, had five working churches by 1942 and intensive pastoral courses which in seven months produced forty priests for the diocese. Altogether, 57 percent of all the surviving church structures in Belorussia were restored to their original use in the course of less than three years of German occupation. There was, however, an acute shortage of priests. The few available priests, most from the formerly Polish part of Belorussia, wandered from village to village, baptizing 150-200 persons per day.

Many churches had been blown up by underground Komsomol terrorist squads on orders from Soviet authorities and underground Communist cells. In Vitebsk, for instance, such a squad perished before succeeding in blowing up the city cathedral. Some Komsomol members committed suicide rather than fulfill such orders.

Spot surveys on religious belief, undertaken by the Germans, showed an incredible one percent atheists in Smolensk and three percent in Borisov. Such figures ought to be taken with a great degree of skepticism. First, only about 20 percent of the pre-war population remained in Smolensk under the Germans. The situation was much the same in other urban centers. Clearly, the large numbers who evacuated east with the retreating Soviet armies contained a much higher proportion of communists, and hence also of atheists, than the predominantly anti-communists who chose to remain. Then also, Soviet citizens are masters at mimicry. Just as they would declare themselves atheists under the Communists, now, seeing the slogan "God is with us!" on the German soldiers' buckles, they thought it safer to call themselves religious believers. The figures of 40 to 70 percent and more of the population regularly attending church services, reported by German counter-intelligence, are a more accurate reflection on the intensity of faith in the Soviet population of the time.

The Ukraine

The Ukraine once again became a crossroads of several conflicting currents. In Eastern Ukraine, the Germans sought to weaken Russian influence by supporting Ukrainian nationalism and church separatism—both of which enjoyed very little support from the local population. At the same time in Lvov, the hotbed of Ukrainian nationalism, the Germans arrested the locally formed Banderist Ukrainian nationalist Government and sent them to a concentration camp (where, however, they were given relatively comfortable living conditions). The Germans further weakened the Ukrainian nationalist cause by placing Eastern Ukraine off limits to the Ukrainian Catholic clergy from Galicia.

As to Orthodoxy, two parallel Church structures arose in the Ukraine: the Ukrainian Autonomous Orthodox Church under the Moscow Patriarchate was formed by a *sobor* at the Pochaev Monastery in Volynia in August 1941; and the Ukrainian Autocephalous Church formed was at a *sobor* in Rovno in February 1942. In contrast with Lypkivskyi's "self-consecrators" of 1921, the new autocephalists had a canonical base, because their founders, as well as those of the autonomists, had been bishops in the pre-war Polish Orthodox Church, which had received its autocephaly from the Ecumenical Patriarchate in 1924. The Autocephalists' canonical problems arose from the fact that the 1942 *sobor* decided to accept the remnants of the Lypkivskyite clergy—who had held their own *sobor* in Kiev in September 1941—without re-ordination.

However, Dionisii, Metropolitan of Warsaw and head of the Polish Orthodox Church, who had lost over 80 percent of his flock and parishes with the Soviet annexation of the Ukraine and Belorussia and the confirmation of these new frontiers by the Germans, decided to grant recognition to the Ukrainian autocephalists, as they in return proclaimed him their supreme metropolitan. Dionisii had no chance with the autonomists, because after the Soviet annexation of eastern Poland in 1939, he had abdicated in writing all authority over the churches in the annexed territories in favor of the Moscow Patriarchate. After that transfer of authority, the Orthodox episcopate of Western Ukraine and Belorussia visited Moscow, where they were officially received into the patriarchal jurisdiction. The only bishop who did not go to Moscow was Polykarp (Sykorskyi). Now, under the Germans, he claimed that he had never joined the Moscow Patriarchate, and therefore had the full canonical right to form a Ukrainian Church with the blessing of his metropolitan, Dionisii. The latter obviously hoped to move to the Ukraine and become the patriarch of that Church (though he was himself a Great Russian). After the Germans refused to let him leave Warsaw, he granted the metropolitan's title to Polykarp; and thus the Ukrainian autocephaly was re-born.

The leader of the Autonomous Church, elected at the Pochaev Sobor and elevated to metropolitanate, was Alexii (Gromadskii). Although the vast majority of Ukrainian parishes and clergy joined the Autonomous Church, her situation was made precarious by the hostility of the German-supported Ukrainian nationalists, whose terroristic arms were the Ukrainian SS-Division Halychyna and the Ukrainian Banderist partisan movement, which became active in 1942. By 1943, the nationalists began to terrorize the autonomist clergy, especially in the rural areas of Volynia and Podolia.

Metropolitan Alexii several times entered into negotiations with the auto-cephalists on the subject of uniting the two Church structures. The negotiations came to naught owing to three factors: first, the autocephalists refused to re-ordain the former Lypkivsyite clergy; second, the clergy and laity of the Autono-mous Church refused to have anything to do with the Autocephalists, claiming that they were a political party rather than a Church; third and most important, the German Command informed both groups that they would not tolerate a sin-gle Ukrainian Church with "Ukrainian politicians in episcopal vestments" par-ticipating in her leadership.[7] One of these politicians was Mstyslav Skrypnyk. Consecrated by Sykorskyi in 1942 as his assistant, he became the *de facto* political commissar of the Church. He was a nephew of Petliura, the founder of the Ukrainian national socialist movement (taken over by Bandera after Petliura's murder in the 1930s) and of its short-lived government in 1918. Before the war, Skrypnyk was a Ukrainian Petliurovite member of the Polish Parliament.

The Banderist partisans responded with wholesale terror to the failure of the amalgamation as well as to the failure of the autocephalists to win over the Ukrainian faithful. In 1943, they killed Metropolitan Alexii and Archbishop Manuil (Tarnovskyi)—the latter probably in revenge for his defection from the autocephalists—and scores of village priests. This brought about a mass defec-tion of rural priests, particularly in Volynia, where the partisans were most ac-tive, over to the autocephalists in 1943-44. In the cities, where it was safer, most parishes remained in the Autonomous Church to the end of the war.

The process of restoring and reopening churches was as swift in the Ukraine as elsewhere. In the Diocese of Kiev, for instance, by 1941 there re-mained only three functioning churches; 798 (50 percent of the pre-revolutionary figure) were operating by 1943: 500 autonomous and 298 auto-cephalous) served by 1034 priests (70 percent of the pre-revolutionary number: 600 were autonomists, 434, autocephalists. Outside of Kiev, which attracted the nationalists because it was the capital, only two other dioceses east of the former Polish border had numerous autocephalous churches: Zhitomir, which was actually the eastern part of Volynia, had 100 autocephalous parishes versus 300 of the autonomists, and Poltava, the birthplace of Petliura and Mstyslav, had 100 autocephalous churches versus 140 of the autonomous. Even there the

---

7 F. Heyer, a German historian and observer of the events in question, observed that whereas the bishops of the Autonomous Church were true monks dedicated to the faith, the Autocephalist bishops were nationalist politicians and basically secular men, whose sermons sounded like political agitation more than the teaching of the word of Christ.

distribution of churches was not proportional to the distribution of parishioners. According to the German figures, 80 percent of the Poltava Diocese believers were autonomists and only 20 percent, autocephalists. More typical were the Dnepropetrovsk and Chernigov Dioceses: in the former there were 10 autocephalous churches to 318 autonomist ones, and in the latter, not a single one, until the Germans assigned one in Nezhin to the autocephalists, but practically no one went to that church, and after a few months it was closed down. The Autonomous Church reopened over twenty monasteries in the formerly Soviet Ukraine by 1943, and had some 2,000 monastics, mostly women, as the Germans banned tonsuring males of working age. The autocephalists had a total of 100 monks and nuns. The seminary of Kremenets in Volynia, closed under the Soviets, was re-opened by the autonomists, who were also about to re-open the Kiev Seminary on the eve of the German retreat. Of the fifteen autocephalist bishops, fourteen emigrated to the West with the retreating Germans; while of the surviving fourteen autonomous bishops six remained with their flocks, and one more returned home soon after the war. At least three autonomist bishops subsequently spent ten years in Soviet concentration camps.

There were some attempts also to reopen Renovationist churches, but the Germans banned them as Soviet agents.

Ukrainian nationalism proved very weak east of the former Polish border; nevertheless, German counter-intelligence underestimated it by claiming that it was non-existent. Likewise, in its reports claiming that 70-95 percent of the population were religious believers, the lower figure may have been realistic, but definitely not the higher one.

Russia

Only relatively small areas of ethnically Russian territories adjacent to the Ukraine fell under German occupation; and the occupation lasted there for a shorter period of time than in the Ukraine; nevertheless, religious revival there was as intensive as in the Ukraine. The surviving bishops of Rostov-on-Don and Taganrog (on the Azov Sea) functioned in their dioceses under the auspices of the Ukrainian Autonomous Church. As occurred in the Ukraine, numerous members of the clergy in German-occupied Russian provinces were deported to Stalin's camps after the return of the Soviet forces, including Bishop Iosif of Taganrog, who had already spent many year in prisons and concentration camps before the war.

Romania

The Romanian Zone of Occupation included Odessa and most of its province, annexed into "Greater Romania" under the name of Transnistria, and most of the Black Sea littoral up to the Crimea; the latter was shared by Romanians and Germans. Missionary work in these areas was conducted directly by the Romanian Orthodox Church. "Transnistria" was divided into three dioceses. 500 of the pre-revolutionary 1,150 parishes were functioning there by 1943. They were served by 600 priests and deacons. Most were Russian-speaking clergy from the Bessarabian Diocese of Kishinev, but there were also a few local Russian and Ukrainian priests who had survived the holocaust. The Odessa Seminary was all but reopened when Soviet forces returned—hence its early reopening under the Soviets. Pastoral courses were functioning in two other towns.

The Romanian Government tried to use the Church as a channel for romanianizing the local population. Attempts were made to conduct church services, as well as religious broadcasts, in Romanian, which the vast majority of the population did not understand. Romanian bishops appointed to "Transnistria" reported on the exceptional piety and religiousness of the population which, according to the reports, could spiritually enrich any Romanian clergyman.

The Church on Soviet Territory

Real changes in the situation of the Church in that part of the USSR which never fell under enemy occupation began after the eventful meeting of September 4, 1943, between Stalin and the three senior Russian hierarchs: Sergii, the *locum tenens*, Alexii of Leningrad, and Nikolai of the Ukraine. Until recently, it was held that the meeting had come as a total surprise to the hierarchs, that they were not aware they were being taken to meet Stalin even when the limousines arrived to pick them up. However, E.I. Lisavtsev, a formerly leading religiologist from the defunct Institute of Scientific Atheism of the CPSU Central Committee's Academy of Social Sciences, claimed that at least Metropolitan Sergii had met Stalin twice before that date: in July 1941 and on the eve of the 1943 meeting. According to Lisavtsev, since both of them were former seminary students, they quickly found a common language, and both were satisfied with the meetings.

But according to secret archival documents, actually notes on the meeting written by Karpov, Chairman of the Council for the Russian Orthodox

Church Affairs (CROCA for short), in the morning of September Stalin summoned him to his suburban dacha in Kuntsevo and requested information on Metropolitans Sergii, Alexii, and Nikolai, as well as on patriarchal elections and on other Church related questions. Malenkov and Beria were asked about the appropriateness of his meeting the metropolitans.[8] Having obtained their approval, Stalin told Karpov to telephone Metropolitan Sergii, invite him to the meeting, and ask him to choose the most appropriate date. Sergii said: "Today." Of course, had Stalin met Metropolitan Sergii before he would hardly have asked Karpov for information about him. In addition, had Stalin and the Metropolitan met in 1941 and reached a mutually satisfying understanding, as suggested by Lisavtsev, then why did Stalin exile Sergii to Ulianovsk in the autumn of 1941 and keep him there until late August 1943, while allowing Metropolitan Nikolai to stay in Moscow? Or was this a dictator's game to test Karpov and his informativeness?

Stalin's meeting with the metropolitans lasted 1 hour and 55 minutes, according to Karpov.[9] The motivation behind the meeting was certainly not that Stalin needed the Church to win the war—after the battles of Stalingrad and Kursk victory had already been sealed. The point was that the Anglican Church had been asking the Soviet Government for some time for the right to pay a high level visit to the Russian Church. Now, on the eve of the Teheran Conference, such a visit would be most opportune for Stalin. He needed the Russian Church to impress a top Anglican Church delegation. By graphically convincing the Anglicans that the Russian Church was doing well and that there were no religious persecutions, Stalin hoped to put additional pressure on English public opinion and on the British Government to support an early invasion of Normandy. Stalin began the meeting by asking the metropolitans what were the most urgent needs of the Church. Metropolitan Sergii replied that the most urgent need of the Church was to convoke a *sobor*, elect a patriarch, and restore the Synod *dissolved in 1935*, as he had been ruling the Church since then without any canonical administrative structure. Preparations for the *sobor*, he said, would take at least a month. Stalin approved everything. He offered the use of military air transport to bring the bishops to Moscow immediately so as to open the *sobor* in four days, on September 8; and so it happened. Stalin then introduced Karpov to the metropolitans as the chairman of a new body—the Council for the Russian Orthodox Church Affairs—and told them that they

---

8 This probably was a show to impress Karpov how democratic Stalin was.

9 GARF, F. 6991c, op. la, item 1.

should henceforth deal with him in all matters concerning Church-State relations. Stalin offered to fully subsidize the *sobor* and to aid the Church financially, but Sergii refused any state subsidies. However, he secured Stalin's promise to allow the reopening of seminaries and other theological schools, "in as many eparchies as the Church would see fit," reopen churches and to re-establish the publication of the official monthly *Journal of the Moscow Patriarchate*. Metropolitan Alexii raised the question of releasing some clergy from prisons and exile and for the right of the recently released clergy to travel unhindered and to be appointed to positions and places as required by the Church. Stalin replied that the bishops should prepare a list of imprisoned clergy and told Karpov to look into both matters. Indeed, a list of a score of incarcerated bishops and priests was submitted by Sergii on October 27, 1943. The list reveals how uninformed the patriarchate was, as many of the bishops listed as living in Patriarch Sergii's humble petition were long dead, having mostly been executed in 1937-38. At the conclusion of the September 4 meeting, Stalin ordered that groceries be supplied to the Patriarchate from special Government storages at official state prices, and that the building of the former German Embassy be requisitioned to serve as the official residence of the Patriarch and as the Patriarchate's offices. Metropolitan Sergii categorically rejected, however, Stalin's offer to subsidize the Church.

In the course of the meeting, Stalin remarked to Karpov that he was not to be a new Over-procurator, but only a liaison officer between the Church and the Soviet Government.[10] This was not to be, however. CROCA's archives reveal the constant and rude interference by its chairman into internal Church affairs, in fact his arbitrary dictatorship over the Patriarch and various Church organs. For instance, Karpov's was the decisive voice in the preparation of the Church Statute of 1945, its main author being Zaitsev, one of Karpov's assistants in the CROCA. When the so-called monastery "consolidation" (a euphemism for their gradual liquidation) began in 1946, Karpov paid no attention to the Patriarch's timid objections and forced him to submit.

---

10 Karpov bore the rank of major general of internal security (NKVD). The fact that Stalin had called Karpov to brief him on Church matters on the eve of the meeting indicates that he had been in charge of Church affairs in the security organs (most likely as Tuchkov's heir). According to the archives, as head of the NKVD for the Pskov Province in 1937-38, Karpov "had badly abused socialist legality, carried out mass arrests of innocents, used perverse means of investigation, falsified depositions of the defendants…in 1941 he was recalled to the central NKVD administration in Moscow." *Izvestiia TseKa KPSS*, No. 11, 1989, p. 52.

The 1943 Sobor

Of the mere nineteen bishops who participated in the Sobor that opened on September 8, two metropolitans, Sergii and Alexii, had been consecrated before 1917; two, the same Sergii and Archbishop Vasilii (Ratmirov), were former Renovationists; at least six were recently released from concentration camps. There were still scores of bishops and perhaps thousands of priests in camps and internal exile. Some were later released and appointed to the newly re-opening dioceses. Many, however, remained in detention unto their death, refusing to sign a declaration of loyalty to Sergii and his policy, which was the Soviet precondition for release. The "archipelago of the catacombs" was still quite numerous at the time, and this gave psychological support to the steadfast bishops and made their steadfastness meaningful. The situation drastically changed in 1945, after the widely recognized leader of the "catacombs," Bishop Afanasii, recognized the canonical validity of the election of Patriarch Alexii and appealed to his followers to rejoin the established Church.

The *sobor* opened with Sergii's speech on the patriotic activities of the Church during the war. Then Metropolitan Alexii called on the members to elect Sergii as patriarch, which they did unanimously. Sergii declared the formation of the Patriarchal Synod of bishops consisting of three permanent members and three additional bishops called to duty by the Synod in rotation. Then Sergii read a statement that any person "guilty of betraying the ecclesiastical cause and of going over to the fascist side...would be excommunicated, and every bishop or priest [guilty of such acts] would be defrocked." A collective address to Stalin thanked him for his "sympathetic attitude" to the Church (sic!).

Although such leading Orthodox theologians as the late Vladimir Lossky, based in Paris, praised Sergii as "the great church leader...who lived the doctrines of the Church...who measured everything against the basic truths of the faith," Patriarch Sergii was himself not so certain when, in his enthronement speech, he admitted: "As *locum tenens,* I felt I was temporary and therefore was not that careful in avoiding mistakes. I reasoned to myself: a patriarch will appear one day; he will correct all my errors."

But his patriarchate lasted only eight months. He died on May 15, 1944, one month before the reopening of the Moscow Pastoral School, which two years later became a seminary and a graduate academy, and of the Leningrad Theological Institute, which also evolved into a seminary and an academy. Sergii, however, drafted their educational programs and gathered their first teaching staffs. He also laid foundations for the revival of diocesan structures, raising the number of diocesan bishops to forty-one by the time of his death. His other achievement was the November 10, 1943, recognition of the originally unilaterally proclaimed restoration of the Patriarchate of Georgia.

As to the reopening of churches, that process was much more rapid on enemy territory. By 1947, there were 14,092 functioning Orthodox churches in the whole Soviet Union, of which 2,491 had been received from the Uniates; 7,547 had been re-opened on enemy-controlled territory during the time of the occupation; and over 3,000 were inherited from the annexed territories of Moldavia, North Bukovina, Carpatho-Ruthenia, Western Ukraine and Belorussia, and the Baltic Republic. This left just over 1,000 churches re-opened over an expanse of 20,000,000 square km., representing Soviet territory never occupied by the enemy. Such a slow pace of the restoration of churches was dictated by the Council of Peoples' Commissars Instruction No. 1325 of November 28, 1943, which stipulated that believers who wanted a church should address their petition to the local soviet, which had the right to reject it, but had no right to authorize the reopening of a church. If the local soviet approved, it had to forward the believers' petition with its affirmative comments to CROCA, which forwarded the petition with its own "preliminary opinion" to the Council of Ministers of the given Soviet republic, which alone had the right to order either to return a church to the believers or to allow them to build one, or to veto the reopening altogether. Thus the time between the submission of the original petition and the actual beginning of church services could be anywhere from one to three years—and this only in the case when all levels approved the decision!

FOR FURTHER READING

Abteilung Fremde Heere Ost. German Armed Forces Documents (microfilms). National Archives and Records Service. Washington, D.C.

Alexeev, W. and T. Stavrou, *The Great Revival* (Minneapolis: Burgess Publishing Co., 1976).

Archive of the Council for the Russian Orthodox Church Affairs and of the Council for Religious Affairs. *The State Archive of the Russian Federation* (*GARF, TsGAOR* prior to 1992).

Armstrong, John, *Ukrainian Nationalism* (New York: Columbia U. Press, 1963).

Balevits, Z., *Pravoslavnaia tserkov' Latvii pod sen'iu svastiki* (Riga, 1967).

Bullock, Alen, *Hitler: a Study in Tyranny* (London: Penguin, 1975).

Chrysostomus, J, *Kirchengeschichte Russlands der neusten Zeit* (see previous chapter).

Dallin, A., *German Rule in Russia, 1941-1945* (London: Macmillan, 1957).

Fireside, H., *Icon and Swastika* (Cambridge, MA: Harvard U. Press, 1971).

Fletcher, William, *Nikolai* (London, 1968).

_____, *The Russian Orthodox Church Underground* (see previous chapter).

_____, *A Study in Survival* (New York, 1965).

Heyer, Friedrich, *Die orthodoxe Kirche in der Ukraine von 1917 bis 1945* (Köln, 1953).

Levitin-Krasnov, A, *Likhie gody* (see chapter 10).

_____, *Ruk tvoikh zhar* (Tel-Aviv, 1980).

_____, and Vadim Shavrov, *Ocherki po istorii russkoi tserkovnoi smuty* (see chapter 10).

Patriarkh Sergii i ego dukhovnoe nasledstvo (see previous chap.).

Pospielovsky, D., "Ot patriarkha Tikhona k mitropolitu (patriarkhu) Sergiiu" (see previous chapter).

_____, *Russkaia Pravoslavnaia Tserkov' v XX veke* (see previous chapters)

_____, *The Russian Church under the Soviet Regime* (see previous chapter).

Regelson, Lev, *Tragediia Russkoi Tserkvi 1917-1945* (Paris: YMCA Press, 1977).

CHAPTER 13

THE FIRST POST-WAR DECADE

Stalin and the Church

Stalin on the whole kept his word: there was no renewal of direct persecutions of the established Church on the pre-war model. However, harassment of believers, as well as of clergy successful in bringing new members to the Church, was renewed.

Intensification of antireligious policy began already after the September 1944 CPSU Central Committee Resolution, which called for the renewal of the anti-religious struggle by propagating "scientific Weltanschauung." If that wording appeared somewhat oblique, the following year the CPSU CC directly instructed the mass media to enhance atheistic propaganda. But consolidation of the post-war antireligious front occured in 1947 with the formation of the "All-Union Society for the Dissemination of Scientific and Political Knowledge," *Znanie* (Knowledge), for short. This organization was structured more deviously than the League of the Militant Godless, which it replaced. *Znanie* recruited genuine scholars, as its aims included the popularization of scientific discoveries and theories, as well as popular lectures on history, art, and science. Lecturers received lucrative honoraria. Thus, by 1972 *Znanie* had 2,457,000 members, including 1,700 members of the All-Union and the constituent republics' academies of sciences, 107,000 university professors and doctors of sciences and arts, among whom were many genuine scholars, decent people who had nothing in common with the popularization of atheism. *Znanie* organized and ran special houses and lecture halls of "scientific atheism" in most cities. *Znanie*'s atheistic activities reached their apogee in the last year of Khrushchev's reign, 1964, when the total annual run of such brochures, journals, and books surpassed 6 million copies. However, precisely because, as an umbrella organization, it succeeded in recruiting so many respectable scholars, the lecturers on atheism appeared more respectable.[1]

The 1945 Sobor and the Life of the Church

After Patriarch Sergii's death, his *locum tenens*, Metropolitan Alexii, who had served as the interim *locum tenens* by virtue of being the senior Russian

---

1   The author cannot vouch for which of the famous Russian-Soviet nuclear physicists had in fact been members of *Znanie,* but many of them were, with no direct obligations to participate in atheistic propaganda campaigns.

bishop, convoked a local *sobor* on January 31, 1945. In contrast to the council of 1943, this *sobor* included parish clergy and laity delegates. The new patriarch, elected unanimously in an open ballot, was also Sergii's choice. Sergii, contrary to the canons, had already named him in his will, as he was obviously uncertain whether the Soviets would permit another *sobor*. Although only three days long, the *sobor* also adopted a statute, which was modeled more on the Roman Catholic papal structure of one-way command from top down than on eastern conciliar traditions. The new statute did not call for regular *sobors* or even diocesan conferences. Theoretically, it gave the Patriarch absolute command over the Church; bishops, over their dioceses; and priests, over the parishes. Even on the diocesan level, it was left up to the local bishop whether to have a diocesan council or not.

Although the author of the Statute was a certain Zaitsev, a member of the CROCA, it is likely that Sergii, directly or indirectly, had a hand at its composition, as it was drafted in his lifetime. His likely participation in its drafting is possibly betrayed by the importance it placed on the clergy, disregarding Soviet laws which simply did not recognize the clergy as a legal entity. If Patriarch Sergii was indeed the Statute's co-author, then it would indicate a dramatic change in attitude toward conciliarism, which Sergii in his younger years had advocated so passionately. He apparently realized that in the age of Stalin's iron dictatorship, the Church was in need of a similar centralization to survive. The toleration and approval of the statute, so blatantly incompatible with Soviet law, indicates either a firm belief at the time that state law would be amended accordingly, or it represents a cynical act on the part of the CROCA once again to keep the Church as a hostage, which could at any time be attacked for contravening Soviet law. This is exactly what happened in 1961. But even this "pro-Church" Statute contained a devious trick, the meaning of which might have escaped even a church consultant: the official seal of the Church was to be registered not in the name of the Patriarchate, but of the patriarch. In other words, even before the election of a patriarch, the candidacy had to be approved by the CROCA, which registered the seal and could simply refuse registration if its candidate was not elected. This resolved the problem of free elections and of having more than one candidate. The same procedure was followed for the diocesan and parish seals in the appointment of bishops and parish rectors.

With regard to finances, the previous ban on membership dues remained in force, and it was not touched by the Statute. Parishes, however, were allowed to pass on some of their income to the diocesan center. The new stat-ute also required parishes to give generous donations to the Peace Fund, which replaced the War Effort Charity Fund after the war and soon became a *de facto* heavy tax on each parish, camouflaged as a voluntary donation. Di-ocesan centers were permitted to contribute both to the central Patriarchate's treasury and to the support of the seminaries. As far as religious education of children was concerned, the Statute followed closely the 1929 Soviet law, which permitted parents to teach religion to their children and even to invite a priest for that purpose, but banned any group teaching involving children of more than one family. During the war and in the first post-war years, how-ever, the state tolerated religious slide shows for children in some churches immediately after a service, with instructional comments made by some dar-ing priests during the shows.

A few days after the *Sobor* the Patriarch and several senior hierarchs, in-cluding Metropolitan Nikolai, were received by Stalin. Metropolitan Niko-lai's sycophantic report on this meeting reveals that Stalin's agreement was obtained to open eight more seminaries in addition to the Moscow Seminary and Academy. In fact, by 1947 eight seminaries (Zagorsk [Moscow], Lenin-grad, Stavropol—in Russia; Odessa, Kiev, and Lutsk — in the Ukraine; and Zhirovichi in Belorussia) and two graduate academies (Zagorsk and Lenin-grad) were operational. Archives reveal that petitions were submitted for the reopening of at least nine more seminaries (Tallin in Estonia; Vilnius in Lithuania; Chernovtsi and Lvov—in the Ukraine; Rostov-on-Don, Iaroslavl, Smolensk, and Novosibirsk—in Russia) and an academy in Kiev. But all the petitions after 1947 were rejected.

The encounter with Stalin must have included a foreign policy agenda for the Church, as on May 28 the Patriarch, accompanied by Metropolitan Niko-lai, left on an extensive political pilgrimage. They traveled to the Holy Land, to Egypt, where they visited the Patriarch of Alexandria, to Damascus, visit-ing the Patriarch of Antioch; and then on to England. This was the Church of Russia's return visit after the Anglican Church's 1943 trip to Russia.[2] The Pa-triarch was received by King George VI and, as the guest of its Archbishop, in York Patriarch Alexii publicly attacked the Vatican, very much in line with the latest Soviet foreign policy, declaring the papacy to be the common enemy of both the Orthodox and Anglican Churches. During this "pilgrimage" Alexii

2 On October 13, 1943, when Karpov mentioned to Molotov that the Patriarch was inquiring about a return visit to England, Molotov responded: "They haven't even opened the second front yet...Let them wait."

managed to bring back under his omophorion the Russian parishes in Alexandria, Damascus, and London. Thus began the Moscow Patriarchate's campaign for the return of the Russian diaspora churches into its jurisdiction.

The Moscow Patriarchate and the Diaspora

As the vast majority of war-time refugees from the USSR found themselves in
West Germany where, thanks to Hitler, the Karlovcians had complete monopoly, most refugee clergy joined that jurisdiction. Thus the reconstructed
post-war "Russian Orthodox Church Outside Russia" (the "neo-Karlovcians")
grew to several times its European pre-war size, when it had merely about half
a dozen parishes in Serbia, another two or three in Bulgaria, two in Germany
(prior to Hitler's confiscation of the Evlogian parishes), and three or four in
the rest of Western Europe.

Numerically, the largest part of the pre-war Karlovcians was in the Far Eastern
dioceses. But by the end of the war, all three bishops in Manchuria (including
Dimitri, the father of Filaret and the future head of the Karlovcian Synod) sent a
sycophantic congratulatory telegram to Stalin on the occasion of his victory—and
then joined the Moscow Patriarchate. Of the two bishops in China proper, one,
Victor of Beijing, likewise joined the Moscow Patriarchate. Only Ioann (John) of
Shanghai remained loyal to the Karlovcians, although he wavered for a whole year
and kept in contact with the Moscow Patriarchate. In Europe, two senior Karlovci
bishops joined the Moscow Patriarchate: Serafim (Sobolev) in Bulgaria, and
Serafim (Lukianov), the Karlovcian metropolitan of Paris. If the Manchurian bishops' only choice was between the Moscow Patriarchate and emigration to China
and later abroad, Serafim of Bulgaria could easily have joined the Bulgarian
Church, as did some other prominent Russian churchmen (including Shavelskii,
the last head of the tsarist military chaplains), if he truly supported the Karlovcian
anti-Moscow stand. As to the Parisian Serafim, he had been a very active Nazi
collaborator during the war: his quick desertion to the Moscow Patriarchate after
the arrival of Metropolitan Nikolai in Paris in September 1945 was likely motivated by his fear of being prosecuted by the French Government for his war collaboration. Another prominent Karlovci hierarch, Hermogen, had collaborated
in Zagreb with the Croat fascists and headed their puppet "Croat Orthodox
Church," whose purpose was to camouflage the fascists' genocide of the Orthodox Serbs. Tito had him executed, and the reconstituted Karlovci Synod posthumously condemned him. Three more Karlovci bishops died during the war.
Metropolitan Anastasii was thus the only Karlovcian European bishop to survive

the war and not to desert his jurisdiction. Hence, the membership of the reconstituted Synod of the ROCOR consisted entirely of refugee bishops from the USSR and Poland, under Anastasii's chairmanship. The only exception was Metropolitan Serafim (Lade) of Berlin who, however, died under mysterious circumstances (after having been savagely beaten) less than three years after the war's end. The other Karlovci veteran was George Grabbe, by that time an archpriest and still the head of the Synod's chancery.

On August 10, 1945, Patriarch Alexii addressed an appeal to the Karlovcians to return to their Mother-Church. Alexii criticized their schismatic activities, but, in contrast with Metropolitan Sergii in 1927, he did not ask for any pledges of loyalty to the Soviet State. Metropolitan Anastasii's response snubbed the Patriarch, addressing the Russian people rather than the Patriarch himself. Anastasii referred to the Patriarchal Church as Soviet, rather than Russian, accused her of betraying the new martyrs, of lies, and of total capitulation before the Soviet power—passing over in silence, however, the similar behavior of seven Karlovcian bishops in much safer conditions than those faced by the Church in the USSR.

The harsh tone of his response betrayed quite a different person from the Anastasii of the 1920s, when he had admitted the guilt of the Karlovcians for the persecution of Patriarch Tikhon by the Soviets and when (in contrast to Metropolitan Antonii, his master) he had recognized the authenticity of Patriarch Tikhon's *Testament*.[3] The Anastasii of the 1940s, according to Archpriest-Professor V. Vinogradov, his former student and friend, was living by the fiction of an imaginary, numerous Catacomb Church in Russia, refusing to hear the truth that there was no other way for the survival of the Church but the one pursued by Patriarch Sergii and his heirs. Similar complaints came from Natalia Kiter, an active member of the "Sergiite" Church until 1941, who complained to Anastasii to no avail that the articles she had written on the life in the Russian Church were appearing in the Karlovcian *Orthodox Russia* "re-edited" into stories about the catacombs. In response to her protests the editors replied: "The truth would be harmful to the ecclesiastical cause in America."[4]

Whatever contradictions there may have been in Anastasii's response, any ties with the Moscow Patriarchate, at a time when its leaders were singing hosannas to Stalin, were psychologically impossible for a Church consisting of recent refugees from Stalin's hell. KGB/SMERSH agents were hunting down

3   Archbishop Anastasii's letters to Prince Gr. Trubetskoi. *Vestnik RKhD*, No. 151 (Paris, 1987), pp. 228-230.

4   Kiter's letters. *Vestnik RKhD*, No. 150 (1987), pp. 235-48.

ex-Soviet citizens in Western Europe, kidnapping and even murdering some of them; and the allies were actively helping that "cause" by repatriating Soviet citizens by force.

In contrast with the pro-Nazi policies of the ROCOR, the "Evlogians" actively participated in the French Resistance, as well as in operations to rescue Jews, at a considerable loss of the rescuers' lives.[5] The victory brought an outburst of Soviet patriotism among many Russian émigrés in France. The septuagenarian Evlogii, succumbing both to senility and to the influence of his acolyte Roshchin, a Soviet agent, fell into that temptation as well. Roshchin arranged Evlogii's secret visits to the Soviet embassy and obtained an invitation from the Moscow Patriarchate for Evlogii to participate in the January 1945 Moscow Sobor. However, as if by some bureaucratic error, the invitation, dated December 20, 1944, was received by Evlogii on 5 February, long after the Sobor. By that time, Evlogii's only wish was to return to the fold of the Russian Church and to die in Russia. His re-unification with the Russian Church occurred in August 1945, during the visit to Paris of Metropolitan Nikolai, who concelebrated with Evlogii, ignoring the late Sergii's 1931 ban on Evlogii and his clergy. After Nikolai's emotional speech at the diocesan assembly of August 29, Evlogii declared his decision to join the Moscow Patriarchate, despite considerable opposition from his clergy and particularly from professors of the St Sergius Theological Academy. Evlogii's only proviso was that the transfer of allegiance could not be made without a canonical release from the Ecumenical Patriarchate. Nikolai then mendaciously assured the assembly that the problem had already been settled with the Patriarch of Constantinople; and he promised that the Moscow Patriarchate would fully respect the autonomy of Evlogii's Church granted to her by the Ecumenical Throne.

It was soon discovered that the Ecumenical Patriarchate had not been aware of any such deals, and that no negotiations had taken place on the subject between Moscow and Constantinople. Hence, although Evlogii personally considered himself to be temporarily an exarch of both Patriarchates, his diocese remained under Constantinople at the time of Evlogii's death in 1946. The decision to stay with Constantinople was finalized after the Moscow Patriarchate had appointed as its exarch Serafim (Lukianov), a former Nazi collaborator and enemy of the Evlogians, instead of Evlogii's deputy, Vladimir (Tikhonitskii), the very popular and saintly archbishop of Nice.

---

5 E.g., Mother Maria and the Priest Dimitry Klipenin. Both were murdered in Nazi concentration camps for having run such a rescue operation.

Vladimir refused to accept Serafim as his superior, and a diocesan assembly gave him full support. Its decision was to remain with Constantinople. Metropolitan Vladimir, seeking to end the émigré schisms, entered into personal negotiations with Metropolitan Anastasii, humbly proposing to subordinate his diocese to the ROCOR Synod on the condition that the latter return under the jurisdiction of the Ecumenical Patriarchate (i.e., to the 1921 status quo). Anastasii refused, perpetuating the diaspora schism.

Patriarch Alexii's reaction to the "Evlogians'" decision to remain under Constantinople was more cautious than that of his predecessor. He restricted himself to a purely canonical exclusion of the clergy of all three diaspora Church structures—the "Evlogians," the American Metropolia, and the ROCOR—from the clergy list of the Moscow Patriarchate.

Now for a few words about the American Russian Orthodox Metropolitan District's ("The Metropolia" for short) relations with the Moscow Patriarchate. Carrying out Metropolitan Sergii's 1927 request to pledge loyalty to the Soviet State was even more absurd in the American context than it was in Europe. Most American Orthodox priests were citizens of the United States or Canada, many were American by birth, and most were of Austro-Hungarian descent, and not Russian. Hence Metropolitan Platon, while assuring Sergii of his acceptance of the pledge, did not collect any loyalty pledges, biding for time. Having obtained no results, Sergii in 1933 ordered Archbishop Veniamin (Fedchenkov), who had remained with Moscow after the Evlogian split, to go to the United States for inspection. When Veniamin reported that no signatures were being collected, Sergii deposed Platon and appointed Veniamin as the metropolitan-exarch for America. Platon did not recognize the ban and continued to rule the Metropolia as de facto a temporarily autocephalous Church. He claimed legitimacy for this decision on the basis of the following acts: Patriarch Tikhon's and Metropolitan Agafangel's encyclicals on the right of establishing temporary autocephalies, which he considered to be valid in the American situation because of the absence there of a local Orthodox Church; and Metropolitan Sergii's encyclical of July 14, 1927, in which he stated that the Orthodox missions in Japan, China, and America had sufficiently matured to be considered as local Churches.

Metropolitan Platon died in 1934. A local *sobor* of the Metropolia elected Bishop Theophilus of San Francisco in his place. He was a widower whose deceased wife had been Serbian. The Serbian connection may have been at least partly responsible for his readiness to react positively to the 1936 appeal of Varnava, Patriarch of the Serbian Church, to come to Sremski Karlovci for a Russian diaspora re-unification *sobor*, at which the Serbian Patriarch would be the mediator. The Sobor proved a failure. Immediately after the formal re-unification the Karlovcians renewed their verbal attacks on Metropolitan Evlogii, and particularly on the St Sergius Theological Academy in Paris. As to North America, the Karlovcian bishops sent there in the 1920s continued to pursue their own separate policies, even after their formal inclusion into the Metropolia. Theophilus' unilateral unification with the Karlovci Synod was very unpopular with his American flock, which felt no affinity whatsoever to a group of White Russian Church politicians. At the American council which Metropolitan Feofil convoked upon his return from Karlovci to approve his act, only 105 delegates voted their support, versus nine nays and 122 abstentions. The latter obviously opposed the act but did not want to embarrass their metropolitan.

During World War II and immediately after its conclusion, the American Orthodox were even more enthusiastically pro-Soviet than those in France. Under that pressure, Metropolitan Theophilus was forced to begin negotiations with the Moscow Patriarchate. The American side insisted that their Church must be guaranteed wide autonomy by the Moscow Patriarchate, including the right to appoint all their bishops and to elect the metropolitan from among their American clergy, subject only to confirmation by the Patriarch of Moscow. Moscow claimed, however, that what the Americans demanded amounted to virtual autocephaly, not autonomy, which at the time she was not prepared to grant. The negotiations collapsed after the council of the Metropolia met in Cleveland in 1946 and ruled to recognize the Moscow Patriarch as the Metropolia's spiritual head, while retaining her complete independence. As a gesture to the anti-Karlovci leanings of the American Orthodox public, the same Sobor resolved to end its administrative connection to the ROCOR Synod, retaining, however, fraternal and liturgical links with it. The four Karlovcian bishops in America present at the Sobor refused to sign this resolution, which, as the council declared, meant their exclusion from the Metropolia's hierarchy. At the other extreme was the minority of American clergy and laity who wanted to rejoin the Moscow Patriarchate at any cost.

Consequently, on the wave of the post-war Soviet patriotism, a small exarchate of the Moscow Patriarchate arose in Western Europe; and in America, a somewhat larger group, consisting of fifty-sixty parishes, evolved out of Metropolitan Veniamin's tiny exarchate created in 1934. Otherwise, the jurisdictional configuration changed little from the pre-war days, except for the growth of the ROCOR which resulted from the refugee migration.

In response to the Cleveland resolutions, the ROCOR Synod, meeting in Munich, resolved to break off all relations with the Metropolia and to set up a parallel ROCOR structure in America. Moreover, it declared the Cleveland Sobor invalid because the voices of the laity were counted there on par with those of the bishops and priests. The ROCOR Synod totally ignored the North American situation of the time, when the atmosphere at the council was emotionally so laden that a real schism would have occurred had the lay voices been counted for less. In fact, it was from that Cleveland Sobor that the independent existence of the Metropolia began. Granted autocephaly by the Russian Mother-Church in 1970, it has become the autocephalous Orthodox Church in America.

The Moscow Patriarchate in the Soviet Bloc and in the Communist World

The real gains of the Moscow Patriarchate were to be had only in countries under Soviet control. In Hungary, the Russian and Hungarian Orthodox parishes became the Hungarian Vicariate of the Moscow Patriarchate. The Orthodox Churches of Latvia and Estonia were fully integrated into the Moscow Patriarchate, followed by the Carpatho-Ruthenian Diocese, which before the war had been under the Patriarchate of Serbia.

The Polish Orthodox clergy and laity, tired of Metropolitan Dionisii's ethno-political maneuvers, began negotiations with the Moscow Patriarchate in 1948 on the annulment of the canonically irregular autocephaly granted by the Ecumenical Patriarchate without Moscow's permission in 1924, to be replaced by autocephaly from the Mother-Church. This was duly granted.

In Czechoslovakia, all Orthodox parishes, including the Carpatho-Ruthenian churches of the so-called "Preshov Rus'," which used to be in the jurisdiction of the Serbian Patriarchate, were consolidated in 1946 into a single Orthodox Church, consisting of three dioceses, under the Moscow Patriarchate. With the resettlement in the Sudeten of the Volynian Czechs, who were Orthodox, the Czech Diocese increased considerably in size, while the Slovak Diocese tripled in size at the expense of the Uniate Church, which was liquidated in 1951. Subsequently, the Church was granted autocephaly by Moscow.

In China, the four Russian émigré bishops were recalled to Russia and appointed to head internal dioceses, while a Chinese Orthodox priest, Simeon

Du, was consecrated as the first Orthodox native bishop. But with Mao's ideological experiments, culminating in the "Cultural Revolution," the Chinese Orthodox Church has virtually disappeared.

The Uniate Issue

The Ukrainian Catholic Church, more commonly known as the "Uniates" or the "Unia," was an eyesore for Stalin. To begin with, as the dominant Church of East Galicia, the cradle and center of Ukrainian nationalism, she was, not unjustly, identified with the separatist movement and with Ukrainian anti-Soviet partisans, who were very active at the time. Secondly, she was under the Vatican, which Stalin hated, primarily because it was an ecclesiastic administration beyond his control. He had more than enough Roman Catholics in Lithuania and Latvia, not to mention Poland and Czechoslovakia, let alone having them also in the Ukraine.

Uniatism, he must have thought, would be easier to liquidate than the Latin Rite Catholic Churches because of the following factors:

1. Its ritual and traditions were almost identical to those of the Orthodox Church;

2. It used the same Church Slavonic and Ukrainian languages as the Orthodox of the rest of the Ukraine;

3. As about 90 percent of the Ukrainians were at least nominally Orthodox, and so had been the Uniates prior to the seventeenth (and in some Western areas up to the late eighteenth) century, the liquidation of the Unia could be achieved under the flag of a return to the ancestral faith and to a spiritual unification with the rest of the Ukrainian nation;

4. A trend to rejoin the Orthodox Church has been present in Galicia and Carpatho-Ruthenia (the pre-war eastern tip of Czechoslovakia, added to the Ukraine after World War II) at least since the 1840s, becoming particularly active in the inter-war period, when over 20 percent of Carpatho-Ruthenians joined the Orthodox Church; while in Galicia the trend was stopped artificially by the Polish Government after some fifty Uniate communities in the Polish Carpathian area had joined the Orthodox Church. Stalin apparently hoped to build on that trend.

Historically, while Uniatism had been diversely associated with Austria, Hungary, the Latin West, and finally Ukrainian separatism, the pro-Orthodox in Galicia and Carpatho-Ruthenia had been identified with russophilism (and russophile panslavism in the nineteenth century). While such sentiments had been widespread and wholly respectable in the past, during the post-war period russophilism began to be popularly, although inaccurately, identified with pro-Sovietism. And pro-Sovietism, to put it mildly, lost all traces of popularity after the first taste of NKVD terror. Although there still existed theologically pro-Orthodox Uniates, one of the most prominent among them being the priest Gavrilo Kostelnik, the prestige of the Russian Orthodox Church declined catastrophically after World War II, particularly in the newly annexed territories, because of her unqualified, if involuntary, support of the Soviet regime and its policies.

Kostelnik headed the Uniate clergy's "Action Group for the Reunification with the Orthodox Church" (henceforth, AGROC). Its work was marred from the beginning by its hand-in-hand cooperation with the Soviet terror machine. Metropolitan Iosyf Slipyi, the primate of the Uniate Church in Galicia, was arrested in 1945, followed by the arrest of the whole Uniate episcopate. Of more than 2,000 Uniate clergy, only 1,270 remained at liberty by February 1946. In the meanwhile, AGROC collected signatures from 997 clergy in support of reunification. On the basis of "the majority" thus achieved, a local *Sobor* of the Uniate Church was convoked by the AGROC in Lvov at the end of February. The *Sobor* was presided over by two bishops, both former Uniate priests and members of AGROC, recently consecrated in Moscow. The *Sobor* declared the Unia liquidated and the historical reunification with the Orthodox Church achieved.[6] The Sobor, however, cannot be considered as canonically valid, not only because of the fraudulently achieved majority vote, as half of the clergy were in prison, but also because bishops of another faith presided over it.

What was the role of the Moscow Patriarchate in that fraudulent act? Its first step was Patriarch Alexii's address to the Ukrainian Uniates on the occasion of the victory, which lamented the fact that they were religiously separated from their Orthodox brethren and therefore could not join them in the same churches in a common prayer of thanksgiving to God for the end of the war. After the Lvov Sobor, he issued another address, congratulating the Western Ukrainians on their return to their historical Church. The wording of both addresses was such that any member of the Orthodox Church could easily sign it—except for its timing: such congratulations coming on the tail

6 Documents in: RTsKhIDNI, fund 125, op. (listing) 125, d.(file) 125; GARF, f. 6991c, op. 1a, d.1.

of the NKVD terror sounded like mockery; especially as the message implied the legitimization of the fraudulent "*Sobor*."[7] Practically speaking, however, by accepting the Uniates the Moscow Patriarchate preserved for the local population most of the former Uniate churches for worship; these churches would otherwise have probably been simply destroyed by the Bolsheviks. Archival documents, moreover, indicate that subsequently most of the ruling bishops were quite lenient to the underground Uniate clergy (see ch. 16).

However, even the official acts of the Moscow Patriarchate in relation to the Uniates cannot be compared with the Uniates' practices vis-à-vis the Orthodox, both in the seventeenth century, as discussed in chapter 5, and again after the re-legalization of the Uniate Church at the end of 1989 (see ch. 16).

A Struggle for Survival

In order to survive in a militantly godless state, the Church had to demonstrate continuously her usefulness to the state. The only field open to the Church for such endeavors was inter-Church or inter-confessional conferences, at which the Russian Church leadership had to defend Soviet foreign policy and/or bring other churches and social movements into the Soviet sphere of influence.

The first such initiative was an attempt to make Moscow into the Orthodox "Vatican," as it were.[8] The occasion was the 500th anniversary of the de facto autocephaly of the Russian Orthodox Church. Celebrating this date was in itself a slight upon the Greeks, as the Russian withdrawal from the jurisdiction of the Ecumenical Patriarchate and the unilateral election of her first independent metropolitan in 1448 had been caused by Constantinople's brief acceptance of papal supremacy. The underlying message of the celebration was thus the religious unreliability of the Greeks contrasted with the Orthodox steadfastness of the Russians. All local Orthodox Churches, as well as representatives of the Anglican Church, were invited. Solemn church services were to be followed by an inter-Orthodox consultation in preparation for a Pan-Orthodox Council. The hope apparently was that the Council, spoken about since the late nineteenth century, would likewise take place in Moscow.

---

7 Levitin's presumption (vd. his *V poiskakh novogo grada*) that the Patriarch had not been aware of the NKVD persecution of the Uniates is refuted by Kostel'nik's letters to the Patriarch, in which he prophetically warned the Patriarch that the Uniate clergy being forced into the Orthodox Church by the NKVD would rebel against the Orthodox Church at the first opportunity. GARF, f. 6991c, op. 1c, d. 32.

8 According to archives, the initiator was Patriarch Alexii. GARF cit., op. 2, d. 65.

But Constantinople responded that the convocation of pan-Orthodox consultations was its sole prerogative. Consequently of the Eastern Patriarchates only the Antiochian was fully represented; the Ecumenical Patriarchate was represented by a minor delegation; neither the Orthodox Church of Greece, nor the Churches of Alexandria and Jerusalem sent any representatives at all. Greek representatives, in fact, participated only in the religious services, and not in the conference. Thus, instead of being a pan-Orthodox consultation, it became a politicized conference of Orthodox Churches from the Communist-controlled states, plus the Antiochians, economically and politically dependent on Moscow. Its main topic was attacks on the Vatican. The only theological issue was a decision not to recognize Anglican ordinations. This question arose because there had been cases in the 1930s of their recognition by the Patriarchates of Constantinople and Alexandria.

The failure of this conference convinced the Soviet Government that the Church was only of limited value. This, no doubt, was an important factor in the increased severity of Soviet religious policy on the internal front after 1948. It coincided also with Stalin's general policy of retrenchment and isolationism at the beginning of the Cold War, the Berlin Blockade, and the Western allies' tough and determined response. Additional elements of that retrenchment included Stalin's decision to end the Communist civil war in Greece, his break with Tito, and the subsequent bloody purges of the Communist Party elites in the East European Soviet satellites, reminiscent of the Soviet Communist Party purge of 1930s.

1949 saw the birth of the Soviet-controlled "Committee for the Defense of Peace." At its Moscow congress in August 1950, Metropolitan Nikolai attacked American actions in Korea, accusing them of such fantastic genocidal crimes as cutting off women's breasts, plucking out eyes, crucifying Korean patriots and scalping them. He alleged that the Americans had built death camps, murdered over 400,000 civilians, applied bacteriological warfare and systematically murdered Korean intellectuals. The very bright and sophisticated Metropolitan must have made up these absurd and grotesque accusations knowing that no one in their right mind in the West could possibly believe such stories, and thus he hoped to neutralize the effect of whatever fraudulent tales he would have to make up in the future. Whether or not the CPSU Central Committee's Department for Agitation and Propaganda (Agitprop) realized Nikolai's trick, the fact is that, whereas in 1945-48 the Moscow Patriarchate was either the initiator or the chief "producer" of such external undertakings, in later congresses and similar enterprises she was merely a participant, an important and useful one, but not of primary importance to Soviet foreign policy. Moreover, the Soviet authorities knew that an element of sincerity was also present in the Russian Church's participation in the peace forums. After the recent war, the bloodiest in Russian history, the Russian people's will for peace was so intense that, under its pressure, the Russian Church was prepared to collaborate with anyone if that could help preserve peace. Consequently, the Soviet leadership did not feel obliged to reward the Church too generously for her peace endeavors.

The role assigned to the Russian clergy was to present the Soviet Government and its policies as peace-loving. This was the price the clergy, particularly bishops, had to pay for the right to perform their minimal pastoral duties. Every bishop and, to a lesser extent, most parish priests, had to be two-faced. The glaring contrast between, say, Patriarch Alexii's and especially Metropolitan Nikolai's propagandistic speeches, on the one hand, and their sermons on spiritual themes, on the other, reveals a tragic state of imposed splitting of the personality. On the one hand, the Patriarch prayed for Stalin, called him in his political "sermons" a military genius who ceaselessly toiled "for the good of the Motherland." On the other, he appealed to his flock to thank God (not Stalin) for the achievement of peace. At the consecration of new bishops, he cautioned them publicly about the hard road lying before a pastor and an archpastor. He appealed to the bishops to be steadfast, to preserve church discipline and Christian morals. But how could morals be taught when lies became an organic part not only of daily secular life, but also penetrated the life of the Church? That horrible contradiction could not but influence the very fabric of the Church, demoralizing both clergy and laity. In speeches and messages on the occasion of the reopening of seminaries, the Patriarch expressed the hope for high moral standards in a new generation of clergy. Comparing the new seminaries with prerevolutionary ones, he pointed out that the latter were schools for the clergy estate; many students were there not because of any inclination to serve the church, but because their father had been a priest. But the students in the new seminaries were there only because of their calling to serve at the altar. He appealed to the students and seminary professors to concentrate on the study of the Scriptures and the Church Fathers. If the new schools did not fully justify his hopes, as the Patriarch himself admitted on occasion, was not at the root of it all this moral dualism, gnawing at every seminarian?

The seven seminaries existing in 1947 fell far short of the needs of the Church, growing as the number of functioning churches continued to rise until the end of 1949, when their total reached 14,479,[9] as compared to 10,544 just before the annexation of the Uniate parishes in 1946. In 1950, the number of Orthodox clergy of all ranks reached its maximum of 13,483, after which it began gradually to decline. The eighth and last seminary, in Saratov, was opened in 1948. All subsequent petitions by the Patriarchate and by local bishops to reopen more seminaries were categorically rejected by the CROCA, except one, in Vilnius, the capital of Lithuania; this petition, however, was rejected by the Lithuanian government.[10] After 1949, the number of churches being closed on formerly German-occupied territories began to exceed the number of churches being reopened in areas which had not been occupied during the war. In the Russian Republic, the maximum number of 3,806 churches served by 3,684 clerics was reached in 1957.

The refusal to allow more seminaries contradicted Stalin's promise in 1943 that the Church could open as many seminaries as she needed. Facing a growing shortage of priests and no prospects for a significant increase in seminary enrollment because of lack of space, bishops were forced to ordain men without theological education. Local bishops tried to raise these clergy's theological knowledge by organizing periodic theological and pastoral courses for ordained priests. Most of the courses lasted no longer than one month. At first, they were concentrated predominantly in formerly enemy-occupied areas, indicating that they had the blessing of (or may have even been initiated by) the CROCA for the purpose of political re-education of the clergy, under the guise of which some theological-pastoral instruction was given as well. But by the 1950s, brief pastoral courses became a frequent phenomenon in the inner areas of the Soviet Union as well. Thus Venedikt, Bishop of Ivanovo, just north-east of Moscow, ran these courses on a regular basis, and even built a dormitory for their participants, probably with an eye to developing them eventually into a seminary.

Periodic diocesan clergy conferences, often of several days' duration, were also convoked by bishops. Whereas in the 1960s-70s they predominantly

9 The official statements in the 1950s of up to 25,000 functioning Orthodox churches and up to 35,000 clergy was a CROCA propaganda lie, as revealed by the CROCA archives available to researchers since 1989.

10 This must have been a political decision by both sides: CROCA did not mind a Russian seminary in the strongly nationalist Lithuania; the Lithuanian national-communists did not want a Russian Orthodox seminary in the national capital, which had no parallel Lithuanian Catholic school, the Lithuanian Catholic seminary being in Kaunas.

bore the character of ideological indoctrination, with an inevitable propaganda speech to the clergy by the provincial official of the CROCA/CRA,[11] in the 1940s-50s, after the obligatory political speech, the rest of the agenda focused on church matters. For instance, the main topic of the Tula diocesan conference in December 1946 was the establishment of a diocesan library and a reading room open to public—which violated the 1929 law.

Complaints by bishops about the clergy shortage become particularly vocal in 1954. They and the Patriarch petitioned the CROCA to allow the establishment of theological-pastoral courses, three to six months in duration. CROCA, though, apparently tolerating sporadic courses, categorically refused to permit their establishment on a regular basis. Then, towards the end of the 1950s, i.e., once Khrushchev's antireligious campaign reached its apogee, pastoral courses disappeared from the scene altogether. The only thing that Patriarch Alexii I achieved in those years was the establishment of an extramural theological program at the Moscow/Zagorsk theological schools in 1951. This was, however, a very questionable concession by the CROCA. On the one hand, three years later, it was planning a reduction in the number of existing seminaries; on the other, towards the end of 1959, the extra-mural section of the Leningrad theological schools, functioning since the late 1940s, was closed by the CROCA on the basis that its existence at Zagorsk was sufficient. Measures to lower the academic quality of theological education began in 1948 with a ban by the Ministry of Higher Education on teaching non-theological subjects in seminaries, including philosophy, logic, pedagogy... This move was, of course, in conformity with Lenin's Decree of January 23, 1918, and the laws of 1929.

In the last chapter, we gave the number of parishes gained by the Russian Church from the formerly enemy-controlled areas. As we saw, the total number of functioning parishes rose almost by 400 between 1947-1949. This growth took place exclusively in areas which had not been occupied by the enemy. The total number of these churches was still a miserable 1,270. The over-bureaucratized, cumbersome procedure for re-opening a church on Soviet-controlled territories, which made progress so slow, was explained in chapter 12.

The following are a few illustrations of the re-opening of churches in the immediate post-war years, which, as far as the Church was concerned, were the most liberal in post-war Soviet history. In the Gorky (Nizhni Novgorod) Province, there

11 The Council for Religious Affairs replaced the CROCA in December 1965, after the amalgamation of the CROCA and the Council on the Affairs of Religious Cults (non-Orthodox) into a single organization.

were 1,101 closed and twenty-two functioning churches in 1945. Petitions for the re-opening of an additional 212 churches were received by CROCA from groups of believers. Of these, only fourteen petitions were approved—a 7 percent success rate. In the inner parts of the USSR, the years 1947-48 appear to have been most generous to the Church: in a single day (March 17) sixty-four petitions (from diverse dioceses) were surveyed and all were approved. But even in those years the waiting period between the submission of the first application for a church and its opening was between one and three years. Many petitions, particularly those gaining approval, came from religious societies which already had a functioning, but not officially registered church served by an unregistered priest. These clearly represented the so-called "catacomb" communities coming into the open, as advised by Bishop Afanasii (see ch. 12).

Archival documents allow us to establish that the following criteria were used by CROCA to approve the legalization of a religious society:

1. Distance to the nearest church of seven to twenty and more kilometers;

2. Registration of an already existing and religiously active community (ex-catacombs in most cases);

3. The given group of believers was known to have collected sizable voluntary donations for the restoration of cities destroyed by the war;

4. Convincing evidence that the given church had been illegally closed in the 30s, i.e., against the believers' wishes;

5. Persistently repeated petitions, especially those signed by large numbers of petitioners, from several hundred to thousands.

These "good" years, however, did not bring, any reduction in the tax burden on the clergy. The minutes of the Synod's sessions are full of complaints by bishops. Thus, Bishop Innokentii of Kursk, with an annual income of 60,000 rubles, had to pay 57,250 rubles in taxes. Tax officials counted the diocesan residence, food, and utilities paid by the diocesan administration as additional taxable income. The Synod decided that he should pay only the tax levied directly on his cash income; the diocese should pay the rest. But this decision did not make the financial situation of the diocese any easier. We may remember that, as far back as 1930, the late Metropolitan Sergii had petitioned the Government to change the clergy taxation category from Article 19, which related to profit making private enterprise, to Article 18, which applied to social and professional organizations. Patriarch Alexii continued to request tax reductions; but the Government finally did reclassify the clergy as taxable under Article 18 only from January 1981!

Although as long as Stalin lived no one dared publicly to contravene the status quo of sorts established since 1943 between the state and the Church, here and there, especially on the formerly enemy-occupied territories, local administrators began to confiscate churches from believers, returning them to their pre-war "masters": clubs, theaters, cinemas, museums, libraries, sometimes workshops, warehouses, and even garages. These actions were based on a decree by the USSR Council of Ministers of September 19, 1946—"On the Liquidation of the Agricultural Statute's Breaches"—and on a second decree which annulled all acts of the occupational forces, as if it were the occupation forces, and not the believers themselves, who had re-opened the churches. Archives reveal that, as early as the end of 1946, some collective farm administrations, for instance, requested that an active church be taken away from a religious community and "returned" to the farm to be used as a granary or warehouse, as it had been bought by the farm before the war from the local soviet for that purpose. Such documents pass over in silence the fact that the church had originally belonged to a parish, and that it was not bought from the parish, but simply taken by force. If the believers successfully appealed the decision to close their church, the "compromise" reached was usually that the church building should go to its pre-war "owner," while the believers either received a village hut to use as a church or were given building materials to build a prayer house. There were cases when the existing church was demolished by order of the authorities under the pretext of its "dangerous state of disrepair," while the prayer house given the believers was in a much worse state of disrepair. The reason for such visibly irrational actions was to reduce the esthetic appeal of religion. Especially in rural areas, the church has always been the most beautiful structure, usually attractively situated on a hill, surrounded by trees, often overlooking a stream or a lake. Its internal decoration was likewise the esthetic focus of the village. A crowded village hut serving as church was quite another matter.

The Council for Russian Orthodox Church Affairs and the Church

From its very inception, the Council began to behave as if it were the master over the Church, although in the law code of no republic was its existence even mentioned until 1975, when the newly revised and amended 1929 laws on religious associations were published.

Who was really in charge can clearly be deduced from the fact that the top copies of the Patriarchal Synod's sessions are to be found in the CROCA/CRA archives. Trushin, the chief CROCA/CRA official for the Moscow Province, was an absolute dictator over the Church. For instance, on a wall in the Moscow Seminary was a framed note in Patriarch Alexii's handwriting, stating that the Pedagogical Institute, which had occupied the building prior to 1944, had left it in a catastrophic state of disrepair. The note thanked the plant management for its excellent restoration work, "bringing the building to an even better condition than before 1917." Trushin ordered the plaque removed (obviously because it made the Church, and implicitly even the pre-revolutionary era, look better than the Soviet state and its institutions). When Trushin went too far, interfering even in the Patriarch's appointment of priests in his cathedral, Karpov apologized to the Patriarch, admitting that while CROCA officials may register or refuse to register priests, their appointment is an internal Church matter. Even this apology, however, demonstrates Karpov's contempt for the Church when he suggests to the Patriarch that he forget the incident as something unimportant in comparison with affairs dealing "with the external activities of the Church."

At the same time, the CROCA continued to extort money from the Church and the clergy for the "Peace Fund" and state loans. Trushin scolded the Patriarch in writing for the stinginess of the Patriarchate's officials, who had donated only 51,340 rubles to the state loan. He then insolently requested the Patriarch to make a personal contribution of 1,000,000 rubles.

According to archival documents, the Patriarch, although in a rather humiliatingly ingratiating tone, repeatedly petitioned Karpov on behalf of imprisoned clergy and stood up for the seminaries. The Patriarch could do literally nothing beyond matters relating to church services without Karpov's approval. For instance, when the Orthodox Church of Albania asked the Patriarch to send them a film on the 500th anniversary celebrations of the autocephaly of the Russian Orthodox Church, the Patriarch had to ask Karpov for the permission to do so.

The late Levitin-Krasnov wrote that the Soviets treated the Church as if she were the plague. A case in point was the reaction of the chief librarian of Kazan' University to Patriarch Alexii's letter asking him to donate duplicate books from prerevolutionary theological schools, held by the university library, to the Moscow Seminary. Instead of responding to the Patriarch's letter, the librarian wrote to Karpov that he was prepared to honor the Patriarch's request, but only on condition that the deal be made between the university library and the CROCA, and that no Church representative would be present at the transaction.

The existence of the Church as a social pariah led to irresponsibility and arbitrariness within the Church organization as well. Church personnel had to address all their grievances against arbitrary and unjust treatment at the hands of their ecclesiastic superiors to the same Karpov. Even the Patriarch asked Karpov to clear the church porches of beggars, among whom are many "obscure and passportless individuals, children with dysentery, contaminating others." He explains why he addresses such requests to Karpov by saying that it would be embarrassing for the clergy to do this, because Orthodox Christians have traditionally viewed paupers as "Christ's brothers." This is similar to Joseph of Volotsk, who wanted to burn heretics at the stake but relegated that activity to the State, as the Church herself may not deprive anybody of life.

Thus, humiliatingly for the Church, even church officials treated the KGB-dominated CROCA as their supreme arbiter! The Church, the clergy, and seminarians had no other recourse against arbitrariness, both within the Church organization and outside. A case in point was an incident on the grounds of the Zhirovichi Seminary in Belorussia. A part of the seminary dormitory building was occupied by an agricultural college. If a seminarian became friendly with a female student at the college, she was subjected to public scolding by the College Komsomol Committee and was placed under Komsomol supervision. As the result of one such friendship, a male Komsomol gang physically attacked a seminarian who was suffering from a curable form of tuberculosis. The physically weak seminarian had no other way of defending himself from the gang beating, but to pull out his pocket knife. He slightly wounded one of the attackers. The court condemned the seminarian to a three-year term in a concentration camp, while the attackers were not even reprimanded. In Odessa, a graduating female high school student was expelled from school for "immoral behavior"—the immorality was her church marriage to a seminarian. These events took place in 1956, the most liberal year, when Khrushchev denounced Stalin and when masses of political prisoners were freed or posthumously rehabilitated!

FOR FURTHER READING

Agitprop documents (Agitation and Propaganda Department and other CP policy documents on religion and atheism). RTsKhIDNI (Russian Center for Documents of the Contemporary History), Fund 17.

Alexeev, Wasilij, "Russian Orthodox Bishops in the Soviet Union, 1944-1953." *Research Program on the USSR. Mimeographed Series,* 61 (New York, 1954).

Alexii (Simansky), Patriarch, *Slova, rechi, poslaniia, obrashcheniia, doklady, stat'ii,* vols. 1-3 (Moscow, 1948, 1954, 1958).

Anastasii, Metropolitan, ed., *Tserkovnaia letopis'* (Lausanne, 1945).

Andreev, Ivan, *Blagodatna li sovetskaia tserkov?* (Jordanville, NY, 1948).

Bociurkiw, Bohdan, "The Catacomb Church: Ukrainian Greek Catholics in the USSR," *Religion in Communist Lands* 5:1 (1977).

Bogolepov, A.A., *The Statutes of the Russian Orthodox Church of 1945* (New York, 1959).

Chrysostomus, J., *Kirchengeschichte Russlands der neusten Zeit* (see previous chapters).

CROCA/CRA. Documents. *The State Archive of the Russian Federation* (GARF, funds 6991 c).

Curtiss, J., *The Russian Church and the Soviet State* (see previous chapters).

Deianiia soveshchaniia glav i predstavitelei avtokefal'nykh pravoslavnykh Tserkvei v sviazi s prazdnovaniem 500-letiia avtokefalii Russkoi Pravoslavnoi Tserkvi, 8-18 iiulia 1948 g., 2 vols. (Moscow, 1948-49).

Evlogii, Metr., *Put' moei zhizni* (see previous chapters)

Fletcher, W., *Nikolai* (see chapter 12).

_____, *The Russian Orthodox Church Underground* (see previous chapters).

_____, *Religion and Soviet Foreign Policy, 1945-1970* (London: Oxford U. Press, 1971).

Grabbe, G., *The Canonical and Legal Position of the Moscow Patriarchate* (Jerusalem: The Russian Ecclesiastical Mission, 1971).

Levitin-Krasnov, A., *Vospominaniia*: v. I: *Likhie gody* (Paris, 1977); v. II: *Ruk tvoikh zhar* (Tel Aviv, 1979); v. III: *V poiskakh novogo grada* (Tel Aviv, 1980).

Marshall, Richard, Jr., ed., *Aspects of Religion in the Soviet Union, 1917-1967* (see ch. 11)

Pospielovsky, D., *A History of Soviet Atheism in Theory and Practice, and the Believer* (see previous chapters).

_____, *The Russian Church under the Soviet Regime* (prev. chs.).

_____, *Russkaia Pravoslavnaia Tserkov' v XX veke* (prev. chs.).

Raz'iasnenie dlia priezzhaiushchikh v Ameriku Di-pi. A neo-Karlovcian brochure of propaganda against the "Metropolia" to prevent post-war displaced persons emigrating to America from joining that Church (New York, 1950).

Spinka, M., *The Church in Soviet Russia* (see prev. chapters).

Stroyen, William, *Communist Russia and the Russian Orthodox Church, 1943-1962* (Washington, D.C.: Catholic U. Press, 1967).

CHAPTER 14

KHRUSHCHEV'S PERSECUTIONS AND THE POST-KHRUSHCHEV RELIGIOUS POLICY

Early Warnings

The year 1954 is memorable in the recent history of the Russian Church because of mutually contradictory CPSU Central Committee resolutions with important consequences for the Church. The first, militantly antireligious, of July 7, 1954, acknowledged that diverse religions, including the Orthodox Church, were attracting young people. It requested the Ministry of Education, the Komsomol, and the trade unions to launch a decisive struggle against religion. It also promised to start a new mass-circulation, antireligious journal in order to neutralize the effect of the religious press, which was in fact limited to the monthly *Journal of the Moscow Patriarchate*, with a circulation of 15,000 copies per issue, the *Ukrainian Orthodox Messenger,* which published a few thousand copies every other month, and the *Baptist Fraternal Messenger,* also published six times annually with a tiny circulation, while the total annual run of antireligious brochures already surpassed 800,000 in 1950. In contrast to the majority of such resolutions, that of July 1954 contained no warnings against insulting religious feelings. It thus invited a return to the 1930s. But then, just as unexpectedly, another Central Committee Resolution, dated November 10, attacked such methods of antireligious struggle as slander, insults, and particularly condemned any form of direct oppression or persecutions.

At the time, there was still a sharing of power between Khrushchev and Malenkov; both were party secretaries, but whereas Khrushchev concentrated on Party work, Malenkov as prime minister concentrated on government affairs. The full-scale persecution of religion began only in 1959, after Khrushchev had achieved full mastery over both the Party and the Government, while Malenkov after his retirement became a church reader. It is thus now beyond doubt that the first resolution was initiated by Khrushchev and his associates, while the second was probably the result of Malenkov's influence. Be that as it may, the November resolution annulled the July resolution, and consequently 1954-56 marked something of a respite, during which (and even at the beginning of 1957) several dozen churches were either built or restored, their total number surpassing that for 1953, but still falling short of the 1949 figure. The promised antireligious journal was likewise delayed by five years. It appeared under the title of *Science and Religion* ("*Nauka i religiia*") at the end of 1959.

The toughening of antireligious policy began to be felt already in 1957 with the gradual introduction of mandatory courses in "scientific atheism" into school and university curricula. At the same time, the staff of the Institute of Scientific Atheism was enlarged, the number of titles and the circulation of its publications were increased, and so-called "individual work with believers" was introduced. Local sections of the *Znanie* Society and of trade unions assigned their atheistic activists to known religious believers individually. These activists would visit them at home and would try to convince them to quit their religious practices. If the believers persevered, their cases would be taken up by a comrade court at their place of work, which could adversely affect the believers' career and/or educational prospects. Much effort began to be exerted to recruit religious renegades from clergy ranks. Between 1959-64, about 200 clergy did leave the Church. Their names soon appeared over various antireligious brochures with such titles as, *We Broke with Religion*. But after the fall of Khrushchev, when Soviet "religious experts" began to take stock of Khrushchev's anti-religious assault, they admitted that the recruitment of clergy renegades had backfired—the response of believers was: "Good riddance! That priest has lied to us, now he will be lying to you. The fewer such priests, the better for us." Several, however, were rather significant figures. One was Alexander Osipov, a former professor of Old Testament at the Leningrad Theological Academy, and three had been seminary teachers: Nikolai Spasskii, an archpriest; the priest Pavel Darmanskii, and a lay theologian Evgraf Duluman.

Remarkably, during these difficult years the Church did not pass these desertions over in silence, but published in its *Journal of the Moscow Patriarchate* (JMP, February 1960) a declaration of excommunication not only of the four professors, listed in the statement by name, but also "of other former lay members of the Orthodox Church who have publicly blasphemed the name of the Lord." In other words, the excommunication was a repetition of Patriarch Tikhon's Excommunication Encyclical of January 19, 1918, although worded more obliquely.

Resistance and Capitulation

Up to 1961, the Patriarchate and the believers tried to resist the new attack on the Church as best they could. The archives contain numerous complaints directed to the Patriarchate and to the CROCA. The Patriarch, too, repeatedly addressed complaints to Karpov, both orally and in writing. Believers, he pointed out, were accusing the Patriarch of inaction in the face of the closing of the very churches which had been reopened under his aegis, and even of co-operating, so they thought, in closing them. At the same time, the Patriar-chate tried to strengthen the Church in preparation for the mounting attacks. Numerous articles appeared in the *Journal of the Moscow Patriarchate* in the course of 1959-60 about the strengthening of ecclesiastic discipline, on the necessity of humility for the clergy, who must remember that they are servants of their flock, not its masters. Extravagant clergy banquets and luxuries were attacked in the *Journal of the Moscow Patriarchate*. The clergy were called to lead eucharistic revival by cultivating frequent communion. One of the most powerful "swan songs" of the Church's resistance, however, was the Patriarch's speech at the Kremlin "Soviet Public Conference on Disarmament" of Febru-ary 16, 1960. The Patriarch declared that he was speaking on behalf of that Church,

> ... which strengthened the legal principles of the family, affirmed the woman's position as a person-in-law, denounced usury and slavery, enhanced a sense of duty and responsibility of the individual...which contributed to the unification of Russia, ...which in the trying years of the Tatar Yoke pacified the khans, de-fending the Russian people from new inroads and ravages...our Church strengthened the national spirit by her faith in freedom...

> She rendered support to the Russian State in its struggle against foreign invaders during the Time of Troubles and in the Fatherland War of 1812. She stood be-hind her people in the last Great Fatherland War as well.

Then he turned to *peace*, the official subject of the agenda, and pointed out that the Bible was the source "of the idea of world peace." In conclusion, he said:

> And yet...Christ's Church, which has been aiming at the well being of all man-kind, is being attacked and insulted by people...The consolation she finds for her faithful in her current situation is contained in ...the following words of Christ: "The gates of hell shall not prevail over the Church."

Pandemonium broke out at the conclusion of his speech. Shouts and pro-tests were heard accusing the Church of illegitimately appropriating the role of maker of Russian culture. At that moment, to protect the Patriarch from being the target of the attacks, Metropolitan Nikolai rose and courageously declared that he had written this speech. Clouds descended over the Metro-politan's head. His situation was made even worse by his sermons of the past two years, which condemned the new persecutions and responded to media attacks against the Church. Nikolai felt that, since Khrushchev's administration had broken the 1943 and 1945 concordats with Stalin, the Church had also been freed from her part of the obligation. The State's response to the Church's attempts to defend herself was a real pogrom in 1960-61. In 1960, Metropolitan Nikolai was also forced to retire, and a year later he was dead. Younger than the Patriarch and up to then in good health, he was taken to a hospital, allegedly to treat a heart condition, and there died of a heart attack. There are strong suspicions that his death was induced.

The *pogrom* of 1960-61, the disappearance of such a staunch adviser as the late Metropolitan Nikolai, and the replacement of the somewhat "domesticated" Karpov with the much tougher Kuroedov[1]—a combination of all these factors must have been the cause of the Patriarch's brief nervous illness which left him a broken man, wholly compliant to the pressure from the State to bring Church by-laws in line with civil religious legislation. The Damocles' sword that had hung over the Church ever since the 1945 adoption of the Statute, without any appropriate amendment of the state laws, now came crushing down over the head of the Church.

The by-laws were amended at an episcopal *sobor* convoked on CROCA's orders by telegrams sent individually to each bishop. The telegrams did not even explain the purpose of the invitation to the Trinity-St Sergius Monastery. As the *sobor* coincided with St Sergius Day, July 18, 1961, on which occasion it was normal for the Patriarch to invite a dozen or so diocesan bishops to participate in the celebrations, each of the invited bishops thought that this was the reason for the invitation. None of them, therefore, was prepared for a conference. Nor were they given any agenda upon their arrival on July 17. Invited to attend the long vigil, which was followed by a supper, they went to bed still unaware of the next day's program. The day began with a long festal liturgy, followed by a festal banquet. Only then were they invited to the *sobor*, at which the Patriarch finally announced an agenda of four points. The first, third, and fourth points related to the Patriarchate's peace initiatives, the decision to join the World Council of Churches, and the enlargement of the Synod. Only the second point raised the issue of the new by-laws, according to which the parish rector was deprived of all power and rights in the church, except "the performance of the cult," to use the Soviet terminology. Absolute

1 And yet in the mid-eighties he was removed for having become "too soft" on the Church; and on his death in 1993 he received an Orthodox Christian burial!

control over the parish now went theoretically to the group of twenty lay persons responsible to the state for the church building and for all that went within it. But in practice, the real power was now held by the parish executive committee consisting of three persons (the warden, the secretary and the treasurer). Although the committee was elected by the "twenty," the election was valid only when confirmed by the local soviet—i.e., de facto by the Party Committee's first secretary. That structure assured the gradual demoralization of the parish, and consequently of the whole Church, from within, as the militantly antireligious state and party officials installed their candidates into the parish executives, who more often than not returned the favor by robbing the church treasury and sharing the "take" with their benefactors. Theoretically, the By-laws still stipulated that the priest was the moral and spiritual leader of his flock. But in practice, he had no legal right to impose any ecclesiastic penances on his parishioners, as he had no rights whatsoever under Soviet law. He could hardly provide spiritual guidance to an executive organ which met and carried out all its business without even contacting him.

The Patriarch convinced the bishops to accept the amendments without a proper debate, arguing that there had been breaches of financial discipline by the clergy and that such facts had seeped into the secular press, which used them as pretexts for propaganda against the Church. CROCA officials were present in the hall throughout the meeting, and in their presence no one dared to challenge the instructions that clearly came from the Kremlin. Adding to the pressure was the fact that, at that very moment, at least two bishops were in Soviet concentration camps: Archbishop Iov (Kresovich) of Kazan', and Archbishop Andrei (Sukhenko) of Chernigov, a veteran of Stalin's camps. Twenty-six priests from the Orenburg Diocese alone were also in prison, and the total of imprisoned clergy was at least in the hundreds. The clergy continued to pay unbearably huge income taxes and, in addition, were forced to make large "voluntary" donations to diverse peace funds. In order to survive, therefore, they had to conceal at least some of the income of the Church, as well as their own. Hence, once the attack on the Church began, the easiest way to imprison a priest or a bishop was to accuse him of tax evasion. The *sobor* delegates hoped that, by removing all financial matters from the clergy's control, they would deprive the State of at least that channel of persecution. Finally, persecutions were increasing at such a rate that the bishops seriously feared a repetition of the 1930s. Precisely at that time, Metropolitan Nikodim (Rotov) of Leningrad and Archbishop Ioann (Vendland) of Iaroslavl', and possibly others, secretly began to ordain priests for the "catacombs". Under such conditions, the request by the Soviet State to change the Statute reassured the bishops at least that there was no intention to annihilate the Church completely. The clergy must not have been aware that Khrushchev, while publicly proclaiming the construction of communism by the year 1980, and launching a seven-year plan at the 1959 Extraordinary CPSU Congress, also stated unofficially at the same Congress that by the end of the seven-year plan he would display on television the last priest in the country. Or his words were simply not taken seriously?

The Clergy of the New Generation

A new, wholly Soviet, generation of clergy, particularly of bishops, made its appearance in this decade. In 1960, the thirty-one year old Archbishop Nikodim (Rotov) stepped into the shoes of Metropolitan Nikolai as the new chairman of the Department of External Ecclesiastical Relations. Nikodim was the son of the First Secretary of the Riazan' Provincial Party Committee and a school teacher. He chose to be baptized as a teenager, in secret from his parents. He was followed by a whole "galaxy" of bishops born in 1925-35. Almost all were graduates of the renewed Moscow and Leningrad theological academies. The very influential Moscow priest, Vsevolod Shpiller, a former émigré who had completed his theology studies in Bulgaria and taught for some time at the Moscow Theological Academy, noted that most of them had come to the Church "through a personal conversion experience. They were brought up...in an actively antireligious environment...Suddenly they perceived the Church in her truth and beauty...and joined her." At the same time, that generation blended with the totalitarian society so completely that, as students of theology, they could not comprehend how the Church could have a separate canon law and its own ecclesiastical courts, and abide by them in a state that had its own laws. Thus, Shpiller continued, they saw nothing wrong with the fact that the Church has no legal person status in the USSR. The Church for them was merely an association of believers, with no juridical context. Shpiller was concerned that they might in the future allow the complete subordination of the Church by the State. It was such a mentality, he thought, that explained the virtually unopposed acceptance of the anti-canonical amendments of 1961.

Persecutions and "Socialist Legality"

Khrushchev justified his assault on religion in terms of the struggle to restore the Leninist socialist legality and to overcome Stalin's legacy, his abuse of Soviet laws in general and of the laws regarding religion in particular. Khrushchev was right, except that he was restoring not Lenin's legislation of 1918 which, though restrictive, allowed "religious propaganda," but Stalin's laws of 1929, which ceased to be strictly observed by Stalin after 1943. Literal adherence to the laws of 1929 would have made the survival of the Church impossible. Hence, in accordance with Khrushchev's new antireligious policy, a secret instruction of March 16, 1961, by the Council of Ministers requested the immediate and complete restoration of the 1929 legislation, especially of the total ban on all forms of Church charity, including financial aid to monasteries and poor parishes by religious centers or prosperous parishes. Signed personally by Khrushchev, this instruction was kept secret not only from rank-and-file believers, but even from the Church leadership, as can be seen in the concern expressed in the report of a CROCA deputy chairman that the Patriarch had somehow learned about the instruction's existence. This is what "socialist legality" meant for Khrushchev, and, for that matter, also for Lenin, the creator of the term. In a letter to Kursky, the commissar of justice and author of the first Soviet Code of Laws, Lenin wrote that, in a socialist state, the law was to be subordinate to the needs of the Party, and the use of terror ought to remain a part of the due process of law.

Naturally, in places where the ban on material support for poorer parishes was fully applied, many rural churches had to be shut, as much of the rural population was migrating either to the cities or to Siberian hydroelectric construction sites. This was true especially of northern Russia, which Khrushchev deliberately depopulated, after discovering that its sparse population could not be subjected to full socialization and sovietization. Among other measures against the Church were oral orders by local CROCA/CRA officials forbidding priests to begin church services in the presence of children, to give communion to minors, and to allow boys to serve as acolytes.

Although none of the Party and State decrees issued in 1959-65 relating to religion mentioned CROCA or the CRA (which replaced CROCA in 1965), it was precisely during this period that these bodies began to act as absolute dictators over the Church. This can be seen also in one of Patriarch Alexii's complaints: "CRA officials have taken full command over dioceses, ignoring the believers' wishes to retain their churches...The bishops reign, but the CRA officials rule." Furov, the CRA deputy-chairman, responded cynically: "The country is building communism, the concern of the Party and the State is to educate the new Communist man, who will be free from religious prejudices. Isn't it clear to you what awaits the Church in twenty-thirty years, when all men will be atheists?"

The Reborn Theological School and Its Destiny

As we have seen, when theological schools were re-opened after the war, Patriarch Alexii had high hopes that they would be better than the pre-revolutionary schools, because the new students were more spiritually motivated. Eight years later, in 1953, he admitted that the results were disappointing, chiefly because of the thirty-year interruption in theological education and the total isolation of Russian theological studies from the developments in the rest of the Orthodox world. As a result, the majority of theology professors were poorly qualified, and students began their studies from zero. The Patriarch emphasized the necessity of a profound study of the Church Fathers and of Scripture, even at the expense of such traditional disciplines as the study of sects and schisms. The Patriarch's statement that contemporary theological schools enjoyed complete freedom, which did not exist in pre-revolutionary schools, sounds ironic in view of the Soviet refusal to allow additional theological schools (and seven years before the closing of most existing schools). In the very same year that the Patriarch made these remarks, 1953, there were numerous examples showing that theological schools lacked freedom. Thus the dean of students of the Leningrad theological schools, Pariiskii, a professor of pre-revolutionary vintage, reported to Karpov an "extraordinary event" amounting to the following: a group of students from the Geological Institute arrived without warning and asked for a tour of the Theological Academy. However much he, Pariiskii, tried to dissuade them, they insisted. He had to allow them in, but before doing so sent a student to instruct all the students to stay in their rooms with the doors closed during the tour. When the geologists were leaving the building, three seminarians walked out of their room and followed the visitors into the courtyard. Their names were duly reported by Pariiskii, who added that the visitors surrounded the seminarians in the yard and began a lively discussion. To put an end to that conversation, Pariiskii told the doorman to call the seminarians back, allegedly for choir practice. "On their return, the seminarians were told to make an immediate deposition as to what questions they were asked by the visitors." Pariiskii added that he immediately reported the case to the Leningrad Provincial Committee of the CPSU. Why, then, did the Patriarch speak of the unprecedented freedom enjoyed by the theological schools in the USSR? Because that same Karpov was present at the meeting where the Patriarch spoke!

By 1955-56, CROCA was worried about the considerable rise in the number of applicants to theological schools, and the tripling of students in the 18 to 22 age group compared to 1952 (311 versus 126), as well as by the growth in their educational level: almost all candidates had complete secondary education. The applicants included even young people with university degrees and members of the Komsomol. In 1957, according to CROCA reports, the number of applicants grew by another 168 persons from the preceding year, reaching a total of 765; but the acceptance rate increased by only 42 students because of the screening by CROCA officials. The Council's chief concern was the rise in the number of applicants with university degrees, and the tendency of Metropolitan Grigorii of Leningrad to accept them. The Council succeeded, however, in eliminating most such candidates through Pariiskii, their obedient servant. This, as well as other cases when applicants to other seminaries were rejected by the CROCA, as cited in official documents, tends to confirm the suspicion that local CROCA officials were orally instructed to allow into the seminaries, to the extent possible, only applicants with mediocre school records. The generation currently at the helm of the Russian Orthodox Church had to pass through this kind of screening, which explains a certain lack of leadership in the Church of the post-Communist era and the obscurantism in the sociopolitical activities and declarations of many bishops and other contemporary Church administrators.

As to CROCA, its involvement was at first somewhat surreptitious, but by 1959 its officials began to interfere directly in the educational process. They objected, for example, to the defense of such dissertations on moral theology which spoke of the necessity for Christian families to educate their children as Christian believers. This, the CROCA pointed out, contradicted Lenin's Decree on the separation of the school from the Church, and it amounted to a condemnation of the Communist education of youth. The year 1959 also saw the number of theology students reach its peak, which may help to explain why CROCA felt the need to interfere. The following represents incomplete data gathered from CROCA's documents:

ENROLLMENT IN THEOLOGICAL SCHOOLS			
	1956/57	1958/59	1959/60
Leningrad Seminary	112	126	?
Moscow Seminary	146	169	160
Kiev Seminary	97	116	80
Minsk (Zhirovichi) Seminary	138	130	95
Odessa Seminary	140	159	109
Volynian Seminary	148 (1957/58)	138	130
Saratov Seminary	102	159	?
Stavropol Seminary	41 (1954-5)	115	82
Extramural section of Leningrad Seminary	302	340	320
TOTAL SEMINARY STUDENTS	1,226	1,452	1,160 ?
Moscow Theological Academy	99	106	103
Leningrad Theological Academy	58	62	?
Extramural, L.T.A	296	?	?
TOTAL ACADEMY STUDENTS	453		

As the seminary program took four years to complete for full-time students and five for extramurals (who had to be ordained priests or deacons to be enrolled), and as the ordination rate was close to 90 percent of the graduates, even after all the screenings the potential of ordinands was about 350 per annum. Thus this system, in the span of a generation, could produce up to 12,000 priests—hardly sufficient for a country with a historically Orthodox population approximating 200 million. The potential declined even further after the closing of five of the above eight seminaries between 1960-65.

The following were typical methods of killing seminaries:

——Refusal by a CRA official to approve a candidate's seminary enrollment on the grounds that he lacked a reference letter from his bishop;

—A young man was being prepared for the seminary by his priest. Result: the priest was deprived of his license for religious propaganda; the candidate was refused enrollment by the CROCA official for having been educated by a "religious fanatic";

—Using diverse pretexts, local governments in the towns where the seminaries were situated refused to issue a residence permit to a newly enrolled seminarian; and conversely, the local government of the city to which the local bishop invited a seminary graduate to come and be ordained, would refuse to issue a residence permit to that seminarian.

—An applicant accepted by a seminary would suddenly be called for military duty.

In 1960, the Soviet authorities closed the Stavropol Seminary on the pretext of its merger with the Saratov Seminary, although the latter had no room for additional students, while the Stavropol Seminary owned four buildings, some newly built by the seminary and some bought and adapted—all at the expense of the Church. After closing the seminary the state confiscated three of the four buildings from the diocese with no compensation. In response to the Patriarchate's protest that, according to the Decree of August 22, 1945, the Church could own real estate, the Government responded that the Church had only a "specific purpose" right of possession: as long as the seminary functioned, the building bought for that purpose belonged to the Church; once the seminary was closed, ownership reverted to the state. Thus the Church was being robbed once again!

The same year that the Stavropol Seminary was closed, so was the seminary in Kiev. And the seminary in Saratov was likewise closed a year or two later.

The seminaries in Zhirovichi (Belorussia) and in Lutsk (Volynia) were never closed officially, but were simply strangled gradually by the above methods. Some applicants were refused registration in the seminary towns, others were called up for military service. As a result, by 1963 neither seminary had any students, and on these grounds the Volynian Seminary was closed in 1963, the Belorussian in 1965.

But then the Soviet authorities decided to make propaganda use of seminarians in 1957, during the pro-Communist World Youth Festival taking place in Moscow. 260 of the most reliable seminarians, thirty-five young seminary teachers and forty politically reliable (or docile) lay members of various parishes were hand-picked and trained to meet and entertain leftist Christian youths from abroad. Their task was to convince the foreigners that there was complete religious freedom in the Soviet Union. Among those chosen were: the now deceased Metropolitan of St Petersburg, Ioann (Sychev);

Peter Buburuz, a prominent priest in Moldavia today; Vakhromeev, a theological academy student at the time, now Metropolitan of Belorussia; Rozhkov, the current rector of one of the largest and most prominent conservative parishes in Moscow, "St Nicholas of the Smitheries"; and Svistun, another academy student, the current Archbishop Makarii of the Ukrainian Orthodox Church (Moscow Patriarchate).

Their work with the foreign youths was successful indeed. A group of young Mexican journalists wrote the following comment in the guest book of the Trinity-St Sergius Monastery: "Thanks to the Soviet regime, to the Soviet people and its Government, religion in the country is held in high esteem."

Monasteries and Churches

At the end of the war, there were 101 monasteries and convents on the territory of the Soviet Union, of which only one was opened with Soviet permission, the Trinity-St Sergius Lavra in Zagorsk (Sergiev-Posad). All the other monasteries were either communities which never closed, because they were situated on territories annexed by the Soviet Union in 1939-1945, or they were newly reopened under the German or Romanian occupation. As early as 1946, the CROCA began to push for the so-called "consolidation" of monastic communities, although there were no signs of any decline in their membership. Thus, by the early 1950s, only 90 monastic communities remained and only 17 by the mid-sixties. Mass closures began soon after the Soviet Government issued a secret order to the governments of the constituent republics "to submit within six months reports on the possibilities of reducing the total numbers of functioning [monastic] communities." The methods of liquidation of the communities varied. Some monasteries were closed by applying the decree invalidating acts of the enemy, although they had been reopened by believers, and not by the occupational authorities (except perhaps on Romanian-occupied territory). Others were closed by raising taxes and simultaneously confiscating arable monastic lands, pastures and orchards, depriving the monastics of the means to support themselves.

A case in point was that of the highly revered Pochaev Monastery in Volynia, which the authorities tried to starve out, failing only because of a concerted action to save it by the local population, with surreptitious support from the Patriarchate. From 1958, the Monastery was taxed 4,000,000 old rubles (400,000 after the 1961 devaluation). Pilgrims were persecuted: they were systematically arrested, beaten—with cases of murder and rape at the hands of the militia [police]—and their would-be donations for the monastery confiscated, in order to deprive the monastery of aid and to isolate it from the population of the surrounding areas. The guest house and all the other buildings, except for the main churches and the monks' residences, were taken away from the Pochaev Monastery in the early 1960s, forcing pilgrims to spend the night inside the churches. The building adjacent to the main cathedral was turned into an asylum for the insane, whose shouts and screams drowned out church services.

As the CROCA examination of monasteries indicated that there were many young people among the monks, nuns and novices, or at least that they had joined the monastic communities as young people (i.e., they were Soviet by birth and education) it was that generation of monastics which was subjected to particular persecution. Some young monks were inducted into the army; others, especially those recently tonsured, were "diagnosed" as schizophrenics, thrown into mental asylums and there terrorized, and not just through the use of psychotropic drugs. At least two young Pochaev monks were murdered: one, thirty-three years old, died in a psychiatric "hospital" after two months of enforced "treatment"; another, twenty-five years of age, died under police interrogation. Both had been absolutely healthy before their arrests. A 1961 decree banning group pilgrimages legalized the terrorizing of pilgrims. Nevertheless, Pochaev was one case in which the Soviets failed to achieve their aim, despite all the above terror and the forcible dispersion of most of its monks, reducing its population from over 150 to some thirty monks by 1965. The monks and the local population wrote numerous appeals for help, describing the horrors, to the Patriarch of Constantinople, as well as to Western Church leaders, the World Council of Churches (WCC), and the United Nations. The Moscow Patriarchate's representatives in the WCC and other contacts transmitted these petitions to the West, and they appeared widely in the Western media; but the Patriarchate's most effective means of preserving Pochaev, as well as such threatened monasteries as those of Zhirovichi in Belorussia, the two convents of Kiev and the Pükhtitsy Monastery in Estonia, was to bring regularly foreign ecclesiastical visitors to these places.

The motives behind the especially harsh treatment meted out to monastics (both before the war and under Khrushchev) are quite clear: the monastic idea of "other-worldliness" is diametrically opposed to the materialistic doctrines of Communism. Even more intolerable was the fact that the monasteries attracted numerous, spiritually thirsty Soviet citizens. In addition, because of the influx of pilgrims from all corners of the state, the monasteries acted as information centers of sorts, where pilgrims and visiting clergy could inform each other on what was going on in their parishes, what was the situation with persecutions; and from here the information often seeped abroad by way of dissidents with their foreign journalist contacts in Moscow. In this way the outside world became aware, through *samizdat*, of the persecutions and their magnitude, of the closure and destruction of churches, which reached massive proportions by the early 1960s. The Diocese of Odessa lost 210 of its 400 parishes; Volynia, 180 of some 450; Kiev lost 17 of its 25 churches; Odessa, 14 of 23; Rostov-on-Don lost eight out of 12. Belorussia, which the Soviets planned to turn into the first Soviet "wholly atheistic" republic, had fewer than 400 working Orthodox churches, as compared to the 1,250 she had had in 1945. But the mass closure of churches was not limited to territories formerly occupied by the enemy. Thus, 15 percent of the parishes in the northern Vologda Province were closed, reducing the total in 1965 to a mere 17 parishes, where before the revolution there had been 800. In the Kirov Diocese, just north-west of the Urals, of 75 parishes in 1955, only 35 remained by 1965.

The pretexts used for closing churches on territories formerly occupied by the enemy have been explained above. The difference between the immediate post-war years and the post-1958 period was only in numbers: scores of churches were closed then, and now, thousands. And on the territories that were never under enemy control, the methods differed but little from those of the 1930s. For instance, the local CROCA/CRA official would deprive a parish priest of registration under one pretext or another, and then he used other pretexts in refusing to register a new priest sent there by the bishop (and the local government refused to grant him a residence permit). After the parish remained without a priest and without services for over six months, it was closed, and the religious society was dissolved by the local government. The law that a person's residence had to be in the same locality as one's place of employment was applied to prevent a priest from another parish from making pastoral and liturgical visitations to a priestless church. Again, after six months without services, the church was closed. As seminaries were being closed, the growing shortage of priests resulted in a proportional increase of priestless parishes. On other occasions, the fire inspector would "temporarily" forbid services in a church, demanding very expensive alterations to the church building. In some cases, a poor village parish could not afford them:

left without resources because of the strict ban on diocesan or inter-parish aid to poor churches, the parish would eventually cease to exist. In other cases, the parish was ready to undertake such reconstruction, but the local soviet would freeze the parish bank account. And because parishes had no legal status in Soviet law, parish executive could not remove their own savings from the bank without the local soviet chairman's counter signature.

Many parishes were impoverished by the anti-candle campaign that was waged in the Soviet media from 1960. The sale of candles in the churches was defined as a hidden form of membership dues, which were banned by law, and for a while churches in many areas were forbidden to sell candles. In smaller, rural parishes, the sale of candles was the main source of income. Although this draconian measure was of a short duration, some churches had to close as a result.

The combination of all the above and other measures resulted in a decline in functioning churches from 13,400 in 1958 to 6,893 in 1988, after the reopening of scores of churches in the mid-80s on the eve of the Millennial year.

What Was Behind Khrushchev's Assault?

In 1959, Khrushchev declared that Communism, "in the main," would be achieved in the USSR by 1980. But Marx stated that "communism begins with atheism." He also "predicted" that once capitalism was eliminated and religion deprived of its material base, religion would wither away by itself. That prediction fooled both Lenin and Khrushchev. But Khrushchev also knew that the construction of Communism was the only justification of the system and of its colossal cost in human suffering and lives. He could not, therefore, renounce Communism, the *sine qua non* whereof was atheism. Hence, if faith in God refused to die by itself, it had to be liquidated by force.

For Khrushchev in the 1950s it was an "either-or" issue. Secret sociological surveys were reporting that destalinization was having a destabilizing effect on society: there was ideological disarray, disillusionment and cynicism among the youth and, conversely, a growing interest in "idealistic" philosophies and in religion. According to reports from "religiologists," more young people began to frequent churches, to sing in church choirs. The experts also observed a religious side effect to Khrushchev's social policies. Namely, for the first time since the revolution, Khrushchev introduced adequate pensions for all women above 55 years of age and men over 60. Consequently, people in these age groups began to frequent churches, ceased to hide their faith, as they no longer depended on a job and ideologically acceptable behavior for survival. By publicizing this observation, Soviet authors implicitly admitted that people were persecuted for their religious views. They also pointed to the esthetic attractiveness of church services, to the intelligent and often good sermons which attracted people, admitting the absence of such factors in secular Soviet life.

To dissuade people from resorting to the sacraments, the Church was ordered in 1959 to keep written records of the passport data of all people participating in baptisms and marriages. The records were then checked by the CROCA/CRA and local government officials, which often led to difficulties at work or school for those involved.

A novelty of the 1950s was these sociological field studies of believers and of the diverse religions extant in the USSR, their teachings and their practices. Of course, the studies were one-sided, pre-programmed to show that religion was on the decline and that believers represented an intellectually backward and unenlightened sector of the population; nevertheless, they were the first sociological studies of that kind with some semblance to scholarship since the 1920s. In practical terms, the studies made little difference as long as Khrushchev was in power. His goal was the liquidation of religion, and he remained faithful to that end until his fall in October 1964. But during the less aggressive, so-called "stagnation" era under Brezhnev, the Central Committee ideologues, who had read the results of the studies in their pre-censored form, gradually came to the conclusion that a brutal physical assault on religion stood no chance of eliminating it. Consequently, some ideas of the early Bolshevik "godbuilders" were pulled out of mothballs, although deprived of even the shallow philosophical arguments of Lunacharskii and his associates. Khrushchev's and Brezhnev's ideologues, incapable of appreciating the mystical depths of religious teachings, saw in religion merely its esthetic side and ethnic traditionalism. They therefore proposed to establish or embellish Soviet civic festivities with rites and ceremonies borrowed from the Orthodox Church, or in the case of Muslim or other minorities, on their religious ceremonies. Thus "wedding palaces" were created, with ceremonies to some extent imitating those of the Orthodox Church. The civic rite of name-giving borrowed some externals of religious baptism, etc. Articles and books written by Soviet religiologists, in the 1960s and early seventies in particular, claimed that once such ceremonies were in place and became esthetically attractive, people would cease going to Church. But this proved to be as "realistic" as

Trotsky's claims in the early 1920s that, once cinema reached the whole Soviet population, people would stop going to church.

FOR FURTHER READING

Akademiia obshchestvennykh nauk pri TseKa KPSS. *Konkretnye issledovaniia sovremennykh religioznykh verovanii* (Moscow, 1967).

The Anglo-Russian Theological Conference, July 1956 (London: Faith Press, 1956).

Arkhiereiskii sobor Russkoi Pravoslavnoi Tserkvi. "Deianiia." *Zhurnal Moskovskoi Patriarkhii* (henceforth *ZhMP*), 8 (August 1961). A *Samizdat* description of the same is found in "Opisanie arkhiereiskogo *sobor*a 1961 g." Radio Liberty Archives: AS 701.

Bilinets, S., *T'ma i ee slugi* (Kiev, 1960).

Bourdeaux, Michael, *Patriarch and Prophets: Persecution of the Russian Orthodox Church Today* (London: Macmillan, 1969).

_____, *Religious Ferment in Russia: Protestant Opposition to Soviet Religious Policy* (London: Macmillan, 1968).

Conquest, Robert., *Religion in the USSR* (New York: Praeger, 1968).

Fletcher, W. *A Study in Survival* (New York: Macmillan, 1965).

Hutten, Kurt, *Iron Curtain Christians* (Minneapolis: Augsburg Publishing House, 1967).

Kischkowsky, A., *Die sowjetische Religionspolitik und die russische orthodoxe Kirche* (Munich, 1960).

Klibanov, A.I., *Konkretnye issledovaniia sovremennykh religioznykh verovanii* (Moscow, 1967).

Kline, George, *Religious and Anti-religious Thought in Russia* (Chicago University Press, 1968).

My porvali s religiei (Moscow, 1963).

Pantskhava, I.P., *Konkretno-sotsiologicheskoe izuchenie sostoianiia religioznosti i opyt ateisticheskogo vospitaniia* (Moscow, 1969).

Pospielovsky, D., *A History of Soviet Atheism*, 3 vols. (Previous chapters).

_____, *Russkaia Pravoslavnaia Tserkov' v XX veke* (Previous chapters).

_____, *The Russian Church under the Soviet Regime*, vol.II (Previous chapters).

Samizdat Archives. Prague: Open Media Research Institute (Formerly: Radio Liberty Research Department, Munich).

Samizdat Religious Archives (Oxford: Keston Research).

Struve, Nikita, *Christians in Contemporary Russia* (London: Harvill Press, 1967).

Valentinov, A., *Religiia i tserkov' v SSSR* (Moscow, 1960).

CHAPTER 15

THE CHURCH UNDER THE DECAYING SOCIALISM: 1965-1988

The 1971 Sobor and the Church in the Post-Khrushchev Era

Patriarch Alexii I died in 1970, at the age of ninety-two. His last act was the signing of a Tomos (Charter) granting autocephaly to the Orthodox Church in America (OCA), the former Metropolia (vd. chapter 13). Had he died before signing it, the consequences for the OCA could have been catastrophic. This was because, in order to receive the Tomos, the Metropolia had to return under the jurisdiction of the Moscow Patriarchate. The "subordination" lasted only half a day before the Tomos was signed "releasing" the newly-born OCA as the fifteenth independent Local Church. Had that formal subordination lasted longer, given the Cold War atmosphere and the Russian Diaspora's understandable distrust of anything emanating from the Soviet Union, including from the Moscow Patriarchate, a major schism would have been created in the OCA, with numerous parishes breaking away. Metropolitan Nikodim, who had responded positively to the Orthodox-American initiatives, appreciated the situation and had an ally in the Patriarch; but many bishops in the USSR, including Metropolitan Pimen, the future patriarch, were opposed to the granting of autocephaly; and so were many Soviet officials. Even that speedy solution of the autocephaly issue resulted in a vicious attack from the Karlovcians, who accused Fathers Alexander Schmemann, John Meyendorff, and Cyril Fotiev, the chief architects and negotiators of the autocephaly, of having sold the Church to the KGB. A number of Russian World War II émigrés fell prey to this propaganda and left the OCA for the ROCOR.

Pimen (Izvekov), was elected patriarch at the Local Sobor of 1971. The election was again open, unanimous, and with only one final candidate, it was more regular than the election of both his predecessors. First, the late Patriarch Alexii did not name a successor in his will. Second, before deciding on Pimen, the CRA (into which both the CROCA and the Council on Religious Cults were amalgamated in 1965) sounded out bishops' opinions individually. Moreover, the CRA first offered the patriarchate to the 78-year old Iosif (Chernov) of Alma-Ata, a long term pre- and post-war prisoner of Stalin's concentration camps and a very popular bishop. Archbishop Iosif declined the honor, not only because of his age, but primarily because he had no theological and very little secular education. He expressed a fear that the more sophisticated 'courtiers' would manipulate him with the help of their erudition. Metropolitan Nikodim's candidacy was rejected by the CRA, at least partly on the basis of an evaluation provided by Archbishop Alexii (Ridiger, the current patriarch) of Tallin in 1967. Alexii had praised Nikodim as a brilliant administrator, leader and intellect. In contrast, Alexii evaluated Metropolitan Pimen as a very mediocre person, rude, passive and lacking any strong will, but popular with the uneducated, pious, old women for his beautiful voice and the emotionally moving way he served the liturgy. "Naturally," the CRA chose Pimen over Nikodim: it did not want any strong leadership in the Church. The KGB completed the task. It strictly warned Nikodim not to run for the patriarchate; while local KGB officials ordered local bishops, under the threat of repression, to vote only for Pimen.

Having gained a patriarch whose temperament was perfectly suited for Brezhnev's "Era of Stagnation," the Soviet authorities could rest assured that he would not cause any trouble, such as, for instance, insisting on the re-opening of closed churches. The late Patriarch Alexii, eighty-six years old at the time of Khrushchev's downfall and broken by the persecutions of the previous five years, apparently had no energy left to renew the struggle for the Church in the last six years of his life. But Pimen, even at 60, was not a fighter. There can be no doubt, however,that he was a true believer. Born in 1910, he chose the monastic tonsure at the age of 17 in 1927, when only those wholly dedicated to the faith did so. In the 1930s he spent time in concentration camps, followed by exile in the distant Uzbekistan. As the war broke out, he was mobilized. Appointed to the political department of the armed forces, he rose to the rank of major, but ended the war in jail, allegedly for desertion. Desertion by an officer in war time was punishable by death; instead, already in 1946 he was at liberty, serving as a monastic priest. According to CRA archives, he was released under the Victory Amnesty; but it is most unlikely that a major of the political department who deserted during the war could be pardoned so easily and quickly. It is much more likely that his arrest resulted from the discovery that, under his major's uniform, was a monk who had concealed that part of his biography. In fact, one CRA report mentions Pimen's tendency to conceal facts in his biography when filling out CV questionnaires. The report adds that Pimen avoided contacts with the CRA until he was reproached for that (probably with a threat of blackmail). Thereafter, he began to visit the CRA regularly for talks. Church people who knew him closely pointed out that, after all his sufferings at the hands of Soviet punitive authorities, Pimen was "extremely fearful of Soviet organs." This made him particularly useful as Patriarch.

As to the 1971 Sobor, besides "electing" the patriarch, it lifted the 1667 condemnation of the Old Ritualists, recognizing them as Orthodox Christians. The late Patriarch Tikhon had proposed the restoration of the Old Ritualists when he was still an archbishop in 1905. The issue had been placed on the agenda of the 1917-18 Sobor, but it was postponed to the 1919 session, which never took place. In 1971 Metropolitan Nikodim initiated the lifting of the condemnation. After the 1971 Sobor, the responsibility for re-unification lies with the Old Ritualist clergy. All they have to do is to reciprocate the act of the Moscow Patriarchate, which they have not so far done.

There were hopes among the clergy and the laity that the Sobor would at least annul the deadly 1961 by-law amendments. In fact, Archbishop Veniamin (Novitskii), a veteran of Stalin's Kolyma death camps, with a group of other bishops, submitted a draft of changes to the 1961 amendments which would restore the canonical status of parish priests and diocesan bishops. But the Sobor ignored the issue after Makartsev, one of the CRA deputy chairmen, warned the bishops individually: "Those bishops who dare to resist the [1961] amendments will have their legs broken."

Two years later, Archbishop Veniamin confided to Archbishop Vasilii (Krivochein) of Brussels (Moscow Patriarchate) that the situation in the parishes was unbearable. A parish meeting could assemble only with the express permission of the local soviet, and no elected parish executive could operate without the approval of its members by the same soviet (i.e., in practice, by the CPSU district committee). Consequently, party stooges, often atheists, were ruling and robbing the parishes, dividing the spoils with local party bosses. As a result, parish and church life was being degraded from within. The authorities, undoubtedly, chose this method of subverting the Church after having failed to extinguish or even diminish the faith by any other means. Indeed, whereas in the 1960s Soviet sociological surveys revealed some 10-15 percent urban and 15-25 percent rural religious believers, a decade later they showed 20 percent urban believers, plus 10 percent "waverers." The following is a table based on a survey of industrial workers in Leningrad, with a typically Soviet categorization of their attitudes to religion:

	1970	1979
A Marxist attitude to religion	27%	10%
Vulgar atheism ("all priests cheat")	17%	4%
A positive attitude towards religion	11%	19%
No answer or no personal opinion	34%	49%
Waverers (between belief and non-belief)	7.4%	8.8%

As the neo-"godbuilding" experiments, with civic festive rites and ceremonies, had failed as well, Soviet religiologists began to concoct a plan of adapting religion to Communism by the use of priests of a new type, who would double as communist ideological workers. This plan was revealed by Kharchev, the *Perestroika* era CRA Chairman, during his speech at the Moscow Higher Party School in the spring of 1988. The subject of the speech was how to make use of the clergy in the building of a Communist society. This experiment, consisting of an ideological re-orientation of the clergy, was attempted with particular intensity under Andropov and Gorbachev, his disciple. The Andropov period was marked by enhanced persecutions against genuine God-seekers and against independent religious seminars and study circles, combined with a somewhat benevolent attitude toward established religious structures, as long as they limited their activities to the mere "performance of the cult." The idea of a priest-propagandist of state ideology had a precedent in the *Spiritual Regulation* of Prokopovich and Peter the Great, with the sole difference being that Prokopovich and Peter the Great never planned to annihilate the faith, while the goal of annihilating any faith in God is a *sine qua non* of Marxist Communism. Thus, since Communism and Christianity are incompatible, instead of a Communist priest there appeared merely some demoralized, opportunistic and disoriented clergy and a general confusion which is reflected in the painful state of the Church and society in the post-communist years, with their alternation between monarchism, fascism, and communism.

In this new "Time of Troubles," by contrast to its seventeenth-century predecessor, the leadership of the Church lacked undisputable authority because of the decades of survival diplomacy, the decades of adaptation in the face of ideological enemy encirclement. As a result, Church leaders failed to provide the nation with clear spiritual direction and moral guidance. The advent of a new "Time of Troubles" was evident. Any remnants of the belief that a socially just welfare state could be built on the principles of Marxism-

Leninism disappeared with the collapse of Khrushchev's promises to construct communism, with the waves of repression during his reign, and particularly during the years of the system's progressive senility under his successors. The liquidation of the so-called "Prague Spring" by Warsaw Pact troops put an end to any illusion of some sort of Marxist democracy and/or "socialism with a human face." The Marxist pseudo-religion proved itself totally empty. And just as the rejection of the Church by the bolshevized revolutionary masses of 1917 was not a denial of faith, but merely its re-orientation from God to the idol of a paradise-on-earth, so after the rejection of Marxist idolatry, the human soul opened itself up to the search for God.

It was towards the late 1960s that dissent in Russia began to turn to such issues as Christianity, the philosophy of history, and problems of spiritual culture in general. A myriad of religious study circles and seminars began to replace the various revolutionary action groups of the previous decade. That change of emphasis and direction reflected itself in *samizdat*'s greater concentration on religious, philosophic, and historical subjects. These changes were followed by a wave of conversions of young intellectuals and students, mostly to the Orthodox faith, during the 1970s and 1980s. But neither the predominantly aged and uneducated church members, who suspected a Komsomol god fighter in every young person, nor the majority of priests were ready for such an influx. Nor was it safe for the Church to extend her welcome to the newcomers. Thus the two—the wave of new converts and the established Church—never fully met, and this was to cause grave difficulties during the post-communist era.

But let us return to the questions of Soviet religious policies during the declining years of communism.

The Council for Religious Affairs

The first publication of the CRA Statute, together with the 1975 amendments to the 1929 Soviet antireligious legislation, was evidence that the crude religious repression was taking on more civilized external forms. The CRA, according to the Statute, de facto possessed the powers of a supreme administrator over the Church. This is clear in point 3 of the Statute:

> The Council...exercises control over the observance of the legislation on cults by religious organizations and the clergy...[it] has the right to take decisions ... on the dissolution of religious associations, on the opening and closing of houses of worship...to verify the activities of religious organizations inasmuch as

their observance of the cult legislation is concerned, and give obligatory directives on the removal of their violations.

Because of the publication of the Statute and of the religious legislation amendments, believers at last became aware of the "laws" which caused their legal impotence. Even this was better than the period of unknown secret instructions of 1962-75, which were codified in the 1975 amendments. In some respects the amendments were worse than the original 1929 laws. For example, the 1929 laws granted the power to open or close churches to local soviets, but the 1975 amendments transferred these powers to the CRA alone. A group of believers could no longer petition the local soviet to license them as a religious society until they were registered by the CRA. Whereas the 1929 legislation stipulated that the local soviet either had to accept or reject in writing an application to open a church within one month, now there was no such time limit; and instead of answering the religious society directly, the CRA simply had to give their opinion on the matter to the government of the given republic, which, within one month, "is to give its recommendation *to the CRA"* [emphasis supplied, D.P.]. Thus the final decision remained with the CRA, but with no time limit. In other words, the CRA was transformed from an organ for liaison between the Church and State into the final decision-making body, thereby depriving the Church of the possibility to appeal unjust decisions.

On the positive side, the 1975 amendments brought the Church a bit closer to legal person status. First, the phrase that the Church was not a legal person was dropped from the revised version of the laws. Second, there was for the first time an enumeration of those things the Church was allowed to own, including: eucharistic vessels and other "cult objects," means of transportation, and buildings, which the Church administration could either lease, buy, or build for its use. These rights had already been given the Patriarchate administratively, on the basis of Karpov's 1945 letter to Patriarch Alexii I. But now they were incorporated into the law code, and the rights were also extended to individual parishes. The only piece of real estate the Church could still not own was a public worship dwelling, i.e., the church per se. This seemed to be a deliberate mockery; but the logic of retaining full control over places of worship by the atheistic state was its ideological aim to gradually reduce their numbers, so as eventually to liquidate them altogether. And indeed, though not as dramatically as under Khrushchev, the number of open churches continued to decline under Brezhnev, from some 8,000 in 1965 to less that 6,800 by Brezhnev's death in 1982.

The situation of the three seminaries and two academies which survived after Khrushchev's pogroms improved considerably during the 1970s, as all three were allowed to expand their physical plant (in Leningrad, at the cost of purchasing off the remaining half of the seminary building from the state for 3,000,000 rubles). Consequently, the total number of students at all five schools, including their extra-mural sections, reached 2,000 by the end of 1970s, higher than when ten schools had been open (eight seminaries and two academies). At the end of the 1960s, Metropolitan Nikodim managed to break the unwritten Soviet ban on accepting students holding degrees from the secular universities into the Leningrad Seminary and Academy. By the mid-seventies, this brought about the existence of a new breed of young priests and theologians from Soviet establishment families: children of party members, of Soviet scholars and officials. This was a major breach in the "Great Wall of China" which the communist regime had tried to build between Soviet society and the Church, isolating the Church into a ghetto by limiting access to the seminaries to the children of clergy and, predominantly, West-Ukrainian peasant boys. The appearance of a new breed of clergy and religious thinkers at the time of the proliferation of unofficial religious study circles, seminars, and their *samizdat* was not a mere coincidence: all these currents influenced and cross-fertilized one another and jointly worked towards the final bankruptcy of Marxism-Leninism.

These new developments, however, had little effect on the traditional clergy cadres, from which most of the episcopate originated. With rare exceptions, the episcopate remained passive and took no advantage of the obvious decomposition of the political system and its growing corruption, in order somehow to broaden the rights of the Church or to obtain some pastoral and teaching rights for the clergy. Such attempts in Stalin's times would have cost many human lives; in Khrushchev's times, they led to an intensification in the closure of churches; in Brezhnev's years, they would at worst have led to the forced retirement of a few bishops and priests. At its stage of advanced senility, the regime would hardly have dared to launch another campaign of mass persecutions.

A case in point is that of two priests, Nikolai Eshliman and Gleb Yakunin. In 1965, they submitted two memoranda: one, addressed to the Soviet Government, criticized the recent persecutions and demanded the restoration of closed churches; the other, to the Patriarch, criticized the bishops' compliance with the CRA's orders and demanded active resistance on their part to the atheistic onslaught and the abolition of the 1961 amendments. Under pressure from the Soviet Government, Metropolitan Pimen, their diocesan bishop and the future patriarch, deprived both priests of the right to officiate until they repented "for disturbing the Church peace." At first, Eshliman and Yakunin were supported by ten bishops; but eventually only two, Archbishops Ermogen of Kaluga and Pavel of Novosibirsk, continued their support of the priests' memoranda. Consequently, both bishops were forced into retirement (Pavel, being a returnee from Paris, was eventually allowed to go back to France and died in the 1970s as the Bishop of Belgium in the Russian West European Diocese of the Ecumenical Patriarchate).[1] Thus no blood was shed in the Eshliman-Yakunin affair (although it can be argued that the regime's reaction might have been different had the Patriarchate itself supported the memoranda). Yakunin eventually spent seven years in a concentration camp, but that was in retaliation for his setting up an unofficial Committee for the Defense of Believers' Rights, i.e., for dissident activities involving Church politics. That and similar cases with Baptist dissidents indicated that a churchman standing up for the Church against the Communist establishment in Brezhnev's time risked his/her own well-being and even freedom, but such actions did not affect the fate of the Church as a whole. Thus the argument that the episcopate's compliance during the eras of Stalin and Khrushchev was the only way to save the Church from total destruction can hardly be justified with respect to the post-Khrushchev period. Unfortunately, as Shpiller mentioned in his letter to Metropolitan Nikodim (see ch. 14), most bishops remained paralyzed from "fear in the marrow of the bones" remaining from the times past, the force of inertia, and the above mentioned attempt to create "a communist priest."

And yet, from the CRA's point of view, not everything was smooth in the Church establishment. A secret report to the CPSU Central Committee by V. Furov, the CRA's deputy chairman, in approximately 1976 (the copy smuggled to the West was undated), boastfully declared that the CRA had full control over the episcopate and that no decisions of the Synod were made without prior coordination with the Council. Yet, the same report divides 57 bishops into three categories based on their loyalty to the regime; and further commentary on the criteria in defining those categories indicated that control over the bishops, and therefore over the Church, was far from complete. The categories ranged from seventeen completely reliable bishops (including the

---

1 Thus, the Moscow Patriarchate did exactly what the late Metropolitan Kirill of Kazan' had flatly refused to do when Tuchkov asked him, as a condition of allowing him to lead the Church, to agree to dress up Soviet government requests to remove clergy from their posts as if they were acts initiated by the Church (see ch. 11).

late Patriarch Pimen and the current Patriarch Alexii II); to the 23 externally loyal bishops, dutifully fulfilling their Soviet foreign policy roles abroad, but deeply dedicated to the Church and Christian teachings, and actively "recruiting" neophytes at home (Metropolitan Nikodim fell into this category); to seventeen ideologically and functionally wholly unreliable bishops.[2] This last category included a number of the younger bishops of post-war formation, such as Archbishop Mikhail Mud'iugin, a professor of metallurgy in Leningrad before his enrollment at the Leningrad Theological Academy in the 1960s, and Archbishop Khrizostom (Martishkin), the deputy chairman of the Patriarchate's Department of External Church Relations.

In Furov's view, the most desirable characteristic of a bishop was his total pastoral and theological inactivity. And conversely, the "worst" bishops were those who preached, ordained numerous priests, brought young clergy candidates to their dioceses, tried to spread the Christian message, and attracted neophytes. Among the bishops most severely criticized for those qualities was the above-mentioned Khrizostom, especially because in his sermons he dared to ridicule dialectical materialism and official Soviet atheism, particularly the argument that God did not exist because the Soviet cosmonauts did not meet Him in outer space. Soon after the publication of Furov's report in the *Messenger of the Russian Christian Movement*[3] and after Khrizostom's return from his visit to the United States, during which he was quite outspoken regarding the "tensions" between the Church and the Communist Party,[4] the Archbishop lost his post in the Department of the External Church Relations and was exiled to the distant Siberian diocese of Irkutsk.

Other CRA reports expressed concern that so many volunteers worked for the Church without remuneration and thus made mockery of the official propaganda that the Church "bought" new members through gratuities and favors. Such reports also complained that even the withdrawal of registration did not stop priests from continuing their pastorate. De-registered priests wandered from village to village and officiated in private dwellings of the

2 Interestingly enough, the former Metropolitan Ioann (Sychev) of St Petersburg, notorious for his anti-Semitic diatribes and cooperation with the national-Bolsheviks and neo-fascists, who as a theology student had been chosen for propaganda contacts with the Western leftist-Christians at the 1957 International (Communist) Youth Festival in Moscow, appeared in Furov's report in the third category.

3 *Vestnik RKhD*, No. 130 (1979).

4 Typically, to be on the safe side, he maintained the artificial distinction between the Government and the Party.

faithful, especially in settlements deprived of a functioning church. The disestablishment of priests only made them more popular among believers.

The status of the Church did not, however, advance in a straight line during the two post-Khrushchev decades. There were changes of direction even in the Brezhnev era: from an oblique critique of Khrushchev's persecutions in 1964-66 and an attempt to revive the "god-building" imitations of the Church, to the toughening of anti-religious policies in the early to mid-seventies, and the somewhat more relaxed, although unpredictable, situation of the last two to three Brezhnev years. While Brezhnev was virtually non-functional for six years prior to his death in November 1982, Andropov's administration began with the death of the Stalinist ideological boss, Suslov, in January 1982. As a former head of the KGB, Andropov was much better informed on the real situation in the country than his party *apparatchik* predecessors. But with his "policeman's" mentality, he knew of only one "cure" for crises: repression. So he tried by force to make the nation work more efficiently, to put an end to corruption and loafing. But he also knew that religious believers were more honest, responsible, and conscientious, drank less and worked more than the atheists. And so, on the one hand, his short reign was marked by a more respectful attitude towards the established religions and their clergy; but, on the other, he increased the use of terror against independent religious initiatives, such as study circles, seminars, religious and other *samizdat* activities. During his rule the number of incarcerated religious activists (both in concentration camps and in "psycho-prisons") reached its post-Khrushchev peak. Yet it was he who agreed in 1982 to return to the Church the St Daniel Monastery in Moscow to mark the Millennium of Russia's Christianity (1988). Here and there, some churches were reopened under Andropov. Kuroedov, the CRA Chairman, published his *Religion and Church in the Soviet Society*, in which he stated emphatically that oppression at work or in educational establishments for religious belief was criminally punishable, and he admitted that such cases had taken place "in the past."[5] The Central Committee's congratulatory message to the Eighth Znanie Congress did not even mention that organization's antireligious work, although that was the main purpose for its creation in 1947!

The reign of Chernenko—from February 1984 to March 1985—was marked by a less tolerant religious policy, including the attempt to take St Daniel's Monastery back from the Church. The Church succeeded in reversing

---

5 Even the 1981 introduction of more favorable taxes on clergy income could probably be credited to Andropov's influence as the very powerful KGB chief at the time.

this decision only with great difficulty, by paying millions of rubles in bribes to high party officials and by agreeing to call it not a monastery but a religious-administrative center, with the Department of External Church Relations as its focal point. It is important to remember that the ideological head of the Party under Chernenko was Gorbachev, and that Chernenko was gravely ill and unable to function for almost half of his thirteen months' tenure. During the latter part of his reign, Gorbachev was the real leader; and the aggressively anti-religious turn must therefore be viewed as predominantly of Gorbachev's making.

Patriarch Pimen and His Time: The Years of Stagnation and Fluctuations in Soviet Antireligious Policies

Communist policy did not change, but the all-out attack of Khrushchev's years gave way to episodic and localized repressions. This was caused not so much by a change of heart resulting from the reevaluation of Khrushchev's persecutions and their fruits, as by the growing de facto decentralization of power and the decadence spreading from the center. Frontier hostilities with China likewise dictated a milder attitude to the Church, as reflected in the restoration and even construction of a handful of churches in those years, particularly in Siberia and Central Asia, relatively close to the Chinese border. The favors granted the Church were minimal, but they nevertheless brought to mind the years just prior to the 1941 German attack, when Soviet authorities suddenly showed great concern for patriotism and began to refer to national historical heroes and heroic events in Russian history, in which the Church was inseparably interwoven.

Simultaneously, however, independent religious seminars and study groups, which consisted chiefly of young people, were mercilessly persecuted. Participants were fired from work and from universities. In 1971, the 61-year-old Boris Talantov, a teacher of mathematics and a veteran of Stalin's concentration camps, died in a prison hospital. He had been imprisoned in 1969 for writing letters to Soviet newspapers protesting against persecutions and arbitrary closure of churches in his diocese of Kirov. Failing to have these published, he distributed them through *samizdat* and also forwarded the letters to the Soviet Government, as well as to the United Nations and the WCC. As a teacher, he had been influential among the young.

The Brezhnev era demonstrated the system's total inability to renew itself after the discrediting of Stalin. The attempt to curtail any discussion of Stalin's crimes, and even to partially rehabilitate him, proved insufficient to halt the ideological crisis and the growth of dissent. The government's response was repressions, imprisonments, psycho-prisons, moderated somewhat by a fear of world-wide publicity, i.e., of Western public opinion. Such acts were unprecedented in post-war Soviet behavior and demonstrated the regime's new sense of weakness and insecurity. Thus a "gray zone" of uncertainty appeared, which was exploited by dissidents arranging orderly protest demonstrations and engaging in *samizdat*.

If there had been an equally daring leader of the Church, he could probably also have taken advantage of that "gray zone" for the benefit of the Church. For example, Patriarch Ilia of the Georgian Church, 44 years old at the time of his election in 1977, succeeded in doubling the number of operating churches and of seminarians during the first five years of his tenure; he also reopened several monasteries and was able to attract large numbers of young people to the Church. His success, no doubt, was at least partly due to the resurgence of Georgian nationalism, which nine years later led to Georgia's declaration of independence. The situation of the Russian Church is quite different. The Russian Federation is too ethnically and confessionally diverse to be simply identified with the historically national Church. Its society is not as homogeneous as that of Georgia, where, for instance, the *samizdat* attack on corruption within the Church, where some bishops cooperated with high party officials in robbing the Church, did not lead to any schism and wholly subsided with Ilia's enthronement. By contrast, in Russia dissidents did not generally join the parish "twenties" and, with rare exceptions, did not participate in the struggle for the re-opening of churches, but rather took on irreconcilably critical posture towards the political collaborationism of the hierarchy. Consequently, the life of the parishes and the struggle for their survival fell predominantly on the shoulders of semi-literate retirees, mercilessly insulted and bullied by Soviet authorities.

The Russian dissident intelligentsia, neophytes in the Orthodox Church, brought into their religious life and activities the same methods they had employed in their secular resistance to the regime. The above-mentioned Talantov is a case in point. Another example was the religio-philosophic seminar led by Alexander Ogorodnikov in Moscow and Vladimir Poresh in Leningrad. It even branched off into other cities such as Smolensk, where its most active member was Tatiana Shchipkova, a professor of French at the local pedagogical institute. Most of the active members of the seminar, including all those named above, were arrested and sentenced to long labor camp terms in 1979-80, and were later amnestied under Gorbachev. The above-mentioned Father Gleb Yakunin formed in 1976 an unofficial Committee for the Defense of Believers' Rights. Its members scrupulously collected data on the oppression and persecution of believers of all faiths, publicizing it by sending protests to the Soviet Government, publishing the information in *samizdat* and forwarding it to the West via Western correspondents and other contacts. In 1980, Yakunin was arrested and sentenced to five years' hard labor and seven of internal exile (he was amnestied in 1987). Nevertheless, his Committee was able to function for four years, which indicated that some activities of this sort were possible as long as the participants were ready to suffer the consequences. Some daring souls, however, failed the test. This was the case, for instance, with a popular Moscow priest, Dimitri Dudko. He actively engaged in catechetical group work preparing adults for baptism. After church services he held public theological question-and-answer sessions. These activities fell under the law banning religious propaganda. After many warnings, and after being transferred from Moscow to parishes in rural areas of the diocese, Dudko was finally arrested in 1980, not so much for his catechetical as for his political activities: he had published several books of his sermons abroad, corresponded with the leader of the ROCOR. In his letters, he called himself a soldier in the army of the Russian Tsar, denounced the Soviet regime, and praised the monarchy. A former prisoner of Stalin's concentration camps, Dudko broke down when faced with the prospect of repeating the experience. During Great Lent in 1980, he was set free after confessing his political "sins" on Soviet television, promising to be a good citizen, condemning the West, and the Western correspondents who had smuggled his writings abroad, for having ideologically misled him. In the post-perestroika years, he compromised himself even further by joining the editorial staff of a clearly fascist weekly, *Den'*, renamed *Zavtra*[6] after the attempted coup of October 1993. The remarkable catechetical achievements of Dudko's contemporary, the late Father Alexander Men' (hideously murdered in September 1990), who brought literally thousands of intellectuals to the Church and published his purely theological works abroad, while keeping aloof from all even vaguely political activities, indicates that the "gray zone" allowed some such activities. Probably, if there had been more people of the caliber of Alexander Men', the "gray zone" itself could have been broadened.

One would think that, had there been a more daring person in Patriarch Pimen's shoes, a person of Patriarch Ilia's caliber (and age) for example, the

6 Which translate respectively as "The Day" and "Tomorrow."

Russian Church could have achieved more during those years, even keeping in mind her less advantageous position than that of the Church of Georgia. Perhaps an indicator of missed opportunities is the fact that, whereas the Baptists managed to register 170 parishes in 1974-78, the Orthodox Church managed to re-open fewer than ten churches in the same span. True, most of the newly registered Baptist churches had been in existence unofficially prior to their registration. But the Orthodox Church also possessed numerous unofficial, unregistered religious communities. Thus a Soviet "religiologist" wrote that the Komi Autonomous Republic of northeast European Russia had only three officially registered Orthodox churches, but over twenty unofficial parishes, not counting the schismatic communities of the so-called "True Orthodox."

Despite the Patriarchate's timidity, there was some movement in the right direction during those years. Thus Yuvenalii, Metropolitan of Kolomna and Krutitsy, who was in charge of the churches of the Moscow Province and who had replaced the shamefully compliant Metropolitan Serafim[7] in 1978, warned Fr Dudko some time before his arrest that, as long as his activities remained purely ecclesiastic in nature, the Church leadership would defend him; but it would do nothing if he engaged in politics. Shortly before Dudko's arrest, the Metropolitan openly visited his parish and, in his sermon, praised him to his parishioners. Similarly, Yuvenalii protected Men' from direct persecutions and arrest, probably using his KGB connections for that purpose, which, according to documents made public by the Russian Supreme Soviet's Commission investigating the KGB's subversion of the Church, had been quite powerful. The same Yuvenalii had gotten in trouble in 1972 after failing to condemn Solzhenitsyn for his *Lenten Letter to the Patriarch* at a press conference in Athens. Solzhenitsyn's letter criticized the Patriarchate for not standing up for religious liberty and Christian education of the young. Yuvenalii merely remarked that Solzhenitsyn was insufficiently informed about the spiritual work of the Church.

The disparaged status of the Church is closely reflected in the following two telegrams on behalf of Patriarch Pimen. The first, on the occasion of Andropov's death in 1984, states:

> During his whole life...he worked selflessly and in total dedication...With heartfelt gratitude we shall always remember Yurii Vladimirovich's favorable understanding of the needs of our Church.

---

7 He is infamous for his public statement (made under pressure) approving the Soviet Government's expulsion of Solzhenitsyn in 1974.

The second one was on the occasion of Chernenko's death in 1985:

> Prayer and memory...A grateful memory for all that which Konstantin Ustino-
> vich has done during his great and productive life...For his selfless work the na-
> tion has rewarded him with the true love of the people...The faithful sons and
> daughters of the Church shall always with heartfelt gratitude remember...Kon-
> stantin Ustinovich's favorable understanding of the needs of the Church...

The wording is the same in both messages, although there had been considerable differences between Andropov's and Chernenko's attitudes to the
Church. While Chernenko was being praised for his "understanding" of
Church needs, the clergy and the faithful were whispering about the harden-
ing of antireligious policies under Chernenko. His death was greeted with a
sigh of relief that the end of the year of national humiliation had come. It was
not only the question that the country had been ruled by such a non-entity,
but that the country was ruled by a "dead soul," to paraphrase Gogol. Nor was
there much sincerity in the first message: everyone knew that Andropov's
"selfless work" consisted of presiding over the KGB, the terror machine, *inter
aliae* aimed at the Church and at believers.

This schizophrenic duality in the behavior of the Church's leadership
could not but negatively affect the whole life of the Church, the spiritual integrity of her clergy and laity. This demoralizing dualism existed on almost all
levels of Church life. In all official statements, for example, and especially at
WCC sessions and at numerous peace forums, the Russian Orthodox hierarchy vehemently continued to deny the existence of any persecution, or even
of limitations on the rights of religious believers in the USSR; but in daily life
the same hierarchy, whenever possible, ignored the punishments meted out
by Soviet organs to members of the clergy. For instance, both Archbishop Andrei (Sukhenko), sentenced to eight years at hard labor in 1961, and Archbishop Iov (Kresovich), sentenced in 1960 to six years at hard labor, were
reappointed by the Patriarchate as diocesan bishops soon after their release.
As they were imprisoned allegedly for criminal acts, their restoration as ruling
bishops implied the admission by the Church leadership that the Church was
being persecuted. Iov's obituary, published in 1977 in the *Journal of the Moscow Patriarchate*, called him "...a man totally devoted to the Church, ...re-
membered everywhere he served as a kind and generous pastor, God-loving
and merciful to people"—as if to emphasize that the verdict of the court
which had sentenced him, allegedly for corruption and bribe-taking, was but
a vile fabrication.

The Role of Dissidents and of Samizdat in the Life of the Church

By the 1970s, samizdat documents on religious persecution began to reach the outside world in such quantities that they could not be wholly ignored, even by such left-leaning bodies as the World Council of Churches. The silence was broken by an impressively documented letter by Gleb Yakunin and Lev Regelson[8] addressed to the WCC General Assembly, meeting in Nairobi, Kenya, in 1975. Despite the resistance of the WCC leadership, the document was read out to the full house by delegates from the Orthodox Church in America, and its text was distributed to all members. The delegates voted in favor of a resolution mildly reproaching the Soviet "restrictions of religious liberty," for the first time since the ROC had joined the WCC. But Dr Ernest Payne, a British Baptist, protested that the issue was not on the agenda and therefore had to be sent to the steering committee. The assembly agreed to this, and under the ROC's pressure the final version of the resolution added the adjective "alleged" before the word "restrictions" and removed any direct reference to the USSR. In 1976, Yakunin and Regelson sent two additional letters, providing further details of persecutions, to Dr Potter, the WCC General Secretary. Potter remained silent on the subject. Only in 1980, taking advantage of a leave of absence by Potter, his temporary replacement, Dr Konrad Raiser, addressed an open letter to Metropolitan Yuvenalii, head of external ecclesiastic relations of the Russian Orthodox Church, requesting an explanation of the unjustified trials and imprisonments of religious believers and clergy in the USSR. In his response, Yuvenalii did not deny the facts, but pointed to the "generosity" of the Soviet state towards those who repented, e.g., Fr Dudko. By stressing that the Church had re-appointed Dudko as a parish priest as soon as he was conditionally released, without waiting for the formal end of the judicial investigation, Yuvenalii implicitly admitted the existence of persecutions and false criminal accusations against religious activists and indicated that the Church considered the Soviet indictments to be fraudulent.

The active dissident religious circles, seminars and human rights committees of various kinds, religious and theological *samizdat*—all these, on the one hand, began at least partly to fill in the gap caused by the ban on such publications and activities and, on the other hand, proved to the world the absence of religious freedom. In some cases, these activities set new precedents. For instance, when

8 The author of *The Tragedy of the Russian Church*, a collection of documents on the post-revolutionary history of the Russian Church, preceded by a brief historical overview by the compiler-author. It circulated in *samizdat* and was published in Paris by YMCA Press in 1977.

Dudko had begun his catechetical question-and-answer sessions, his ruling bishop, Serafim of Kolomna and Krutitsy, applied pressure through threats, bans, and transfers to other parishes. But by the end of the 1970s, similar sessions were being held on a regular basis after vespers by Archbishop Kirill (Gundiaev), rector of the Leningrad theological schools, with hundreds of students from secular educational institutions in attendance.

The above memorandum by Eshliman-Yakunin also set a precedent. Twelve years later, in 1977, a similar memorandum was addressed to Brezhnev by Feodosii, the ruling bishop of the Poltava Diocese. Paralleling the Yakunin-Regelson letters of 1975-76, the bishop reported cases of arbitrary despotism by local CRA officials, who literally robbed churches of their last penny in the name of enforced, although nominally "voluntary," contributions to the Peace Fund. Left penniless, the smaller rural parishes were unable to keep their churches in an appropriate state of repair, whereupon the local authorities, with the approval of the CRA, would close them down as "unsafe for use." The bishop followed his criticism and complaints with a draft proposal for new religious legislation, which would grant the Church the status of a legal person and general religious freedom. As he predicted in the memorandum, he soon lost his diocese. The Patriarchate was forced to move him to the smaller diocese of Astrakhan', but also demonstrated its support for his action by raising him to the rank of archbishop.

During the same decade, Soviet antireligious publications noted that more young people were attending church than before. "School children," they reported, "predominantly demonstrate a positive attitude towards religion." Eighty percent of religious families taught religion to their children under the direct influence of the clergy, who preached that atheism was satanic. Soviet religiologists singled out Filaret, Metropolitan of Belorussia, for having "advised his priests to gather all the children wanting to receive communion into one group and to give them catechetical instruction just before the beginning of the liturgy." This was in Belorussia, which, in Khrushchev's time, had been projected to become the first territory wholly "freed from religion"—where priests had been ordered by the CRA not to begin a service as long as any children were present in the church and to refuse communion to school children!

Even some official representatives of the Moscow Patriarchate abroad began to be more outspoken in the last decade of the communist regime. Foremost among these was the Protopresbyter and Professor Vitalii Borovoi, the ROC representative at the WCC headquarters in Geneva. In a sermon at the Moscow Patriarchate's London cathedral in 1980, he spoke of Russia as a land which produced more Christian martyrs in the twentieth century than all Christendom did in the entire history of the Church. He spoke about the influx of young people, of university students and the intelligentsia, into the Church even as it had seemed that, with the passage of the old generation, the Church would wither away. He gave the current Russian Church no credit for this influx, as she was not engaged in active missionary work, but could only keep the doors open for neophytes, whose appearance he saw as God's miracle. A few months earlier, in 1979, speaking in New York, Fr Borovoi declared that the reason the Soviets were still in power was because the nation saw no moral alternatives. The Western powers could have served as such an alternative model had they retained their Christian identity and followed Christian principles in practice and as a matter of policy.

Patriarch Pimen's behavior and public statements contrasted unfavorably with these early signs of gradual self-emancipation. In 1973, Pimen read a statement in Geneva denying not only violations of human rights in the USSR, but also the existence of any social injustice or material want.[9] His 1982 speech at the United Nations was essentially similar, despite the events in Nairobi and the imprisonment of Fr Yakunin.

The extreme timidity of the Patriarchate and the behavior of the Patriarch were a subject of debate in *samizdat*. Some, such as Solzhenitsyn, criticized the Patriarch for his total submission to Soviet orders,[10] arguing that in the conditions of the time the Patriarch, having behind him a flock of many millions, risked nothing if he spoke out. Others, including the late Fr Sergii Zheludkov, an active *samizdat* author who had lost his clergy registration for alleged religious propaganda, maintained that Solzhenitsyn risked only his own life, while the Patriarch—"a bird in a golden cage," as he called him—would have risked the fate of the whole Church. Zheludkov argued

9 The late Fr Alexander Schmemann commented at the time: "The Patriarch's statement...is so blatantly mendacious that passing it over in silence would amount to treason. The statement...was made even as...a new wave of persecutions has been unfurled against all independently minded people, against all expressions of faith, spirit and freedom."

10 However, after his expulsion from the USSR in 1974, Solzhenitsyn, in his letter to the Third Council of the ROCOR (Jordanville, fall 1974) emphasized that he could criticize the Patriarchate only as long as he was in that Church's flock inside Russia. The moment he crossed the border, he lost the moral right to write such letters. These words were a reproach to the Karlovicians for daring to attack the Moscow Patriarchate from their cozy Western safety.

that under Soviet law and in the current structure of the Church, the faithful were not a single flock but atomized individuals, because parishes as such did not exist. Closely linked was the *samizdat* discussion on the most appropriate structure of the Church in a totalitarian-antireligious state. Some argued that, since the center of the state system was weakening and local party bosses increasingly behaved like independent feudal lords, a decentralized Church was preferable, in which each diocese could deal separately with local administrations. As it was, the Church was centralized only on paper, and the Patriarchate had no power over local dioceses, which were controlled by the local CRA officials and party bosses, while the real power in Moscow resided in the central CRA office, not the Patriarchate. Whenever a diocesan bishop became "over-active," the CRA would force the Patriarchate to restrain him or remove him from his diocese; while in a decentralized structure the bishop would have to deal only with local authorities. Others argued that, even with decentralization the central CRA would remain in charge. At present it controlled the dioceses through the Patriarchate, which had at least some weight in its dealings with the CRA. But should the links between the dioceses and the Patriarchate be weakened, the CRA's control over the former would become even greater than it already was. All these discussions indicated the senility of the system, pointing to changes in the future, if not at present.

Among the real gains during the last Soviet decade was the opening of a Church factory in Sofrino (some forty kilometers from Moscow) in 1980. The Patriarchate had been asking for the permission to establish a central factory to produce church goods since 1946. In 1981, the Publishing Department of the Moscow Patriarchate erected a spacious modern building. Under the Communist regime, however, the Department's chief output was intended for Western consumption: records of church music, propaganda books, and brochures about the Russian Church in foreign languages, etc., while little was produced for domestic consumption. Yet, it created an important base for the future, should there be political changes in the country. Another improvement came in the form of a response to the Patriarchate's petitions, dating from as far back as 1930, to reduce the tax burden on the clergy. As of January 1, 1981 the taxation category for clergy was altered from that of private business (article 19), where the maximum tax amounted to 81 percent of one's income, to the category of professional self-employment and cooperatives (article 18), with a maximum tax of 69 percent. Was this a fair deal? The maximum tax rate for state employees and workers at the time was 13 percent of their income.

FOR FURTHER READING

Academiia obshchestvennykh nauk pri TsKKPSS. *Konkretnye issledovaniia sovremennykh religioznykh verovanii* (Moscow, 1967).

Anderson, John, *Religion, State and Politics in the Soviet Union and Successor States* (Cambridge University Press, 1994).

Bloch, L., Sidney and Reddaway, P., *Russia's Political Hospitals* (London, 1978).

Bourdeaux, M., *Faith on Trial in Russia* (London, 1971).

_____, *Patriarch and Prophets: Persecution of the Russian Orthodox Church Today* (London, 1969).

_____, *Religious Ferment in Russia: Protestant Opposition to Soviet Religious Policy* (London, 1968).

_____, and Katherine Murray, *Young Christians in Russia* (London, 1976).

Davis, Nathaniel, *A Long Walk to Church. A Contemporary History of Russian Orthodoxy* (Boulder, CO: Westview Press, 1995).

Dudko, Priest Dimitri, "Kreshchenie na Rusi," *VRKhD*, No. 117 (1976).

_____, *Our Hope* (Crestwood, NY: St Vladimir's Press, 1977).

Dunlop, John., *The New Russian Revolutionaries* (Belmont, MA, 1976).

_____, *The Faces of Contemporary Russian Nationalism* (Princeton, NJ, 1983).

Ellis, Jane, *The Russian Orthodox Church: a Contemporary History* (London, 1986).

Gagarin, Iu., *Religioznye perezhitki v Komi ASSR* (Syktyvkar, 1971).

Goricheva, Tatiana, *Die Rettung der Verlorenen* (Wuppertal, 1982).

Hebly, J.A., *The Russians and the World Council of Churches* (Dublin and Ottawa, 1978).

Konstantinow, Fr. Dimitri, *The Crown of Thorns* (London, Ont., 1973).

Kuroedov, V. A., *Religiia i tserkov' v sovetskom obshchestve* (Moscow, 1984).

Levitin-Krasnov, A., *Dialog s tserkovnoi Rossiei* (Paris, 1967)

_____, *Zashchita very v SSSR* (Paris, 1966).

Meerson-Aksenov, Michael and Boris Shragin, eds., *The Political, Social and Religious Thought of Russian 'Samizdat'—an Anthology* (Belmont, MA, 1977).

Pomestnyi sobor Russkoi Pravoslavnoi Tserkvi, 30. 5-2. 6, 1971 g. (Moscow, 1972).

Pospielovsky, D., *A History of Soviet Atheism in Theory and Practice* (see previous chapters).

_____, *Russkaia Pravoslavnaia Tserkov' v XX veke* (see prev. chs.).

_____, *The Russian Church under the Soviet Regime* (see prev. chs.).

Powell, David., *Antireligious Propaganda in the Soviet Union: a Study in Mass Persuasion* (Cambridge, MA, 1975).

Reddaway, Peter (ed.), *Uncensored Russia* (London, 1972).

Religion in Communist Lands. A Keston College quarterly (Keston, England, 1971-1991).

Religion, State and Society. A follow-up to RCL (Oxford: Keston Research, 1992-).

Scarfe, Alan, ed., *The CCDBR Documents: Christian Committee for the Defence of Believers' Rights in the USSR* (Glendale/Orange, CA, 1982).

Shalamov, V.T., *Kolyma Tales*. (New York, 1980).

Simon, Gerhard, *Church, State and Opposition* (London, 1974).

Solzhenitsyn, A.,ed., *From Under the Rubble* (London, 1975).

Struve, Nikita., *Christians in Contemporary Russia* (London, 1967).

Yakunin, Fr. Gleb and Lev Regelson, *Letters from Moscow* (San Francisco, 1978).

Zheludkov, priest S., *Pochemu i ia khristianin* (Frankfurt/M., 1973).

CHAPTER 16

THE CHURCH UNDER PERESTROIKA AND THE AGONY OF COMMUNISM

Gorbachev and Religion

Gorbachev's ascent promised no relaxation in Soviet religious policy. He had been the ideological party boss during Chernenko's regime, which had taken a hard line against religion. In addition, the Central Committee Plenum preceding the 27th Party Congress called for the intensification of ideological work; while the new CPSU Program adopted at the 27th Congress in the spring of 1986 again called for the dissemination of "scientifically atheistic Weltanschauung for the overcoming of religious superstitions." And, as of old, the Program's section on "Atheistic Upbringing" placed the struggle against religion next to such vices as corruption, alcoholism, and theft of state property—i.e., faith in God was still treated as a pathological deviation from the norm.

Gorbachev's chief ideologist, Yegor Ligachev, Second Secretary of the Central Committee, began an antireligious offensive in press editorials in September 1986, attacking the intelligentsia for "flirting with a god."[1] Then, at an All-Union Conference of Deans of Social Science Faculties in October, Ligachev attacked the Russian intelligentsia for associating morality with Christianity. Symptomatic was an incident that occurred roughly at that time at the New Jerusalem Museum at Istra. One of its scholars was a religious believer; moreover, she dared to invite two scholar-priests from the Moscow Theological Academy for scholarly consultations. This cost her her job. When museum employees sent a letter of protest, a spokesman from the CPSU Central Committee informed them that the firing was in full conformity with *perestroika*, which also included an intensification of atheistic work.

This proved to be the last antireligious campaign. It ended not as a tragedy, not as a drama, but as a farce, when one of the top Soviet "scientific atheists," Kryvelev, was devastatingly ridiculed in the liberal journal *Novyi mir* for his uncouth attacks on the novelist Astafiev's Christian short stories.

Several factors contributed to the "sudden" courage of the intelligentsia: the failure of the system to respond to dissidents except through terror wholly

---

1 A popular Soviet propaganda quotation from Lenin.

discredited the Soviet system; Gorbachev's appeal to Soviet writers, on the eve of the 1986 Writers' Congress, to help him in the struggle against alcoholism, for the moral restoration of the nation.[2] But the intelligentsia had matured since Khrushchev's days, when it was ready to return with full loyalty for even a partial liberalization of the censorship of literary publications. In those days, most of the intelligentsia was so distant from religious problems that it hardly noticed Khrushchev's persecutions. The new intelligentsia of the 1980s was radically different from its positivistic predecessors. With the moral bankruptcy of Communism, materialistic positivism was likewise compromised, and there was a widespread openness to religion. The Chernobyl nuclear disaster further discredited the communist system, because the accident was caused by the incompetence of unprofessional, politically appointed administrators, as well as the Soviet planning system irresponsibly setting dates for commissioning plants irrespective of the state of their safety features, against the better advice of experts. There was also a mystical element in the disaster. The Ukrainian word *chornobyl'* means wormwood; and within days the relevant passage from St John's Revelation (8:10-11) was recited across the country:

> ...there fell a great star from heaven, burning as it were a lamp, and it fell upon the third part of the rivers, and upon the fountains of waters; and the name of the star was called Wormwood...and many men died in the waters, because they were made bitter.

These words aroused eschatological expectations, as well as associations of Chernobyl and its architects with Satanism. Masses of people, and far from only the uneducated, rushed to the baptismal font. This atmosphere made it imperative that Gorbachev soften his religious policy if he hoped to obtain the intelligentsia's cooperation. The other factor leading to a change in Gorbachev's religious policies was the need to end the arms race. He feared imminent economic collapse and a growing technological gap, which precluded the possibility for the Soviet Union to compete with the US in "star wars" research. Gorbachev understood that, in order to achieve better relations with the United States and the rest of the Western world, in order to end the Cold War and to obtain Western credits, he had to take some steps towards democratization in the Soviet Union. He knew that religious freedom was an important international measuring stick of the degree of freedom in a country. And a perfect pretext for a radical change in religious policies was the forthcoming Millennium of Russian Christianity in 1988.

2 Gorbachev's appeal was merely reported in the Soviet press, but a detailed paraphrase of his words appeared in *samizdat*.

1987, on the eve of the Millennium, marked the turning point in Soviet religious policies. In 1987, Gorbachev flew to Washington for further negotiations with American President Reagan, taking with him a plane load of representatives from the Soviet elites, including the leaders of all the major religions in the USSR. While negotiations were taking place at the White House, religious leaders of both the USSR and the USA were praying at the Washington National Cathedral, and then they issued a joint declaration condemning the arms race of *both* states.[3] In the course of that same year, *Science and Religion*, the main Soviet anti-religious monthly, was transformed into a forum for atheists and religious believers. However, in a subtle if indirect way, the journal continues to discredit Christianity by opening its pages also to the occult, to astrology and black magic, presenting these as aspects of religion. Given the general religious ignorance in post-Communist Russia, such a mixture of the occult with Christianity can easily lead to confusion, mixing their faith with superstition and magic—and thus discrediting religion in the eyes of non-believers. This new direction of the journal may or may not have been deliberately planned by the atheists running it.

The millennial celebrations were preceded by three major international theological conferences organized by the Moscow Patriarchate in Kiev, Moscow, and Leningrad. For the first time, secular Soviet scholars participated alongside clergy and theologians from the seminaries. Some of the Soviet scholars, including the top Soviet space scientist, the academician Boris Raushenbakh, presented profoundly theological papers and openly demonstrated their religious faith. Only the third conference, in 1987, received wide coverage in the Soviet press, including the naming of the participating secular scholars. This represented the first such direct admission that religion was not the exclusive domain of the uncouth.

On April 29, 1988, there occurred a widely publicized meeting of Gorbachev with the entire Holy Synod of the Russian Orthodox Church. This was the first such encounter since the 1943 and 1945 meetings with Stalin. The difference was that the latest meeting came at the request of the Synod (although Kharchev, then head of the CRA, later claimed that the initiative was his), which presented to Gorbachev a memorandum containing a list of Church grievances, and requesting that the Church be recognized as a legitimate public organization, a legal person with all appropriate rights, and

---

3 This marked the most explicit official criticism of the policies of the Soviet Union by the Russian Orthodox Church and other Soviet registered religions to date.

asking that state legislation governing religion be changed. Gorbachev gave an affirmative promise. A month and a half later, the historic Millennial Sobor of the Russian Orthodox Church took place.

The Millennial Sobor and Its Consequences

Meeting on June 6-9, 1988, this was the first council of the Russian Church since the seventeenth century unrelated to the election of a patriarch.

The New Statute

The most important act of the *sobor* was the adoption of a new Statute of the Russian Orthodox Church. This, despite the Sobor's brevity, was not a mere formality. Thus, a majority of the council forced the bishops to shorten the maximum intervals between general (local) *sobors* from ten to five years, between episcopal *sobors*, from five to two years. The parish rector was granted the prerogative of chairing all parish meetings *ex officio*, even though the draft prepared by the episcopal council preceding the Sobor stated only that he may chair such meetings. On the whole, the new Statute brought the structure of the Church closer to Orthodox canons and abolished the uncanonical 1961 amendments.

Yet, it was a far cry from Statute passed by the 1917-18 Sobor. The new Statute did not provide for any elected representatives of the clergy and/or laity in the central administration of the Church. The Patriarchal Synod remained a self-electing body consisting of five senior bishops as *ex officio* members, and five diocesan bishops chosen in turn by the Synod for six-month terms. The 1988 Statute recognized the parish as the basic self-governing institution of the Church, with the right to object against a priest appointed by the bishop; but there is no clear stipulation as to whether the bishop must abide by the parish decision. Bishops are likewise appointed by the Patriarch and his Synod—whereas the 1917-18 statutes allowed parishes to choose their own priest or a candidate for ordination, and diocesan conferences could elect a bishop or a candidate for consecration as their bishop. Nevertheless, the new Statute was a great improvement over the Stalinesque statute of 1945. The new Statute required each bishop to have a diocesan council elected by a diocesan congress. It also defined the limits of power of the patriarch; as in the 1917-18 decisions, he became merely the chairman of the Synod and of all general and episcopal councils. General *sobors* received supreme judicial power over the patriarch. The retention of the old authoritarian structure of the Synod, however, make it practically impossible to convoke such a judicial *sobor* without the Synod's approval. In fact, although the Statute has provisions for an ecclesiastical court, eight years after its adoption the Church still lacks any juridical bodies. This, as well as an electoral representative Church body at the Patriarchal level during the long intervals between general councils, is badly needed, especially now when the authority and credibility of many senior bishops has been undermined by the discovery of KGB documents indicating their former contacts with that body (most likely involuntary). As a result of the discrediting of some members of the Synod, their arbitrary disciplinary actions, such as the banning or defrocking of a priest, carry little moral authority: the censured priest immediately claims to be a victim of political persecution and thus gains public sympathy, regardless of his guilt or innocence.

A case in point is the defrocking of Fr Gleb Yakunin in November 1993. Following the bloody confrontation between the Supreme Soviet and President Yeltsin in October 1993, in which some priests were on the side of the legislative body, others on the side of the executive, the Moscow Patriarchate banned further clergy participation in federal or local legislative bodies. The Patriarchate also received numerous letters from believers protesting the presence of priests wearing cassocks and pectoral crosses on televised broadcasts of parliamentary debates, passionately attacking their opponents and calling them names. This contradicted the traditional Russian image of the priest as a peacemaker and mediator. The Synod ordered all priests running for Parliament or local legislatures to withdraw their candidacies. All but Yakunin submitted. Consequently, he was defrocked, and overnight he became a "martyr" in the eyes of public opinion, particularly abroad. The action was interpreted as a personal vendetta on the part of the bishops, because Yakunin had been active in uncovering KGB documents which listed them by rather transparent code-names as collaborators. Yakunin continued to play the part of martyr by publicly attacking the Synod and the patriarch, even though he had himself earlier admitted that the Patriarch had made him a compromise offer to apply for a position with the executive branch of the government rather than the legislative, which is so much in the public eye. Moreover, although the ruling to forbid clergy participation in parliament was wise in the circumstances, it contradicted the decision of the 1917-18 Sobor. According to the canons, only another general council can overturn the decisions of a previous general council. Thus, even if expediency made the above Synod's decision necessary pending its approval by a future local council, there was no basis for defrocking a priest who acted in accordance with the canons established by a legitimate *sobor*, whose authority had not been challenged. Perhaps the Synod could have suspended him for insubordination, but defrocking is a punishment for heresy or major moral transgressions, which was certainly not the case with Yakunin. Had an appropriate ecclesiastical court existed, it might have found a more legitimate solution.

The Statute is often neglected also with respect to the life and rights of parishes. Before the adoption of the new state laws on religious freedom in October 1990, the Statute could not be fully applied, because the Soviet authorities recognized only the 1929/75 laws as binding. But after the adoption of the 1990 legislation, which explicitly recognized the legal validity of the statutes of registered religions, it was the Church leadership itself which often ignored its own statute.

A case in point is the story of the dynamic Moscow missionary community headed by Fr Georgii Kochetkov. A former economist and an adult convert, Fr Georgii studied at the Leningrad Theological Academy until he was expelled by the KGB for running a clandestine catechetical institute for adults during the Andropov era. Returning to his native Moscow, he started another clandestine catechetical school while working as a night watchman. Only in 1989 was the Church able to ordain him, and he received a ruined church in the industrial town of Elektrougli, some thirty miles from Moscow. By then, he had already assembled a small community of recent converts. In 1990, the community succeeded in gaining a small space for religious services in the beautiful early seventeenth-century church of the Meeting of the Vladimir Mother of God Icon in Moscow, occupied by ugly cubicles of restorers' workshops. In the course of the next three years, the community gradually managed to rid itself of these cubicles and to evict their occupiers. By that time, the Vladimir Mother of God community surpassed 1,000 members, 90 percent of them recent converts. The community runs a one-year catechetical program preparing adults for baptism, as well as giving a course of basic theology to formally baptized but theologically ignorant Christians. After "graduating" from the catechetical program—which has some 800 students all over the country, most studying by correspondence—some choose to continue their theological studies for another five years at the Higher Orthodox-Christian School, directed by Fr Georgii, where they receive thorough theological training with a strongly missionary emphasis. In addition there is an Orthodox high school and a kindergarten, as well as a scout troop attached to the church. The community also runs a charity food and clothes distribution center. Fr Georgii's pastorate differs from that of most other priests in many ways, which arouses considerable suspicion and wrath on the part of the conservatives. He refuses to baptize those who do not undergo at least one year of catechetical preparation (and baptizes them only during the celebration of the Paschal All-night vigil and at Pentecost). He russifies the Church Slavonic language by using modern Russian for words and expressions which are incomprehensible for those who have never studied Church Slavonic, i.e., 99 percent of the population. In this he is in fact carrying out what one of the brightest bishops of the Russian Church, Kirill of Smolensk, called for at the 1988 Sobor, when he stressed that the Slavonic language was not understood by believers, and that by keeping it the Church was in danger of becoming a museum. Kirill also called for liturgical reform, to make the liturgy meaningful to the modern man. This is exactly what Kochetkov has been doing. He insists on congregational singing and on frequent communion. At the end of the Liturgy of the Catechumens, he tells the unbaptized catechumens and non-believers to leave the church; he orders those Orthodox who are not prepared for Communion to move to the church vestibule; and then he shuts the doors so that only communicants remain for the Liturgy of the Faithful. His parish is divided into groups of fifteen to thirty people, each with its own spiritual adviser responsible to the priest. In addition to the Sunday and other services, each such group normally meets once a week for an *agape* meal followed by bible reading, discussion, and socializing.

In 1993, as the church was becoming too small for a community of nearly 1,500, the parish managed to acquire another church one block away, which had been occupied by a naval museum. The parish's hope was that one or more of their theological school's graduates would be ordained to serve in the second church. In February 1994, however, Kochetkov received an order from the Patriarch, who is also the ruling bishop of the Moscow (City) Diocese, to vacate the Vladimir Mother of God church and to move to the other church. The reason given was that the Mother of God church, which was originally part of a monastery, should become a monastic chapel once again. The church was named the Moscow annex of the Pskov Monastery of the Caves, and a handful of morally dubious monks, supported by an extremist-chauvinist brotherhood, moved in with scandals and hurling insults at Fr Georgii and his community. The community had made tremendous sacrifices in both finances and labor to restore the first church. In the spring of 1994, they were hard at work restoring their new church, though with less enthusiasm, suspecting that once that church was repaired they might be forced to get out again. At the time of this writing this is not a likely prospect. In August 1994, the Pskovian monks, with the support of some Cossacks, attacked Fr Kochetkov's theological school, ransacking the library and hurling icons from the windows of the icon-painting workshop into the street below (the Militant Godless could hardly have done better!). The Patriarchate's order that the monks should share the building with Kochetkov's community and its schools was largely ignored by the monks, who eventually physically threw the community out in 1995. With generous donations by parish members—women were donating their rings, earrings and pendants—and some financial help from such Western Christian organizations as the Roman Catholic "Church in Need" Foundation, the parish succeeded in purchasing two large adjacent apartments. These were converted into classes and lecture halls, and within a few weeks all programs of the community resumed their work. The lack of proper support from the Patriarchate and its failure to discipline unruly monks and other extremists contradicted the resolutions of the December 1994 Council of Bishops which called for liturgical and linguistic reforms, missionary activation, and the development of an Orthodox social doctrine for modern era—i.e., precisely what Kochetkov has been doing. Yet Fr Georgii had been punished for the work hailed as absolutely necessary by the Episcopal Council. The expulsion was a blatant contravention of the Statute's assertion of the parish as an autonomous legal entity of the Church.

The lawlessness of seven decades of Communism undermined general respect for law and human dignity, as well as tolerance for opinions other than one's own; while ignorance of theology and of church history reduced peoples' understanding of the Church, resulting in the idolizing of such particularities as the alleged "holiness" of the Slavonic language, contrasted with the "profanity" of using Russian in the liturgy. Thus Fr Kochetkov has been accused of heresy, and conferences of conservative churchmen even petitioned the Synod, unsuccessfully, to submit him to an ecclesiastical trial. Fr Kochetkov is hated particularly by fascists and anti-Semites, because his community has attracted numerous Jews seeking conversion to Christianity.[4] Graffiti depicting David's star with threatening anti-Semitic slogans have appeared periodically on the walls of his church.

4 This is also true of the communities initiated by or following in the steps of the late Fr Men', who was of Jewish background himself. These communities, such as the Cosmas and Damian Church near Tverskaia Street, have likewise been subjected anti-Semitic attacks. Fr Men', a prolific writer, preacher, and the most successful missionary pastor of the intelligentsia, who brought literally thousands to the Church, was savagely axed to death on Sunday, September 9, 1990, on his way to church to serve the liturgy.

The Millennial Sobor also canonized nine new saints and sent an amazingly humble and truly fraternal address to the emigre "Russian Orthodox Church Outside Russia." In contrast to the Patriarchate's previous appeals to this church group, the new statement did not condemn them as schismatics and did not demand their return under the Moscow Patriarchate, but merely invited them to reestablish peaceful fraternal relations with the Russian Church in a unity of worship. The initiator of this new approach was Metropolitan Anthony (Bloom), the Moscow Patriarchate's bishop of Britain. In his speech at the Sobor, he praised the ROCOR for retaining the Russian spiritual traditions and for passing them on to the younger generations of Russian emigres, as well as for publishing large quantities of service books, which are used even by the Moscow Patriarchate's parishes inside Russia. The humility of the Moscow address to the Karlovcians lay in the fact that it treated the tiny schismatic ROCOR, consisting of some 200,000 members, fraternally, as an equal.

The ROCOR responded to this appeal by issuing a resolution on May 16, 1990, to ignore the Moscow Patriarchate and to begin to set up ROCOR parishes and dioceses in the USSR under the name of "The Free Russian Orthodox Church" (FROC). The resolution repeated the hackneyed Karlovcian allegation that God's grace was absent in the sacraments of the Moscow Patriarchate's churches; but then it claimed that grace was present, nevertheless, in the services and sacraments of those priests who were true to their calling and who did not cooperate with the Soviet regime. Thus the ROCOR made the validity of sacraments dependent on individual priests and on their political behavior, de facto denying the Church as the mystical body of Christ—this was precisely the so-called "Donatist" heresy (third-fourth centuries), condemned by the Ecumenical Councils. The resolution invited such priests to join the FROC after repenting for having served in the Moscow Patriarchate. The irony of the situation is evident: why should priests, whose sacraments were valid and who had maintained that validity at the risk of their lives by refusing to compromise with the Soviet power, repent before émigré hierarchs, who enjoyed the freedom and comfort of Western democracies?

What actually happened—and as admitted in 1992 even by Karlovcian bishops—was that most of the several scores of priests who joined the FROC did so for purely expedient reasons: they had a personal quarrel with their bishop, committed some misdemeanor or had serious defects of character or morals, hoped for a better career in a smaller Church and expected that a Western-based Church would be wealthier and would provide travel abroad.

Most of the three or four local priests consecrated bishop by the ROCOR were suspended by the latter within less than three years for "serious moral transgressions." The first of them, Bishop Valentin of Suzdal', gathered a council of some sixty FROC parishes in 1993, at which it was decided to temporarily break with the ROCOR owing to their incomprehension of the situation in Russia, and to proclaim a temporary autocephaly. This left only some thirty or so parishes in Russia under ROCOR. Of these, several, together with their priests, have returned through repentance to the Moscow Patriarchate in the course of 1994-95. One cause for the above break with the ROCOR was a scandal over anti-Semitism in late 1992, when two ROCOR clergymen from the United States, Fr Victor Potapov and Bishop Ilarion, organized a press conference in Moscow at which they condemned anti-Semitism, disavowed a blatantly anti-Semitic interview earlier given by their chief hierarch, Metropolitan Vitalii, to the Moscow national-Bolshevik weekly *Den'*, and condemned two Moscow ROCOR priests and a France-based ROCOR bishop for supporting the fascist and anti-Semitic Pamiat'. Bishop Valentin participated in that press conference. However, on his return to America. Fr Potapov was censured by the ROCOR Synod and forbidden ever again to get involved in Russian affairs on the threat of suspension. Shortly after this, Bishop Valentin was suspended by the ROCOR Synod, allegedly for grave moral transgressions. He responded by convoking the above "*sobor*" and proclaiming autocephaly.

Social and National Stratification, and the 1990 Sobor

During the communist era most believers, even of diverse confessions, felt themselves united, so to speak, against aggressive atheism. With the end of persecution and repression, believers began to shrink back into their particular confessional niches. Dissidents, as well as those believers who had openly stood up for their faith in the past and had suffered the consequences, began to call leaders of the "registered" religions to account for their past close cooperation with communist authorities, demanding repentance for their former fraudulent denials of religious persecutions in the USSR.

The politicization of the World Council of Churches and the use of its general assemblies by religious organizations from the socialist camp led to a broad revulsion against the very idea of inter-confessional Christian cooperation. The Karlovcians have used this political peg in their wholesale condemnation of ecumenism *per se*, and the WCC in particular.[5] In Russia, the ROCOR has an aura of "purity" because of its uncompromising condemnation of communism. Few Russians, however, are aware of its close collaboration with the Nazis, while their right-wing sympathizers do not care, as they are themselves admirers of Hitler. Just as the ROCOR, they associate communist internationalism, and therefore also any internationalism, including Christian ecumenism, with a mythical Judeo-masonic plot against Russia.

With the open and widespread celebration of the Millennium, with the broad visibility of the clergy in television debates and at televised solemnities, the Orthodox Church was transformed almost overnight from an oppressed, persecuted and ridiculed institution into a most fashionable one. Just as in the fourth century, when the recently persecuted Christianity, which had embraced only some 2-3 percent of the population of the Roman Empire, became the official religion of the empire and brought large proportion of the religiously ignorant population into the Church, so after its Millennium the Russian Orthodox Church began to attract the masses.

The vacuum left by the bankruptcy of communism began to be filled with nationalism, which, however, inherited all the ills of Soviet society, and most of all a sense of the external enemy. Marxism spoke about the external and internal class enemy, which was blamed for all the problems and failures of the socialist system. Nationalism, with its notion of national superiority, blames all national problems on other nations.

For Ukrainian nationalists, the scapegoat became the Russians and the Russian Orthodox Church which, they claimed, was a form of spiritual imperialism. In Galicia, a center for the most extreme Ukrainian nationalism, the Uniate majority identified the whole Orthodox Church with Moscow. As we have seen in chapter 13, the role of the Russian Orthodox Church in Stalin's liquidation of the Unia was predominantly passive. Moreover, CRA documents have revealed that some Orthodox bishops in Galicia, such as Archbishop Palladii of Lvov and Ternopol in the 1960s, secretly helped the persecuted and clandestine Uniate clergy. By contrast, when the Uniate clergy, returning from the concentration camps and internal exile, unofficially began to organize Uniate religious life in Galicia in the 1980s, the Soviet authorities generally turned a blind eye, while the Ukrainian Orthodox reacted with overt hostility, instead

---

5 They continued, however, to receive subsidies from the WCC as a Church of refugees—the only Orthodox Church to be thus subsidized.

of giving a sympathetic hand to their Uniate confreres (even if they did not agree with them theologically). For example, in 1986 Archbishop Makarii (Svistun), and in 1989 the then Exarch of the Ukraine, Metropolitan Filaret (Denisenko), issued mendacious declarations that Uniatism had ceased to exist and that what passed for Uniatism was merely chauvinistic hooliganism.

The Soviet Government was quicker than the Orthodox to recognize the Uniates. In September 1988, the Chairman of the Ukrainian CRA declared that the Uniate Church was not banned. In December 1989, after Gorbachev's audience with the Pope in Rome, the CRA officially legalized the Uniate Church in the Ukraine, giving it a status equal to all other registered confessions.

The Uniates began to re-establish themselves with a vengeance. Even before their official legalization, they formed an unofficial *Committee for the Defense of the Ukrainian Catholic Church*, presided by Ivan Ghel, a recent prisoner of conscience who, while in a Mordovian concentration camp, engaged in beating Ukrainian prisoners who dared to have Russian and/or Jewish friends. Among his victims was a Galician Orthodox priest, Vasyl' Romaniuk. In 1977 an international prisoners' comrades' court of honor ruled that Ghel's "behavior was unworthy of the status of a political prisoner" because of his instigation of international hatred. Now, as the head of the above "Committee," Ghel was crisscrossing Galicia with a bus-load of strong-arm adherents, physically attacking Orthodox parishes and turning them over by force to the Uniate Church. As extreme nationalists had won the local elections in the Galician provinces, they supported Ghel's activities and even provided OMON special police forces for such actions. Most of the formerly clandestine Uniate priests and bishops had had little or no theological education, and their adherence to Ukrainian Catholicism was often motivated more by nationalism than by any theological considerations. Such clergy typically did not moderate Ghel's strong-arm methods. All attempts of tripartite and tetrapartite negotiations with the participation of representatives from the Vatican, as well as Russian Orthodox, Ukrainian Orthodox and Uniate delegates, failed. Proposals to divide churches in proportion to the number of adherents of either religion in each particular town or village, and the provision of alternative space or building materials for the minority religion in those villages where there was only one church building, came to naught as the Uniates insisted that all church structures that had belonged to the Uniates prior to 1946 should be returned to them, regardless of who was in the majority. The Orthodox argument that in this case, all church structures that had been Orthodox prior to 1596 (including the Uniates' main shrine, the St George Cathedral which had remained Orthodox through most of the seventeenth century) should be returned to the Orthodox Church, had no effect.

It should be noted that, before the legalization, even Ghel advocated (at least in theory) the proportional division of churches. He believed that, as soon as the Uniate Church was legalized, almost all Western Ukrainians would return to it. The Uniates changed their stand once it was discovered that, even in the Lvov Province, about half of the population remained Orthodox. A 1992 survey indicated that 42 percent of the ethnically Ukrainian population of the province declared themselves Orthodox, as against 45 percent Uniates. Counting the ethnic Russians, who make up 15 percent of the Lvov city population and 5 percent of the rest of the province, and of whom 70 percent claimed to be practicing members of the Orthodox Church, the two religious populations are about even. But an indicator that pressure has been used against the Orthodox is that in 1992 only 800 churches were still in the Orthodox hands, as contrasted with 1200 Uniate.[6]

More or less simultaneously with the Uniate revival in Galicia, there appeared an autocephalist movement among the Orthodox of Galicia and neighboring Volynia. In their strategy, however, the Orthodox autocephalists once again ignored the canons. Ioann (Bodnarchuk), the archbishop of Zhitomir (in eastern Volynia), who had begun the rebellion in 1989, invited a self-proclaimed "catacomb bishop" of Tula, Vikentii, to participate in the consecration of the first "autocephalous" bishops—Bodnarchuk's two brothers. Vikentii, however, was actually an impostor: he had been a deacon in the Moscow Patriarchate until he was found guilty of sexually violating young boys. After being defrocked and having served a term of imprisonment, he resurfaced in 1988. He went to the United States and tried unsuccessfully to convince the Karlovcians that he was a catacomb bishop. In 1990, failing to gain recognition, he declared himself a Uniate in his native Tula, and Volodymyr Sterniuk, the Uniate Metropolitan of Lvov, appointed him the Uniate bishop for Russia.[7]

Such were some of the problems facing the new Patriarch, Alexii II, elected at the June 1990 Sobor following the death of the 79-year-old

---

6 Ian Bremmer, "Post-Soviet Politics and Political Integration in Lviv," *Working Papers in International Studies*, I-94-13 (Stanford: Hoover Institution, October 1994).

7 The Vatican Cardinal for Uniate affairs, Liubachivsky, on his return to the Ukraine, is known to have reprimanded Sterniuk for that action. The current status of "Vikentii" is unclear.

Patriarch Pimen. This was the first council since 1917 at which a genuine secret ballot, with multiple candidates, occurred.[8]

Born in 1929 in Estonia into a family of Russian émigrés, the son of an Orthodox priest of aristocratic background (German-Swedish on his father's side), Alexii chose the monastic vocation after graduation from the Leningrad theological schools. He soon became the archbishop (later metropolitan) of Estonia and also chancellor of the Moscow Patriarchate. In 1986, he was removed as chancellor for having written a letter to Gorbachev full of concern for the moral decline of Soviet society. He then proposed that the Soviet state should change its religious policy and allow the Church a role in the moral renewal of the nation. The "punishment" was not severe: he was appointed Metropolitan of Leningrad. But he was removed from the leadership of the Church in the years when Pimen had already lost his mental faculties, and the chancellor functioned as the real head of the Church. Otherwise, Metropolitan Alexii had been a political conformist (see Furov's assessment, ch. 15), but his cautious diplomacy preserved the Church in Estonia from Khrushchev's pogrom; and it was largely thanks to him that the Orthodox convent of Piukhtitsy in Estonia not only survived, but even grew both quantitatively and qualitatively under his supervision, becoming spiritually the healthiest monastic community in the Russian Church and currently the "hot house" of female monasticism in Russia.

The new Patriarch's first assignment from the Sobor was to protest the Soviet bureaucrats' revision of the first version of the draft law on religious freedom. The revision was not in the Church's favor and was carried out without any consultation with Church representatives. After the Patriarch's personal remonstration to Gorbachev, Church representatives were invited to participate in the preparation of the final text. The compromise product of this cooperation was respectively, the USSR Law on the Freedom of Conscience and the Russian Republic's Law on Religious Freedom, both issued in October 1990. For the first time since 1918, the state laws on religion ceased to contradict the statutes of the Church.

8 At the council of bishops immediately preceding the Sobor, all diocesan bishops possessing Soviet citizenship and at least forty years of age could be voted for. The number of candidates was reduced to three after several rounds of voting and elimination. The following day, the Sobor had the choice of electing one of the three or adding another candidate, provided at least twelve members of the Sobor proposed that candidacy. In order to be elected patriarch, the candidate had to gain over 50 percent of the votes. After two rounds, Alexii, the 61-year-old Metropolitan of Leningrad, finally received the required number.

The legislation of the Russian Republic was more sympathetic to the Church than that of the Soviet Union. Fourteen months later, however, the Soviet Union ceased to exist, and so its law can be ignored in our discussion. The Russian Law abolished the CRA, recognized the Church as a social organization and as a person-in-law, with the right to own property, including churches and other buildings. The law recognized not only actual religious societies, i.e., parishes, but also the whole hierarchical structure of the Church, by stating that it recognized such form of religious organization as required by that religion's canons. The law confirmed that Russia was a secular state, in which neither atheistic nor religious organizations are subsidized by the state; they must finance themselves through private donations and other private sources. The registration of a religious community became an act of certification instead of authorization. In fact, a religious community was no longer obliged to register in order to exist. A non-registered community simply did not possess the status of a person-in-law. The law permitted the teaching of religion in church-related Sunday schools, as well as in private schools. In public schools, headmasters and parents now received the right to introduce the teaching of religion as an optional subject, outside of the regular class schedule. The teaching of religion in a purely informative manner, however, unrelated to any particular confession, could be included in a school curriculum at the discretion of the school.[9] Believers and unbelievers have equal rights, and the government may not place any obligations on religions. Religions, however, have the right to participate in public life and may use the mass media for disseminating their ideas. Although the law provided for tax exemption for donations to churches, to the date of this writing no laws have been passed to that effect, and in most cases no tax reductions are given to donors. The income and profits of enterprises run by the Church were freed from the prohibitive taxes of the Soviet era and were treated as those from any other business.

The law stipulated that military personnel should have the right to attend religious services in their free time. Such a formulation, however, left an atheistic officer the possibility to keep his soldiers from attending church by assigning them army duties. The law permitted the Government to declare religious feasts as state holidays. As a result, on the Patriarch's petition, Christmas and Easter were soon declared state holidays by Yeltsin. The law and subsequent decrees by Yeltsin gave the Church priority in reclaiming property that

9 It is through this clause that "Moonies" and other, seemingly innocent, totalitarian sects have since taken over religious education in many state schools. This is now of great concern both to parents and to the Church.

had belonged to the Church before the Bolshevik confiscations. The fulfillment of these decrees has gradually become quite smooth with respect to church buildings, but the restoration of former rectories and other dwellings to the Church has met with tremendous resistance from local governments, and particularly from the businesses that operate out of them. Moreover, the new law has not been followed by the adoption of clear procedural laws, thus making the full realization particularly of property rights very problematic.

The Church has been hit very hard by the galloping inflation of the 1990s, especially since it coincided with the return of thousands of ruined monasteries and churches to the Church. The total number of operating Orthodox churches of the Moscow Patriarchate, for instance, has grown from 6,800 in 1988 to over 17,000 by 1997, and monasteries, from eighteen to over 300. Restoration costs are astronomical. Another extremely necessary but very costly operation is theological education: the total number of theological schools has grown from five in 1988 to over sixty-five in 1997. At the same time, the falling incomes of the majority of church members have considerably reduced their capacity to donate. The Church has also suffered from a manifold increase of taxes on profit and on land use. Here the Church is officially treated like any profit-making enterprise, not fairly, in view of her colossal expenses on education and the restoration of churches, most of which are culturally and historically important works of art. In real practice, however, many local administrations take this into consideration and either reduce their taxes on church properties or waive them altogether.

The Patriarch, the Church, the Society

As Patriarch, Alexii II has repeatedly rejected the idea of a church-state symbiosis, arguing that unless all 100 percent of the population are practicing members of the Church, turning the latter into the state Church reduces her to the role of a truncheon. And if a Church is used as a truncheon she breaks apart. But he sees the Orthodox Church as a national-historical Church, responsible to God for the spiritual and moral state of the nation. He has therefore taken a stand on civic matters. In January 1991, he condemned the bloody Soviet Army attack in Lithuania, appealing to Russian soldiers to abstain from fulfilling criminal orders; simultaneously he called on President Gorbachev to abstain from using force against the separatists in the Baltics. At Yeltsin's inauguration as the first president of the Russian Republic, the Patriarch gave him his blessing and appealed to him to rule mercifully, humanely and not to try to change human nature by force, as the Communists had tried to do. During the August 1991 putsch, the first day of which coincided with the Feast of Transfiguration, the Patriarch ordered that the army and the government not be commemorated during the liturgy; and on the second day, August 20, he wrote an address dissociating himself from the Putschists, appealing to them to prove their legitimacy by letting Gorbachev's voice be heard and to abstain from the shedding of blood.[10] Three days later, in his address to the Church and the clergy, the Patriarch condemned Communism as the source of the Putschists' actions and as an ideology which denies all absolute moral foundations, and thus humanity's responsibility to others and to God. On numerous occasions, the Patriarch has condemned anti-Semitism and any version of extreme nationalism. Finally, in the fall of 1993, while a guest of the Orthodox Church in America at festivities inaugurating the bicentennial of Orthodoxy in America, the Patriarch curtailed all his engagements as soon as he heard about the confrontation in Moscow. He flew back to Moscow and offered the mediatory role of the Church leadership in the confrontation. Both sides technically accepted the offer. But whereas the Yeltsin side was acting in good faith and believed that the conflict would be settled without bloodshed, the Supreme Soviet side, it turned out, simply used the Church mediators to play for time and, instead of seeking a final agreement, began the armed rebellion.

Preservation of the unity of the Russian Orthodox Church has been one of the new patriarch's priorities. In Ukraine, Metropolitan Filaret, the patriarch's exarch, irritated because he was not elected patriarch, suddenly ceased to be a russifier who used to forbid services in Ukrainian, and became a Ukrainian nationalist, supporting autocephaly. He found encouragement and support from the nationalistic Ukrainian *Rukh* movement and from his close friend, Leonid Kravchuk, the first Ukrainian president, who likewise changed his stripes from being the chief Ukrainian communist ideologist to a nationalist. The Patriarchate responded to Filaret's overtures by 1991 by granting to the Ukrainian Orthodox Church complete internal autonomy, in accordance with the decision of the 1917-18 Moscow Sobor. The issue of autocephaly, however, as well as Filaret's extreme despotism, corruption, and his blatant breach of celibacy (required by the monastic status of bishops), made Filaret very unpopular among his clergy. Many letters from Ukrainian parishes and from several Ukrainian diocesan bishops to the Patriarchate protested that, if there was a break with

10 Written in the evening of August 20, published on the 21st in the morning.

the Russian Church, they would reject their allegiance to Kiev and remain under Moscow. Filaret responded by retiring bishops and banning priests who opposed his policy. All this drew the attention of the media, which exposed all his abuses as well as his particularly close cooperation with the KGB, revealed by that agency's documents. Details about his intimate life were also published, including the fact that he had fathered three children.

The Patriarchate convoked an episcopal council in Moscow in May 1992, with the full participation of bishops from the Ukraine, including those removed by Filaret. All but two Ukrainian bishops voted against autocephaly and demanded his immediate retirement. To avoid scandal, an agreement was reached that Filaret would return to Kiev still as metropolitan, convoke a council of bishops, offer his resignation, and let the bishops elect his replacement. Filaret swore on the Bible and the cross to fulfill that request. And the Council, in its public statement thanked him for the service he had rendered to the Church in the past, announcing his "voluntary" retirement. No sooner had Filaret returned to Kiev, however, than he announced that the "Muscovites" had twisted his arm and that his pledge was therefore invalid. He declared that he was joining the autocephalous Ukrainian Church as the exarch for Mstyslav (Skrypnyk), the émigré Ukrainian autocephalous bishop living in New Jersey, who had been elected patriarch by the Bodnarchuk autocephalist group in 1990. In response to Filaret's insubordination, another Council of Bishops defrocked Filaret, reducing him to the status of an ordinary monk. A council of all Ukrainian bishops but two, convoked in Kharkov, elected Metropolitan Vladimir (Sabodan), a Volynian Ukrainian, as the new head of the Ukrainian Orthodox Church under the Moscow Patriarchate.

Filaret ignored not only these bans, but even his new "patriarch," who refused to recognize Filaret as his exarch and ordered him to submit and go into retirement. Following Mstyslav's action, the autocephalists split, predominantly along geographical lines: the autocephalists of Galicia remained under Mstyslav and refused to have any dealings with Filaret; the majority of the Volynian and East Ukrainian autocephalists remained under Filaret. The Galician autocephalists adopted the old name of the "Ukrainian Autocephalous Orthodox Church" (UAOC for short); Filaret's group took the name of the "Ukrainian Orthodox Church-Kievan Patriarchate" (UOC-KP); and the Moscow Patriarchate's autonomous Ukrainian Orthodox Church, by far the largest Church in the Ukraine with some 7,000 parishes, became known as UOC-MP. In Galicia, the dominant Orthodox Church became the UAOC where, because of her Ukrainian nationalism, she managed effectively to stop the further expansion of Uniatism. As we have seen, the traditional believers in Galicia (discounting Latin-Rite Roman Catholics, sectarians, etc.) are split about evenly between Uniatism and Orthodoxy. The "Filaretists," despite President Kravchuk's support and the use of local OMON and paramilitary Banderist formations who physically attack and confiscate churches, remain a minority Church even in nationalistic Volynia and other areas west of the Dniper, while in Eastern Ukraine they are almost non-existent.

In 1993, after Mstyslav's death in America, both autocephalous Churches elected their own separate patriarchs, neither of whom is recognized by any of the canonical Orthodox Churches. The UAOC elected a seventy-seven year old priest, Petro Yarema, as "Patriarch" Dimitri. The UOC-KP elected the above-mentioned priest Vasyl' Romaniuk as "Patriarch" Volodymyr. Although even among his adherents Filaret failed to be elected to the top office, as the "Patriarch's" deputy and controller of all finances of UOC-KP, holding the alcoholic "Patriarch" on the leash, he continued to run the Church as he pleased. This and his failure to obtain recognition by the Ecumenical Patriarchate even after his and the then President Kravchuk's visits to Constantinople, has resulted in the desertion of eight of his bishops to the Moscow Patriarchate in 1994. Accepted through repentance, they brought back to the UOC-MP several monasteries and hundreds of parishes. As of late 1996, each of the impostor-patriarchates holds about 1,200 parishes.

In the spring of 1995, "Patriarch" Romaniuk suddenly died in mysterious circumstances, after he had attempted to audit the finances of the Kievan Diocese headed by Filaret. There are strong suspicions of Filaret's hand in his death. Filaret is believed to have intimate links to the Kievan criminal mafia. Following Volodymyr's death, Filaret succeeded in being elected "patriarch."

It must be said that, despite the uncanonical basis of the UAOC, its relations with the UOC-MP on the local level appear to be quite cordial. This is partly the result of their geographic separation, partly because both of them continue to be harassed by the UOC-KP and by nationalistic west-Ukrainian local authorities and local paramilitary forces, but most importantly, because Metropolitan Vladimir (Sabodan) of the UOC-MP has declared his support for the principle of autocephaly, as long as it is achieved canonically and without causing schisms in the Church.

In Russia, too, nationalism has raised its ugly head, attempting to take control of the Church in order to use her as an ideological lever. As so often happens, at the base of that distortion lay a good intention. Soon after his election, Patriarch Alexii II called on the laity to become active in the Church, to form fellowships (the Russian term is "brotherhoods") to engage in missionary, educational and charitable activities. Similarly, he called on young people to form an Orthodox Youth Movement. But it soon transpired that, although there were millions of individual faithful, there was no sense of Orthodox community or of an Orthodox public as a collective whole. Under the Communists, the parish could not exist as a community, in which each member could feel personally responsible for the parish, and particularly for its social, educational and other activities. Instead, there was the "twenty" electing an executive committee of three persons who ran the parish, and the individual, anonymous worshipers tried to "dissolve" into the crowd as soon as they left the church. Indeed, with a tiny number of churches serving huge numbers of believers, there could be nothing but an anonymous crowd of worshipers.

Parish communities and "brotherhoods" (fellowships of both sexes) began to be formed in some of the newly re-opened churches of the late 1980s and 1990s. In fact, some priests had organized secret brotherhoods in their parishes even under the Communist regime, including, for example, the late Vsevolod Shpiller, Alexander Men', and Dimitri Dudko. But these were only exceptions. Elsewhere, the vacuum began to be filled by rightist-radical and the so-called "red-brown" elements, often former Communist and Komsomol activists who now covered themselves with a mantle of "Orthodoxy," but whose intentions had little to do with the Church or Christianity, and whose methods remained those used for advancing in the Komsomol and the Party. Their intolerant and hostile attitudes towards "others" were simply carried over from their former training and experience. It was these extremists who took control of the Union of Orthodox Brotherhoods formed at the Brotherhoods' First All-Russian Congress on October 12-13, 1990, even before the adoption of the new state religious legislation; i.e., the congress, strictly speaking, was illegal.

Among the leaders of the Union are genuine Nazis, who have published portraits of Hitler and excerpts from *Mein Kampf* in some of their bulletins. Their statements and articles have demanded the "separation of Christ from the Old Testament" and the rejection of the Old Testament by the Church as a "satanic book" (sic!). They equate Judaism, and in some cases even Roman

Catholicism and Protestantism, with Satanism. They became particularly vocal after finding an ally and "ideologist" in the late Metropolitan of St Petersburg, Ioann (Sychev), who took the *Protocols of Zion* literally and believed in a satanic "Judeo-Masonic" plot against Russia. He readily published diatribes in such fascist and national-Bolshevik newspapers *as The Day (Den')*, *Tomorrow (Zavtra)*, and *Soviet Russia (Sovetskaia Rossiia)*. Ioann himself, however, privately admitted that he did not write these articles. His "red-brown" ghost-writers needed and used his name to make their writings sound authoritative and credible to an uninformed public, indoctrinated during the communist era to fear an enemy within and now craving to find a scapegoat for their past and present sufferings. The tracts that appeared under his name were fervently "patriotic," depicting Russia as a saintly martyr, suffering throughout her history from crafty Jewish designs. Russian bishops who sat with Ioann at Synod sessions claim that he was incapable of any coherent thought and was totally inarticulate. A case in point was Yeltsin's appeal, in the spring of 1994, asking all public figures to sign a statement of social consent placing national interests above those of individual factions and parties. Church leaders all signed the statement—all but Ioann, who signed a Communist declaration which actually called for the overthrow of the government. When confronted by the Synod, Ioann expressed his surprise: he thought that he and the Patriarch had signed the same statement. He was obviously flattered by the role of leader of Russian patriotism assigned to him by the "red-brown" manipulators.[11] The Synod did not dare to retire Ioann out of fear that he might have joined the ROCOR (he had often expressed his sympathy for it) and, since he had been made into such a symbol by the radical right, numerous priests and members of the laity would have followed him.

The current "fashion for religion," combined with religious and theological ignorance as well as with a general insecurity and fear of the unknown, promote an eschatological mood, a certain mysticism, the easy acceptance of myths and all sorts of esoteric teachings. Hence the spread of the occult, both imported—such as Moon's "Universal Church," the Hare Krishnas, etc.—and home-grown—such as the Theotokos Center, the White Brotherhood, or the preachings of a certain "Patriarch" Vissarion in Siberia. On the other hand, the

---

11 Part of his "patriotic" campaign was his resolute struggle against the use of the Russian language in Church services. He claimed that services in that language would be blasphemous, because Russian is the language of criminals and prostitutes.

country has been flooded by numerous American sectarian preachers, mostly from the southern United States. Many of them preach a Calvinist theology of prosperity, which is rather tactless in view of the present poverty in Russia, thus implying that Americans are a God-chosen people while the Russians are damned by God. Such activities, as well as their total ignorance of and lack of respect for the Russian spiritual culture and traditions, turns Russians against the West and against Western Christianity in general, which they tend to identify with these misguided American preachers. The tiny rate of recruitment achieved by American preachers is completely disproportionate to the expense and energies that go into their campaign. Their few recruits come either from among those Russians who admire everything American or who join the sects out of despair because they cannot understand the Orthodox services, conducted in the largely incomprehensible Slavonic, or are unable to find a spiritual home in the Orthodox Church. In contrast with sectarian meetings, newcomers are not welcomed, as a rule, in an Orthodox church. No one helps them to understand the service, invites them to catechetical meetings or makes them feel comfortable. Exceptions to that "rule" exist in communities such as those of Kochetkov and of the followers of the late Fr Men', as we have seen above, but they are few and far between. Generally, the Orthodox do not even try to compete with the Protestant groups in explaining their faith to strangers. They don't preach in city squares, they do not visit homes unless invited. The harmfulness of the missions lies not so much in their recruitment of new members, but rather in causing general dismay in the Russian population, which expected that with the collapse of Communism the Church would provide them with guidance. Today, the multitude of sects and their overt or implied hostility to the Orthodox Church has engendered a general disappointment with religions, which the Russians now perceive as little better than political parties, constantly fighting and undercutting each other.

Although the barbarity, brainwashing, and psychic traumatizing of youth by totalitarian occult groups such as the White Brotherhood, the Theotokos Center, and others has been clear for quite some time, the Moscow Patriarchate denounced them publicly much more slowly than the Protestant sectarians. Such indecision may lie in the fact that the eschatological expectations of those groups is widely shared by the Orthodox as well. Only in 1993 did the Patriarchate finally officially condemn these and other occult groups.

As to the foreign Protestant missionaries, the Patriarch petitioned the Government in April 1993 to form a mixed commission, consisting of representatives of the Government and the major registered religions of Russia, which would have the right for the next five to seven years to permit or restrict foreign missions. The Supreme Soviet then drafted a bill allowing foreign preachers to preach in Russia only if they were invited by one of the established Russian religious centers. Under pressure from the liberal domestic and foreign media, Yeltsin vetoed the bill.[12] Liberals were in an uproar, claiming that the Supreme Soviet and the Patriarch were trying to infringe on religious freedom in Russia. Indeed, at first glance it did appear strange that the Patriarch, who had repeatedly rejected any role by the state in religious affairs, was now asking the State for help. But it must be pointed out that the Patriarch did not ask for any special privileges for the Orthodox Church alone, but for the right of all Russian confessions to have some control over foreign missions. Secondly, he asked that such limits be set for a limited period of time, in the course of which he hoped that the Church would acquire sufficient numbers of well-educated clergy and theologians and would have sufficiently educated her flock in order to withstand the foreign onslaught.

Having recognized the need for the development of Orthodox mission work, one would expect that the Patriarchate would welcome and support the few successful missionary efforts that do exist, such as the above-named communities. But the patriarchate has avoided conflict with the radical brotherhoods, fearing that they might cause schisms in the Church. Knowing that the clergy and parishes attacked by the radicals were profoundly dedicated to the Church and would not break ecclesiastical discipline, the Patriarchate chose not to defend them in the face of attacks from the "red-brown" Union of Brotherhoods. The Patriarchate's fears were probably exaggerated, because most truly church-centered brotherhoods broke their links with the Union after its Third Congress in June 1992 in Leningrad, at which even the Patriarch was attacked as a Zionist agent for having met in New York with the American Rabbinate and having presented them a memorandum on the common Biblical heritage of Jews and Christians. The Patriarch did not respond, even though some priests, under the influence of the Union of Brotherhoods, stopped commemorating his name at the liturgy. How is it possible to explain such meekness in the face of an organization whose anti-Semitism

---

12 This may have been one reason why some priests and bishops sympathized with the Supreme Soviet rather than with Yeltsin during their bloody confrontations in October 1993.

and racial hatred is incompatible with Christianity? Is he afraid that the Union, in the current conditions of extreme moral and ideological instability and disorientation, will attain control over the ignorant masses, who are embittered and full of wrath against that invisible enemy? In short, the mood today is similar to that which brought Hitler to power in 1933.

The Patriarchate wants to avoid a split at any cost. Probably it felt that the Union's attacks would decline if they were met with silence. In any case, at its Fourth Congress in 1993, the Union expressed its loyalty to the Patriarch in return for his greeting to the Congress. Was the price paid for that loyalty worth it? The price was at least the temporary silence of the Patriarch, who only two years earlier had appealed to the liberal intelligentsia to become active members of the Church in order to help the Church became a dynamic organism, facing the future rather than the past. He stressed that not all was right in the past, that not all was worthy of emulation, and he condemned anti-Semitism and any form of extreme nationalism in many of his early statements. But in 1993, the Patriarchate did not react even to the resolution of the Fourth Congress demanding the canonization of Ivan the Terrible for his alleged struggle against the Jews. The Congress also called for the restoration of the Oprichnina, Ivan's terroristic police, in order to purge the country of its "judaizers."[13] It also requested the canonization of Nicholas II, with the formula "murdered by the Jews."

Only after the turbulent summer of 1994 did the Patriarchate finally decide that the extremists had gone too far and had somehow to be checked. This was the summer of the described pogrom against Fr Kochetkov's Higher Orthodox School, as well as a number of so-called "theological conferences" convened by the extreme right, each attacking Fr Kochetkov and the "Menevites." The final straw may have been the conference on November 14-15, under the auspices of the St Tikhon's Institute in Moscow, which unsuccessfully tried to achieve a consensus to request the Patriarchate to submit Fr Kochetkov to an ecclesiastical trial. To the surprise of the rightist radicals, the Episcopal Council of November 28-December 2 ignored their demands and passed resolutions which implicitly approved the missionary, liturgical, charitable, and educational efforts of those priests and communities whom the above conference had attacked. The most important resolutions of the Episcopal Council were then

13 A rationalistic, anti-Trinitarian heresy with strong Judaic elements, disseminated in Russia in the 15th century by several Lithuanian Jews. For some unclear reasons, the "red-browns" consider the Men' and Kochetkov communities to be modern Judaizers.

formally approved by the Synod on February 22, 1995. The Synod set up commissions on educational reforms, missionary work, etc., and ordered that each brotherhood submit its statute to its diocesan bishop within a six-month period for approval. Similarly, the Union of Brotherhoods and the Union of Sisterhoods were requested to submit their statutes to the Synod. Henceforth, only those brotherhoods and sisterhoods whose statutes had received the approval of their hierarchs could operate under the auspices of the Church. Those who will fail to submit their statutes within the stipulated period "will be considered as having no connection to the Church."

It is to be hoped that the resolutions of the December Episcopal Council and the regulations issued by the February 1995 Synod session will be adhered to by the Church leadership and implemented on the local level as well. It is, however, unrealistic to expect clarity of direction and stability from the contemporary Church leadership. As human beings, with typically human faults, they are an inseparable part of a nation living through a deep crisis of identity, searching for the meaning of its horrible twentieth-century experience and for a new way of life, humiliated by the revelations of terror and tortures committed by their fathers and brothers, incompatible with the myths of Holy Russia, resulting in a constant temptation to find scapegoats rather than coming to terms with the national guilt.

As an institution and an assembly of believers, the Church is inseparable from the nation. She has come out, after all, from under the same rubble of seven decades of totalitarianism as the rest of the nation, badly wounded and traumatized.

FOR FURTHER READING

Anderson, John, *Religion, State and Politics in the Soviet Union and Successor States* (Cambridge University Press, 1994).

Davis, Nathaniel, *A Long Walk to Church. A Contemporary History of Russian Orthodoxy* (Boulder, CO: Westview Press, 1995).

The Journal of the Moscow Patriarchate for 1986-95.

Furov, V., "Iz otcheta Soveta po delam religii—chlenam TsK KPSS." *Vestnik RKhD*, No. 130, 1979.

Kyrlezhev, A., "Bog v epokhu smerti Boga." *Kontinent*, No. 2 (72), 1992.

Nezhnyi, A., "Ego blazhenstvo bez mitry i zhezla," *Ogonek*, Nos. 48 and 49, November-December, 1991.

Pospielovsky, D., "Church and State under Gorbachev: What to Expect?" *Gorbachev and the Soviet Future*. Lerner, Lawrence W. and Donald W. Treadgold, eds. (Boulder, CO and London: Westview Press, 1988), pp. 164-187.

_____, "Impressions of the Contemporary Russian Orthodox Church: Its Problems and Its Theological Education," *Religion, State and Society*, vol. 23, No. 3 (Oxford: Keston Institute, 1995).

_____, "The Russian Orthodox Church in the Post-Communist Commonwealth of Independent States," *Modern Greek Studies Yearbook* (University of Minnesota, 1993) vol. 9, pp. 227-266.

_____, *Russkaia Pravoslavnaia Tserkov' v XX veke* (Moscow, 1995)

EPILOGUE

Some General Remarks

Almost a decade after the adoption of the current Church Statute, the Russian Church still lacks anything resembling a proper ecclesiastical court system, although the Statute stipulated its creation. The arbitrary rule of the CRA during the Communist era has simply been replaced by the arbitrary rule of the Synod and the diocesan bishops. As in the past, there is no *sobornal* interaction between the laity, the parish clergy and the episcopate; rather, there is only pyramidal, one-way communication. Some bishops are totally despotic and prevent a proper development of clergy and laity initiatives;[1] others delegate freedom of arbitrary power to their parish priests. This can be beneficial in cases of dedicated, intelligent and popular priests, but it can lead to very negative results where the priest is despotic, narrow-minded, or uneducated, as is often the case today. The growth of seminaries and the increase in student numbers, however spectacular, cannot keep up with the quantity of churches now being reopened.

Despite the emphasis in the 1988 Statute on the importance of the parish as the basic unit of the Church and on laity-clergy interaction, the parish community is still defined, in accordance with the old Soviet laws, as consisting of no less than twenty believers registered by the State as people responsible for the parish.[2] Consequently, in most parishes it is precisely the twenty-or-so persons registered with the state who are treated as the parish community, and it is they alone, together with the parish clergy, who constitute the twice-yearly general parish meetings mandated by the Statute. In order to survive economically, however, the parish must number close to a thousand, given the low incomes prevailing in present-day Russia. In other words the laity are reduced to passive attendance at services, thus precluding the development of any real parish-community life. Only a minority of priests, mostly of the younger generation and well-educated, have created real parishes in which every regular communicant is a full parish member with the right to vote in parish meetings. When

---

1 A case in point may be the Diocese of Kostroma whose well-meaning, good-natured and sincere bishop proved to be incapable of delegating responsibility, the result of which has been the virtual collapse of a theological school begun with much enthusiasm in 1991.

2 The 1990 State laws reduced that to "no less than 10 persons." See also: *Ustav ob upravlenii Russkoi pravoslavnoi Tserkvi* (Moscow Patriarchate, 1988), pp. 28-36.

the priest is transferred, however, nothing guarantees that the old system will not be reimposed, and believers will again be reduced to the role of mere worshipers and passive bystanders in relation to parish affairs.

Another problem of Church discipline and authority is the appearance of uncanonical parallel jurisdictions, as discussed in the previous chapter. The scandal with the former Metropolitan Filaret of Kiev, now the unilaterally proclaimed Patriarch of the Ukrainian Orthodox Church-Kiev Patriarchate (UOC-KP), could have been avoided had he been defrocked at the 1990 Council of the Russian Church (*Sobor*) or soon thereafter. Instead, this occurred only in 1992, and only after scandalous revelations about Filaret appeared in the secular press. Had his removal from the ranks of the clergy been carried out in an open trial, he would not have been able to play the card of offended Ukrainian nationalism as effectively as he did.

The existence of the ROCOR parishes in Russia and of Bishop Valentin's "Free Russian Church," splintered off from the ROCOR, further undermines canonical discipline. Whenever a priest of the Moscow Patriarchate quarrels with his bishop or does not want to carry out an order from the Patriarchate, he can join one of the splinter groups, declaring himself to be a true anti-Communist and accusing the leadership of the Patriarchal Church of having been collaborators. The following examples are indicative of the problem.

Lev Lebedev, a priest of considerable intellectual and scholarly erudition but an alcoholic, was suspended in 1991 by his bishop, Yuvenalii of Kursk. Lebedev then joined the ROCOR and published a brochure in which he presented his departure from the Moscow Patriarchate as a voluntary act of principle.[3]

Even more "colorful" is the story of Archimandrite Adrian of Noginsk (Moscow Province). In response to scores of complaints by parents that their children who attended Adrian's parish school had been sexually violated by him, the Patriarch ordered his removal from his position as rector of the Noginsk Cathedral. Refusing to heed the order, Adrian shifted his cathedral to the jurisdiction of the ROCOR. After a few months, the ROCOR likewise suspended him for immorality, and so did Valentin of Suzdal a little later. Finally Adrian went to Filaret in Kiev, who consecrated him bishop and appointed him exarch of the Kiev Patriarchate for Russia.

3 His medical record from his university student days to 1967 can be found in GARF, F. 9661s, op. 6, d. 91, ll. 3-7.

Directly related to Adrian's case is the *cause célèbre* of the priest Gleb Yakunin, discussed in the previous chapter. Having failed to gain a reversal of the defrocking order (for his refusal to give up his candidacy for the Duma), Yakunin went to Kiev in 1995 and was accepted into the clergy ranks in Adrian's "exarchate" by the very Filaret whom he had been unmasking and condemning as a major KGB agent ever since 1991.

The existence of parallel Church "jurisdictions" thus seriously undermines Church discipline and the moral authority of the Church in the eyes of the nation. Had there been full openness in the Church, due process of law and the strict observance of canon law, such cases would hardly have been possible. For example, while a closed session of the 1992 *Sobor* of Bishops condemned and defrocked Filaret,[4] its public statement expressed gratitude to him for his great contribution to the Church, thus giving the impression that he was retiring voluntarily. As we saw in chapter 16, Yakunin's suspension contradicted the rules adopted by the Moscow Sobor of 1917-18, rules which could be altered only by another full council.[5] Thus the current Church leadership not only functions without proper ecclesiastical courts, but it also ignores its own canon law, further undermining discipline in the Church at all levels. There is no real leadership in the Church, and, as one authoritative member of the clergy described the situation to this author, "There is Orthodox theology and an Orthodox *oikoumene*, there are individual Russian Orthodox parishes and communities, even occasional dioceses and some good seminaries, but there is no single unified national Russian Orthodox Church." This statement may be an exaggeration, but it represents a wide-spread feeling among the Orthodox Christians in Russia that the Church lacks proper leadership.[6]

4 The form of defrocking in itself was canonically questionable, because the *Sobor* allowed him to return to Kiev while still a metropolitan and declare his own retirement on the election of his replacement. This gave him the leeway to act as he did.

5 Arkhiereiskomu soboru Russkoi pravoslavnoi Tserkvi. APELLIATSIA. Sviashchennik Gleb Yakunin, October 27, 1994. Ms. includes the Moscow Patriarchate's FAX information for the Media of November 3, 1993. The tone of that appeal to the Episcopal Council is very respectful, in contrast to his open letter to President Yeltsin of 21 March 1995, in which he condemns the Patriarchate as Stalin's creation and quite transparently appeals to the President to take drastic measures against the Russian Church leadership. (Another Ms.). For confirmation of his links with Filaret of Kiev. See L. Aleinik, "V Moskve izdana klevetnicheskaia biografiia o. Gleba Yakunina," *Russkaia mysl'*, 18-24. I. 1996.

6 This is also a legacy of the totalitarian collectivist system of the past seven decades, which repressed the personality in the human being and induced a fear of personal responsibility and initiative. This almost precluded the development of real leadership qualities, instead producing manipulators. Characteristically, all totalitarian leaders, from Lenin and Hitler to Mao and Castro, were born and educated in "bourgeois" societies. The communist bosses born under Communism who replaced the first generation leaders, have been

Theological Education

The mushrooming of new Orthodox theological schools of all kinds, both under direct ecclesiastical administration and privately founded, run and funded, is remarkable indeed. In the 1950s, there were eight undergraduate seminaries and two graduate academies in the late in the whole USSR; the number dropped to three seminaries and two academies in the late 1980s. At present, the CIS has approximately:

—21 seminaries (15 in Russia proper), some of which have expanded their course of studies from four to five years, on a par with secular universities;

—four graduate academies (2 in Russia);

—five theological faculties or departments in secular universities (3 in Russia);

—two Orthodox universities and four institutes (one of the latter, inter-Christian with an Orthodox department) aimed at theologically educating the general Russian intelligentsia, but also containing a specialized Church-related theological faculty for those aspiring eventually to ordination. There are also two institutions in Russia which call themselves "Higher Orthodox Schools," with a thorough theological education of five to seven years and at least 21 two-year junior theological schools (15 in Russia)—many of them aspiring to evolve into full-fledged seminaries. In fact most of the new seminaries began in this fashion.

Yet most of these schools leave much to be desired. They all suffer from the following major deficiencies: an extreme shortage of funds, forcing them to operate at what any Western society would consider to be far below poverty level; inadequate libraries or a virtual absence thereof (except in those schools that had not been closed: Sergiev-Posad [Moscow], St Petersburg, and Odessa); an extreme shortage of qualified teachers; and the virtual absence of modern theological textbooks. In fact, four or five textbooks by some contemporary Orthodox theologians have appeared in the last few years, but those penned by regular seminary professors leave much to be desired. Textbooks written by independent Orthodox theologians are ignored or even banned by the administration of the most conservative seminaries, even when they bear an imprimatur from the Patriarch. With very few exceptions, seminary professors produced by theological schools of the Soviet or post-Soviet

typical "committee people," not real leaders. This is one of the main reasons for the leadership crises in the contemporary post-Communist societies.

era are too timid and uncreative to be theologically productive, let alone intellectually original and daring in research and publications, as the education they received was targeted at preserving the pre-Revolutionary legacy. Moreover, the traumatic experience of the 1920s Renovationist Schism contributed to a fear of and revulsion against any new ideas in theology, including those of the Russian religio-philosophic renaissance which began in the last pre-Revolutionary decades and then continued at the St Sergius Orthodox Theological Institute in Paris established by the great Russian theologians expelled by Lenin in 1922.[7] Although that new Russian theology had revived the almost forgotten Patristic thought and the legacy of the early Church in place of the Western scholasticism imported during the eighteenth and nineteenth centuries, the very fact that this new theology was chronologically close to the Revolution and was then clouded in the confusion of Renovationism made it highly suspect in the minds of churchmen educated in Soviet-era schools, who had to function in the general Soviet environment of dogmatism and isolation. In contrast, it is the independent, mostly self-taught theologians, often neophytes of the 1960s-1980s, who have been intellectually open to the "new" Russian theology, as well as generally to the Christian thought of the twentieth century. These "Varangians," either self-taught or who had received their theological education after graduating from secular universities, are among the most popular professors in theological schools. Their open-mindedness, however, proved unpalatable for such arch-conservative institutions as the Moscow Theological Academy and Seminary, from which most of them were expelled in 1993-95. At this school, a kind of censorship has also been practiced by its librarian. Its reading room, for example, contains pro-communist and national-Bolshevik (extreme chauvinist) newspapers, but not democratic and liberal ones. One of the best Russian-language Orthodox periodicals, published in Paris, has similarly remained uncatalogued and thus unavailable for general student readership. The present educational system relies almost entirely on regimented study by rote, and the teaching load borne by the professors and students is too heavy to be conducive to an atmosphere of academic freedom and intellectual debate, without which no creative and productive scholarship can occur.

---

7 E.g., Georges Florovsky, George Fedotov, Semen Frank, Sergei Bulgakov, Vasilii Zenkovsky, Nicolas Afanasiev, Vladimir Lossky. The traditions of these scholars and of the Paris School have been inherited and continued by St Vladimir's Orthodox Theological Seminary in Crestwood, NY, transplanted onto the American soil by such products of the Paris School as: Alexander Schmemann, John Meyendorff, Serge Verkhovskoy. and others.

The leadership of the Church constantly complains about the spread of aggressive foreign missions and diverse totalitarian cults, both foreign and domestic. Only a well-educated, theologically erudite, and intellectually liberated clergy and laity can be an effective match to such cults and sects. Not only does seminary education leave much to be desired, but the seminaries do not appear to be a priority in the Church's budget: they are funded on the residual principle.[8] The first priority seems to be the monasteries, of which over 340 have been returned to the Church since 1987, although most have only a handful of monks and are unable to support themselves, let alone undertake proper repairs costing millions of dollars. Another priority is the reopening and costly repair of churches, which are generally returned in a ruined state. Instead of using interim chapels, Church authorities insist on their full, extremely costly, restoration, including the gilding of domes. Moreover, the Patriarchate tends to ordain graduates of the two-year junior theological schools originally meant to train catechists and psalmists, rather than the graduates of the independent theological schools, even though all of these schools have been approved by the Patriarchate's Department of Theological Education. These independent institutions train Christian missionaries for the modern world, maintain fraternal contacts with Western Christian denominations, enjoy an atmosphere of intellectual freedom, and cherish the legacy of twentieth century Russian theology, both pre-Revolutionary and that which developed in the diaspora.[9] In short, the graduates of these schools are much better trained to face the challenges of the modern world and thus to carry on an effective Orthodox mission, yet the Patriarchate keeps them at arm's length and avoids ordaining them.

---

8 In actuality, most of the funding for theological education in Russia comes from diverse Western Christian foundations, e.g.: the Dutch-German Roman Catholic *Church in Need* Foundation, the German Lutheran Church and many of its individual parishes, and the Swiss Protestant foundation *Faith in the Second World*. Some support comes from the new Russian enterprises and their owners, e.g., the Tobolsk Seminary in Siberia is largely financed by *Gasprom*, the Siberian gas-extracting monopoly with its main office in Tobolsk.

9 Among such schools could be named: the Higher Orthodox Theological School of Moscow directed by Father G. Kochetkov and its namesake in Krasnoiarsk, directed by Fr G. Persianov; the Orthodox universities of Moscow and Volgograd, the St Andrew Biblical-Theological Institute of Moscow; the Open Orthodox University named after Fr Alexander Men' in Moscow; the Smolensk Theological Seminary; the St Petersburg Christian Humanities Institute; the Orthodox Theology Department at the Moscow University Faculty of Journalism, and probably the Orthodox Theological Faculty that is in process of establishment at the University of Novgorod. Some potential for a positive evolution is visible in such schools as the seminaries of Saratov, Kursk, Belgorod, Minsk, and Tomsk. There is hope that after a period of decline the theological seminary and academy of St Petersburg will return to its past glory.

Proselytism and the Occult

As we have seen, proselytism is a serious problem in today's CIS, and the Orthodox Church, now emerging "from under the rubble" (to use Solzhenitsyn's expression) of seven decades of isolation and suffering financial poverty, is at a strong disadvantage before the wealthy, aggressive, professionally trained Western and Eastern (mostly Korean) missionaries, who enjoy an almost limitless supply of literature and all sorts of modern communication gadgets. Nevertheless, the success of the Fundamentalist Protestant (mostly Evangelicals) and Roman Catholic missions is very limited, especially given their vast efforts. The following statistic illustrates this point: whereas the percentage of the population calling themselves believing Christians has grown in Russia from 27 percent in 1990 to 40 percent in 1992, a total of fewer than two percent declared themselves to be members of Protestant and Roman Catholic Churches combined, i.e., about four percent of all believers. But, whereas in 1990 80 percent of Christians declared themselves to be members of the Orthodox Church (i.e., 18 percent of the total population of Russia), in 1992 only 38 percent of Christians called themselves Orthodox—i.e., the net percentage of Orthodox in the total population declined by three percent in two years, while the total percentage of Christians grew almost by 50 percent. In other words, about 58 percent of people believing in Christ belonged to no particular confession.[10] Other and more recent soundings indicate the continuing growth of the religious sector in the Russian population, although some findings have been rather bizarre. For instance a survey conducted in 1995 by the respectable All-Russian Center for the Study of Public Opinion gives the following results:

Orthodox Christians	53%	Hindu (probably Hari-Krishna)	0.1%
Other Christian faith	2%	Non-believer	28%
Islam	3%	Uncertain	13%
Other religions (e.g., Judaism)	1%		

But responses to the question "What role does religion play in your life?" revealed that a high proportion of the so-called believers were in fact agnostics, probably declaring their religious affiliation on the basis of having been baptized, circumcised, or otherwise initiated into a religion at a certain stage in their lives, but no longer practicing it. Thus only 4 percent of the respondents claimed that religion was a fundamental factor in their lives; 19 percent ascribed a significant role to religion in their lives; 30 percent said the role

---

10 A. Kyrlezhev, "Bog v epokhu smerti Boga," *Kontinent*, No. 2 (72), 1992, p. 265; S. Filatov & L. Vorontsov, "Kak idet religioznoe vozrozhdenie v Rossii?," *Nauka i religiia*, No. 5, 1993.

played by religion in their lives was insignificant; 19 percent said religion played "practically no role"; 14 percent said they were atheists; and 13 percent were uncertain.[11] In other words, according to the above opinion poll, only 23 percent of the population can be considered to be committed religious believers, with the Orthodox forming 19-20 percent, indicating growth of only 1-2 percent in practicing Orthodox believers since 1990, and no growth at all for the "other" Christians (Catholics and Protestants). The same conclusion must have been reached by most of the Evangelical preachers (mostly from the southern part of the USA), as by 1996 their presence in Russia declined markedly. Mormon door-to-door missionaries were about the only ones this writer encountered in the streets of Russian cities in 1996, but even they were not as numerous as in the early 1990s.

However, it has been estimated that up to three to five million Russians may have fallen prey to totalitarian and brainwashing "New Age" sects, both imported and domestic. Among the former are: Hubbard's "Scientology," Moon's "Unification Church," the followers of the "Krishna Consciousness," etc. The most aggressive and dangerous domestic sects include: "The White Brotherhood," "The Theotokos Center," and Vissarion's new "Church of the Last Testament."

Scientology needs no explanation to a Western reader,[12] but one of its victims has given a good explanation for why it and similar totalitarian sects attract former Soviet citizens:

> In the [current] critical years when the only true, all-conquering, universal and salutary teaching has collapsed, inevitably there will remain its long-lasting echo in the form of thirst for...another all-conquering, universal and true teaching. Hubbard's teaching, in the very words of its not-too-modest founder, claims to be all that.

The cited *Izvestiia* report describes numerous cases of broken marriages, mental disorders, and suicides among Hubbard's Russian followers. Yet

---

11 "Rossiianam dorogo pravoslavie, a ne religiia," *Segodnia* (a respectable Moscow daily), 2. IX. 1995.

A probe of the Moscow population conducted by the Academy of Sciences sociological department found that 44 percent of the population considered themselves to be religious believers: 35 percent Orthodox, 5 percent Christians without any Church affiliation, 0.5 percent were Roman Catholics, Protestants and Old Ritualists combined, 1.5 percent Jews, ! percent Muslims. "Skol'ko veruiushchikh v Moskve?" *Moskovskii komsomolets*, 25 January, 1996.

12 However, the following details, cited in a well-researched article by three investigative journalists, may not be generally known: one, that Hubbard had begun his career as a science-fiction writer; two, that at a conference of writers in 1949 he allegedly declared: "If you want to become a millionaire, the best way to do so is to establish your own religion." After having established Scientology he allegedly once said: "I am selling particles of the blue sky," D. Dokuchaev, S. Marzeeva & E. Iakovleva, "Prodavtsy neba," *Izvestiia*, 12.IX. 1996.

Scientology legally functions in Moscow thanks to its approval in 1994 by the Russian deputy-minister of health. Although this functionary has since lost his job, Hubbard's center continues to operate legally in Moscow (although without an official license), having no difficulty in attracting students for its courses in such quack "sciences" as *dianetics* and *detoxicology*, costing from $100 to $1,000 and amounting to para-psychological brainwashing people into alleged "re-living" of their "previous" lives, purportedly in order to turn them into *supermen* freed from such "false emotions" as empathy, and who will have no fear of hurting or even harming others, "when this is required in the name of justice."[13]

Vissarion's *Church of the Last Testament*, by contrast, is entirely home-grown, but in its totalitarian character it responds to the same described above. Vissarion is a former policeman who, according to some reports, allegedly lost his job for alcoholism in 1990 at the age of 30. Vissarion then declared himself to be Jesus Christ who has come into the world to save it and to unite all religions and spiritual teachings into one universal religion. In April 1994, he declared Minusinsk in the Siberian Sayan Mountains and its region to be "the promised Land, the New Jerusalem." Thousands of people from all over the CIS flocked to him, at his request selling all their possessions and handing everything over to him. Surprisingly, many of Vissarion's followers are well-educated urban people, as described in a letter written by one such follower. She writes about a life in primitive huts with no amenities, electricity, radio, or medical services, haunted by hunger, cold, depression. and thoughts of suicide, in some cases actualized. Her own gradual self-emancipation from Vissarion's "hypnosis" was stimulated by the sight of her hungry children, who constantly begged her to go and secretly buy bread, the consumption of which had been banned by Vissarion. She could not stand the sight of hungry children and the fits of hysteria in both children and adults caused by hunger. The tension over food nearly reached a breaking point, after which Vissarion eventually permitted his flock to eat everything but meat, eggs, and fish. She cites cases of nervous exhaustion, which caused temporary paralysis in otherwise healthy people. Vissarion's message was for people to leave behind the sinful world around them which was quickly approaching Doomsday, and to condemn all those who remain in it. And indeed, those responding to his call have condemned the real world and real people. For this reason her husband, a very talented and formerly very

13 Obvious borrowings from Nietzsche, see *ibid.*

successful scientist, although he agrees that there is something wrong with the whole idea, and admits that for him the only way out is suicide, refuses to leave the colony because "he has never made a mistake before." There is no mutual love in the colony and a great deal of frustration: its inhabitants have no property, no money, no jobs, nowhere to return to, even if they wish to leave. The writer herself finally moved her children out to her relatives. She was lucky enough to find a very compassionate young Orthodox priest where her relatives live. He baptized her elder son and became his godfather. He blessed her to return to the colony to help others free themselves from their delusion. Just as the above description of motives that lead people to Scientology, the author of this letter concludes that Vissarion's success is a result of "the 70-year-long [dominance of] atheism, complete religious ignorance, and perverse notions regarding the freedom of the human person."[14]

What can the Church do about these harmful cults, to which citizens of the formerly totalitarian political systems appear to be particularly vulnerable? Because of the impact of these cults, some clergy and a considerable number of the laity are increasingly supporting the position that the Orthodox Church should once again become a state religion, despite repeated warnings from the Patriarch against any Church-State symbiosis.[15] In practice, however, there are already signs of such a symbiosis in real practice. For example, only one religious leader, Patriarch Alexii II, was present at President Yeltsin's inauguration in August 1996. Had Yeltsin been a practicing Orthodox Christian, this could have been justified as a normal blessing by his spiritual father. But in a joint TV appearance with then President Gorbachev in 1991, both presidents declared themselves to be atheists, although Yeltsin added that he was superstitious and felt good in church. In light of such an attitude by the president, the presence of the Patriarch and his words of blessing were clearly meant to have national significance, and the presence of other major national religious figures would certainly be expected. In May 1996, a shipment of children's Bibles sent from Finland to the Russian Pentecostal Church was delayed by the Moscow customs officials pending the approval of their contents by the Moscow Patriarchate.[16] This is a dangerous precedent, and these examples only show how

14 A. Zubov & T. Venslavskaia, "Esli vy veruiushchie liudi, pomolites' o nas ...," *Russkaia mysl'*, 5 - 11. IX. 1996, p. 8.

15 As recently as August 1995, his answer to the question, "Would you want the [Orthodox Church] to become the state Church?" was: "Such a situation has never been beneficial to the Church." Natalia Zhelnorova, interviewer: "Ne vsiakomu dukhu verte," *Argumenty i fakty*, No. 33, 1995.

16 Keston News Service FAX report by Lawrence Uzzell.

clumsy any form of Church-State symbiosis is from the very beginning. The whole course of the history of Russia, as well as that of most other nations, militates against any direct state interference into religious matters.

But there are also indirect ways. One such attempt was the creation, in August 1995, of a "President's Council on Interaction with Religious Associations," which consisted of representatives of all the registered religions of Russia (Orthodox, Old Believer, Muslim, Buddhist, Jewish, Roman Catholic, and several Protestant Confessions), with Anatolii Krasikov as its executive secretary. Krasikov is a former journalist who specialized on religious matters ever since Vatican II, and later for some time served as Yeltsin's press secretary. The novelty of the Council was that it was a direct voice of the relevant confessions, and not a bureaucratic institution, and that at the same time it had the potential to foster inter-religious cooperation on the highest level, as well to transmit authoritative and direct information on religious matters to the President and the central Government. Alas, the institution proved to be too novel and probably too independent from the bureaucratic machine to be tolerated by it for long time. It existed for only about six months when, in the spring of 1996, it was replaced by a purely bureaucratic body bearing the same name and presided over by the head of the President's Administration, an establishment bureaucrat. Representatives of the major faiths remained, but the membership was expanded to include representatives of state departments, provincial administrations, etc. Obviously at home in bureaucratic matters, the bureaucrats and the clergy will run this new Council.[17] Should not this have served as an early warning to the churches not to enter into too close a relation with the state apparatus, if already on the level of a purely consultative body the bureaucracy succeeded in quashing an independent inter-religious institution? But when issues such as introducing religious education into school curricula or providing subsidies for theological education to build up cadres of well-educated clergy, arise, then the bureaucracy responds: "Oh no, this is a secular state with separation of Church from the State. Religion cannot be taught in state schools, nor can the state support theological schools." And, to the present day, even private donations to religious organizations and churches are not tax-deductible.

17 See respectively: "Polozhenie o Sovete po vzaimodeistviiu s religioznymi ob'edineniiami pri Prezidente Rossiiskoi Federatsii," *Sluzhba kommunikatsii OVTsS*, 30.VIII. 1995; N. Petrov interviewing Krasikov: "U kazhdogo svoia vera, no edina Rossiia," *Rossiiskaia gazeta*, 30.8. 1995; A. Krasikov, "Revnopravie-ne ravnovelikost'," *Rossiiskie vesti*, 24.XI.1995; "Pervoe zasedanie Soveta po vzaimodeistviiu s religioznymi ob'edineniami pri Prezidente," *Information Bulletin. Department for External Church Relations.* Moscow Patriarchate, 15 May 1996, p. 7.

Concluding Remarks on Some Events in the Church Life

Probably the most important event in recent Church life was the full Council of Russian bishops held in December 1994. Shortly before the council, the red-browns went into a period of high activity, which included some acts of violence, such as the attack on Fr George Kochetkov's Higher Orthodox Christian Theological School by a group of monks led by the hegumen Tikhon (Shevkunov) in the late summer of 1994. Shevkunov had already succeeded in forcing Fr George and his parish out of the Meeting of the Icon of the Vladimir Mother of God Icon church just half a year earlier. The monks raided the school, threw icons out of the school's iconographic section and books from its library into the yard down below, just as the Bolsheviks had done in the past.[18] As if this was not enough, in November 1994 a group of the most reactionary clergy organized a pseudo-theological conference on renewal movements in the Church under the auspices of the allegedly neutral St Tikhon Theological Institute of Moscow, with the purpose of condemning Kochetkov, the late Alexander Men', and his followers. The resolution of the Conference was addressed to the forthcoming Bishops' Council with the hope that it would condemn the targeted clergy.[19]

The resolutions of that largest Council of Bishops since 1918, with 128 voting members, dashed the reactionaries' hopes. Recognizing the morally very disturbing state of society in the CIS, with record numbers of divorces, abortions and suicides, the Council formed a task force to develop a *social doctrine of the Church*, to be presented for approval to the next All-Russian Sobor (long overdue at the time of this writing). It approved the current economic and democratic reforms in Russia, but appealed to the Government to take better care of the poorest elements in society.

Turning to strictly ecclesiastical issues, the Council adopted the following decisions:

—that the education of future clergy be given first priority, with the aim in the near future of ordaining only persons with full theological education, raising the status of the undergraduate seminaries to that of the universities by expanding them from a four to a five year program;

18 "Further Incidents Affecting the Catechetical School of Father Kochetkov," *Sourozh: a Journal of Orthodox Life & Thought*, No. 58. London, November 1994, pp. 47-48.

19 Iuri Tabak, "Khronika odnoi konferentsii," *Russkaia mysl'*, 24-30. XI. 1994, p. 8.

—that the Church should aim at providing all schools with optional religious classes and sufficiently qualified teachers of religion approved by the Church, thus putting pressure on the appropriate state authorities to expand the legal rights for such programs;

—that the network of Sunday schools be expanded to assure their availability to all children.

Contrary to the reactionaries' position, the Council approved the Moscow Patriarchate's ecumenical contacts and canonized Father Alexander Khotovitsky, martyred by the Bolsheviks, who had been a very enthusiastic ecumenist during his missionary years in the United States.

As mentioned in chapter 9 above, the agenda of the Great Moscow Sobor of 1917-1918 included major liturgical reforms, including the russification of the liturgical language, the abbreviation of church services and the keeping of the central sanctuary doors open throughout the services, the recitation aloud of the so-called "secret" prayers of the Eucharistic Canon, an abbreviation of the annual fasting periods, and the issue of the liturgical calendar (Julian or Gregorian). However, because the Sobor was forced by the Bolsheviks to dissolve without concluding its work, all these issues remained in the form of recommendations by the Agenda Commission to the Sobor. The 1994 Bishops' Council once again raised these issues, although in the following oblique form:

> Missionary work is inseparably linked with the need of the immediate restoration of a full-blooded church life in the dioceses and parishes. It is absolutely necessary to apply more efforts in the sphere of religious education, catechization and evangelization. Orthodox missionary work must take into consideration the diversity of contemporary society [followed by an enumeration of the diverse professions and social groups, including prison inmates and the armed forces personnel]…It is necessary to emphasize especially missionary work with the youth, including the development of special religious services and talks for children and teen-agers.

Thus, although the issue of liturgical language was not raised directly, it is evident that special services for the youth and the development of missionary work inevitably include the use of the vernacular, as all Orthodox missions have always been conducted in the vernacular of the given people, including the missions among the Volga-Urals tribes, in Siberia, and in Alaska.

As the most active and successful missionaries are precisely Fr Kochetkov and the priests who can loosely be termed disciples and followers of Fr Men', and several parishes,[20] and as all of them have replaced Slavonic with the spoken Russian for at least some parts of the services, the decisions of the Council were a cautious and tacit blessing of their work and, eventually, of the russification of church services.

The Council also ruled that each Orthodox Brotherhood (or fellowship) had to belong to a particular parish and to be active in parish work (educational or charitable), and that it was required to submit its statute to the diocesan bishop, without whose approval the brotherhood could claim no connection to the Orthodox Church. This ruling effectively reduced the Brotherhoods' political activities, resulted in the closing of the most radical of them, and virtually silenced their central organization, the *Union of Russian Orthodox Brotherhoods*.

Finally, the Council also extended the ban on clergy participation in legislative bodies from the Russian Republic to all CIS countries.[21]

But the two years that have passed since the 1994 Council have witnessed no marked progress in the implementation of any of its decisions.

Our report would be incomplete without mentioning several events in the life of the Church in 1995-96, at least one of them being of crisis dimensions, not only for the Russian Church, but for the whole Orthodox *oikoumene*—the issue of the Orthodox Church in Estonia. Ever since the establishment of the first Orthodox communities by Russian missionaries in Estonia in the eleventh century, and up to 1924, the Estonian Orthodox Church had been under Russian jurisdiction. In 1921, when Patriarch Tikhon granted it internal autonomy within the Russian Patriarchate, 17 percent of ethnic Estonians, including the president of that new state, belonged to the Orthodox Church. In 1923, however, the Estonian Government for political reasons forced the Church to move under the *omophorion* of the Ecumenical Patriarchate, which accepted the Estonian Church without seeking its canonical release from the Moscow Patriarchate, thus contradicting the canons, but with the proviso that this was an emergency measure resulting from the impossibility for the Russian Church to administer the life of her daughter church abroad. Obviously, under the Soviet occupation in 1940 and again in 1945 the Estonian Church's allegiance to the Moscow Patriarchate was

20 Which include the Cosmas and Damian Church in Moscow, a small monastic community near Kolomna, and several parishes in the provinces.

21 This ruling nullified Yakunin's claim that the decision of 1993 was aimed specifically at him.

restored. A group of Estonian Orthodox, however, including some priests and the ethnically Estonian Metropolitan of Tallinn, Alexander, emigrated to Sweden and set up an Estonian Synod in Exile in Stockholm, under the jurisdiction of the Ecumenical Patriarch. In 1953, Metropolitan Alexander died in Stockholm. Left without a bishop, the Estonian parishes in diaspora were simply absorbed into the Ecumenical Patriarchate. The Synod-in-Exile ceased to exist by virtue of the absence of any bishops. In 1978, Dimitrios, the Patriarch of Constantinople, officially declared the 1923 acceptance of the Estonian Church into the jurisdiction of his Patriarchate null and void as a result of the restoration of normal relations with the Moscow Patriarchate.

In 1992, soon after the restoration of Estonia's independence, a local council of the Estonian Orthodox Church declared its loyalty to the Moscow Patriarchate, on the conditions of the restoration of internal autonomy. Such autonomous status was granted by the Moscow Patriarchate in the same year, and this new status of the Church was immediately reported to the Estonian Government. Then, in August 1993, the Estonian Ministry of Internal Affairs, instead of confirming the statutes of the Estonian Church, suddenly granted recognition as "The Estonian Orthodox Apostolic Church" to the sole Estonian parish in Stockholm whose elderly rector had decided to return to Estonia, and refused to legalize the Moscow Patriarchate's Church under the above name. This action was followed by letters sent by the Estonian prime minister and president to the Ecumenical Patriarch in Constantinople, asking him to accept the EOAC into his jurisdiction, which he did in January 1996. In response, the Moscow Patriarchate suspended communion with Constantinople. Realizing that the majority of the local Orthodox Churches, including those of Antioch, Jerusalem, Serbia, and Bulgaria, sided with Moscow and criticized the uncanonical behavior of the Ecumenical Patriarchate, the latter agreed to begin negotiations with the Moscow Patriarchate. These concluded in May 1996 with a compromise agreement, giving each Orthodox parish in Estonia the right to choose its jurisdictional preference. The majority of Estonian-speaking parishes (numerically more than half of the 80-odd Orthodox churches there, but containing fewer than 30 percent of Orthodox believers) chose to go under Constantinople, while the Russian speaking parishes, some of the mixed parishes, and the majority of the priests remained under Moscow. Although it would be next to impossible to find a canonical justification for this compromise, it was the only realistic solution in the conditions where the ethnic Estonians associate any affiliation with Moscow with the recent Soviet occupation. But the large and oppressed Russian minority in Estonia, deprived of access to Estonian citizenship and thus to civic rights enjoyed by Estonians, cherishes the Russian Church as their only spiritual link to Russia. Re-unification of the Orthodox Church in Estonia will have to wait until both communities rise to sufficient spiritual maturity to see themselves primarily as Orthodox Christians united in faith and disregarding their ethnic differences.[22]

Another major problem in Russian Church life once again became apparent in connection with Patriarch Alexii's first official visit to Germany in November 1995. At a service in the main Berlin cathedral, he publicly apologized to the German nation for the Communist tyranny that had been imposed by the Soviet Union. The Communist and the national-Bolshevik (Nazi-fascist) press rose up in arms, accusing him of committing national treason and insulting the Russian nation. A Moscow priest, speaking on a phone-in program on a private, Communist Party, Moscow radio station, agreed with a caller's attack on the Patriarch for the apology and then used the opportunity to vent his own anti-Semitism, protesting against the presence of so many people of Jewish background in churches. He accused the Jews of killing Nicholas II and declared that it was unpleasant for a Russian to go to confession to a "Jewish priest."[23]

What is the connection between the Patriarch's apology and the issue of anti-Semitism? In fact, it is a part and parcel of the syndrome of a victorious nation. The notion that the victor is always right is not only an unfortunate fact of historical injustice, but also of the self-consciousness of the winner. In the case of the CIS, and of Russians in particular, this syndrome is further complicated by the myth about Holy Russia, and of the Russian people as a "God-bearing nation." In this way of perceiving reality, it is next to impossible to accept that those very "God-bearing" Russians were sadistic *chekists* (a common name for secret police in the USSR) or Red Army soldiers who crucified priests, destroyed churches, desecrated altars, and burned icons. Surely, this

22 The situation was the reverse in pre-war Estonia, where ethnic Estonians constituted the majority of the Orthodox Church members and Russians were in the minority, with their Russian parishes within the Estonian Church. For more details of the Russo-Greek quarrel and reconciliation, see the *Information Bulletin*. Department for External Church Relations, Moscow Patriarchate, 4 March 1996, pp. 1-32, and 1 July, 1996, pp. 1-8.

23 He means, of course, converts from Judaism. According to a recent poll, 25 percent of Russian Jews are converts to Christianity, 8 percent consider themselves to be adherents of Judaism, the rest being agnostics, atheists, or members of other non-Christian confessions. Only one-fifth of the Christian Jews, however, are members of the Orthodox Church, the rest being either non-denominational, Catholic, or Protestant. See also the open letter to the Patriarch protesting the priest's anti-Semitism and the Patriarchate's toleration of such persons in the ranks of the clergy, Vladimir Erokhin, *Russkaia mysl'*, 5-10. I. 1996.

could only have been done by Jews, they argue, the whole Communist terror being presented as a Judeo-Masonic plot against Russia and the Orthodox Church. Therefore Russians have nothing to apologize for.[24]

Such views are not shared by most Russians, but they are typical of right-wing monarchists, as well as of communists; the sole difference between them is that the former view the evil of communism as a foreign importation, while the current Communist Party, having been purified from its Jewish element, is patriotic and therefore, in its view, presents no more threat to Russia and to the Russian Church. The communists, of course, see no reason to apologize for any part of their past. However, when pressed, they also denied any responsibility for atrocities by blaming them on the internationalists of the early Communist Party, primarily Jews: Trotsky, Zinoviev, and others. It is precisely this similarity of mentalities that led some Orthodox clergy to support the Communist Party in the presidential elections of 1996.

The Patriarch, although he gave several hints that he would support Yeltsin, maintained that both he and the Patriarchate must officially maintain complete political neutrality for the sake of preserving the unity in the Church. Even before the 1995 Duma elections, the Patriarch stated that the Church would not

> associate herself with any political movement or party, inasmuch as members of the Church can be found in every one of them. We welcome those party programs which express a concern with the moral state of our society. We consider that the freedom gained in the democratic process must be preserved irrespective of who wins the elections.[25]

He was even less specific on the eve of the 1996 presidential elections when he declared once again that all political parties were acceptable to a Christian, and then expressed the hope that Orthodox Christian voters would make the right choice, without indicating what this was. It might be expected that as a Christian leader, he would at least declare that a Christian could not vote for a party that preached and practiced genocide, whether racial or class-based, nor for a party whose ideology included a militant atheism aiming at the liquidation of religion. It is not surprising, then, that some clergy came out openly and with impunity in support of Ziuganov and his Communist Party. After all, no

---

24 For attacks on the Patriarch's apology to the German nation, see N. Selishchev, "Samooplevanie i samopredatel'stvo," *Pravda*, 20. XII. 1995; V. Lakatash, "Za chto izvinialsia patriarkh?" *Pravda*, 30. XI. '95; "Eshche raz o pokaianii," *Sovetskaia Rossiia*, 13. I. '96.

25 V. Zapevalov, "Ego Sviateishestvo zavoevyvaet serdtsa nemtsev," *Literaturnaia gazeta,* 22.XI.95.

other party made as many pronouncements on spirituality and the necessity to morally purify Russia as Ziuganov's nationalist-communist bloc! In his appeal to the nation, co-signed by ten Orthodox clergymen and 25 lay scholars and writers, Ziuganov promised to struggle for the restoration of the family and family values, for the general moral regeneration of the nation, to ban the spread of pornography and of moral license in the media, and to impose limitations on the activities of foreign missionaries.[26]

The group of clergy supporting Ziuganov was headed by Alexander Shargunov, an erudite Moscow priest highly respected in certain right-wing circles, formerly a leading poet and a dissident. He is the founder and leader of the "Public Committee for the Moral Restoration of the Fatherland," which publishes an irregular journal called *Antichrist in Moscow*, containing a peculiar mix of sensible concerns, wrong priorities, and dangerous misinformation. The Public Committee's appeal for moral revival is but an abbreviated version of Ziuganov's appeal. Among the borrowings from the latter is the claim that "the moral catastrophe [in Russia] has no parallels in national history. Russia has never known such crimes." Have Shargunov and his companions forgotten the scores of millions murdered during the years of Communist terror? When Professor Nikita Struve, the editor of the highly-respected Russian language journal of religion and Christian philosophy, reminded Shargunov of the Communist terror and added that this was infinitely worse and more demoralizing than all the pornography in the world, particularly since an offensive television program could simply be turned be off, but that the Communist terror could not, the very next issue of *The Antichrist* accused Struve of supporting pornography and named him (along with this author) a servant and agent of the Antichrist; and Struve's periodical, *The Messenger of the Russian Christian Movement*, which the Patriarch had publicly praised as the best Orthodox publication, was condemned as pseudo-Christian, harmful, and serving the Antichrist. The same issue of *The Antichrist* also condemned all forms of ecumenism as anti-Christian, although the Patriarch is a veteran participant in and supporter of inter-Christian ecumenism.[27]

The March 1996 issue of *The Antichrist* contained the following appeal to the Christian Orthodox electorate to vote for the Communist Party:

26 And what about Vissarion, the White Brotherhood and other domestic totalitarian sects?

27 Struve, "Antikhrist v Moskve?" *Vestnik RKhD*, No. 172 (1995), pp. 3-4; D. Pospielovsky, "Nekotorye problemy sovremennoi Russkoi Pravoslavnoi Tserkvi," *ibid.*, pp. 198-231; Sviashchennik Stefan Krasovitskii, "Aforizmy sera Genri ili Struve v Moskve," *Antikhrist v Moskve*, 2 (1996), pp. 85-89; Shargunov, "Beseda pered vyborami 17 dekabria 1995 g.," *ibid.*, pp. 61-68.

...we believe that by God's will that force is being used today to stop the dissolution of Russia. Just as Zhirinovsky two years earlier...saved Russia, similarly this can be done today by the communists...

Whom should we vote for then? For them who...have not defiled themselves by a deliberate violation of the Commandments—who do not kill, do not steal, do not give false witness...for them who have courageously raised their voices against murder and moral corruption...

Are the Communists, who have exterminated entire peoples in the USSR for 70 years, not guilty of murder? Having deprived millions of people of personal property, are they not guilty of theft? Having promised universal happiness, plenty, and peace, but having brought only poverty, deprivation, blood and tears, are they not guilty of false witness?[28]

The immediate reaction of the Patriarchate was a suprisingly noncommittal statement that Shargunov and his group of clergy, who had declared their support support for Ziuganov on TV, expressed their own private opinions as free citizens but not that of the Church; and the Patriarch, and the Patriarch, who was scheduled to consecrate a new iconostasis for Shargunov's church, refused to do so. What was expected from the Patriarchate or at least from the Patriarch as "a private citizen" condemning Shargunov's behavior and reconfirming the incompatibility of Christianity with Marxism. Was the silence on such a basic issue of ideas and values the price the Patriarchate was paying in order to preserve a make-believe unity in the Church? But what sort of unity is it when theological books by an Orthodox publisher and bearing the imprimatur of the Patriarch's blessing, are banned for use in some seminaries and from sale in parish bookstores by some clerics; when a respectable septagenarian priest and chaplain to the Orthodox Youth Movement, a prisoner of conscience of Soviet times, Valentin Chaplain (a medical doctor and professor of music) is banned from reverencing relics in a nearby monasterey headed by the Patriarch's namesake, Bishop Alexii?

28 It is hard to believe that Shargunov, a former dissident, has such a short memory. Nor could such amnesia be ascribed to Father Dimitri Dudko, who had spent years in Stalin's concentration camps and was constantly harassed by the KGB in the Brezhnev era for his brave sermons and his active catechization of adults. Yet he is now a member of the editorial board of *Zavtra*, the major national-bolshevik weekly, calls himself its spiritual advisor and has appealed in the newspapers "for an alliance of communists with Orthodox Christians," because "Ziuganov is a true communist...and a patriot with an Orthodox tenor of life." People of this ilk are simply blinded by the myth of the Holy Russia, which leads them to see all the horrors of the former Communist regime as a foreign importation, a product of the Elders of Zion and their legacy. In Ziuganov and his supporters, they see genuine Russians, and this alone is for them a guarantee that Ziuganov's Communism will be free from atrocities, but will still be sufficiently authoritarian to satisfy their longing for an autocrat.

From the timidity of the Patriarchate it would appear that the pro-communist or pro-fascist clergy constitute a very significant force in the Church. In actuality, the clergy supporters of Ziuganov, at least publicly, constituted fewer than a dozen priests and probably two bishops—the above-mentioned Alexii and Tikhon, head of the Patriarchal Publishing Department. To this party also belonged the late Ioann, Metropolitan of St Petersburg, and perhaps Metropolitan Gedeon of Stavropol in the Northern Caucasus.

In actuality, according to the Analytical Center of the Federation Council, the proportion of politically inactive people is twice as high among the Ortho-dox laity as in the population as a whole.[29] But among those believers who have declared their political preference, the proportion of centrists, leftists, and rightists is the same as among the unchurched. Among the clergy, and espe-cially among the bishops, centrists (among them the Patriarch) constitute the majority. For this reason, the Church plays a positive role in strengthening the state and discouraging people from participating in any actions that might de-stabilize it; although there are quite a few extreme nationalists among the monastics and some parish clergy. Among the 138 bishops, extreme national-ists constitute approximately 15 percent. The liberal (open and ecumenically inclined) clergy constitute a relatively small contingent, but they include the best educated and the most active priests in the field of education, charity, and mission. The report laments that the political democrats have ignored this last group of clergy at their own peril, and thus leaving them without the external political support enjoyed by the radical and right-wing clergy.[30]

It is not unlikely that such findings contributed to the Patriarchate's decision to finally take a more affirmative action to prevent such cases as that of Shargu-nov's group in the future. The Council of all Bishops of the Russian Orthodox Church of February 1997 issued a resolution forbidding priests, parishes and other organizations to participate in political actions, propaganda and politi-cal electoral campaigns.

29 The Analytical Center calculates that, although 70 percent of the population of Russia are baptized Orthodox, only 5 to 10 percent are practicing church members. In fact, as pointed out before, those going to church at least weekly and taking communion at least monthly are a mere 2-3 percent of the population of Russia.

30 Sergei Ivanenko, "Politicheskie predpochteniia pravoslavnykh," *Moskovskie novosti,* No. 51, 1995.

INDEX